W9-CUA-095

Punch—King of Puppets
From a music cover, 1843

Fr.

The History of the English Puppet Theatre

BY

GEORGE SPEAIGHT

AUTHOR OF
"JUVENILE DRAMA: THE HISTORY OF THE
ENGLISH TOY THEATRE"

WITH MANY ILLUSTRATIONS IN HALF-TONE

JOHN DE GRAFF
NEW YORK

FOR ANTHONY

who also loves Punch

A NOTE UPON NOTES

THE author of every serious work of history must decide how he is going to treat the problem of notes and references. He must balance his duty to scholarship and posterity against the irritation of breaking the continuity of his narrative; the foot of the page against the end of the text.

In this book I have provided notes for two purposes. Firstly, to give the original authority of every reference to puppet history; and, secondly, to amplify my text with interesting information of secondary importance. These notes are placed at the back of the book. It is not necessary—nor advisable—to refer to them, one by one, while reading the text, and the general reader may well read the book without looking at the notes at all. I would suggest, however, that the inquiring reader may care to glance through the relevant notes after each section of a chapter has been read. In this way his memory may be refreshed, his curiosity satisfied, and his knowledge enlarged.

I hope that this procedure will enable my notes to assist and not annoy, to aid the scholar and divert the curious, and to be easily ignored by the rest.

G. S.

ACKNOWLEDGMENTS

IT is a pleasure to record my grateful thanks to the many people who have assisted me over the years in gathering material for this book, and without whose co-operation many important discoveries would have gone unrecorded. In particular I must express my deep acknowledgment to the late Paul McPharlin, beside whose fine history of Puppets in America I am proud to place my own, and to Mr Gerald Morice, whose articles have enriched the puppet revival of our time with many fascinating sidelights on history from which I have freely drawn; also to Miss Sybil Rosenfeld for many entries from eighteenth-century records and advertisements, to Mr Edward Kersley for valuable clues on Punch's iconography, to Dr James G. McManaway for the discovery of early playbills in American libraries, to Dr J. E. Varey for sharing with me the results of his researches into the history of Spanish puppet shows, and to Mrs D. Gislingham, for allowing me to consult the manuscript memoirs of her father, Richard Barnard; and to Miss Amina Chatwin, Miss M. Hartley, Mrs Judith Philip, the late Alfred Loewenberg, Mr Harry Beard, Mr Richard Findlater, Mr Eric Halfpenny, Mr Victor Neuberg, Mr John Stead, Mr Richard Southern, and to many other correspondents, who will, I hope, accept this collective expression of gratitude. I also acknowledge the courteous assistance of the staffs at the British Museum Reading and Print Rooms, the Gabrielle Enthoven Collection at the Victoria and Albert Museum, the Horniman Museum, the Guildhall Library, the Public Record Office, and the Westminster, Richmond, Kensington, and York Public Libraries. Finally, I am indebted to the owners of the originals of my illustrations for their kind permission to reproduce them here.

CONTENTS

ILLUSTRATIONS

Except where otherwise acknowledged, all illustrations are reproduced from originals in the collection of the author.

Chapter I

MEDITERRANEAN MIMES

Masks and Puppets

THERE are two kinds of emotion in the theatre. We may be moved by the personality of the actor or by the impersonality of the actor. We may be thrilled by the fire or the lucidity of a Kean or an Olivier, or we may be lifted out of ourselves by the sad, impassive miming of a Pierrot; by the haunting gestures of masked dancers; or by the traditional horseplay of a circus clown. Our imagination will give life to the inscrutable countenance of the marionette.

This book tells something of the story of the second of these theatres—the impersonal theatre. It is not the rival but the complement of the other, the actor's theatre; it is the symbolic rather than the naturalistic element in the dramatic entity; it is the theatre of stock characters, of mimes, masks, and puppets.

The puppet is, indeed, the complete mask—the mask from which the human actor has withdrawn. And often, stranded on the boards of its little stage above the high-water mark of the ebb and flow of dramatic fashion and development, the puppet has preserved for centuries a theatre elsewhere lost and forgotten. The story of the puppet theatre in England is not only the strange and curious history of travelling showmen and a popular art; it is an essential chapter in the history and development of the European theatre. And before we can understand it aright we must first learn something of the popular theatre and the puppets of Europe, from which it sprang.

The puppet theatre has not always been a children's theatre, but it has always been the theatre of the people. The wealthy and the sophisticated too have loved the puppets, but as a light diversion or a passing fancy; their elemental appeal has always found an enduring response from the simple and the pure in heart, from peasants and labourers, from artists and poets, from the child-like spirit in man.

It is, perhaps, a romantic fancy to imagine that puppets preceded the human theatre; they did not form it, but reflected it.[1] And so for the beginning of our story we must go back to the first stirrings of the drama in Europe, and to the mimes and masks through which it was expressed.

Greek and Roman Mimes

The husbandry of the vine has not changed greatly in three thousand years. Then as now, steep valleys ran down to the Ægean Sea; then as now, peasants toiled through the hot summer to raise a precarious crop from a stony and arid soil; then as now, the harvest was gathered in with prayer and hope, and brought home with celebration and rejoicing. And after all was done there would be food and wine for the labourers, and songs in praise of Dionysus—or Bacchus—the god of wine and fertility. Encouraged by the wine they had drunk, we may imagine one reveller after another leaping into the firelight with a dance, a song, or a speech. Smearing their faces with the dregs of wine, these humble peasants would escape for a moment from the awkward cages of their bodies and strut as gods in some primitive ritual. In the spring the gods would be invoked again, and we learn that processions would wind from every village across the fields and vineyards of Greece, praying that Nature would stir again from her cold sleep, and carrying with them as the symbol of the fertility upon which their lives depended, erect upon a pole, a gigantic phallus.

As the centuries passed, the improvisations of a Bacchanalian orgy grew to a pattern, and a religious ritual became increasingly dramatic. The drama was born. The stories of the gods and of the mortals who defied them, cast in the rigid mould of Greek Tragedy, were enacted in vast amphitheatres and written down in words that can still thrill us to-day; but side by side with this Comedy, Farce, and Mime were shaped by the universal delight in mimicry and buffoonery, and by the sixth century before Christ the existence of a popular drama can be discerned.

The rustic revellers had given to this form of theatre elements that it was never to lose. It was a drama of stock types rather than of individual characterization, probably largely extempore, and the actors wore masks upon their faces. Fights and beatings were frequent, and—no doubt as some protection from the stick—the actors were grossly padded upon their stomachs and buttocks; hanging between their legs—an obscene relic of the Dionysiac processions—swung a formalized phallus. The plays, like those of Tragedy, brought the gods to earth, but here as the equals of men to share the scrapes and the indignities of our common lot: Dionysus, Apollo, Heracles, Jove himself, were displayed in burlesques of the divine mythology; and intermingled with these there ran simple sketches of domestic life and homely family farces.

Little of this was written down, and hardly any literary records have survived. Our knowledge of its very existence can be gleaned only from a few stray hints, a few vases and terra-cotta statuettes. No one can definitely say where or when these rustic farces were first performed, or exactly how they developed into a form of professional theatre. There is said to have been a type of Dorian Mime that originated at Megara,

THE HOOK-NOSED MASK OF A ROMAN COMIC ACTOR

From a terra-cotta statuette.

By courtesy of the Trustees of the British Museum

from which the Old Comedy of Aristophanes was derived. It is certain that the Greek colonists in Sicily and Southern Italy brought with them a native form of popular drama, the Phylax Comedy, which had distinct points of resemblance to what we know of the Dorian Mimes, and about which we have—thanks to the survival of a number of vases painted with dramatic scenes—excellent pictorial records. The Phylax Comedy disappeared with the decay of Greek influence, but its place was taken in Italy at about the time of the birth of Christ by a roughly similar form of native drama, originating from the Oscan district now known as Campania. This was the Atellan Farce.

Running through these five hundred years of folk-drama, hinted at in the Dorian Mime, painted in the Phylax Comedy, and at last named in the Atellan Farce, there may be discerned a succession of stock characters or masks. There is Bucco, the comic slave; Maccus, the country bumpkin; Pappus, the old dotard; Dossennus, the sharp-tongued hunchback; Manducus, grinding his teeth and frightening the children; and perhaps Cicirrus, the "cock man," a dashing fighter who crows about it afterwards. Vulgar, often obscene, always vigorous, grotesquely masked and padded, these characters remind us that classical art is not entirely represented by the smooth perfection of the Venus of Milo, and that the range of classical drama is not fully conveyed by the sixth form in white sheets declaiming the Greek play.[2]

The Dark Ages

With the collapse of Roman civilization in the fifth century after Christ there disappeared the formal theatrical entertainments that had flourished under it. Some of the more literary comedies were preserved in manuscripts, but the elaborate mimes and the spectacular circuses were disbanded, while the great theatres and amphitheatres for which they were designed fell into ruins.

It is usual to imagine that all forms of dramatic activity in Europe were completely suspended until the slow evolution of a new religious drama began to make itself apparent in the eleventh century. It is difficult, however, to believe that the primitive impulses that had stirred the Mediterranean peoples so powerfully would easily be forgotten, and it is probable that some form of popular secular folk-drama did, in fact, continue to exist up and down Europe throughout the Dark and Middle Ages. It is certain that minstrels, jugglers, acrobats, and wandering showmen of all kinds still made their way from Court to Court and castle to castle; they sang songs, trained animals, mimicked people, walked on their hands, danced and tumbled; they sometimes wore masks. It is not certain that they ever acted anything that we would call a play to-day, but they did at least constitute a corps of professional semi-dramatic entertainers. And if these Court performers rested always on the music-hall side of drama their presence and example may have inspired their humbler colleagues—the village amateurs—to preserve and embroider the old dramatic fertility games that had been enacted at springtime and autumn for longer than anyone could remember. To this day there can be seen in the Balkans a simple play of birth, death, and resurrection, acted from door to door by local villagers, that may—in its essentials—date back to before the Dorian Mime. In England the old mummers' play of St George can still sometimes be seen, and many people still living can recall its serious performance, with a combat, a death, and a restoration to life as the unchanging elements in a confused buffoonery. The origins of the mummers' play are completely lost to us—no certain written records of earlier than the eighteenth century are preserved—but in its elements this too must surely go back to some pagan dramatic ritual re-enacted and reshaped in English villages for centuries, secretly, away from the eyes of chroniclers and urban busybodies.

How much of this tradition, if any, was absorbed into the religious cycles of miracle plays, which grew up between the tenth and thirteenth centuries, need not concern us here. It is sufficient only to draw attention to the existence of a thread of semi-dramatic activity running through the long course of European history from the first stirrings of an agrarian culture in Attica to the Greek colonies in Italy, the pomps of Rome, the sports of peasants, and the by-play of minstrels; and in this thread perhaps a few stock incidents and plots, but more certainly a series of stock characters and types, known by their costumes and their masks—the old grey-beard, the braggart warrior, the country bumpkin, the sly servant, wide-mouthed, long-nosed, warted, bald-headed, hook-nosed, and hunchbacked.[3]

The Commedia dell' Arte

By the end of the fifteenth century the great urge for religious drama that had swept across medieval Europe had worked itself out. New classical and secular ideas were in the air, and it was at this moment in history that there appeared in Italy the extempore form of drama known as the Commedia dell' Arte.

Travelling with the mountebanks through the Italian provinces we hear of strange characters who gathered a crowd with their jokes and acrobatic buffoonery before the master of the show came to the selling of his medicines. These *zanni*, as they were called, were distinguished by their curious costumes, by their grotesque masks, occasionally by a phallic symbol, and by their regional accents. Before long we hear of them deserting the pedlars of medicine and forming themselves into small troupes of actors and actresses, sometimes attached to a Court and sometimes tramping the roads from village to village. The plays they performed have been preserved only in the form of scenarii, or rough plots, and they were re-created for each performance with improvised speeches.

The dramas themselves grew to fit the pattern of the stock characters who made up each little company. There would be at least two straight characters, the Inamorati, or Young Lovers, who were not masked; probably two old men, Pantalone, a Venetian merchant, and the Dottore, a pompous jurist from Bologna; perhaps the Capitano, a boastful but cowardly soldier of fortune; and several *zanni*, as comic servants, inn-keepers, and other plebeian roles. The *zanni* were the life and soul of the piece with their witty or foolish answers and their ingenious *lazzi*, or comic business. They might go under the names of Arlecchino, Brighella, Scapino, Mezzetino, Pulcinella, Scaramuccia, Burattino, or many another.

Within this framework the changes could be rung on hundreds of domestic comedies and farces. The basic plot was, of course, the romance between the young lovers, in the course of which Pantalone was sure to be made a cuckold or to lose his daughter by the tricks of the *zanni*. Each actor played the same part in every play, and if contemporary reports are to be believed there were among these Italian comedians some of the most brilliant actors in history.

It is extraordinarily tempting to trace these comic characters back to the stock masks of the Atellan Farce, and to the Greek mimes. The connexion was taken for granted by the antiquaries of the eighteenth century and the romantics of the nineteenth, but under the cold light of twentieth-century criticism any clear textual evidence for such a derivation is found to be almost non-existent. The most recent tendency among scholars seems, however, to favour a qualified return to the earlier theory. This is not a matter that can ever be proved in indisputable terms; an enormous gap of over a thousand years stretches between the last records of the Atellan plays and the first of the Italian Comedy; we can only conjecture that the basic stock types lived on as the sub-dramatic grotesque figures of popular festival, ready to be brought once more into the light of literary comment by the brilliant improvisations of a generation of natural comedians.[4]

Pulcinella

For the purposes of this study there is one character among the *zanni* that interests us particularly.[5] Pulcinella was not the oldest or the most important of the comic servants, but he did acquire a considerable local prominence in Naples. As far as can be ascertained, he first appeared as a regular mask in these plays in about 1600; he was first depicted under this name in 1618 in the curious series of designs made from birds' feathers constructed by Dionisio Minaggio, the Governor of Milan's gardener;[6] and again in about 1622 in the wonderfully expressive engravings of Callot.[7] Here we see a shambling *zany*, dressed in the loose white shirt belted outside his trousers that was in essence the daily costume of the sixteenth-century Italian peasant; his nose appears to be slightly—but not ridiculously—hooked.

During the next century this figure and mask became standardized. He acquired a high floppy pointed hat, and the nose of his black half-mask became grotesquely hooked to form the most striking aspect of his appearance. Apart from his mask, there was little difference between his general attire and that of Pedrolino, who is so familiar to us in his French character of Pierrot.

A Picture of Policianelo, made from Bird's Feathers by Dionisio Minaggio in 1618

By courtesy of McGill University, Montreal

In character Pulcinella had grown from the Neapolitan peasantry; he could play any part in any play, usually in a humble role, but in spirit he was always the primeval peasant, a slow-witted country booby, but with the cunning and guile of his race. With the years he developed other more farcical characteristics; he was gross of speech, indecent in gesture, and a braggart who ran away at the sight of danger, but even when he was most a buffoon he was ever one of the *lazzari*.

We must, above all, clear our minds of preconceived illusions. The genuine Neapolitan Pulcinella was not, and never has been, humpbacked, nor dressed in bright colours, nor fond of fighting, nor a wife-beater.

Much ink has been spilt in discussing his origin. Various actors claimed to have "invented" Pulcinella, but it is most unlikely that so primordial a character was ever originated by any one individual. It may well be that the mask in the Italian Comedy was evolved from a long-established character of popular festival, and many attempts have been made to trace his descent from the stock figures of the Atellan Farce. But the only evidence for these theories rests on certain grotesque statuettes from the Roman period, which may not even represent actors at all, and none of which really bears much resemblance to the typical Pulcinella that we know to-day.[8] There is a hooked nose here, or a humped back there, but it may well be argued that these are found in nature in all ages, and that it is straining probability to insist on fanciful derivations of these physical grotesqueries from a remote classical past.

THE PULCINELLA OF NAPLES, C. 1800

The truth surely is that these flamboyant creatures of Mediterranean fancy cannot be fitted into tidy modern classifications; any attempt to track neat family trees across the lost millennium is too great a simplification. But this hook-nosed Neapolitan peasant, foolish and sly, boastful and cowardly, is an immortal human type that was not invented by anyone in 1600, but had been living for one, two, who knows how many thousand years before he joined Scapino, Fricasso, Cocodrillo, Bagatino, and the rest of these capering mountebanks as they danced and clowned their hungry way through Renaissance Italy.

The Italian Comedy Abroad

It was not long before these companies of actors began to travel beyond Italy, and to bring the gesticulating grotesques of the Italian Comedy to France, Spain, Holland, Germany, and England. Everywhere they were greeted with the delighted patronage of the Courts and the scandalized protests of the Puritans. In the year 1577 the Gelosi Company visited Paris, and was soon followed by others; the Italian language was generally understood at the French Court, and so much of the performance depended on purely visual effects that little was lost by those unfamiliar with the dialogue. In time, however, as the Italian comedians became more securely established in France, they began to perform in French, and by 1680 they had acquired sole possession of their own theatre at the Hôtel de Bourgogne, where they gave daily performances. Their success, however, roused some jealousy, and their alleged indecencies gave offence. In 1627 they over-reached themselves by poking fun at Mme de Maintenon, and a severe retribution fell on them: their theatre was immediately closed, and the company dispersed. The *zanni* and *lazzi*

Hunchbacked Clowns at the Marriage Festivities of Henri IV and Marie de Medici in 1600

of the Italian Comedy remained only in the theatres of the fairs, in the humble popular milieu from which they had sprung.[9]

Italian players had reached England by 1573, performing "certain pastimes" before the Mayor of Nottingham, and the next year appearing before Queen Elizabeth. Their art was not appreciated everywhere, however, and a popular preacher attacked "the unchaste, shameless, and unnatural tumbling of the Italian women." Four years later a famous Arlecchino, Drusiano Martinelli, appeared in London, and we learn at this time that the requirements for a performance consisted of "a mattress, hoops, and boards with trestles."[10] It is clear that these pastimes still owed a great deal to the circus, and that the first Italian players were acrobats as much as actors. Although they never took the firm root in London that they had in Paris, the Italian Comedy was not without its

THE FRENCH POLICHINELLE, AS DEPICTED BY M. MAZURIER IN THE BALLET "POLICHINEL VAMPIRE," 1823

influence upon the budding Elizabethan drama, and its characters, certainly Pantaloon, were known by Shakespeare. It was, however, by more devious channels than the legitimate stage that the *zanni* eventually triumphed here.

Although he was never a leading actor, Pulcinella travelled with the other characters across the Alps. By the middle of the seventeenth century he was established in France as Polichinelle, in his familiar role of stooge to a quack doctor, but quite lacking any of the grotesque physiognomy that we should expect to-day. But here in France another influence was at work; there had, it would seem, long been a folk tradition of hunchbacked fools in the French popular farces and merrymaking, and in some way this humpback became fathered upon Polichinelle.[11] At the same time he began to pad his stomach in an absurd counter-poise to his back, and to deck himself in finery, with an elegant ruff, and buttons down the front of his resplendent coat. The rough Italian peasant was developed into something more fantastic and Gallic. By 1688 he can be found in prints in the shape so familiar to modern eyes. This is the character depicted by Watteau, by Lancret, and by Meissonier.

In due course the French Polichinelle returned to Italy, and had some influence upon his native originator; in Venice, in particular, Pulcinella became generally hunchbacked and wore a tall, round rigid hat—like a deep inverted flower-pot—instead of a pointed floppy one. This is the Pulcinella as drawn by Tiepolo.[12] But in Naples, his birthplace, and in Rome, the original Pulcinella—on the stage, in carnival, or as a puppet—remained unchanged.

We do not know whether Pulcinella came to England with the Fiorilli troupe in 1673, when they were loaded with gold and silver plate and returned to play daily in the palace at Whitehall as if it was a public theatre. But if he did he would have found himself not unknown to London society, for his reputation and his mask had gone before him. Punchinello the puppet had already staked a prior claim upon our hearts.

Chapter II

PUPPETS IN EUROPE: FROM SOCRATES TO LOUIS XIV

Types of Puppets

A PUPPET is an inanimate figure moved by human agency. This definition excludes dolls on the one hand and automata on the other, but it is sufficiently wide to include a large variety of figures and methods of manipulation. A simple classification is into Flat Figures and Round Figures. Flat figures may be moved from the side, like the characters in an English Toy Theatre; or their limbs can be actuated into a semblance of spasmodic jerkings by strings pulled from below, like the toy called a Pantin, or Jumping Jack, that was quite a craze in England in the mid-eighteenth century. Flat figures can also be held between a strong light and a translucent screen, and thus become Shadow Figures; these can be pushed on from the side, or moved by rods held horizontally like the shadow puppets of the Karageuz Theatre in Greece and Turkey, or by rods held vertically from below, like the shadow puppets of Java and Bali, or by strings from below, like the Ombres Chinoises of eighteenth-century France and the Galanty Show of nineteenth-century England. Shadow puppets can be made of opaque materials, to give a black-and-white effect, like the shadow shows of Java and the Ombres Chinoises; or of translucent materials, to give coloured shadows, like those of China and Greece.

Round figures can be operated either from above or from below. If moved from below with rods to the body and hands they are known as Rod Puppets, and this is a type traditional to both Java and the Rhineland. If made smaller, with a hollow cloth body to fit over a man's hand and articulated by his fingers, they are called Hand or Glove Puppets, and this type is found all over Europe, and also in China. There are numerous combinations of hand and rod puppets.

A complete figure with articulated limbs, moved from above, is a Marionette. These were originally controlled by one rod or stout wire to the head, with perhaps strings to the hands and feet. Folk puppets of this kind can still be seen performing in Sicily, in Northern France at Amiens, and in Belgium at Brussels and Liège. Within the last hundred years or so the general method of manipulating marionettes has come to be by strings alone, and a high degree of naturalism and perfection has been obtained.

This does not completely exhaust all the types of puppet. There are the Japanese Puppets, each carried by a man in full view of the audience, and manipulated by sometimes two or three assistants, with strings and levers in its back, like a ventriloquist's dummy; there are Jigging Puppets, or *Marionnettes à la Planchette*, made to dance on the ground by a cord running through their breasts from the showman's knee to a vertical post; there are Finger Puppets, in which the showman's two fingers are the puppet's two legs; and there are Living Marionettes, in which the puppet's body, worked by rods from behind, hangs from the head of a human manipulator.

In this book I shall write often of 'puppets,' and when I do so it means that the exact type is not clearly known, or that I am referring in general to all types. Whenever possible, however, I shall specify the type of puppet with which I am dealing. In their long history, and in the many countries in which these little figures have played their interpretation of drama, first one type and then another has risen to popularity; no one type can be described as better than the others, but each has its own individual characteristics, and for each there is a certain type of suitable dramatic material. The shadow figure, for instance, can convey an atmosphere of magic and mystery, or represent a scene pictorially, though it is by no means confined to such themes; the rod puppet can appear without any incongruity in exalted themes of epic poetry and drama, thanks to the sure control of its wide, eloquent gestures; the glove puppet is a natural at knock-about farce, quick, witty dialogue, and at bringing in 'audience participation'; the marionette is the most human of all puppets, the nearest to life, but there is a danger of sterile naturalism in its present perfection, and the marionette really finds its mark with the slight exaggerations and wicked caricatures that lie so easily within its grasp.[1]

Greek and Roman Puppets

There are two possible starting-points for a history of puppets. The first doll that moved its arms could have gradually developed into a domestic amateur puppet show; or the first statue of a god that amazed its worshippers with movement could have gradually acquired more and more of a dramatic role in the priestly mysteries. Possibly both these elements played their part before finally coalescing in a professional popular entertainment, but on the analogy of the human theatre we must expect to trace a more probable descent from the religious derivation.[2]

Herodotus has described an old Egyptian custom that closely parallels the Dionysiac processions. The women in their village festivals used to carry with them an image of the god of fertility about twenty inches high, fitted with a phallus of nearly the same length that could be erected by strings.[3] (Before we titter or blush at such gross foreign obscenities let us remember our own Giant cut in the turf at Cerne Abbas. There could be no more elemental or fundamentally right beginning for our story.) There are records of other Egyptian statues that turned their heads or gestured with their hands at the right moment; no doubt strings were led through their bodies to the touch of an adroit priestly manipulator. These moving images can be paralleled all over the world, in pagan and Christian countries, but our interest in the puppet lies with its dramatic use; we cannot be sure how far these jointed idols lent themselves to any theatrical purpose. Among the numerous wall-paintings that have been preserved illustrating almost every feature of Egyptian life there does not seem to be a single illustration of any kind of puppet show. We should note the existence of the puppet in ancient Egypt, but may be sceptical of the existence of a puppet theatre.

When we move to the Greek civilization there are definite indications not only of the existence of moving statues and of highly elaborate automata, but of the use of puppets as a form of dramatic entertainment. A frequently misquoted but extremely interesting reference is found in the *Symposium* of Xenophon.[4] This short work describes a dinner-party in Athens in the summer of the year 421 B.C. It was at the close of the greater Panathenaic games, and the city was crowded with the competitors and their followers; no doubt entertainers of all kinds had made their way to Athens for the festival. The banquet was given by Callias, a wealthy dilettante, to a brilliant company of guests, including Socrates, and the host had hired a man from Syracuse to give them an evening's entertainment. His troupe consisted of a girl who played the flute, an acrobatic dancing-girl, and a handsome boy who danced and played the cither; they also performed a mime in which Ariadne, dressed as a bride, waited for Dionysus, who came in to her and loved her, carrying her off to the bridal couch. We are told that this was performed with great beauty and expressiveness, and at the conclusion "those who were unwedded swore that they would take to themselves wives, and those who were already married mounted horse and rode off to their wives that they might enjoy them."

No puppet show was presented on this occasion, but when Socrates, during the evening's discussion, asked the Syracusan of what he was most proud, expecting this to be the handsome youth he employed, the entertainer replied, "Fools, in faith. For they give me a livelihood by coming to view my puppets."

It is just possible that in this reply the Syracusan was referring, metaphorically, to the boy and girl he had trained. But even if this is admitted the use of such a metaphor clearly shows that puppets were an accepted form of entertainment at this time. It is, however, far more probable that the phrase can be given its literal meaning, and that in this Sicilian entertainer, with his troupe of musicians, acrobats, dancers, and puppets, we see the first recorded puppet showman in history. No doubt the human performers were considered more appropriate to an intellectual dinner-party, and the puppets were reserved for the amusement of the common populace.

Six hundred years later Athenæus recorded that "the Athenians yielded to Potheinos the puppet player the very stage on which Euripides and his contemporaries performed their inspired plays."[5] This must have been the great Theatre of Dionysus at Athens, but it is a mistake to imagine that this is a proof of the high artistic regard in which puppets were held. During this period of dramatic decadence the theatre at Athens was used even for exhibitions by conjurors and sword-swallowers, but Potheinos must have been a well-known and successful entertainer to have been able to present a performance in that vast amphitheatre. He is, too, the earliest named puppeteer in history!

With this one tantalizing exception, there is not a single description of a definite puppet performance in the whole corpus of Greek and Roman literature. But puppets were certainly known, and there is no lack of literary and metaphorical references, comparing man to the marionette. For instance, Horace, in 30 B.C., could write that "you are moved like a wooden puppet by wires that others pull";[6] Philo, at about the time of the birth of Christ, that "all these, as in marionette shows, are drawn with strings . . . each in the attitudes and with the movements appropriate to it";[7] and two hundred years later Apuleius, in a frequently quoted passage, refers to "those who impart gestures to the wooden figures of men, when they draw a string to the limb that they wish to move, the neck turns, the head nods, the eyes roll, the hands are ready for every purpose, and the whole is seen, not ungracefully, to live."[8]

These references to the life-like movements of contemporary marionettes, which could be multiplied almost indefinitely, seem to indicate the high degree of perfection that the art had obtained. But the simile between man and puppet is so easy—not least in our own days of puppet emperors and puppet dictators—that there is a considerable danger of our treating these purely literary metaphors as strictly technical descriptions. Cleverly constructed marionettes must have been fairly common, for there are regular references to them from 400 B.C. to A.D. 400 by both Greek and Latin authors; but there is singularly little mention of serious puppet drama, and there are indications that as entertainment the puppets were rated rather low. Aulus Gellius, for instance, in about A.D. 150, complains that men are in reality "ludicrous and laughable, like marionettes."[9] At about the same time the Emperor Marcus Aurelius gives a concentrated and scornful picture of the vain show in which the lives of most men are passed—"a procession's vain pomp, plays on a stage . . . scurrying of startled mice, marionettes dancing to strings."[10]

A considerable number of small jointed figures in clay or terra-cotta have been discovered in the graves of Greek and Roman children, and they are sometimes assumed to be marionettes.[11] As the largest of these, however, are not more than seven or eight inches high, it is unlikely that they could ever have been performed for any public professional purpose. It is possible that some of them may be relics of home puppet theatres, but their operation is always extremely crude, and there is certainly no suggestion of the nodding heads and rolling eyes described by Apuleius. These little figures may have been inspired by the wooden marionettes of professional entertainers, but they hardly ever copy contemporary theatrical characters, and for the most part they are probably no more than jointed dolls.

It is quite clear from the passages already quoted that stringed marionettes were a familiar form of puppet in classical times. The usual Greek word for puppet, *neurospastos*, is derived from *neuron*, which means a cord made of sinew, and this—quite apart from the many metaphorical references to puppets on their strings—clearly proves that marionettes were the standard form of puppet in this period. The probability is that the main weight of the figure was supported by a stout wire to the head, and a few of the jointed doll figures that have survived still retain a short length of rod rising from the tops of their heads.

There is an indication, however, that glove puppets were also known in ancient Greece, probably before 500 B.C. There is a word *koree* used to describe an exceptionally long sleeve that completely covers the hand,

and—for no apparent reason—this identical word is also used for a small statue or figurine.[12] I do not think that this association has been pointed out previously in this connexion, but it is reasonable to suppose that the glove puppet, which is a small figure on the end of a long sleeve covering a man's hand, provides the missing link to connect these two completely dissimilar uses of the same word.

We know, therefore, that puppets were used in Greece for entertainment some five hundred years before the birth of Christ, and possibly much earlier; that their use had spread to Sicily at an early date; and that they became firmly established in Italy during the Roman power. We know the kinds of puppets that were used. But we know nothing whatever about the kinds of plays, if any, in which they performed. They may never have acquired a truly dramatic character at all, and have contented themselves with what they have always done very well—music-hall and variety tricks. But the line between the circus and the stage is not always easily drawn: we have seen how the acrobatic dancers of the Syracusan could also perform a mime with an exquisite histrionic art, and it is difficult to believe that the Syracusan's puppets could not also turn at will to drama or comedy. The Greek theatre with its masked actors on stilt-like boots was one-half a puppet theatre already, and few forms of drama lend themselves more readily to the stilted dignity of puppet actors than does the Greek. Whether the tragedies of Sophocles and Euripides were ever performed by the *neurospasta* we do not know, and it would be rash to guess. But it is certain that wherever puppets have flourished in their long history they have always fastened on the popular un-literary drama as their especial province; and we may feel quite sure that in the puppet shows of Greece and Rome the crudely comic characters of the Dorian, the Phylax, and the Atellan Farces had their place—the fat cook, the learned doctor, the comic slave, the "cock fighter," the glutton, and the hunchback.

Medieval Puppets: The Minstrels

Among the mimes and actors who were driven by the invading Goths from their comfortable if decadent employment in the circuses of Imperial Rome there went the puppet men. Here and there there must have been private houses that welcomed these showmen to play for a party, and in the villages the old shows must still have been enjoyed, but the official world in the towns was unsympathetic. The barbarian conquerors despised the soft Mediterranean culture and all its arts; and the new

Christian Church, still smarting from the mimicries of pagan pantomimes, condemned the whole race of entertainers as brands fit for burning. The puppets, however, seem to have escaped, for the most part, direct attack, but whether this was because their entertainments were innocuous or beneath contempt we can hardly decide.

From some eight centuries, from A.D. 400 to 1200, no written records of puppets in Western Europe seem to have survived, but there are indications that they still flourished in the Byzantine Empire. In the sixth century the Bishop of Alexandria referred to the little wooden figures that were shown at weddings, and were moved by some kind of remote control in the actions of dancing;[13] and in the twelfth century the Archbishop of Thessalonica, commenting on the classic authors, marvelled at the regard in which Potheinos, the puppet player, had been held by the Athenians, dismissing the puppets of his own time as unworthy of serious attention.[14] It is possible that the puppets and the mimes, as well as other graces of Roman civilization, found a safe retreat under the patronage of Constantinople until life was sufficiently settled for them to return to Western Europe.[15] But many entertainers must have remained in the ravaged provinces of the old Roman Empire, unrecorded by contemporary writers, and among these the puppet showmen were almost certainly to be numbered.

The traditions of the mimes, with their mimicry and circus tricks, were gradually absorbed into that of the bard, with his staider recitations of epic poems, and by the tenth century we begin to see the emergence of the great army of minstrels, gleemen, jongleurs, and trobadors who flocked to every Court in Europe and followed in the retinue of every baron, with their old ballads and new love songs, their tricks, and—sometimes—their puppets.

Not all the minstrels followed the Court: there were some, we are told, who hung around taverns and village greens, strumming at some instrument, singing coarse songs, imitating birds' cries, and showing off the tricks of learned dogs. Such a one must have been the Perrinet Sanson, whose name a chance reference has preserved for us, who gathered his audience in a French village with a drum and trumpet to see the performance of his company—his wife and children, a bear, a horse, a nanny-goat, and his puppets.[16] This was comparatively late, in 1408, but for centuries before this such little bands of human and animal entertainers must have wandered across Europe, carrying, sometimes, puppet shows with them.

Although the puppets seem for the most part to have been confined to the more lowly and popular minstrels, there were times when they too were seen in the houses of the great. In the early-thirteenth-century Provençal romance *Flamenca* there is a description of a great feast given on St John's Day at Bourbon, in the Auvergne, in honour of the King and Queen of France. After High Mass the whole company of many thousand knights and ladies, with their servants, sat down to a banquet in the great hall. After the meal was finished they washed their hands (for they had been eating with their fingers), the cloths were taken away, wine was brought, and silk-covered cushions for them to lean against, and then:

Up stood each jongleur in the hall
And bent to make his music call
A note more sweet, a key more mellow,
Than from the instrument of his fellow.
Here did a minstrel sing his lay,
While one upon the harp did play,
And one upon the fife, or flute,
One on the rote, one on the lute;
And some recited, or made merry,
To the accompanying psaltery,
Or to the whistle, or the bagpipe,
The musette, Jew's Harp, or the panpipe.
Here one that made the puppets play,
Or gave a juggling knife display,
One somersaulted on the ground,
Another capered in a round,
One tied his body in a loop,
Another dived straight through a hoop;
Each one, in fact, did his own turn.

Then the company danced, with all the two hundred jongleurs to play the music; and in the afternoon a joust was held by the knights on horseback, while the ladies watched from the windows; and after vespers had been sung by all the company in church they took supper and went tired to bed.[17]

In this vivid picture of an aristocratic feast, in the high summer of European chivalry, we see performing the same tumblers, dancers, and puppet players that had graced the banquet of Callias, seventeen hundred years before.

There are many other references to puppets and puppet players throughout the fourteenth and fifteenth centuries,[18] but few of these give any clear description of what the puppets actually were. It seems certain that at least three kinds of puppet were known in the Middle

Ages. There is a well-known illustration in the twelfth-century Codex of the Herrad von Landsburg,[19] once at Strasbourg, showing a boy and a girl manipulating two puppet knights on a table by means of a pair of horizontally held strings. It is clear that these are actually jigging puppets, and probably this is more of a domestic game than any kind of dramatic entertainment, but as we have clear evidence of the existence of this kind of simple puppet we must always consider the possibility that the *bastaxii* so popular among the minstrels were often of this type.

MINIATURE FROM "THE ROMANCE OF ALEXANDER," 1344

By courtesy of the Bodleian Library

The existence of glove puppets is confirmed by two extremely important miniatures in the well-known fourteenth-century *Romance of Alexander* in the Bodleian Library.[20] Each of these represents a glove-puppet booth of roughly similar pattern, with a curved roof over the stage. In one a puppet with a club seems to be threatening a woman; in the other two knights are fighting with swords, while two other puppets look on. The booths are of the familiar pattern, with drapery concealing the operator, or operators, for in the second case it would require two men to put four figures into movement. There is, however, one extremely interesting feature of these booths that has not yet, I think, received comment. At the two front corners of each booth there are a pair of embattled turrets, projecting slightly forward; in one illustration a castellated edge is carried right across the stage to connect the two turrets. There is no other indication of scenery. Now, the name for this kind of glove-puppet booth is in Italian *castello*, in Spanish *castillo*, and in French *castellet*, meaning a castle, and it is reasonable to suppose that these portable booths, the most suitable type of theatre for a travelling showman, were regularly made in the likeness of a castle, with ramparts and battlements above which the puppets could very naturally appear from the waist upward.

It is very probable that marionettes were still known throughout this period, but it is difficult to find any clear evidence of their survival, and the easy similarities between man and marionette, so common among the early Christian philosophers, seem to be singularly absent from the writings of medieval authors. In general it can be said that the marionette, requiring a fairly bulky and permanent type of stage, comes into prominence during periods of material prosperity, but that the glove and other more portable types of puppet tend to displace it in times of social unrest, when entertainers are forced into a vagabond life. There is, however, an interesting remark in a Provençal romance of 1318 which gives us a clue: the hero was set upon by twelve robbers, and in the terrible combat that followed he strikes the head of one robber from off his shoulders, and it flies through the air to strike another robber in the face and kill him. "There are two good comrades," cried William, "for the dead has killed the living with a kiss. In the same way do the puppets slay each other by knocking together."[21] This summons up irresistibly a mental picture of the knightly marionettes of the folk-puppet theatres of Sicily and Flanders, as they still perform to-day, with the heavy figures swung across the stage by their rods to clash together in the centre. It is indeed difficult to believe that the author had not seen some such combats in the puppet theatres of his day.

It is clear that the puppet plays made a feature of great combats, and in the age of chivalry, in a booth that was made to look like a castle, what would be more natural? We shall probably not go far wrong if we imagine the puppet theatres of the medieval minstrels to have presented the same stories as those that they sang at the camp-fires and in the great halls; not the elaborate love poems of the troubadors, but the old traditional tales of ancient Greece, of Priam, Helen, Ulysses, Hector, Achilles, and Æneas; tales from the Bible, of David and Goliath, Samson and

Delilah, and the fall of Lucifer; tales of chivalry and legend, of the Knights of the Round Table, Gauvain and the lion, Lancelot and Perceval; tales of history, of Julius Cæsar, of Charlemagne, and of Clovis; and tales of popular romance, of the Old Man of the Mountain, of the Fair Unknown, and of the scarlet shield found by the herald at the gate.[22]

Medieval Puppets: Religious Drama

The story of puppets in the Middle Ages may be traced through another line of succession—religious art and religious drama. We have seen the part that jointed and articulated images played in the temples of Egypt and ancient Greece, and these homely mysteries were to be repeated in due course in Christian churches. It was not, however, until the end of the eighth century that the Christian Church in the West began to permit the use of the fully sculptured crucifix. The early centuries of persecution had forced upon Christians the secret use of such symbols as the fish and the lamb, but as it became more and more important to present a simple popular exposition of the Faith the arts of painting, sculpture, and even "moving sculpture" were all harnessed to the service of religion.

One of the most famous of these medieval "puppet images" was the Rood of Grace at Boxley, in Kent, where a crucifix was preserved that was said to have been made, probably in the fifteenth century, by an English carpenter during imprisonment in France. The figure was evidently jointed so that it could move its limbs, and it is even reported that the eyes did "move and stare in the head like unto a living thing, and also the nether lip likewise to move, as though it would speak."[23] Another English jointed figure of this period illustrated the Resurrection of Our Lord, "which put his legs out of the sepulchre, and blessed with his hand and turned his head."[24]

These figures were, no doubt, intended as striking illustrations of the Gospel story, and there is no need to imagine any priestly cunning behind their manipulation; but they attracted the especial venom of the reformers, and several were publicly destroyed at Paul's Cross. "The wooden trunk," we are told of the Boxley Rood in 1538, "was hurled among the most crowded of the audience. And now was heard a tremendous shouting; he is snatched, torn, broken in pieces, bit by bit, split up into a thousand fragments and at last thrown into the fire; and thus was an end of him."

Another type of moving image in medieval churches were the automata, usually moved by part of the mechanism of a clock. Several examples of these are still intact and in working order to-day—at Wells Cathedral, for instance, and at Strasbourg, and there is a pleasing reproduction in the Horniman Museum.

Interesting though these examples of puppet figures may be, they do not in any way constitute a puppet *theatre*. It is tempting to think that some of these jointed statues may have presented short excerpts from the Scriptures, and thus have opened the churches to the great surge of religious drama that swept through medieval Europe, but there is no evidence whatever to suggest that the religious mystery plays originated from any kind of puppets. The Christmas Crib, for instance, as we can see it erected in many churches to-day, seems to have been derived from, rather than to have inspired, the human Nativity plays.[25] A traditional nativity play performed by puppets can be seen to this day in Flanders, in Hungary, and elsewhere in Europe,[26] but these must be regarded as fascinating survivals of the old liturgical dramas, rather than as their originators.

FIGURE OF CHRIST SITTING ON AN ASS, DESIGNED TO BE DRAWN ROUND THE CHURCH

South German, sixteenth century, about half life-size.

Victoria and Albert Museum. Crown copyright

There are, however, instances of plastic figures being used in a semi-dramatic manner to illustrate the liturgy.[27] In the Palm Sunday ceremonies an almost life-sized image of Christ sitting on an ass, mounted on four wheels, was sometimes drawn into the church; there is a fine German figure of this type in the Victoria and Albert Museum. This custom goes back to the tenth century. The Ascension Day service, from the fourteenth century, sometimes showed an effigy of Christ being drawn up into the roof of the church through a ring of silk cloths to represent clouds, while similar figures of a dove and an angel could be raised and lowered by cords. Sometimes an effigy of the Devil was thrown down on to the ground at the same time. At the feast of the Assumption a recumbent image of Our Lady was sometimes carried up to heaven, in the roof of the church, in the hands of angels.[28] At Pentecost the figure of a dove was sometimes lowered through a hole in the roof, and swung above the heads of the congregation like an enormous censer, breathing out sweet perfume. This particular ceremony was still practised in St Paul's Cathedral at the beginning of the sixteenth century.

In none of these instances do the images actually possess movement of their own, and it is straining the sense of the word to describe them as puppets. But the use of these figures in a dramatic form, and the existence of jointed and articulated religious images, did eventually result in the actual representation of religious puppet plays in churches by the end of the Middle Ages. By the end of the sixteenth century the Spanish bishops were forbidding the representation of "the actions of Christ, the Blessed Virgin and the saints, either in churches or elsewhere, with clay images moved in some kind of ordered motion,"[29] and there is an interesting reference of about the same period to a similar performance in England at Witney, in Oxfordshire, then the centre of the flourishing Cotswold wool trade. "In the days of ceremonial religion," wrote Lambarde, a sixteenth-century antiquary,

> they used at Witney to set forth yearly in manner of a Show, or Interlude, the Resurrection of our Lord and Saviour Christ, partly of purpose to draw thither some concourse of people that might spend their money in the town, but chiefly to allure by pleasant spectacle the common sort to the liking of Popish mommetrie; for the which purpose, and the more likely thereby to exhibit to the eye the whole action of the Resurrection, the priests garnished out certain small puppets, representing the persons of Christ, the Watchman, Mary, and others, amongst which one bore the part of a waking Watchman who (espying Christ to rise) made a continual noise, like to the sound that is caused by the meeting of two sticks, and was thereof commonly called Jack Snacker of Witney.[30]

It is interesting to see the intrusion of a comic local character into this early religious spectacle; comic local characters were to continue to intrude into every kind of spectacle on the puppet stage for the next four hundred years, and they had probably been doing the same thing for at least two thousand years previously.

These religious puppet dramas probably borrowed something from the secular exhibitions of the minstrels; they were perhaps more common in the fifteenth and sixteenth centuries than the scanty records would lead us to imagine. In England and other Protestant countries the Reformation dealt a death-blow to puppet plays in churches, though—as we shall see—secular puppet shows continued to present Biblical themes for many years to come. The essential development of liturgical religious drama was, however, by this time long past; and from 1300 onward religious plays had increasingly escaped from their liturgical origins and ecclesiastical settings into the free air of the cathedral steps and the streets. As so often in our story, the puppets remained long after the actors had fled. But even in Catholic countries the puppet shows were soon to be expelled from all churches; the Reformation only hastened in England a sense of propriety that was spreading throughout all Europe.

Puppets are, however, strangely suited to display the divine mysteries in rôles where the human actor is all too conscious of his humanity. There is no doubt that religious drama can still to-day, as it has in the past, be interpreted with curiously moving effect by the hieratic gestures of the marionette.

Italian Puppets

The first puppet showman of whom we have any record was a Sicilian, and right up to our own times the Italians have shown themselves supreme masters of this art. It is natural to suppose that the legacy of the Roman marionettes was carefully nurtured in the peninsula, but until an Italian scholar turns his attention to a subject that has already been carefully traced by French, German, English, and American historians the story of the puppets in Italy, the fount of all European puppetry, will remain to some extent a closed book.[31] We may certainly assume that itinerant entertainers of some kind kept the Roman tradition alive, and we know that elaborate displays of puppet-like figures were shown in Italian churches,[32] and that the mystery plays—or *Saccre Representazione*—of the Middle Ages made use of various inanimate figures, as elsewhere in Europe.

By the sixteenth century we begin to find written evidence of the popularity of puppets as a form of entertainment in Italy, and three distinct types are clearly differentiated. The first of these are the jigging puppets, which had been illustrated four hundred years before, and which are now described as consisting of two dancers, whose movements were controlled by a single thread passing from the musician's leg to an upright post, and who danced most divertingly together to the sound of the bagpipes.[33]

Marionettes were described by Gerolamo Cardano in the mid-sixteenth century as able to "fight, hunt, dance, play at dice, blow the trumpet, and perform most artistically the part of cook."[34] Even allowing for the exaggerations which all literary observers seem to consider appropriate to their descriptions of puppets, it is clear that the Italian marionettes were by this time playing some quite elaborate dramas.

A hundred years later Francesco Saverio Quadrio, a learned Jesuit with a truly catholic curiosity about the world around him, wrote so fully and with so much practical detail and sympathetic interest of the various types of puppets that it seems worth while to translate his descriptions as fully as possible.[35] It must be remembered, however, that these were not written until about 1740, though they may substantially describe the situation of 1640.

The marionette theatre, he writes, should be a

> small stage, well lit above and below, in front of which is stretched a net of very fine thread, and within which the spectators will see the *fantocci* exit, enter, and walk as if they are living persons. The puppets are extremely well made, with the head of *papier mâché*, the bust and thighs of wood, the arms of cords, the hands and legs of lead, all well dressed in silken clothes, with shoes, hats, hoods, and other things usually seen on the persons of living beings. Each of these puppets has attached to its head an iron rod, wherewith it is moved here and there by the operator, who controls and manages it without being seen, and who has four threads of silk, or of some other material, two fixed to its hands and two to its feet, whereby he causes the figure to walk, jump, gesticulate, dance, and make sounds, so that one would think one saw on the stage a law-court, a boarding school, a dance, or the playing of a violin sonata or a guitar, or such actions as are required, copying life to the life.

The net placed in front of the stage was to confuse the eyes of the spectators so that they did not notice the strings, or the very prominent rod, by which the marionettes were moved. The use of cord for arms, permitting all kinds of backward-bending joints, would be very much sneered at by modern puppeteers, but the evidence of men like Cardano and Quadrio should be sufficient proof that the Italian puppet showmen of the Renaissance were past-masters of their art in the manipulation of their figures.

An alternative type of puppet is described by Quadrio as follows:

> Let a high stage be arranged, such as is used in an ordinary theatre, provided with scenes of the usual size. Place on the stage a few wooden boards, grooved in channels, which are to serve as slots within which figures about

> two feet or more in height, and made of *papier mâché*, representing various characters, are to stand or travel. These figures are then to be moved from one end of the channel to the other, as required, by means of concealed counterweights, some of which hang by a wire attached to the shoulders of each figure, and are intended to serve the purpose of manipulating the figures and arranging them in various graceful and appropriate attitudes; these counterweights are worked by men hidden under the stage, or in some other convenient place.

This somewhat complicated procedure was devised at the end of the seventeenth century by Bartolommeo Neri, a machinist and painter.

A much later description of this kind of figure can be found in an English puppet manual of the late nineteenth century,[36] which provides a valuable supplement to Quadrio's tantalizingly vague explanation:

> The Italian marionettes are about four feet high, so that a small dwarfish boy is not unseldom known to be put upon the stage among the dummies, and so enhance the illusion and perplex the spectators. . . . The figures, from their weight, have to be counter-weighted by the wire from the head running up over a pulley-wheel, and ending in a weight behind the scenes. . . . The figures keep in the space between the grooves in which the scenes run, and to appear nearer or farther from the audience would have to be shifted at the side round into the new opening. This restriction prevents the wires which work them being entangled. They are worked from below or at the side. The front sink, the flap of scenery which crosses the front of the stage above, is made of network, to confuse the eye when seeking for the wires.

These figures seem to have been some kind of rod puppet sliding in grooves, with the weight supported from above. Ingenious though the installation may have been, it must have been difficult to portray the rough-and-tumble of a lively drama with such complicated apparatus, and its use must inevitably have been limited.[37]

Glove puppets, also, are referred to as performing in the *piazzas* in the early seventeenth century. These *burattini* are described as rounded figures, fitting into the tips of the fingers of a man concealed in a *castello* covered with cloth.[38] Quadrio says that they were the most popular and usual type of puppet in his day, and that the booths were set up at cross-roads or in the *piazzas*. Their entertainment was sometimes rather coarse, but it was skilfully presented and told. One of the characters in the Comedia dell' Arte was named Burattino, and it is often suggested that he gave his name to this type of puppet, but this is almost certainly a mistake, for the character of Burattino is seldom, if ever, found in any puppet show. It is far more probable that this type of puppet derived its name from *buratto*, a coarse native woollen stuff from which its costume, comprising the bulk of its body, was made; and that the *burattini* were already well-known when one of the human actors in the improvised comedy was nicknamed Burattino on account of his small stature and vivacious movements. The earliest recorded use of this name applied to a human character is in 1585.

With these Italian puppets we have, for the first time, some particulars of how they spoke. Paolo Manucci describes the *burattini* as speaking "with a sort of whistle"; Quadrio provides a very full explanation of this:

> No less various are the methods by which the players make the voices of each sort of figure. Those who are concealed in a *castello* of cloth . . . usually use a *pivetta*, held inside the mouth, by which means they alter the voice according to the character they are manipulating. And usually one man recites the whole *burletta*, changing his voice according to the characters.
>
> In another type of little theatre a reader stands hidden behind the backcloth, with a written text of the play before him. The speeches are marked in various colours to warn him when to change his voice; for instance, red signifies a female, turquoise a male, and green a comic voice. The figures are moved by another man.
>
> In another method each operator speaks for the figure he is moving, and each one has a *pivetta* in his mouth, either longer or smaller or more open or more closed, to produce the correct voice of the character he is playing; and this is done so cleverly that if the *fantoccio* had a voice of its own it could not be more natural.

The *pivetta* was some kind of tube concealed in the mouth, and we shall find an opportunity later in this volume to examine its structure more closely; its effect is to produce a piercing cry that attracts people to the show, and at the same time to provide a certain un-human timbre for the voice of the puppet.

After so many centuries of vague hints and accidental allusions we have at last reached, with these descriptions of Quadrio, a clear knowledge of the construction of Italian puppets. Of their high quality, too, and of their great popularity there seems to be little doubt. Quadrio admits that "this diversion fills the minds of the onlookers with cheerfulness, and as a result is extremely dear to the people." But not every one shared the simple curiosity of this humanistic Jesuit, and a disgruntled classical scholar at the end of the sixteenth century could deplore that the art of puppets, once thought worthy of the skill of men of science and learning, had now fallen—like the arts of Æsop and Roscius—into decadence, and would soon be no more than "the miserable get-penny of a gang of rude, ignorant, and sordid mountebanks."[39]

While we know a great deal about the construction of these Italian puppets of the sixteenth and seventeenth centuries, we still know practically nothing about the plays in which they performed. Quadrio thought that "the farces, to tell the truth, are of small account," and yet he commends "the honourable conduct displayed in the speeches, and the suitability and moderation of the little fables treated." No doubt the puppets played in Italy, as they have elsewhere, some of the sacred mysteries that they had brought from the churches, old legends of the countryside and fables of chivalry; and into their robust popular dramas we may feel certain that the puppet showmen introduced the comic regional characters of the country, the heroes of provincial folklore and legend, the grotesque masked *zanni* who were—at the same time—pulling wry faces at the stalls of mountebank doctors and banding together into companies of the Italian Comedians.

We cannot say who came first, the puppets or the actors. It may be significant that Pulcinella's name, perhaps derived from a chicken or a turkey, assumed a diminutive form. This may suggest that here, at least, the puppet preceded the actor. It is tempting to believe that the immortal characters of the Italian Comedy played their first parts on the stage of a puppet *castello*; but there is no real evidence to support such a claim; in history the function of the puppet seems to be to preserve rather than to originate dramatic types. What is certain is that the rebirth of the Italian puppet theatre sprang from the same mimetic surge and instinct that threw up the Commedia dell' Arte, and that when the Italian Comedy was long dead and a matter only for the wrangles of historians the characters that it had inspired still stamped and squeaked their vigorous courses as actors of wood.

But if, as we shall see, the characters of the Commedia dell' Arte were preserved in the puppet shows long after they had disappeared from the human stages, is it not possible that the characters of the Atellan Farce were equally preserved in the puppet shows of the Dark and Middle Ages to provide at least the inspiration for the rebirth of the improvised comedy in Renaissance Italy? This is not a theory that can be proved by reference to texts, but we may venture to accept the axiom, supported by the analogy of every puppet show in history, that *if* the characters of the old Greek and Roman mimes survived in any dramatic form whatever in medieval Italy, it was on the puppet stages that they were to be found

The puppet theatre may, indeed, provide the missing link to connect the stock characters of classical farce with the masks of the Italian Comedy.

Polichinelle

With the Italian actors who travelled across the Alps into France there went the Italian puppets. We have seen that puppets were well-known in France from the displays of the medieval jongleurs, and by the end of the sixteenth century we learn from a contemporary allusion that "at the drolls, the mountebanks, and the puppets you would find Tabary, Jehan des Vignes, and Franc-à-Tripe, all hobbling, and the hunchbacked fool of the French farce."[40] The French puppet theatre was clearly, by this time, a vehicle for the display of the popular comic characters of native folklore, and its dramatic status is firmly established.

With the arrival of Italian showmen, however, the French puppet show seems to have been lifted from the status of a fairground booth to that of a fashionable entertainment. By the sixteen-forties a puppet theatre had been established in Paris on the left bank of the Seine, on a pitch near the gate to the Pont Neuf,[41] by a showman named Brioché, who was probably an Italian originally called Briocci.[42] He is said to have been a tooth-drawer as well as puppeteer, and he certainly attracted attention to his booth with the antics of a monkey dressed up in the latest dandy's fashions, for there is a story that Cyrano de Bergerac, passing by one day, thought that the monkey was making fun of his nose, and whipping out his sword stabbed the creature to death. In 1669 Brioché and his son, who succeeded him in the business, were invited to the Court for some months to entertain the nine-year-old Dauphin.

These puppet theatres of the market-places and of the fairs were not itinerant glove-puppet *castellos* set up in the open air, but covered booths, outside which players and animals performed to attract a crowd. A poem of 1666, describing the fair of St Laurent, paints the picture well:

Here in the street upon a stage
Two shabby Harlequins engage
The passers-by to pause and gape
At the droll antics of their ape.
We pay our penny, and we go
Inside to see the puppet show;
But while, within, we wait and stand,
We're pushed and elbowed, squeezed and jammed,
As stiff as pasteboard queens and kings,
Until at last the play begins.[43]

Unfortunately we are told nothing about the play itself, except that the pickpockets were active during its performance. Apparently no seats were provided for the audience, on the principle that two can stand in the space in which one can sit.

By the middle of the seventeenth century references to puppet showmen and their performances begin to become frequent, and they were generally welcomed as an amusing idle diversion. Evelyn noted two puppet theatres in Paris at the residences of French aristocrats; they played in elegant little theatres in formal gardens, or at the commencement of fashionable balls.[44] He was a little shocked, however, to observe the aristocratic patronage bestowed upon an entertainment that in England was still confined to the fairground.

Many features of the Italian marionette theatres can also be traced in France. The fine net stretched in front of the stage is apparently referred to in some accounts of expenditure at Court in 1713, when a tinsmith was paid over thirteen livres for "iron wire which he fixed in front of the [puppet] theatre, 12 tin reflectors, and 6 small candlesticks for taking the lights."[45]

The *pivetta* too was introduced under the name of *sifflet-pratique*. By the eighteenth century it was accepted so universally that permits for the performance of puppet plays would be marked "on condition that no speaking is allowed except with the *sifflet de la pratique*."

By far the most important innovation, however, brought by the Italian puppets were the characters of the Commedia dell' Arte, shadowing and exaggerating the human performers. We have already seen that Francatrippa had insinuated his way on to the French puppet stage by 1600, but he was soon to be ousted by another character even more grotesque, whose humpback, pigeon chest, and hook nose marked him out as a ready model for the woodcarver's chisel. In Italy Pulcinella may have been only one among many puppets, but in France, in the early years of the seventeenth century, he assumed, for the first time in all their glory, the fantastic shapes that we know to-day, and was hailed as Polichinelle, the chief hero of the marionette stage.

By 1649 the Polichinelle of Brioché was so well-known that his name was adopted as the author of a political broadsheet addressed to his fellow-countryman Cardinal Mazarin. "I can boast without vanity," he is made to write,

> that I have always been more flocked to and more thought of by the people than you. . . . I have been received like a noble citizen in Paris, while you, on the contrary, have been chased like a louse out of church.

I am Polichinelle
Who acts as sentinel
At the Porte de Nesle.

A few years later, in what may be only an imaginary anecdote, Brioché is described as setting out on tour "with his little wooden Æsop, twisting, twirling, turning, dancing, laughing, and talking—this eccentric grotesque, this ludicrous hunchback, named Polichinelle. His companion was called Voisin."

In about 1705 a charming letter in verse written to Marie-Louise, thirteen-year-old daughter of James II, by "Count" Anthony Hamilton paints a pretty picture of a puppet show at the local festival of Saint-Germain-en-Laye:

Serving-maids and laundry-girls,
In Sunday clothes and well-brushed curls,
With their beaus in clean starched shirts
(For laundry-girls are dreadful flirts),
Are come to see, for little pay,
The showing of a puppet play.
In the granary there was seen
The savage Rape of Proserpine,
With changing scenery as well,
And there the famed Polichinelle,
The hero of these little plays,
Although a bit free in his ways,
In no way made the ladies blush;
They smiled and laughed at him so much![46]

Polichinelle went on to appear in plays on every subject under the sun—*Polichinelle Grand Turk*, *Polichinelle Magician*, *The Wedding of Polichinelle*, *The Loves of Polichinelle*, and so on; for many years no puppet show was complete without his appearance as compère, hero, or clown.

It is not entirely clear to what extent Polichinelle is merely Pulcinella under a French name. We have seen that a hunchback was a traditional figure of French farce before Pulcinella ever came from Italy, and we have also seen how the physical appearance, and probably the character, of the Polichinelle of 1688 differed from the Neapolitan peasant of the original Commedia dell' Arte. Charles Magnin, the erudite French puppet historian, goes so far as to claim that, "despite his Neapolitan name, Polichinelle seems to me an entirely national type, and one of the most spontaneous and vivacious creations of French fantasy."

It is clear that in France the puppet Polichinelle was far more important than the human. It must be emphasized that, except in Naples, the Italian Pulcinella was only a minor character among the human *personaggi*, and if he ever generally headed the cast it can only have been in the puppet theatres. We do not find records of human Polichinelles of any great importance before the Hôtel de Bourgogne engraving of 1688—and even here he is only a minor character in the background. But Polichinelle the puppet was already a byword by 1649. The human Polichinelle seems to be derived rather from the French marionette than from the Neapolitan peasant.

After the expulsion of the Italian players in 1697 the puppets remained as the only representatives of Italian Comedy in France. They had an eventful and important part to play during the eighteenth century at the theatres of the fairs and of the boulevards in the struggle against monopoly in the theatre; but that is a story that we cannot follow here.

For the purposes of this history we have now traced in parallel paths the story of the popular theatre and of the puppet theatre from the dawn of European civilization to the seventeenth century; and we have seen how the Italian puppets, in a reincarnation of the traditions of Greece and Rome, travelled across Europe, giving new life to the puppet stages where they passed, with Pulcinella the hero of their booths. Now only the English Channel lay before him.

Chapter III

THE ENGLISH CLOWN

The Fool

THE story of the English puppet theatre cannot be considered in isolation. It is directly derived from the larger picture of the European puppet stage and the European popular theatre, which we have already traced; and it is also part and parcel of the English popular drama, of pantomimes and drolls, clowns and jesters. Before following the detailed story of puppet shows in England we must first establish their relationship with the English clown and the English fool.[1]

The first fool was the village idiot, whose drivelling inanities sometimes seemed to conceal wisdom and prophecy, and it is a pleasing mark of primitive societies that the lunatic has sometimes been revered and cared for as one "possessed by God." When this simple awe had largely vanished the "natural fool" was still given a place at Court and in the houses of the great. He represented the safety-valve in feudal society, the simpleton who could answer back to bishop and king, the fool with licence to poke fun at anyone, the instigator of coarse practical jokes. But the wit of the lunatic must always have been an uncertain factor, and before long there grew up alongside these "natural fools" the profession of "artificial fool," or private jester. These were sane men, often recruited from the ranks of the minstrels, who paid for their keep with their wit. The jesters were the intimates of kings and princes, sharing their tables and painted with their families; cities and corporations maintained their own fools; taverns and brothels provided clowns to entertain the customers. If their jokes were too dull they were in danger of dismissal, but if they were too pointed they were in danger of a whipping. It must have been an attractive but an uncertain profession.

It had its own uniform. This was not worn every day, but only for masques or ceremonial occasions, but its general features have been well recorded and are very familiar. The coat and hose were motley or particoloured, often in red, green or blue, and yellow; the head was covered by a hood, like a monk's cowl, sometimes decorated with ass's ears, and sometimes with the head or the comb of a cock; bells jangled from the skirts and elbows of the coat, and from the peak of the hood, which was often drawn up to a point and curled forward. The jester carried in his hand a mock sceptre, or bauble, which was a short stick decorated at the end with a fool's head; to this was sometimes attached an inflated bladder, with which he could deal out mock blows. An alternative fool's dress was a long petticoat, sometimes with a fox-tail, a calf-skin, or feathers.

The elements of this costume, which was worn universally throughout Western Europe, probably date back to Roman times. We have already met the use of feathers and the "cock" type; the eared hood is recorded during the Roman Empire; the "fool's cap" is in essence the Phrygian cap, or *pilos*, worn in the Phylax and Atellan Farces; motley seems to have been the traditional wear of Roman mimes.

The practice of keeping a private fool outlived the Middle Ages, and reached its glory in the Renaissance; it died out only in the seventeenth century. When the divine right of kings was questioned freely by Parliaments there was no need for a licensed jester to remind monarchs of their humanity; the Court fool was the first victim of democracy. But society still needed a jester to point a finger of scorn at current abuses, a wit licensed to fool at the mighty in their seats, a clown excused—like the Lord of Misrule—from the Ten Commandments. The people could not house their fool at home, but they kept him for their satisfaction and their delight in the theatre.

The Vice

Buffoonery had very soon crept into the religious plays, and the ecclesiastical authorities, finding themselves unable to curb it, finally expelled the entire drama from the churches. The shepherds were shown as country bumpkins, Noah's wife as a shrew, Herod raged like the villain of a melodrama, and the grotesque Devils slipped across the border from horror into farce as they dragged the sinners into the smoking jaws of Hell. It was the particular genius of the Gothic spirit to bind these gross ingredients with the sincere representation of a religious epic.

By the fifteenth century the simple playing of Biblical stories began to be succeeded by plays still religious, or at least moral, in tone, in which the characters represented personifications of human virtues and vices; these were the moralities. These didactic compositions needed light relief even more than the scriptural episodes, and this necessary duty seems to have devolved upon the chief of the vicious characters, who came to be known, from the actors' description, as the Vice. This character, therefore, was a rogue and a sinner, tempting the virtuous characters, and at the same time a comical buffoon. He was quarrelsome, a braggart, and always getting into fights, but often a coward as well. Something of the private jester seems to have been absorbed into the performance, too, for he could play the fool or the idiot at times. Little of the savour of these performances can be recaptured to-day from the printed texts, which must be numbered among the least approachable relics of our national drama.[2]

Certain elements of the comic business can, however, be safely reconstructed. One of these was backchat with the audience:

> How say you, woman? You that stand in the angle?
> Were you never acquainted with Nichol Newfangle?

Nichol Newfangle was the Vice of *Like will to Like*, a sixteenth-century interlude. Other tricks were to speak in nonsensical or meaningless gabbles, to weep loudly and grotesquely in sorrow, and to delight in perversions and pretended misunderstandings. In a passage from the same play Newfangle is supposed to repeat a mock eulogy to the Devil:

> LUCIFER. All hail, O noble prince of hell!
> NEWFANGLE. All my dame's cows' tails fell down in the well.
> LUCIFER. I will exalt thee above the clouds.
> NEWFANGLE. I will salt thee and hang thee in the shrouds.
> LUCIFER. Thou art the enhancer of my renown.
> NEWFANGLE. Thou art Hance, the hangman of Calais town.

And so on.

At the end of this play the Vice was carried off by the Devil to eternal damnation, but it was doubtful whether even this prospect subdued him, for he made his exit riding on the Devil's back as if it was a horse. This piece of comic business made a great impression on Samuel Harsnett, who recalled in 1603 how

> it was a pretty part in the old church plays, when the nimble Vice would skip up like a jack-on-apes onto the devil's neck and ride the devil a course, and belabour him with his wooden dagger, till he made him roar, whereat the people would laugh to see the devil so vice-haunted.[3]

Shakespeare, in *Twelfth Night*, referred to the "old Vice . . . who with dagger of lath, in his rage and his wrath, cries ah, ha! to the devil," and we shall be reminded later in our story of the interest of this traditional finale to the last religious dramas; but an examination of the surviving printed texts shows that it was no means universal. Often the Vice was led away to prison or hanging at the end of the play; once, indeed, he was saved from hanging only by the breaking of the rope; and so far as the literary records go it would seem that the common end of the Vice was on the gallows.

The costume of the Vice was, at least sometimes, the same as the Court jester, though it followed no set pattern. Often he carried a wooden sword, the "dagger of lath" already referred to. Sometimes he may have been hunchbacked, for a clown once exclaims, "Such a deformed slave did I never see."[4]

During the second half of the sixteenth century the morality form of drama died out. The Vice lingered on, shorn of his moral qualities, as a mere buffoon, the stage clown of the Elizabethan theatre.

The Elizabethan Clown

> And let those that play your clowns speak no more than is set down for them; for there be of them that will themselves laugh, to set on some quantity of barren spectators to laugh too; though, in the mean time, some necessary question of the play be then to be considered: that's villainous, and shows a most pitiful ambition in the fool that uses it.

Thus Hamlet in 1600, and there can be little doubt that here Shakespeare speaks from his heart. The clowns of the early Elizabethan dramas were ubiquitous; "I would have the fool in every act," exclaimed a character in *The Careless Shepherdess*, and "Dost thou not know a play cannot be without a clown?" in *The Pilgrimage to Parnassus*. The clown needed no dramatic connexion with the plot of the story, but was dragged in quite irrelevantly to amuse the groundlings. Sir Philip Sidney complained that the dramas mingled kings and clowns "not because the matter so carrieth it, but thrust in the clown by head and shoulders to play a part in majestical matters, with neither decency nor discretion."[5]

The business of the Elizabethan stage clown was not written down, and once again we can only reconstruct it from hints and allusions. *The Pilgrimage to Parnassus* of about 1598 gives a good description: "Why, if thou canst but draw thy mouth awry, lay thy leg over thy staff, saw a piece of cheese asunder with thy dagger, lap up drink on the earth, I warrant thee they'll laugh mightily." "Enter the clown beating a soldier, and exit" is the surprising stage direction in one old play, which might serve equally well in the toy-theatre script of a Victorian harlequinade! In character the stage clown was a lover of ease, food, and drink, and a hater of hard work; he was sometimes dishonest and a thief; he was fond of practical jokes, but was frequently duped; a coward and a braggart, he seldom stood up to a serious fight; he spoke either in the rude and vigorous vernacular or in extravagant and absurd declamations, especially when in love, but when married he was plagued with a shrewish wife; he was always indulging in horseplay, acrobatic tricks, rough-and-tumble fighting, and crude buffoonery; he could mime laughter, terror, or drunkenness; sometimes he would let his voice be heard off the stage before making an appearance, and then show only his head between the curtains, while, we are told, the audience roared with laughter. He would often sing snatches of songs and ballads, and dance, accompanied by the pipe and tabor, between the acts, and in the jig which so often concluded the programme.

The character represented by the clown was usually a rustic, or a servant, only occasionally a true jester or Court fool. He did not normally wear the jester's motley, but some kind of russet countryman's garb with floppy trousers, or the long mottled-green petticoat of the idiot. Sometimes a more extravagant dress was assumed, with large shoes, enormous waistcoats, vast ruffs, and top-heavy hats, and the wooden sword, or bat, was still sometimes carried.

Some of these English clowns were played by actors who must have been brilliant performers. The most famous of all was Richard Tarleton; he seems to have largely invented the jig as a form of light musical entertainment, and was renowned for his improvisations and his repartee with the audience. In appearance he was a short, thick-set fellow, with curly hair, a squint, a comically flattened nose, and slightly hump-backed; he died, greatly mourned, in 1588.[6] His pupil was Robert Armin, who was the clown in Shakespeare's company and wrote a book about fools. William Kemp was also a famous composer of jigs, who gained fame by the publicity stunt of dancing a morris all the way from London to Norwich; he took four weeks over it, accepting challenges as he went, and fêted all the way. The English theatrical companies which visited Germany in the middle of the sixteenth century always took a clown with them, who became known as the "English John"; the character of "Pickle Herring," who became extremely popular in Germany, was introduced by Robert Reynolds.

The clown was the lineal descendant of the Vice, and was no doubt influenced by the domestic fools, by the rustic bumpkins in whom we have always rejoiced, and to a limited extent by the example of the Italian *zanni*. But England was rich in native comedians, and she had little to learn even from the Italians. The success of the stage clown, however, made his unheralded and ridiculous incursions into the regular drama a confounded nuisance, of which many other authors besides Shakespeare bitterly complained. It was Shakespeare, however, who solved the dilemma by successfully incorporating the clown into the dramatic structure of his plays as a Bottom or a Dogberry, or as a true domestic fool.

The Elizabethan clown flourished for comparatively few years, from about 1580 to 1630, and towards the end of this period he was regarded as an outmoded provincial convention. In the theatres of the Restoration there was no room for the old English stage clown, and soon Italian mimes were to conquer the British stage. The rough, pugnacious but witty character evolved by Tarleton and Kemp from the comic traditions of the religious drama seemed to have had its day.

Survivals of the Clown

Banished from the legitimate stage, the clown survived for many years in the drolls performed at the fairground theatres. Here at Bartholomew and Southwark Fairs in London, on plots of waste ground at Charing Cross or Lincoln's Inn Fields, at country fairs, barns, and taverns, the mountebanks' stages were set up, and short, garbled extracts from recent dramatists were mingled with old English legends and Biblical stories. Well into the eighteenth century these unpretentious strollers preserved upon their boards the clowns of the English tradition—John Swabber, Simpleton the Smith, John Bumpkin, Jack Pudding, Merry Andrew, Trusty, Squib, and Strap, dressed sometimes in the rough clobber of the yokel and sometimes in the motley of the fool. The story of these theatres of the fairs still needs telling, and we cannot follow in any detail the part that the clowns played on the portable stages of Pinkethman, Lee and Harper, Hippisley, Fawkes and Pinchbeck, and many others; they certainly represented a not unimportant branch of the English popular theatre, which has hitherto received less attention than it deserves.[7]

By the middle of the eighteenth century Harlequin had established himself even on these stages, and the old English comics were driven into the background; by the end of the century they had disappeared. It was, of course, only a temporary defeat, and in the next century the true native comic genius reasserted itself in the clown of the harlequinade and of the circus. But these were specialized rôles, and the funny men of the music-halls were individuals rather than types; the ubiquitous traditional fool must be searched for in a yet deeper layer of folk entertainment.

In remote corners of the countryside the rustic amateurs went on playing debased versions of Elizabethan masterpieces for many centuries.

There are descriptions of such performances in the eighteenth century at Craven, in Yorkshire, where adaptations of *The Merchant of Venice* or Heywood's *The Iron Age* were diversified with a clown, dressed in a loose motley garment, with a fox's brush as tail, and a fur cap, carrying a wooden sword.[8] Similar shows were being given in Shropshire at least as late as 1777, where the stage consisted of two wagons, upon which sat a chairman who also acted as prompter. Not more than two actors appeared at a time, and the most usual subjects were Prince Mucidorus, St George and the Dragon, Valentine and Orson, and Dr Forster (Faustus); a fool wearing a paper mask, bells at his knees, and a hareskin cap with ass's ears played a prominent part in every piece.[9] Even at the beginning of the nineteenth century interludes were being freshly written and acted in Wales, in the Welsh language, with titles like *Riches and Poverty*, *A Vision of the Course of the World*, or *Pleasure and Care*, which were quite fantastically similar to fifteenth-century moralities. In these too a fool made an appearance, sometimes to introduce the play at the beginning and dismiss the audience at the end.[10]

The fool too was absorbed into the more spontaneous merrymaking of the traditional folk festivals.[11] On Plough Monday, the first Monday after Twelfth Night, a decorated plough was pulled round English villages, followed by the local lads in clean smocks and ribbons, and preceded by Bessie, a man dressed up as a girl, and a fool in a fox's skin, with the tail dangling behind. In the Sword Dance, which was often given at the same time, Toms or Clowns, with painted or masked faces, would caper round the dancers with antic gestures. In the May Games at the beginning of May, with the setting up of the maypole and the crowning of the May King and Queen, there went the Robin Hood plays and similar festivities in which the fool often played a part. A curious May Day procession was reported from Hertfordshire in 1823, headed by two men with blackened faces, one dressed as a woman in rags and tatters, and the other, with a large artificial hump on his back, carrying a birch broom; these were known as Mad Moll and her husband. They were followed by other pairs more elegantly attired, in every case the women being played by men. Here and there the company stopped for a dance, and if the audience crowded in too closely Mad Moll's husband went to work with his broom, sweeping the road-dust into the faces of the crowd and chasing them about with his broomstick. In all these rural games and sports the morris was regularly danced, and in this too a fool, originally dressed in correct jester's motley, sometimes made up one of the team.

The most interesting and highly developed of these dramatic folk-plays is the Mummers' Play. Here, beside the stock characters of King George, the Turkish Knight, and the Doctor, there were always certain subsidiary figures to introduce the play and make the collection at the end, and some of these appear to be indisputable clowns. The chief of these is called Jack (recalling the Jacks and Johns of the stage clowns)—Johnny Jack at Salisbury, Little Jack at Brill, Fat Jack at Islip, Happy Jack at Hollingbourne, Humpty Jack at Newbold, and at Loughborough

> Here comes I old Hump-backed Jack
> With my wife and family on my back.
> My head's so big, my wit's so small,
> I've brought my fiddle to please you all.

The Jack of the mummers was nearly always padded like a hunchback.[12]

I do not wish to press the parallel too far, but it is perhaps significant to find this purely English tradition of the hunchback clown running like a thread from the old Vice to Tarleton and the clown of the mummers. There is no need to invent prehistoric 'derivations' from Dossennus or even Pulcinella; a humpback is grotesque, and grotesques make simple people laugh, whatever the country or the century; but it is important to establish that the humpbacked comedian belongs to all countries. He has an English as well as a French and an Italian lineage.

Chapter IV

PUPPETS IN ENGLAND: FROM CHAUCER TO CROMWELL

The Middle Ages

THERE can be little doubt that the minstrels who had exhibited puppets in France at least as early as the thirteenth century must have crossed the sea to England; French was the language of the Court in England as in France, and the jongleurs were, besides this, international entertainers, like the circus performers of to-day. But unfortunately there is no clear documentary proof of the existence of puppet shows in England at any time during the Middle Ages.

The word 'puppet' was, however, known in fourteenth-century England, and was used by Chaucer at least twice:

> . . . let this man have place,
> He in the waist is shaped as well as I;
> This were a popet in an arm to embrace
> For any woman small and fair of face.

The sense here is ironical; Chaucer, who is describing himself in this passage, was corpulent, and he means, jokingly, that a small woman would never get her arm round his waist like she would a puppet! Similarly, in describing a pretty girl:

> In all this world, . . .
> There was no man so wise, that could he thench
> So gay a popelote, or such a wench,

"Thench" means imagine, and the sense of "popelote" must be a pretty little thing.[1]

It is, of course, possible that Chaucer's "popet," evidently derived from the Latin *pupa*, meant no more than a doll, and it was sometimes used in this sense in the sixteenth century. But there are illustrations of some thirty or forty years earlier to suggest that he may have had a true puppet, in its modern meaning, in his mind.

These are, of course, the Bodleian miniatures to *The Romance of Alexander*, already described in Chapter II, whose provenance and history we must now examine in greater detail. This manuscript was written in Picard dialect by an unknown scribe in 1338, and the illustrations by Jehan de Grise were finished in 1344. In addition to illustrations to the text, a great many delightful genre scenes of popular games, dances, and amusements have been painted in the lower borders of the pictured pages; these have no connexion with the text. This beautiful manuscript seems to have been produced in Flanders, and at first glance it might seem that this interesting Flemish volume can be of no evidence for English conditions. A careful examination, however, suggests that, in the words of J. J. Jusserand, the book "appears to have been compiled for English people, perhaps on English soil." The rubricator seems, from his style, to have been Anglo-Norman, and the placing of the grotesque drolleries at the bottom of the pages may indicate English workmanship. The illuminator seems to have been familiar with both French and English customs. Finally, all the recorded owners of the manuscript, from the fifteenth century on, were English. There are, therefore, some grounds for believing that this medieval glove-puppet show, in its little 'castle,' was of a type familiar not only on the Continent, but in England during the fourteenth century.

Apart from this intriguing glimpse, no further references to puppets in medieval England seem to have survived. We may believe, with some confidence, that they never in any way acquired the status of an important popular entertainment, but that they played some part for many centuries in the repertoire of itinerant minstrels, alongside the dancers with "the obscene motions of their bodies," the maskers with their animal heads, the tumblers and the jugglers, the performing bears, apes, horses, and dogs, at taverns and ale-houses or in the great halls of the nobles.

We have already recorded the religious articulated images in English churches—the Rood of Grace at Boxley, the Pentecostal dove at St Paul's, and the puppet play of the Resurrection at Witney. This play, derived no doubt from the religious tradition of moving images, was probably presented by marionettes, and was almost certainly being performed by 1500.[2] It is the earliest recorded religious puppet play in Europe, and it is, in fact, the earliest named puppet play of any kind in European history. It seems probable that marionettes of some kind were occasionally employed in the open-air miracle plays that succeeded the church performances, and these must have been manipulated from pageant wagons. In 1599 the Mayor of Chester made himself unpopular by trying to abolish certain abuses that had crept into the performance of the local plays, including men dressed up farcically as women and devils, and "god on strings"; and a stage direction in a Cornish mystery of 1611 calls for "every degree of devils of leather and spirits on cords."[3]

Finally, an entry in Sir Thomas Eliot's Latin *Dictionary* of 1538 translates *gesticulator*, a posture-master or mime, as "he that playeth with puppets," and it seems at last certain that a puppet player was an accepted character in the English scene. The references to puppets in medieval England are scarce and doubtful, but even among these few records there is sufficient authority for us to believe that both glove puppets and marionettes, used in a fully dramatic manner, were familiar forms of popular entertainment by the fifteenth century, and that a tradition of both secular and religious puppet shows had been established here long before the Elizabethan Age.

Shows and Motions

In August of the year 1561 Lady Katherine, Duchess of Suffolk, recorded in her Household Accounts the payment of *6s. 8d.* to "two men which played upon the puppets."[4] Here, at last, is documentary proof of the itinerant puppet show in England, and during the next hundred years we can record an ever-increasing flood of references to the puppet theatre as a popular form of entertainment. "Let nothing that's magnifical . . . be unperformed," wrote a dramatic poet in 1588;

> . . . see that plays be published,
> May-games and masques, with mirth and minstrelsy,
> Pageants and school-feasts, bears, and puppet-plays.[5]

Let the common people, wrote Burton in 1621, "freely feast, sing, dance, have puppet-plays, hobby-horses, tabers, crowds, and bag pipes."[6] Nine years later the magistrates at Bridport observed a troupe of players who "wander up and down the country with blasphemous shows and sights which they exercise by means of puppet-playing, not only by day but late in the night . . . so that the townsmen cannot keep their children and servants in their houses." The showmen had even been attacked in the pulpit by the local preacher, and the court ordered them to leave the county.[7] Here was a sure enough sign of popularity!

"O excellent motion! O exceeding puppet! Now will he interpret to her," writes Shakespeare in 1595.[8] It seems clear enough that a "motion" is an Elizabethan term for a puppet or a puppet play, and if this is the case the popularity of puppets at the dawn of the seventeenth century must have been indeed widespread, for these motions are referred to again and again by contemporary writers. Motions have been accepted as synonyms for puppets by all the competent authorities, and in many cases this is quite certainly the sense of the word, but if we examine the references carefully we shall find that the term was used extremely loosely to describe *any kind* of moving mechanism—quite apart from the twelve alternative meanings allotted to it by the *Oxford English Dictionary*. As the exact definition of this common term is vital for the study of Elizabethan puppet shows, it will unfortunately be necessary for us to turn aside for a moment and consider the matter in greater detail.

As a natural extension of its meaning of 'a movement,' the term 'motion' seems to have been applied to all moving figures. Sometimes these were actuated by clockwork, sometimes by water-power,[9] sometimes they were figures on a barrel-organ;[10] they may have been incorporated in some form of peepshow or "portraiture."[11] A form of 'motion' that may well have been displayed in England is described by Spanish writers of the sixteenth and seventeenth centuries as being carried round the country by foreign showmen. This consisted of a box divided by horizontal and vertical divisions into compartments, in each of which small figures were given movement by clockwork or by the manual turning of a handle. The scenes represented incidents from the Gospels or the lives of saints, and from its shape this type of automata was known as a *retablo*, or reredos.[12] Automata and peepshows are fascinating examples of human art and skill, but they are not puppet shows. To dub the whole world of Elizabethan motions as puppets may seem natural enough to orthodox students of the theatre, but it is really about as accurate as to lump the theatre, the cinema, and the magic lantern together as 'pictorial entertainment.' The puppet theatre takes its place beside these other popular shows and motions, but it alone possesses the element of spontaneous dramatic art, and can lay claim to a higher position in the hierarchy of entertainment.

Whatever these motions were—and they were certainly sometimes genuine puppet shows—they came in the first place from Italy. In 1573 the Privy Council requested the Lord Mayor of London to permit "certain Italian players to make show of an instrument of strange motions"; the Italians evidently had friends at Court, for this request was followed by a sharp order within five days when the permission had not been granted.[13] Between 1619 and 1640 there are continual references to Italian motions touring the countryside, like the three men and assistants who showed "an Italian motion with divers and sundry stories in it" at Coventry; at Norwich an interesting point was raised when a man produced a licence to show an Italian motion, but because he said "his motion was no Italian motion but made in London" he was not allowed to show it there. The term began to go out of use by about 1650, and soon became archaic, but in 1663 the Master of the Revels could still provide three different classifications among the mountebanks, rope-dancers, conjurors, and dancing horses for "clockwork motions, ordinary motions, and extra motions."[14] We cannot hope to know, now, exactly what kinds of motion these shows provided; what is certain is that by the end of the sixteenth century Italian showmen had popularized various kinds of entertainment introducing moving figures. It is sufficient for our purpose to note the popularity of the new shows, and to exercise a proper caution before equating them invariably with puppets.

A most valuable description of a motion is provided in Chettle and Day's play *The Blind Beggar of Bethnal Green* of 1600.[15] Here a couple of rogues, called Canbee and Hadland, cheat a countryman named Stroud, and decide to go underground to avoid the hue and cry. They plan to make their way to Holborn, where "there's an odd fellow snuffles in the nose that shows a motion about Bishopsgate," who will let them use his show, in which disguise they reckon they'll "live like young Emperors."

A little later, however, Stroud and his servant come up to town, and pay a visit to the house in which the motion is shown. The room seems to have been quite small, for he asks, "Shall I see all Norwich in the corner of a little chamber?" to be told, "You shall see it . . . 'tis in this house . . . 'tis called a motion." The master of the motion enters and describes the show as follows: "Gentlemen, the first conceit you are to see is tumbling . . . you shall likewise see the famous city of Norwich, and the stabbing of Julius Cæsar in the French Capital"—he is corrected to the effect that it should be the Capitol in Rome—"by a sort of Dutch Mesapotamians. . . . You shall likewise see the amorous conceits and love songs betwixt Captain Pod of Pye Corner and Mrs Rump of Ram Alley, never described before. . . . Or if it please, you shall see a stately combat betwixt Tamberlaine the Great and the Duke of Guise the less, performed on the Olympic Hills in France." At this point Stroud in impatience tears off the showman's mask, revealing Canbee beneath, and the performance proceeds no farther.

What sort of motion was this? It was almost certainly a puppet show, for when Stroud's man smashes the show up he declares, "I have confounded their motion . . . to the utter undoing of all motion-mongers and puppet-players."

The show must have consisted of a series of short items. An acrobat; a view of the important town of Norwich, perhaps painted in aerial perspective like Visscher's familiar view of London; a historical scene of the death of Julius Cæsar; a bawdy song between two familiar London characters; and an exciting fight between Tamberlaine and the Duke of Guise (the instigator of the Massacre of St Bartholomew)—probably for no better reason than that these two figures happened to be at hand. Norwich, Julius Cæsar, and the Duke of Guise are mentioned as being featured in other puppet shows of this period. This puppet show, even though it never actually began, helps us considerably in forming a picture of the Elizabethan motion; we can see it as a robust, unsophisticated entertainment, drawing its subject-matter from the chronicles of history, its characters from the heroes of the past, all jumbled together with no attempt at historical accuracy, and spiced with topical allusions.

Fortunately the text of one English puppet show of this period has been preserved by the inclusion of a puppet play in Ben Jonson's *Bartholomew Fair* of 1614. This is such an important piece of evidence that it must be examined in detail. The setting of the play is at Smithfield during the time of the Fair, and it presents a fascinating panorama of low life in Jacobean London. The puppet show is one of the shows at the fair, and is presented by a showman called Leatherhead. The full value of the puppet play can be appreciated only by reading the entire text, which is somewhat vulgar for modern taste, but the following abridged extract of its opening scene will give an indication of its quality. The title is announced as "The ancient modern History of Hero and Leander," and it is introduced by Leatherhead standing in front of the stage (the stage directions are modern and conjectural):

LEATHERHEAD.

Gentles, that no longer your expectations may wander,
Behold our chief actor, amorous Leander.

[LEANDER *appears on the stage and stirs a barrel.*

With a great deal of cloth, lapped round him like a scarf,
For he yet serves his father, a dyer at Puddle-wharf. . . .
Now, as he is beating to make the dye take the fuller,
Who chances to come by but fair Hero in a sculler;
And, seeing Leander's naked leg and goodly calf,
Cast at him from the boat a sheep's eye and a half.

[HERO *is rowed across the stage in a ferry-boat, and makes signs to* LEANDER.

Now she is landed, and the sculler come back.
By and by you shall see what Leander doth lack.

[*The boat returns, rowed by* COLE, *the ferryman.*

LEANDER (PUPPET).
Cole, Cole, old Cole!

LEATHERHEAD.
That is the sculler's name, without control.

LEANDER (PUPPET) [*shouting loudly*].
Cole, Cole, I say, Cole!

LEATHERHEAD [*to the puppet*].
We do hear you. . . . Is the dyer turned collier? How do you sell?

LEANDER (PUPPET) [*to* LEATHERHEAD].
A pox on your manners; kiss my hole here, and smell.

LEATHERHEAD [*to the puppet*].
Kiss your hole and smell! There's manners indeed! . . .

LEANDER (PUPPET) [*to the ferryman*].
Here, Cole. What fairest of fairs was that fare thou landest but now at Trig Stairs? . . .

COLE (PUPPET) [*leaning out of his boat*].
It is lovely Hero.

LEANDER (PUPPET).
Nero?

COLE (PUPPET) [*hitting* LEANDER *over the head with his oar*].
No. Hero! . . .

LEATHERHEAD [*to the audience*].
Leander says no more, but as fast as he can
Gets on all his best clothes, and will after to the Swan.

[*Exit* LEANDER *with his barrel, to change clothes.*
[*The ferryman starts to row.*

Stay, sculler!

COLE (PUPPET).
What say you?

LEATHERHEAD.
You must stay for Leander,
And carry him to the wench.

COLE (PUPPET) [*leaning out of the booth and striking him on the head*].
You rogue, I am no pander! . . .

LEATHERHEAD.
Oh, my head, my head!

And so on. The contumacious Cole was evidently the type of the London waterman, the ancestor of many a cabman and taxi-driver since.

And so the robust and vulgar little drama goes on its way in verses as crude as its humour. Leander is rowed across the Thames to the inn where Hero is drinking; Cupid, disguised as a barman, puts a love potion in her drink; and she has a ridiculous love scene with Leander, which is interrupted by the arrival of Damon and Pythias, two quite irrelevant characters who are continually quarrelling and fighting. Leatherhead

THE PUPPET-SHOW SCENE FROM "BARTHOLOMEW FAIR," AS RECONSTRUCTED FOR THE OLD VIC, 1950

Puppets made by John Wright.

Photo John Vickers

helps the story along with a running commentary, and is often interrupted by the puppets, and once again assaulted by them. In the midst of the *mêlée* a Puritan bursts in and denounces the show as a profanity; Leatherhead cannot answer his theological arguments himself, but he puts up one of his puppets, King Dionysius, to debate with him. The argument is finally clinched in favour of the puppets when the Puritan denounces them for masquerading males as females, and Dionysius draws up his costume to show a sexless puppet body beneath!

The plot of the puppet play is a ridiculous mixture and parody of two classical legends that were well-known to the Elizabethans.[16] In the original story Leander was a youth of Abydos, who fell in love with Hero, a virgin priestess of the temple at Sestos; they used to meet secretly at night by Leander swimming across the Hellespont, guided to his destination by a lamp which Hero placed in the window of her tower. One night a great storm was raised by the disapproving gods, the lamp was extinguished, Leander was drowned, and Hero, on seeing his dead body, threw herself also into the waves. Damon and Pithias were devoted friends; upon one being condemned to death by King Dionysius the other pledged his own life as surety; their names were handed down in popular legend as examples of perfect friendship.

The point of the joke is the transplanting of these classical legends into a setting of low life in seventeenth-century London; similarly, Romeo and Juliet were played by costermongers in nineteenth-century burlesques. There are some hints that Ben Jonson's puppet play had, in fact, been written some fifteen years earlier, perhaps for the real puppet stage.[17] *Hero and Leander* was something of a literary squib, written with the tongue in the cheek, but it was clearly closely modelled on the contemporary puppet dramas, and it certainly is a genuine play for puppets, with its knock-about funny business, its vulgarity, and its repartee between the showman, the public, and the puppets. Although it still leaves some problems unanswered, it lifts the story of the English puppet theatre from surmise into literature.

No such building as a puppet theatre existed at this time, when theatres for living actors were only a recent innovation; the puppet shows were presented in temporary booths or in hired rooms at fairs, at inns, and on busy street corners. From the mass of vague contemporary allusions it is possible to establish five pitches in London at which puppet shows were given:

1. Bartholomew Fair. This was held at Smithfield in August. The earliest indication of motions here is in 1600.[18]

2. St John's Street, north of Smithfield. At a puppet play here in 1599 "the house fell and hurt between 30 and 40 persons, and slew five outright, whereof two (they say) were good handsome whores."[19] This was probably an inn, hired for occasional performances, and not the Red Bull Theatre which is believed to have been erected in this street (perhaps on the same site) in about 1605.

3. Holborn Bridge, across the river Fleet in Holborn. Canbee's show in 1600 was in this area. *The Actors' Remonstrance* of 1643 complains of

"the famous motion of *Bel and the Dragon* so frequently visited at Holborn Bridge these passed Christmas holidays."

4. Fleet Bridge, across the river Fleet in Fleet Street. In 1599, "they say there's a new motion of the city of Nineveh, with Jonas and the Whale, to be seen at Fleet Bridge";[20] in 1605, "'twere a rare motion to be seen in Fleet Street. Ay, in the Term";[21] in 1651, "I would have showed him at Fleet Bridge for a monster. I would have beggered the Beginning of the World, the strange birds from America, and the puppets too."[22] This was a popular pitch for shows and freaks of all kinds.

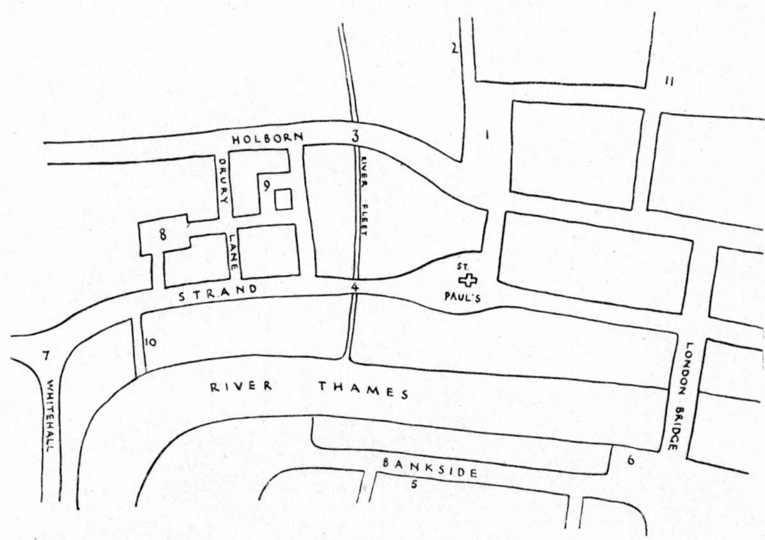

PLAN OF LONDON SHOWING PLACES WHERE PUPPET SHOWS WERE PERFORMED IN THE SEVENTEENTH CENTURY

1. Bartholomew Fair, Smithfield; 2. St John's Street; 3. Holborn Bridge; 4. Fleet Bridge; 5. Paris Garden; 6. Southwark Fair; 7. Charing Cross; 8. Covent Garden; 9. Lincoln's Inn Fields; 10. Salisbury Change; 11. Moorfields. *Off the Map.* May Fair.

5. Paris Garden, on Bankside. In 1584 Lupold von Wedel, a German visitor to England, described some kind of puppet show set up for comic relief in the circular arena here, after bull- and bear-baiting was over; it was "a device in which a man displayed a number of little men and women, dancing, wrestling, and talking together; and at the end one of the little men threw pieces of white bread into the crowd, who scrambled to pick them up." The entertainment concluded with a firework display.

An oblique reference of 1592 to "Paris Garden, wherein he will so tamper with the interpreter of the puppets" confirms the presence of puppet shows in this popular Elizabethan pleasure resort.[23]

The London performances were, however, comparatively unimportant for the puppet showmen, and the majority of these made their living by touring the country. We find records of them at Gloucester in 1582, at Southampton in 1585, at Stratford-on-Avon in 1597, at Coventry in 1599, at Dover in 1610, at Leicester in 1626, at Worcester in 1630, at Norwich in 1635, and so on. The motion men joined the great army of vagrants who were milling across England at this time; there were discharged soldiers and shipwrecked sailors, landless peasants and unemployed labourers, gipsies, fraudulent beggars, poor Toms, tinkers, pedlars, ballad-sellers, fortune-tellers, fencers, jugglers, minstrels, and players.

The old kindly and sometimes abused charity of the monasteries was no more, and country gentlemen were seized with terror at the spectacle of these swarming bands of rogues and vagabonds. Attempts were made to raise charitable alms for deserving cases, and against the rest the law struck savagely: offenders had the lobes of their ears branded and were publicly whipped. No doubt the Elizabethan Vagrancy Acts were aimed chiefly at the thieves and beggars, but every kind of travelling entertainer was a potential vagabond and was specifically included in their scope—"jugglers, pedlars, tinkers, and petty chapmen," as well as "fencers, bearwards, common players in interludes, and minstrels wandering abroad"; but there was a loophole left for "players of interludes belonging to any Baron of the realm, or any other honourable person of greater degree, to be authorised to play under the hand and seal of such baron or personnage." Thus to say, as is so often said, that actors were classed with rogues and vagabonds is extremely misleading; all the best acting companies had grown up as the personal entertainers of noble households, and when they began to venture outside to make their living from public performances they still carried the prestige of their patron's name. When they travelled in the provinces their presence was not always welcomed by the local councils, but they were, at least, on the right side of the law.

The puppet showmen certainly tried to take advantage of this loophole in the law by entering into the service of the nobility. Lord Chandos, for instance, in addition to his regular company of players, gave his patronage to a bearward and to some puppet players, who were at Gloucester in 1590; one puppet company, claiming royal patronage, appeared as Her

Majesty's Puppet Players in 1582, and perhaps the same show was travelling in 1585 as "the Queen's Bearward, with a lion, a porpintyne, and puppets." The noble patronage of puppet shows never became general, as its function was taken over by the Master of the Revels, who was authorized to issue a licence to all travellers presenting "any play, show, motion, feats of activity and sights whatsoever," and the possessors of this were enabled to escape the Vagrancy Laws. By 1614 Leatherhead could claim that "I have the Master of the Revels hand for it," and these licences became so valuable that they were sold from one company to another. A case was tried at Banbury in 1633, where it was discovered that an actor who had obtained a "Commission from the Master of the Revels" hired it to two men who "went with it with a puppet-play until they had spent all"; they then pawned the commission for four shillings; another actor finally redeemed it for twenty shillings down, and either ten or twenty pounds to follow. One is left sympathizing with the poor price the puppeteers obtained when they parted with the licence, and envying the profit made by the pawnbroker![24] When licences could not be obtained honestly, or bought second-hand, they could be forged; in 1630 a man was tried at Worcester for showing a "motion with divers stories in it" with a forged licence.

On arrival at a new town the showman's first duty was to present himself and his licence at the town hall and obtain permission to perform. It was often the custom for him to give a performance before the mayor and aldermen, and their friends, for which he would receive such payment as was thought proper, before setting up his theatre at an inn or other convenient place. The records of the payments for these performances have sometimes been preserved. For instance, Gloucester rewarded Her Majesty's Puppet Players with 22*s*., but this was exceptionally generous; ten or twelve shillings was the average payment, sometimes dropping as low as 3*s*. 4*d*. or 2*s*. 6*d*. Dover paid a puppet player 1*s*. to go away without performing!

These seventeenth-century town records have preserved, by a lucky chance, the names of many puppet showmen, and what they were paid; less often did they record what they acted. These puppets certainly never performed any of the literary dramas of the day, and statements to this effect made by nineteenth-century historians show a fundamental lack of understanding of the sub-world of popular entertainment in which they flourished. If their playlets had any counterpart in the living theatre it was probably the homely English jig, a semi-dramatic ballad sung and danced by three or four characters. The Elizabethan puppet shows were the dramas of an unlettered and conservative class of the people, to whom the Biblical and moral dramas of the old religion were still a living memory, and the Biblical themes that had quite disappeared from the human stage were still preserved by the puppets. The Devil was in a puppet show at Coventry in 1599, and we hear of plays on the stories of Babylon and Nineveh, Bel and the Dragon, Jonah and the Whale, the Creation of the World, the Destruction of Jerusalem, and so on; these were remembered, no doubt, because they were good and familiar stories, rather than for any explicit religious reason. Side by side with these went famous episodes from history, the whole frequently spiced with incongruous topical allusions, as when the notorious brothels of Sodom and Gomorrah were seen to be demolished by a crowd of Elizabethan apprentices. Subjects were sometimes borrowed from popular plays in the human theatre, and it would appear that Marlowe's *Tamburlaine* and *Massacre at Paris* and Shakespeare's *Julius Cæsar* were drawn upon. As we have seen, heroes from the history of all ages might be ridiculously jumbled together in a slapstick buffoonery, and the story was conveyed in the crudest of jog-trot verse.[25] But despite the ignorance and illiteracy of the showmen, we cannot doubt that the puppet shows played some part in preserving the stories and legends of our tradition among their humble audiences. Any startling contemporary event was chronicled by the puppets, too, and Leatherhead recalled *The Gunpowder Plot* as the most popular piece he had ever presented. The performances were helped along with tricks of various kinds, including fireworks and crackers,[26] and we may be sure that the 'business,' if not the actual characters, of the 'English Johns'—the Elizabethan stage clowns—found a place on the puppet stages. The texts themselves—with the exception of *Hero and Leander*—were never printed; they were certainly of no literary value whatever, and were probably seldom even written down.[27]

If the Italian motions were genuine puppet shows they would almost certainly have presented the *zanni* of the Commedia dell' Arte in their extempore dramas, but it is curious that there is no evidence whatever of any Continental influence upon the subject-matter or the characters of the Elizabethan puppet plays; they remained firmly rooted in the native tradition. It seems probable that the Italian motions were essentially non-dramatic examples of pictorial mechanism, and that the puppet shows of Elizabethan and Jacobean England were a purely native growth.

Despite the many references to motions and puppets in the literature of the time, it is by no means easy to say what types of puppets were in use.

I would hazard the guess that the complete absence of the well-worn simile on man moved by strings in Elizabethan writings strongly suggests that marionettes were, at least, not *well*-known. The type of puppets used in the *Bartholomew Fair* play is not specified, but they are brought out in a basket before the show, and this strongly suggests that they must have been glove puppets. Quite apart from this, the whole slapstick business of the puppet play, and especially the beating of the showman's head by the puppets, indicates—to my mind, conclusively—that the play was envisaged for glove puppets.[28] Similarly, the performance at Paris Garden described by von Wedel, with puppets wrestling and throwing things into the audience, inevitably suggests a hand-puppet show; as this was presented in something like a circus ring, with the audience in three tiers all round, the booth was probably a circular open-topped one, without any kind of backing. It is not clear how the manipulators inside were hidden from people in the galleries; perhaps the puppets moved in slots cut in a solid stage floor above the operators' heads.

There are two other indications which confirm that glove puppets were the usual form of puppet show during the first half of the seventeenth century; Sir William Davenant's poem *The Long Vacation in London*, written before 1642, describes the popular entertainers of the town as follows:

> Now vaulter good, and dancing lass
> On rope, and man that cries, hey pass . . .
> And man in chimney hid to dress
> Puppet that acts our old Queen Bess;
> And man that while the puppets play,
> Through nose expoundeth what they say,
> And man that does in chest include
> Old Sodom and Gomorrah lewd. . . .
> All these on hoof now trudge from town,
> To cheat poor turnip-eating clown.[29]

The "man in chimney hid" can only refer to a man standing up in the long, narrow booth used for glove puppets. There is a vaguer, but very suggestive, description in Jonson's *Poetaster*,[30] of 1601, of a man with a torn doublet as "what's he with the half arms there, that salutes us out of his cloak, like a motion?" Now, a glove puppet, of which the arms are merely the finger and thumb of the manipulator, does just exactly give the effect of having "half arms" sticking—as if from the elbows—out of its costume, and it would be difficult to apply this vivid pen-picture to any other kind of 'motion.' Marionettes may have been known, but the typical English puppet of the age of Shakespeare seems to have been a glove puppet.[31]

These puppets may have been roughly carved figures for the most part, but they were capable of at least one effect that is seldom achieved even to-day: like the Roman marionettes described by Apuleius, they rolled their eyes. In 1609 Ben Jonson referred to "the French puppets, with the eyes turned with a wire," and a Notts villager, lamenting the inability of his neighbours to present a puppet show, complained that "they'll be out in turning up the white of the eyes."[32]

We now also, for the first time in European history, find mention of an altogether different kind of puppet—the shadow show. One of these is actually represented in Ben Jonson's *A Tale of a Tub*, of 1633. It is performed at the end of the play by In-and-In Medlay, a cooper, as a private entertainment in a house, and is apparently intended to represent a pictorial summing up of the previous incidents of this not very amusing play. A large empty saltpetre tub is fitted with oiled lantern-paper round its upturned rim, upon which—it would appear—various cut-out silhouettes are pasted. In the centre of the tub a light is fixed which shines through the paper, and whose heat turns the circle of paper round by means of windmill-vanes to which it is fixed. The whole outfit is hidden behind a curtain until the performance is ready to begin. The show is given in five "motions," or separate tableaux, and Medlay sits in front to "interpret," or describe, each scene as it comes into view.[33]

Jonson would certainly not have introduced this shadow show unless the idea was a familiar one to his audience. The setting of the play is described in the Prologue as "at Wakes and Ales, with country precedents and old wives' tales," and the shadow show seems to have been an unsophisticated rustic entertainment. Perhaps some of the motions were, in fact, shadow shows.[34]

An essential feature of the Elizabethan puppet show was the 'interpreter,' or man who stood in front of the stage to describe what was going on and to backchat with the puppets. Sometimes he may merely have described the action that was being presented by mute puppets upon the stage; sometimes he may have spoken for the puppets—Leatherhead said, "I am the mouth of them all"—and sometimes he certainly introduced each character as it appeared and talked with them. In 1607 Dekker referred to old plays "which every punck and her squire (like the interpreter and his puppet) can rand out by heart they are so stale,"[35] and we have already seen how Canbee, Leatherhead, and Medlay played this part.

The origin of the interpreter may be that some puppet shows were brought by foreigners, Italians or French, who could not speak English, and so hired a native to stand outside the booth to translate, or interpret, what was being said. But, quite apart from any difficulty of language, the interpreter seems to have been needed to translate the puppets' speeches even when they spoke in English. A character in a play remarked that "puppets will speak such corrupt language, you'll never understand without an interpreter";[36] and it is very noticeable in *Bartholomew Fair* how often Leatherhead repeats for the benefit of the audience remarks made by the puppets. One of the spectators even asks, "What was that, fellow? pray thee tell me, for I scarce understand them."

The voice of Leatherhead's puppet was described as "neighing" and "hinnying" with a "treble creeking," and the high-pitched, affected voice of a merchant's wife was compared to "a feigned treble, or one's voice that interprets to the puppets."[37] We have already seen that the Italian and French puppet shows used some kind of device in the mouth of the speaker to give a distinctive tone to the puppets' speech, and there is no doubt that something similar was used in England. There are indications, however, that this effect was sometimes produced not so much by an actual squeaker as by giving a nasal twang to the speech by holding, or placing a clip over, the nose. Dekker describes how a justice, on meeting some Londoners at a time of plague, "started back . . . held his nose hard between his forefinger and his thumb, and speaking in that wise (like the fellow that described the villainous motion of Julius Cæsar and the Duke of Guise who—as he gave it out—fought a combat together) . . . cried out in that quaile-pipe voice. . . ."[38] We recall that Canbee's friend who showed a motion "snuffled in the nose," and a Notts villager, on the suggestion that he should put on a puppet play, exclaimed, "Absurd . . . there's none of us can speak in the nose."[39] Similarly, the poem by Davenant already quoted refers to the "man that while the puppets play, through nose expoundeth what they say." When speaking in this manner, or with any kind of impediment to clear enunciation, the meaning of the words is easily sacrificed to mere sound, and an interpreter of the puppet's speech was found to be useful.

Of the puppet showmen we know some names, and not very much more. A famous performer, referred to several times, was Captain Pod.[40] The travelling entertainers whose names have been preserved do not appear to have been actors of any standing; the small companies were fluid, and a man would pass from one to another quite easily. Sometimes one man would travel round on his own, but we often find cases of three travelling together, sometimes with several assistants as well. As many as twelve might travel in one troupe, and a company of this size presupposes an elaborate production.

An interesting point is that at least two female puppet performers are recorded. Although women had come with the Commedia dell' Arte acrobats, no actress had as yet appeared on the English stage. It is also worth noting that, although many of them displayed Italian motions, the names of all these showmen are English or Welsh. Whatever tricks it may have borrowed from foreign visitors, the English puppet show was a truly indigenous art.

Of the puppet showmen in literature, Leatherhead was also the proprietor of a Toy Booth at the fair; Canbee and Hadland were pure rogues —"we have a hundred tricks when we want cash," they declared; and Shakespeare describes Autolycus, the pedlar and ballad-seller in *The Winter's Tale*,[41] as an exhibitor of performing monkeys and a showman who "compassed a motion of the Prodigal Son, . . . and, having flown over many knavish professions, settled only in rogue." In this thieving, singing vagabond, haunting wakes, fairs, and bear-baitings, we have, no doubt, a fair picture of many of the minor puppet showmen of the time:

> Jog on, jog on, the footpath way,
> And merrily hent the stile-a:
> A merry heart goes all the day,
> Your sad tires in a mile-a.

There are a few more details of the puppet shows that can be pieced together to enlarge our picture. Plays were announced by bills,[42] which were sometimes pictorial,[43] and the time of performance was signalled by beating a drum and hanging out a flag or banner, just as in the human theatre. The price of admission for a fairground show was twopence for gentlefolks, and so presumably a penny for the rest, and the same show might be repeated nine times in an afternoon at a fair if it was very successful. This puts the duration of each performance at under half an hour.[44] But when we discover the number of spectators admitted to each performance we receive a surprise: in expatiating on the success of *The Gunpowder Plot* Leatherhead says, "There was a get-penny! I have presented that to an eighteen or twenty pence audience, nine times in an afternoon." We have already seen that the admission charge was a penny, and it would appear that Leatherhead was quite pleased with an audience of eighteen or twenty people for each performance. This seems very little, even nine times in an afternoon! However, some fifty people were hurt when a gallery fell down at the puppet play in St John's Street, so the audience there may well have been several hundred.

We must, however, not be led away by our enthusiasm into imagining these shows and motions as something more important than they were; they must take their modest place with the tumblers, the vaulters, and the conjurers. Sometimes they were signalled out for ridicule as a "ridiculous idle childish invention";[45] sometimes for attack, along with minstrels and interludes, as "ministers of vain pleasures, enchanting men's ears with poisoned songs, and with idle and effeminate pastimes corrupt noble wits";[46] but often they were ignored: puppets are not specified by name in any of the Vagrancy Acts, nor in the manifestos forbidding resort to all places of common assembly during times of plague. To set the Elizabethan puppet shows in their right place they must be seen as one of the minor popular entertainments of that pleasure-hungry age, patronized by the riffraff and women of the streets, by country gentlewomen and provincial gallants on their occasional visits to town,[47] or by wondering rustics at wakes and fairs. They must be seen with all the other strange sights of a brave new world:

To see a strange outlandish Fowl,
A quaint Baboon, an Ape, an Owl,
A dancing Bear, a Giant's bone,
A foolish Engine move alone,
A Morris-dance, a Puppet play,
Mad Tom to sing a Roundelay,
A woman dancing on a Rope,
Bull-baiting also at the Hope;
A Rhymer's Jests, a Juggler's Cheats,
A Tumbler showing cunning feats,
Or Players acting on the Stage,—
There goes the bounty of our Age.[48]

Vulgar and crude though they may have been, these puppets were a virile element in the popular theatre; known and loved by Shakespeare's audience, certainly known by Shakespeare himself, they played their own small part in the emerging splendour of the English stage.

The Commonwealth

In September 1642 the outbreak of the Civil War gave the puritan merchant element in Parliament a heaven-sent excuse to close the theatres, and, like the temporary restrictions of other wars, this one became permanent. In 1647, when the fighting was over, severe laws were passed to ensure that the theatres remained closed; any player discovered in the exercise of his vocation was to be whipped, and every person found witnessing the performance of a stage play was to be fined five shillings. Despite all this the art of the theatre was never entirely suppressed; there were private shows sometimes in noblemen's houses, and at Christmas-time or at Bartholomew Fair the officer of the guard might be bribed and a few stealthy performances gabbled through; or crude drolls, adapted from the popular plays of the old time, were presented by stealth under the description of rope-dancing. And, above all, the puppet plays, too lowly for legal interdiction, continued unhindered.

This was, at first, the cause of bitter complaint by the actors. In a pamphlet published in 1643 called *The Actors' Remonstrance or Complaint for the Silencing of their Profession* the author complained that although the theatres were closed, not only did the barbarous and beastly bear-baitings continue unchecked, but

> puppet plays, which are not so valuable as the very music between each act at ours, are still kept up with uncontrolled allowance; witness the famous motion of *Bel and the Dragon* so frequently visited at Holborn Bridge these passed Christmas holidays, whither citizens of all parts repair, with far more detriment to themselves than ever did the plays, comedies, and tragedies [at our theatres].

The pitches at Holborn and Fleet Bridge continued in use, but the great centre for puppet shows in London was at Smithfield in August during the time of Bartholomew Fair—as, indeed, it had been a generation before, in the time of Ben Jonson. A pamphlet of 1641 had described the

> strange sights and confused noises in the Fair. Here, a knave in a fool's coat, with a trumpet sounding or on a drum beating, invites you and would fain persuade you to see his puppets; there, a rogue like a Wild Woodman, or in an antic shape like an Incubus, desires your company to view his motion. . . . I think there are more motions in a day to be seen [here], than are in a term in Westminster Hall to be heard.[49]

The puppet show was evidently announced by drum and trumpet, like Perrinet Sanson's over two hundred years earlier, with the 'barker' dressed up like a jester or a clown. In 1647, when the penalties against actors were made more severe, John Warner, the Lord Mayor of London, made an effort to banish the puppet shows from the Fair; in the next year, however, his Worship died, and the puppets were left masters of the field, ready to add insult to defeat by caricaturing the late John Warner on their stages. A broadsheet elegy of November 1648 laments:

> Here lies my lord Mayor, under this stone,
> That last Bartholomew Fair no Puppets would own.
> But next Bartholomew Fair, who liveth to see,
> Shall view my Lord Mayor a Puppet to be.[50]

In 1655 the "Ancient Song of Bartholomew Fair," another piece of rough versifying put into the mouth of a visiting rustic, gives a little further information:

> For a penny you may zee a fine puppet play,
> And for twopence a rare piece of art. . . .
> Their zights are so rich, is able to bewitch
> The heart of a very fine man-a;
> Here's Patient Grisel here, and Fair Rosamond there,
> And the History of Susannah.[51]

A penny was still the usual entrance-fee; patient Grisel, fair Rosamond, and Susannah were all heroines of the puppet plays.

A revealing and vivid picture of the plays and puppet 'business' of this period is to be found—most unexpectedly—in a speech made in Parliament by Henry Cromwell in 1659; he is referring to his late father, Oliver, and claiming that despite current criticism he would be remembered in the future as a popular hero.

> For though men say he had a copper nose . . . his name still lives. Me thinks I hear 'em already crying thirty year hence at Bartholomew Fair, "Step in and see the Life and Death of brave Cromwell." Me thinks I see him with a velvet cragg [collar] about his shoulders, and a little pasteboard hat on his head riding a tittup a tittup to his parliament house, and a man with a bay leaf in his mouth crying in his behalf, "By the living God I will dissolve 'em," which makes the porters cry, "O brave Englishman." Then the Devil carries him away in a tempest, which makes the nurses squeak and the children cry.[52]

Although Cromwell did not specifically state that he was thinking of a puppet show, there is, I think, no doubt at all that that was in his mind. His racy description tells us—as, of course, we already knew—that historical characters were often introduced into the performances, and that the Devil, whom we have already met in the previous century, appeared at the end of the show in the medieval tradition and carried off the characters. The reference to the "man with a bay leaf in his mouth" who spoke for the characters may imply that the speech was almost unintelligible—the equivalent of speaking 'with a plum in his mouth'—or perhaps literally describes one method, which practical experiment has failed to elucidate, of producing the distinctive puppet squeak.

At this time the puppet show was, for most people, the only form of theatre available, and it flourished accordingly. But the puppets, who had played for so many centuries a modest and inconspicuous part in the entertainment of simple folk, were not, perhaps, of a quality to fit them for the prominent place they now occupied and the important rôle they had to play. Complaints were made of their wretched performances; puppet plays and rope-dancing had become so common and stale by 1653, we are told, that, tired by the very monotony of these entertainments, audiences were growing scarce. A contemporary writer begged "that such fools-baubles as puppet-plays" should be flung by, and real plays allowed.[53]

Once again, as in the first centuries of Christianity, when the public playhouses were closed and the actors exiled, the drama was preserved in the puppet booths. Roughly hewn and barbarous though the puppets may have been, garbled and vulgar the drolls they presented, untaught and illiterate the showmen who performed them, yet here the divine spark of the theatre found a home, and for eighteen long years of English history the drama knew no other stage.

Chapter V

PUNCHINELLO

The Restoration

IN the year 1660 Charles II came back as king to England. Bonfires were lit on the hills, wine ran in the streets, and the maypoles were set up again; in the words of a contemporary broadside, "little children did much rejoice, and ancient people did clap their hands, saying golden days began to appear"; men danced the morris again and sang ballads, and the playhouses opened their doors. There were to be some bitter dregs in the cup of popular rejoicing, but the froth at the top was pure joy.

Following the new king from his exile in the Courts of France and Holland there came his own faithful royalist retainers, and then the hangers-on and tradesmen of the Court, the bearers of Continental fashions—costumiers, dancing masters, chefs, entertainers, and puppet showmen.

On May 9, 1662, a Londoner with a pretty taste for the arts, Mr Samuel Pepys, noted in his diary that he visited Covent Garden to look at a picture hanging in an alehouse, and went "thence to see an Italian puppet play, that is within the rails there, which is very pretty, the best that ever I saw, and great resort of gallants." A fortnight later he brought his wife to see it, after a silly play at the opera, and noted that "indeed it is very pleasant. Here among the fiddlers I first saw a dulcimer played on with sticks knocking of the strings, and it is very pretty." On October the 8th of the same year this puppet theatre performed before the King at Whitehall; a special stage was set up for it in the Queen's Guard Chamber, and the Lord Chamberlain sent an order to the Jewel House for a gold chain and medal, worth twenty-five pounds, as a reward for the performer, "Signor Bologna, alias Pollicinella."[1]

A new character had appeared to thrust his presence into the English puppet theatres. As Pollicinella, Polichinelli, Punctionella, Polichinello, Punchinnanella, or Punchinello the English grappled with his unfamiliar syllables until he was finally shortened to plain Punch.

The plan of this book should now be apparent. If the reader has followed it so far he will now have been led by four separate but parallel paths to the moment in history when they converge upon the cobbled square at Covent Garden where, in 1662, an Italian showman presented Pollicinella in his puppet booth. We have traced the rise and development of the popular theatre in Europe, with its flowering in the Italian Comedy and its cast of comic masks; we have traced the development of puppets in Europe carried from one country to another by Italian showmen, and the establishment of Pulcinella as the hero of their dramas; we have traced the tradition of the ubiquitous English clown running through the popular theatre from the morality plays to the mummers; and we have traced the fortunes of the English puppet show to the collapse of Cromwell's Commonwealth. Here, inside the rails at Covent Garden, these strands may be joined together. Punchinello had arrived in England.

We are fortunate that at this time a Londoner with a keen interest in every form of dramatic entertainment should have noted in his diary the existence of six different puppet theatres between 1662 and 1668. Guided by Pepys, with some corroborative detail from the State and parish records, we can form a fairly good idea of the relative importance of puppet shows in Restoration London.

Encouraged, no doubt, by Signor Bologna's success, at least one other Italian puppet showman crossed to England, and set up his booth at Charing Cross; Pepys took his wife here on November 10, 1662, to show her "the Italian motion, much after the nature of what I showed her a while since in Covent Garden. Their puppets here are somewhat better, but their motions not at all." (By "motions" he may mean the manipulation of the figures, or perhaps the plays they acted.)

The next year, on August the 6th, Pepys was taking a convivial party home, with some merry kissing in the back of the coach, when they broke their journey "though nine o'clock at night," to look at "a puppet play in Lincoln's Inn Fields, where there was the story of Holofernes and other clockwork, well done." This seems to have been a simple play presented by automata, perhaps similar to the German Clockworks that he saw at Bartholomew Fair that year; these performed

> the Salutation of the Virgin Mary, and several scriptural stories; but above all there was at last represented the sea, with Neptune, Venus, mermaids, and Ayrid on a dolphin, the sea rocking, so well done, that had it been in a gaudy manner and place, and at a little distance, it had been admirable.[2]

Lincoln's Inn Fields was the site of a cluster of wooden sheds used for "puppet plays, dancing on ropes, mountebanks, etc.," for the demolition of which the inhabitants of the square petitioned the King in 1664, because "multitudes of loose disorderly people are drawn thither."[3]

Four years later another Italian puppet showman set up his booth in London, at Moorfields, an open space to the north of Holborn where wrestling and other sports were held. On August 22, 1666, Pepys took a small party here by coach, "and there saw 'Polichinello,' which pleases me mightily"; he also saw Mary, his late chambermaid, there, which possibly pleased him even more! A week later he took a jaunt out to Islington in the evening, ate a custard there, and on his way home called in to see "'Polichinello,' which I like the more I see it." Two days later he took another party out to Moorfields to see the puppets, but was "horribly frighted to see young Killigrew come in with a great many more young sparks; but we hid ourselves, so as we think they did not see us." After the play they went on across the fields to Islington, and there ate and drank and made merry, and came home singing.

A few hours later the Great Fire that was to burn half London to the ground had begun to spread from Pudding Lane. For many months there were other things than puppet shows to engage the citizens' attention; but by the next year what may have been the same show had established itself in a booth at Charing Cross, the open space at the top of Whitehall. This waste ground had been railed round, and was used for executions, and by various mountebanks. On March 20, 1667, Pepys took his wife "to Polichinelli at Charing Cross, which is prettier and prettier, and so full of variety that it is extraordinary good entertainment"; on April the 8th, after going to a poor play at the King's house, he went on "to Polichinello, and there had three times more sport than at the play"; and on October the 24th of the same year he went "to Charing Cross, there to see Polichinelli," but missed the show because the performance had already begun.

The proprietor of this puppet show paid a rent of about seven pounds a year to the parish of St Martin-in-the-Fields; in 1667 these payments are recorded as from "Punchinello, the Italian puppet player for his booth at Charing Cross," and in 1668 as from "Mons. Devone for his Playhouse."[4] Evidently the humble booth proprietor was giving himself airs, and this seems to have led to a clash with the law, for Gervase Price, the Sergeant trumpet, descended upon him with a demand for the payment of twelve pence a day, as due to him from every unregistered player: the theatre was, at this time, a monopoly in the hands of the King and the Duke of York, and unlicensed playhouses in London were not permitted. The puppet player, whose name is now given as Anthony Devotte, sought the assistance of the Master of the Revels, whose licence he held, and Sir Henry Herbert gave him a letter to the Lord Chamberlain, claiming that "Devotte is not in the notion of a player, but totally distinct from that quality and makes show of puppets only."[5] In the end the Sergeant seems not to have proceeded with the case, but trouble still lay ahead, and in 1672 "Anthony Devolto" was forced to petition the King to put a stop to several proceedings that were being brought against him "for matters relating to the keeping his sport of Polichinello at Charing Cross." The King, "having in a gracious favour to the petitioner allowed him to place himself at Charing Cross," gave orders that provided he demeaned himself without offence he was not to be prosecuted further.[6]

We do not know in what circumstances Charles II originally gave his patronage to this Italian puppet player, but he was soon to show his interest still further.

In November of the same year "Antonio di Voto, punchenello" was granted a licence from the Lord Chamberlain, on the King's orders, to play drolls and interludes with living actors, provided that he did not employ any of the actors from the two royal London theatres, or act any of the plays usually performed there.[7] He immediately celebrated this by announcing—in what is probably the earliest-known English printed playbill—a representation of *The Dutch Cruelties at Amboyna*, with the humours of the valiant Welshman, and twice daily performances of farces and drolls, "acted by men and women."[8]

It is not quite clear whether the puppets were now entirely displaced by human actors; the theatre was certainly still known as Punchinello's booth. In 1673 there was a dispute with the churchwardens as to who should pave the waste ground by the booth. Devoto no doubt found the mud a nuisance for his patrons, but thought he paid quite enough in rent as it was; the churchwardens naïvely record how much they paid their witnesses at the inquiry![9] Soon after this the booth must have been removed to make way for the statue of Charles I, which had been loyally hidden during the Commonwealth and was set up at the top of Whitehall (where it still stands to-day) in 1675. During the slow erection of this statue, while the site was still concealed by a hoarding, a contemporary poet complained:

What can the mystery be that Charing Cross
  These five months continues still blinded with boards?
Dear Wheeler impart: we are all at a loss,
  Unless Punchinello is to be restored.[10]

But Punchinello was not restored. To-day the fine statue of Charles I marks the site of one of the earliest and certainly one of the best puppet theatres in London. Devoto's playhouse may only have been a crude booth, but it had gained the patronage of the King, and in its day it must have been presenting one of the best entertainments in a city avid for entertainment. This is almost certainly "the famous Italian puppet play" seen by Evelyn;[11] and Pepys, for all his gossiping excursions into low life, was no fool and a good judge of theatre, and if he could turn from the Restoration drama to Polichinello, and find it three times more sport than at the play, we may indeed feel that the crude Elizabethan puppet drolls had been touched with magic.

Memories of a highly successful puppet theatre at this period were still preserved in 1750 when Colley Cibber noted in his *Apology for his Life*

> that I have been informed, by those who remember it, that a famous puppet-show in Salisbury Change (then standing where Cecil Street now is) so far distressed these two celebrated companies [the King's and the Duke's] that they were reduced to petition the King for relief against it.

Unfortunately this petition, if it ever really existed, has not been preserved; the date must have been before the union of the companies in 1684. The authority for this story is second-hand and not very good, and no other references to this show seem to have been discovered. There may be a confusion here with Devoto's theatre, but perhaps there was another show, rivalling it in popularity.

Puppets were still a popular show at the fairs, and here the old English tradition continued for a time undisturbed. At Southwark Fair, on September 21, 1668, Pepys found it very dirty, but "there saw the puppet-show of *Whittington*, which was pretty to see; and how that idle thing do work upon people that see it, and even myself too!"

At Bartholomew Fair, on August 30, 1667, he walked up and down, "and there, among other things, find my Lady Castlemayne at a puppet play, *Patient Grizill*, and the street full of people expecting her coming out." To his surprise she is greeted with respect when she appears, and drives away in her coach without so much as a hiss or a rotten apple! Five days later he takes his wife and his chief clerk to the fair and saw "Polichinelli." This may have been Devoto's show from Charing Cross,[12] or it may indicate that the Italian hero was already finding a place in the traditional English puppet plays. The next year, on August the 31st, he saw "Polichinelle" here. A ballad of 1686 enumerates the attractions of Smithfield:

Here are the rarities of the whole fair!
Pimper-le-Pimp, and the wise Dancing Mare;
Here's valiant St George and the Dragon, a farce,
A girl of fifteen with strange moles on her ar—,
Here is Vienna Besieged, a rare thing,
And here Punchinello, shown thrice to the King.[13]

Evidently James II (who had come to the throne the year before) was as generous a patron of Punch as his brother. Puppet shows too found their way into the Frost Fair of 1684, when the Thames froze solid and was covered with booths.[14]

The travelling showmen had their regular circuits, like judges. All the summer they toured the country wakes, and came up to London for Bartholomew and Southwark Fairs in August and September; then they wintered in town, finding a pitch in a busy thoroughfare to hang out their painted showcloths. If trade was thin a puppet play, a juggler (or conjuror), an animal freak, and a mountebank might join forces to make up one grand show—"and admit the cutpurse and Ballad-singer to trade under them, as Orange-Women do at a Playhouse."[15]

There were vast numbers of these itinerant performers now roaming through the country, and the Master of the Revels waged an energetic but often unsuccessful campaign to compel them to register themselves and purchase his licences. A town like Norwich, which was then the second city in the kingdom with some 29,000 inhabitants, was visited by puppet shows almost every year, and the town council complained in 1660 of the puppet shows and lotteries "which diverted the meaner sort of people from their labour in the manufacturies," and begged an order from the King empowering them to limit the stay of these unwelcome entertainers in the city. Capitalism and puritanism made a common front against the unpretentious pleasures of the labouring masses, but it was three years before the King gave his grudging consent.[16] The puppet players of Norwich seem to have been famous throughout England, for Davenant referred in 1663 to "the new motion men of Norwich, Op'ra-Puppets."[17] This town had figured (surprisingly) as the subject of puppet shows in the previous century.

These country strollers played the old Biblical dramas which were still remembered by the common people—*The Creation of the World* or *The Wisdom of Solomon*; favourite stories of the mistresses of English kings—*Henry II and Fair Rosamond*, or *Edward IV and Jane Shore* (but the performer announced it as Henry IV, and was corrected by the town clerk); and old English legends like *Whittington and his Cat* or *Maudlin, the*

Merchant's Daughter of Bristol. These stories had been shaped for centuries by ballads and story-tellers; they were the staple fare of chapbooks and drolls; the puppet theatre was one more link in the handing down of a folk literature. But something new was on the way; we have already seen it in London at Covent Garden, at Charing Cross, and at Bartholomew Fair; now it was to reach Norwich. In 1670 Mr Peter Dallman was given permission to "make show of one motion show consisting of three dancing monkeys, a piece of waterwork, and a polichanella." For the next fifteen years this showman was to pay regular visits to the town, playing for three weeks at a time at the Angel Inn, and by 1683 he had discarded the monkeys and the waterworks and was announcing his show as "His Majesty's Puntionella."[18] "Punchinella" had appeared at Cambridge by 1673, presented by Robert Parker;[19] no doubt other local records could tell a similar story. It is clear that within ten years of the first appearance of the Pulcinella puppet in England he had acquired sufficient popularity for English puppet showmen to adopt his name and character for their own provincial shows.

We are not told very much about the nature of these "Punchinello" performances: Pepys's descriptions are tantalizingly vague. It was obviously an Italian puppet show, but it probably came via France, for the spelling is often closer to "Polichinelle" than to "Pulcinella." Pepys refers to a dulcimer in the orchestra, so there must have been a good musical accompaniment. It is probably safe to assume that the performance relied largely on music, singing and dancing, and buffoonery of the Commedia dell' Arte tradition. If different plays were presented their names were not recorded; the name of the chief performer was sufficient title for the show. We do not even know if the language used was English or Italian. The Covent Garden theatre of Bologna was a fashionable show, "a great resort of gallants," who might have understood the foreign tongue, but four years later the "Polichinello" at Moorfields was patronized not only by Court sparks like Killigrew, but also by Mary, the servant-maid, and it evidently had a wide popular appeal; perhaps the singing was still in Italian, but some explanation must have been provided in English. The shows taken round the country by puppeteers like Peter Dallman were no doubt copied from the Italians in London, but they must have been adapted for rustic audiences, and the device of the 'interpreter' was still in use. The name of one of these has, by some chance, been preserved: Phillips was remembered for many years as a famous Merry Andrew, who had once played the fiddle at a puppet show, "in which capacity he held many a dialogue with Punch, in much the same strain as he did afterwards with the mountebank doctor, his master, upon the stage." He is said to have had the advantage of his fellows in being properly educated. A late-seventeenth-century print

MERRY ANDREW FROM TEMPEST'S "CRIES OF LONDON," C. 1690

shows a Merry Andrew, who may be Phillips, looking something like Pulcinella; no doubt he made himself up as a bigger version of the puppet whom he introduced. This engraving may, therefore, be—at one remove—the earliest illustration of Punchinello in England. It shows him with a hunchback, a great protruding belly, lined with big buttons down the front, and an untidy ruff; he is carrying a stick of some kind, and it looks as if it is made of several thin layers of lath, which would clack together with a jolly crack whenever he hit anyone; he has no hat or mask.[20]

Little information is available about the type of puppets at this time, but there are a few hints which suggest that it was the marionette that was now normally employed. The stage built in Whitehall Palace in October 1662, presumably for Bologna's performance, measured 20 feet by 18 feet, and was high enough off the ground for a door to be let into its side. This presupposes an elaborate fit-up, and is more than many marionette companies would require to-day. No glove-puppet booth could require anything so large. The fitting of the door to give access under the stage is suggestive. No doubt good use was made of trap-doors for apparitions and disappearances! In 1664 John Locke, in a letter written from Cleves, describes the Christmas crib in the local church, with the figures of the Virgin, Joseph, shepherds, angels, and so on:

> Had they but given them motion it had been a perfect puppet play, and might have deserved pence a piece; for they were of the same size and make that our English puppets are; and I am confident, these shepherds and this Joseph are kin to that Judith and Holophernes which I had seen at Bartholomew Fair.[21]

This very valuable description summons up in our minds a pleasant picture of heavily carved wooden marionettes, two or three feet high; the European tradition of crib figures is still sufficiently alive for us to be able to recapture in our imagination the rough, crude vigour of these seventeenth-century puppets.

There is also an indication of 1675 that the puppets could fly:

> Players turn puppets now at your desire,
> In their mouths nonsense, in their tails a wire,
> They fly through clouds of clouts and showers of fire.[22]

The indication that they were moved by wires is confirmed by an allusion to the statesmen, who

> Behind the curtain, by court-wires, with ease
> They turn those pliant puppets as they please.[23]

From now on the analogy between politics and wire-pulling was to flow very easily from the pens of the pamphleteers. Another reference in a ballad of the period indicates that puppets could skip (the whole passage is so pleasant that I cannot forbear quoting it in full):

A rare shite 'tis indeed, I needs must say,
To see men skip like puppets in a play.
To act the mimic, fiddle, prate, and dance,
And cringe like apes, is a le mode France;
But to be resolute, one to fight with ten,
And beat 'em's proper unto English men.[24]

Flying and skipping are, of course, impossible for glove puppets, but are particularly natural effects for marionettes. Another allusion refers to "a giant in a puppet show"[25]—a character that can be easily introduced on to the marionette stage.

Complicated marionette trick figures were being employed at this time for special effects in the human theatres. Ravenscroft's *Dame Dobson*, of 1683, describes a cunning conjuring old woman who pretended to possess magic powers, one of whose tricks was to have the dismembered limbs of a human carcass thrown down the chimney into her reception room, which then "joined themselves together, the body erected and walked about."[26] The same trick figure was used again the next year at Dorset Garden in Mountford's pantomime version of *Doctor Faustus*, when his limbs were seen "all torn asunder by the hand of Hell," but came together in a dance and song to bring down the curtain. One of Dame Dobson's customers admitted that "the device was very neat and cleverly performed, but how 'twas done I don't apprehend," but puppeteers will recognize here an old friend—the Dissecting Skeleton—in what must surely be his first appearance upon any stage. Whether this effect was also worked in the marionette theatres we do not know, but it seems very likely.

The Italian puppet theatres probably displayed fairly elaborate scenery, with machinery for changing the scenes and working the flying effects. When Signor Bologna was performing plays by Molière in Paris, at the Foire de Saint-Laurent, in 1678 he boasted that his "changes of scenery and numerous machines" had been adapted to the new stories, in which his "Roman Polichinel" was completely at home.[27]

We have already seen that glove puppets seem to have been the most common type of puppet in the first half of the seventeenth century, and we are now faced with the discovery that marionettes seem to have usurped that position for the second half of the century. The explanation of this change is, I think, that the Italian puppets whose prettiness so delighted a critical spectator like Pepys must have been marionettes, and the popularity of Pulcinella swept this type of figure to the fore. The old Elizabethan glove puppet, with its tawdry fit-up and violent cudgellings,

GLOVE PUPPETS GATHER A CROWD ROUND A MOUNTEBANK'S PLATFORM

A necklace of teeth indicates that the man was a tooth-drawer. A watercolour by Marcellus Laroon, the Elder, c. 1690

By courtesy of the Trustees of the British Museum

was driven into the background—the last resort of the poorest country strollers. That is the simplest and most probable answer to the problem, but, baldly stated like that, it almost certainly oversimplifies the question: John Locke's letter, for instance, suggests that the old English religious puppet plays were presented by marionettes, perhaps in an unbroken tradition from *The Resurrection* at Witney. The whole question of the nature of these early puppets is involved and difficult; we are dependent upon hints and surmise, and it is dangerous to dogmatize.

The puppets by this time were finding their way into the nursery, and in 1682 we have the first reference to a home puppet theatre. Sir Thomas Browne, in a letter to his daughter-in-law about his nine-year-old grandson, Tommy, writes:

> He is in great expectation of a tumbler you must send him for his puppet show; a Punch he has and his wife, and a straw king and queen, and ladies of honour, and all things but a tumbler, which this town [Norwich] cannot afford; it is a wooden fellow that turns his heels over his head.[28]

These, obviously, were some kind of marionettes. Punch was evidently a favourite with the children already, and for the first time we hear that he has a wife.

The popularity of the puppet inspired a few attempts to transfer Pulcinella to the human theatre. At the end of Shadwell's *The Sullen Lovers* of 1668 "a little comical gentleman to entertain you with" is announced, and turns out to be "a boy in the habit of Pugenello," who "traverses the stage, takes his chair, and sits down, then dances a jig." Dancing while sitting on a chair must have enabled the actor to kick both his legs about as if defying the laws of gravity, thus providing an amusing imitation of a marionette's movements. Exactly the same effect is employed in the ballet *Petrouchka*. Pepys found the play tedious, "but a little boy, for a farce, do dance Polichinello, the best that ever anything was done in the world."[29] Despite this glowing report, Punchinello never gained any great success as a human actor; he was, and has remained, intrinsically a puppet.

The success of this Italian visitor was to be reflected in other surprising ways. A gun was christened Punchinello from its shortness and bigness; and Pepys heard a fat child in a poor alley off Long Acre nicknamed Punch by its parents, "which pleased me mightily, that word being become a word of common use for all that is thick and short."[30] We must try to approach the seventeenth-century Punchinello with open minds. What impressed people was his shortness and fatness: there is no mention at present of a hooked nose or a ferocious temper.

The Revolution

In 1688 James II was driven from his throne; Englishmen, no doubt, were glad to get rid of the foreign foppishness, the immorality, the Popish mummeries, and the Continental fashions of the Stuart Court. Punchinello had come over with Charles; was he to be sent packing with James?

England was not to see much more of Italian puppet shows for a hundred years, but Punchinello had been taken to our hearts; the gallants no longer crowded to his fashionable little theatres, but the "meaner sort of people" were flocking to his booths in the villages and at the fairs. When Ned Ward described, in his vivid, racy way, a visit to May Fair in 1699 he found there one company of actors, some rope-dancers, a handful of low "boosing-kens," and "a Puppet Show, where a senseless dialogue between Punchenello and the Devil was conveyed to the ears of the listening rabble through a tin squeaker, which was thought by some of 'em as great a piece of conjuration as ever was performed by Dr Faustus." Of the crowd here Ned Ward declared that he had never beheld in his life "such a number of lazy, lousy-looking rascals, and so hateful a throng of beggarly, sluttish strumpets." In the same year he visited Bartholomew Fair, and passed by with contempt "a couple of Puppet shows, where monkeys in the balconies were imitating men, and men making themselves monkeys, to engage some of the weaker part of the multitude, as women and children, to step in and please themselves with the wonderful agility of their wooden performers."[31]

From these passages we may learn a little more about the seventeenth-century puppet shows. We have already encountered the Devil at Coventry in 1599 and in the fairground puppet dramas of the Commonwealth; here he is now playing opposite Punchinello. He is referred to again by Samuel Butler in the sixteen-seventies, ridiculing the plan of Greek tragedy:

> Reform and regulate the puppet-play,
> According to the true and ancient way;
> That not an actor shall presume to squeak,
> Unless he have a licence for't in Greek:
> Nor devil in the puppet-play be allowed
> To roar and spit fire, but to fright the crowd,
> Unless some god or demon chance to have piques
> Against an ancient family of Greeks.[32]

This reminds us again that the old Elizabethan firework effects were still popular; and its reference to the puppets' squeak corroborates Ward's interesting account of the tin squeaker through which their speeches were spoken. This is, of course, none other than the Italian *pivetta*, variants of which we have already noticed in England. That Punchinello spoke with a special kind of voice is made certain by an instruction for a character in Otway's *Friendship in Fashion* of 1678 to "speak in Punchinello's voice."[33] In another passage Butler ridicules foreign fashions:

> [Hats] with broad brims sometimes like umbrellas,
> And sometimes narrow as Punchinello's.[34]

Here we have another glimpse of Punchinello's costume—the high, narrow-brimmed conical hat that we have met so often already. And an idea of his character is given by a seventeenth-century ballad:

> He was such a fellow
> when he danced a Jig,
> He kissed like Punchanello
> or a sucking pig.[35]

Evidently an uninhibited lover!

The theatres in which the puppet shows were given at the fairs must have been, like the other booths, transportable wooden sheds with a kind of balcony on which the performers paraded outside; sometimes performing monkeys were used, like Brioché's, to attract a crowd. We must be careful to rid our minds of preconceived notions: the puppets performed, like the actors, inside a theatre, for which one paid for admission. There is no suggestion so far of free performances in the open air.

Something of the flavour of the puppet shows of this period can be obtained from the puppet play introduced by Tom D'Urfey into the third part of his *Comical History of Don Quixote* of 1695.[36] This retells the story of Don Quixote and the puppets, from Cervantes, but the play is given a purely English setting; Master Peter arrives at a wedding-feast with his motion, and is invited to give a puppet show; at Don Quixote's request he presents the story of Don Gayferos and Melisandra. The play opens with the Emperor Charlemagne seated, surrounded by his knights, while Master Peter, standing with a rod in his hand in front of the stage, explains that the Emperor is impatient at the delay of Don Gayferos in leaving to rescue his wife, Melisandra, who has been captured by the Moors. At last Don Gayferos enters:

> Great is my sorrow, high and mighty sir,
> That I this journey did so long defer;
> But this a little may excuse the same,
> Myself have had the stone, my horse was lame.

But now all things are suiting to my mind,
My horse is well before, and I behind;
I'll free my spouse, spite of what e're retards,
From the curst Moorish king and all his guards. . . .
I'll fetch her spite of bars or iron lock,
And you to-morrow, sir, by five a clock
Shall find her in my bed without her smock.

The second scene discovers Melisandra at the Moorish Court, and opens with a duet by two puppets, representing a Captain and a Town Miss, singing a contemporary ballad. Melisandra then resists the Moorish king's advances:

MELISANDRA.
My love, long since locked up, is given away,
And of that lock my husband has the key.
MOOR.
But for that casket I a picklock have.
MELISANDRA.
A picklock suits a thief, sir, not the brave.
MOOR.
We all are thieves in love's free commonweal,
And know the treasure sweetest when we steal.

But his pleas and threats are of no avail, and Melisandra is dragged off to imprisonment in a tower.

Don Gayferos now rides in on his horse, and calls to his wife. She appears at the window of the tower and climbs out down a rope of sheets, but half-way down her skirt unfortunately catches on a hook:

DON GAYFEROS.
Why sighs my love?
MELISANDRA.
Alas, I'm hung in the air.
DON GAYFEROS.
I'll cut thee down, with a swift lover's care.
MELISANDRA.
Ah, sir, not for the world, my knees are bare,
And something may indecently be shown
You may not peep upon, though 'tis your own.
DON GAYFEROS.
In such distress, we the best means must prove;
To save your modesty, I'll wink, my love.

So she gets safely and modestly down to the ground, mounts up behind her husband, and rides off. The Moors, however, discover her flight and pursue her; they were just on the point of engaging in battle with Charlemagne's army when Don Quixote, who had been following the proceedings with unconcealed anxiety, drew his sword and hacked the puppets to pieces in the belief that they were real people.

At the actual performance these puppets were, apparently, represented by children, and the play of Don Gayferos is a Spanish story that was never performed in England, but the setting of the show and the speeches of the puppets are undoubtedly true to English conditions. The interpreter standing in front of the stage and the rough rhymes of the little play, with their puerile vulgarities, are in the same spirit as *Hero and Leander* eighty years earlier. These simple verses, a genuine expression of popular literature, represent the tradition of the English puppet play that was to endure for another century.

Just before the end of the seventeenth century the puppets gained the dignity of inspiring a poem—and a Latin poem at that. Joseph Addison, then a fellow at Magdalen College, Oxford, had amused himself by composing a number of Latin poems in a mock-heroic style on such mean and trivial subjects as the Battle of the Pigmies and the Cranes, the Barometer, the Bowling Green, and the Puppet Show. Here, at last, we have a full and fascinating description of the quarry that we have chased for so many centuries through so many vague and recondite allusions.[37]

The setting of the theatre is painted in the opening phrases:

Where some Buffoon from gaping crowds provokes
Peals of loud mirth by tricks and vulgar jokes,
From far and near, the gay and curious come,
Enter the booth, and fill the spacious room;
Not undistinguished are the honours there,
But different seats their different prices bear.
At length, when now the curtain mounts on high,
The narrow scenes are opened to the eye;
Where wire-partitions twinkle to the sight,
That cut the vision, and divide the light.
Ingenious artifice! of sure deceit,
Since naked prospects would betray the cheat.
And now the squeaking tribe proceeding roams
O'er painted mansions, and illustrious domes;
The Drama swells, and to the wondering eyes
Triumphs, and wars, and solemn consults rise;
All actions that on life's great stage appear
In miniature are represented here.

But one there is, that lords it over all,
Whom we or Punch, or Punchanello call,
A noisy wretch, like boatswains always hoarse,
In language scurrilous, in manners coarse;
Large is the buckle that his vest controls,
His mimic eye with living motion rolls,
His belly turgid of enormous size,
Behind his back a bulk of mountain lies.
His limbs a bulk and strength superior boast,
And uncontrolled he struts, and rules the roost,
Chatters, and laughs immoderately loud,
And scolds and swaggers at the pigmy crowd.
E'en when some serious action is displayed,
And solemn pomps in long procession made,
He uncontrolable, of humour rude,
Must with unseasonable mirth intrude.
Scornful he grins upon their tragic rage,
And disconcerts the fable of the stage;
Sometimes the graceless wight, with saucy air,
Makes rude approaches to the painted fair,
The nymph retires, he scorns to be withstood,
And forces kisses on th'unwilling wood.

Not so his fellows of inferior parts,
They please the theatre with various arts;
Lascivious sport, in circling turns advance,
And tire their little limbs in active dance.
Sometimes a train more glorious to behold,
With gems resplendent and embroidered gold,
In robes of state attired and rich array,
Displays the pomp of some illustrious day.
Small nobles, tiny peers, a splendid throng,
And wooden heroines pass in state along,
With active steps the gentle knights advance,
And graceful lead the ladies to the dance. . . .

Yet oft their sports are lost in loud alarms,
Whilst eager fly the dapper chiefs to arms. . . .
Now swords, and spears, and murdering guns they bear,
And all the fatal instrument of war;
The scenes with crackers' dreadful bursts resound,
And squibs and serpents hiss along the ground,
Whole troops of slaughtered heroes strew the stage,
The crimes of dire revenge and civil rage.

Soon as the fury of the fight is o'er,
And War's tumultuous din is heard no more,
Their former cares the jovial tribe renew,
And all the pleasant arts of peace pursue.
Heroes of old, in happier ages born,
Whose godlike acts the Sacred Page adorn,
On this low stage in miniature return.
There you may see a venerable band
Of Patriarch-Sires in hoary order stand,
Their faces furrowed, as they once appeared,
And their chins cloathed with silken lengths of beard. . . .

Now sing we, whence the Puppet actors came,
What hidden power supplies the hollow frame,
What cunning agent o'er the scenes presides,
What hand such vigour to their limbs supplies.
The artist's skill contrives the wooden race,
And carves in lifeless sticks the human face;
Then shapes the trunk, and then the parts assigns,
And limbs to limbs in meet proportion joins;
Then ductile wires are added, to command
Its motions, governed by a nimble hand.
And now, directed by a hand unseen,
The finished puppet struts before the scene,
Exalts a treble voice and eunuch tone,
And squeaks his part in accents not his own.

The information gleaned from Addison's poem may be briefly summarized. A Merry Andrew, or clown of some kind, gathered a crowd outside the booth; there were different prices for different qualities of seats; a fine-wire mesh was stretched across the proscenium opening to hide the manipulation of the puppets from being seen (as at Saint-Germain in 1713, and as described by Quadrio in 1744);[38] painted scenery and a curtain were used; the puppets spoke in shrill and strident voices (no doubt produced by a squeaker, as described by Ward); Punchinello[39] was larger than the other puppets in size, with a big belly and a hump-back (still no mention of the nose); fireworks were still a popular stage effect; the puppets were made of wood, and are quite certainly marionettes; Punchinello's eyes rolled (like the French puppets described by Ben Jonson, and the Roman puppets described by Apuleius).

The light this poem throws on the character of Punchinello is one of its most valuable features. Once again, we must forget all about babies and wife-beating and approach the matter with completely open minds. He is described as a vulgar, loud-mouthed buffoon, lording it over the other puppets; an ardent, if unromantic, lover; and a boisterous intruder into the serious scenes of the play.

Is this the sly comic servant of Italian tradition, the half-wit, falling into trouble and getting out of it, mime, acrobat, and *zany*? There are elements, no doubt, of the Commedia dell' Arte tradition; the name shows an unmistakable genealogy from Pulcinella to Punch: the hump and the belly, though not features of the early Pulcinella, certainly belonged to Polichinelle; of the costume, the hat and perhaps the buttons alone remain. But there is another influence here: we remember the loud-mouthed Vice of the moralities and the ubiquitous clown of the Elizabethan stage; Hamlet's complaint rings home again; the shades of boisterous old comics stir; the English stage fool has found a new body.

It would be ungenerous to minimize in any way the great part Italian, and possibly French, puppet showmen played in the establishment of puppet theatres in England, and in the evolution of the character of Punch. Their rôle has been recorded here with every care, and we are for ever their debtors. But in the last analysis their part was a secondary one. Throughout history foreign puppets have acted always like a transfusion of new blood into English puppet shows, but the old unpretentious, solid English tradition was always there to receive it. Puppets played here long before the Italian motions set the town talking, and comic braggarts strutted on our stages long before Pollicinella set up his booth at Covent Garden. Punchinello may trace an ancestry as far as Imperial Rome and Attic Greece, but Punch belongs to England.

Chapter VI

THE TALK OF THE TOWN: PUPPET THEATRES IN EIGHTEENTH-CENTURY LONDON

Powell from the Bath

AS we pass into the eighteenth century the age of bravura is succeeded by the age of elegance, panache by decorum, coarseness by sensibility. Bawdy Restoration comedy gave way to domestic sentimentalities, Italian singers and dancers nearly drove the legitimate drama from the stage, and the shallow, artificial world of London Society discovered a delicious source of amusement in the little satires and artificial heroics of the puppet theatre. On a superficial view, few periods of history can have been so sympathetic to the puppets as the eighteenth century, and never before could the puppets so naturally hold up the mirror of ridicule to their masters. Never before or since have the puppets played quite so effective and so well publicized a part in fashionable Society; never before or since have puppet theatres so successfully made themselves the talk of the town.

The first, and the most famous, of these fashionable puppet shows was that directed by Martin Powell in the Little Piazza at Covent Garden. We first hear of Powell at Bath in 1709, when he was playfully alluded to in the pages of *The Tatler*.[1] Bath was then just springing into popularity as a fashionable spa; a few people went there for the waters, but all Society flocked there between May and September to be seen, to gossip, to dance, play cards, and gamble. By 1705 its first theatre was opened, and the puppets were not far behind. A more suitable spot for a light hot-weather entertainment could not be imagined. The performances seem to have been on traditional lines: they included *The Creation of the World*, with a scene showing Punch and his wife dancing in Noah's Ark, a jig, rope-dancing, a ghost, and a lover hanging himself; they were announced by a drummer parading the streets on horseback. All this was very typical of other puppet shows of the period. That winter

Powell came to London, and by January 1710 he was giving performances at a theatre in St Martin's Lane. *The Tatler* jokingly complained that he was drawing most of the female spectators away from the opera,[2] and Aaron Hill wrote a prologue for Drury Lane lamenting how the taste of the town had been cast

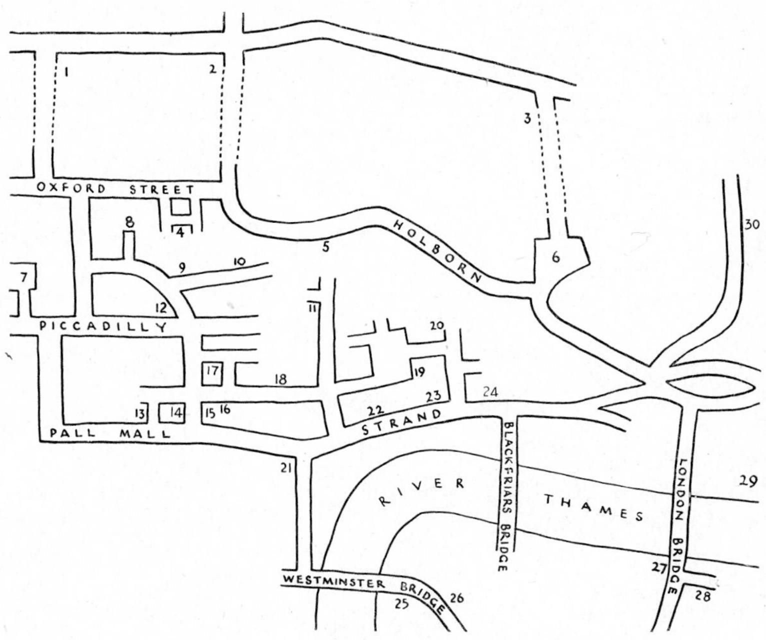

Plan of London showing Places where Puppet Shows were performed in the Eighteenth Century

1. Marylebone Gardens; 2. Tottenham Court Fair; 3. Sadler's Wells Theatre; 4. Cassino Rooms, Great Marlborough Street; 5. The King's Head, Oxford Market, St Giles; 6. Bartholomew Fair, Smithfield; 7. May Fair; 8. Saville Row; 9. Hickford's Great Room, Brewer Street; 10. The King's Arms, Compton Street; 11. Punch's Theatre, Upper St Martin's Lane; 12. 22 Piccadilly; 13. The Great Room, 24 St Alban's Street; 14. The Opera Room, Haymarket; 15. Little Theatre, Haymarket; 16. The Tennis Court, James Street; 17. Hickford's Great Room, Panton Street; 18. The Nag's Head, James Street; 19. Punch's Theatre, the Little Piazza, Covent Garden; 20. Covent Garden Theatre; 21. Spring Gardens; 22. The Scenic Theatre, Strand; 23. Exeter Change, Strand; 24. Lyceum Theatre; 25. Astley's Amphitheatre; 26. The Apollo Gardens; 27. Southwark Fair; 28. The Chinese Academy, Tooley Street; 29. Tower Hill; 30. Spitalfields Market. *Off the Map.* The Royalty Theatre, Wellclose Square; Ranelagh Gardens, Chelsea.

. . . at one huge throw
From opera—Good Lord! to puppet show,

and suggested that the dramatists had better copy the playlets of the puppets:

So might our ruined stage look big again,
And break our rivals in St Martin's Lane.[3]

In May the Four Indian Kings, who were Red Indian Chiefs from Canada visiting London and seeing all the sights, were invited to a performance at this theatre. Their presence at the Haymarket a week earlier had filled the house, and every entertainment in Town was vying in boasting of their patronage; their attendance in a box was thought a far greater attraction than whatever happened to be on the bill. If they really visited the puppets they saw a military spectacle of the victory of Malplaquet, with the battle between the allied forces under Marlborough and the French Army; needless to say, Punch appeared as a British soldier. Performances at this theatre seem to have been given every night at seven o'clock, and the prices were boxes 2*s*., pit 1*s*., and gallery 6*d*.[4]

Presumably Powell returned to Bath for the summer of 1710, but he was back in London the next winter, and early in 1711 he announced that "Punch's Theatre, or Powell from the Bath," would remove from St Martin's Lane to the Seven Stars—presumably a tavern or coffee-house—in the Little Piazza at Covent Garden, "being a place both warmer and fitter to receive persons of quality." He now began to advertise regularly in the daily Press, and it is possible to build up a very complete picture of his various London seasons.[5]

His first season opened in January 1711 and ran for four months. After the usual summer at Bath, with visits to Bristol and Oxford, he returned to Covent Garden in November and ran a six-month season until May 1712. After another summer break—which was the accepted custom at all London theatres—his third season opened in November 1712 and ran to May 1713. It was a fine record, but he had shot his bolt: his fourth season opened as usual in November 1713, but was prematurely concluded by Christmas that year.

During these three seasons Powell produced twenty plays. Many of these were based on legendary tales from ballads and chapbooks, the staple fare of puppet shows everywhere, like *The History of Sir Richard Whittington*; *Friar Bacon and Friar Bungay*; *Chaste Susannah, or the Court of Babylon*; and *King Bladud, the Founder of the Bath*, a play that Powell made his own, which retold the traditional story of how the medicinal springs at Bath were discovered by a herd of leprous swine in the time of the ancient Britons, with a topical epilogue showing ladies and gentlemen of the day bathing in real water at the new baths. These traditional stories were, however, alternated with more sophisticated fare: there were a few satires of contemporary society, like *Poor Robin's Dream, or the Vices of the Age exposed*, based on a ballad of the day in which the gallants, the bullies, the whores, the quacks, and the tradesmen were miraculously reformed, Newgate was empty, and poets had guineas in their pockets. And there was a series of operatical burlesques in which classical stories like *Hero and Leander*, *The Destruction of Troy*, and *Venus and Adonis* were presented "in imitation of the Italian Opera," with some very spectacular scenery. In *The False Triumph*, for instance, the Greeks and Trojans were exactly dressed in the ancient manner, and "at Paris's triumph the stage is to be beautified with trophies, the side scenes representing elephants with castles, in which are Syrians holding forth splendid banners, with Indians on horseback, bearing curious trophies." And then Signior Punchanella appeared in the rôle of Jupiter, descending from the clouds in a chariot drawn by eagles, and sang an aria to Paris. The piece concluded with a prospect of Troy in flames. None of these plays had ever been acted in the human theatre, and only one of them was ever printed.[6]

The guying of the new craze for Italian opera was to be Powell's best line, and brought him wonderful publicity: *The Spectator* thought that "the opera at the Haymarket, and that under the little Piazza in Covent Garden, [were] at present the two leading diversions of the town," and went on solemnly to compare the two productions, with the conclusion that there was one thing "in which both dramas agree; which is, that by the squeak of their voices the heroes of each are eunuchs; and as the wit in both pieces is equal, I must prefer the performance of Mr Powell, because it is in our own language." This is, of course, a dig at the Italian *castrato* singers. In the same issue the sexton of St Paul's, Covent Garden, is supposed to write a letter complaining that when he tolls his bell for daily prayers his congregation now takes it as a signal that the puppet show is about to begin, and that, while the church has a very thin house, Mr Powell is playing to a full congregation.[7] This letter was, of course, a joke written by Steele, and not the serious missive that so many commentators have imagined. But it is, nevertheless, a fair indication of the success of the Piazza Puppet Theatre.

In addition to the main play in each programme, there were a number of supporting turns, like a puppet in imitation of a famous rope-dancer called Lady Isabella, and "Signior Punchanello encountering a lion in the amphitheatre, and slaying it." This was a skit on the opera *Hydaspes*, in which Nicolini had to fight a lion on the stage—an encounter that had provoked both admiration and ridicule about the town. Powell's lion was actually a live pig, who danced a minuet with Punch before the combat![8]

The plays were produced for short runs of about one week each at a time—a very modern system of repertory quite unknown in the human theatres of his day. Including the diversions, the performances lasted for two and a half hours, so they must have been quite substantial productions. The theatre was lit with wax candles, and every effort was made to render it "a place commodious and fit to receive the nobility and gentry of both sexes"; ladies wearing masks—the sign of a prostitute—were not admitted, and half-price admission half-way through the programme—the bane of the London theatre for over a century to come—was never allowed. Performances usually began at six every evening, and prices were 1*s.* for the pit and 2*s.* for the boxes. For important first nights the prices were sometimes raised by sixpence, and tickets were sold "by subscription"—that is, reserved for season-ticket holders. These rates compared favourably with the 3*s.* and 5*s.* prices at Drury Lane, and were a great deal cheaper than the Opera House, where subscription tickets cost 10*s.* 6*d.*

Covent Garden was at the heart of fashionable London. Punch's Theatre was certainly not built as a theatre, but there were many large rooms used as coffee-houses and auctioneer's galleries in the houses behind the Piazza, which stretched round two sides of the square, and it was one of these that was converted for the puppets. Probably it was situated at No. 20, the large house at the south-east corner of the square, which possessed a downstairs room measuring about 50 feet by 100, seating perhaps 300 people.[9] Publicity for the theatre was obtained from advertisements in the Press, and from playbills distributed to coffee-houses. Press advertising was in its infancy at this time, but Powell used it effectively and with imagination; his copy still makes good reading to-day.

After the collapse of his fourth season at Covent Garden Powell made a brief reappearance in March 1714 at the Great Masquerading House in Spring Garden. This Spring Garden (there were several of them) was at Charing Cross, the site of an old pleasure-ground that had been built over since the Restoration. Powell continued playing here all that month, and even announced—in familiar accents—that it was "a place more convenient for the reception of persons of quality and distinction";

but after that he disappears from our records. There is an allusion to him at Bartholomew Fair,[10] and if this is reliable he must have abandoned his summer season at Bath. No doubt he went on playing for many years before simpler and more popular audiences, and it seems probable that he toured in Europe,[11] but the publicity that had pursued him for so long now passed him by, and the remainder of his career lies in shadow.

During the years at Bath and Covent Garden Powell's name became famous even to people who had never seen his show, and he became something of a national 'character'; he was 'used' by the authors of several political pamphlets as the imaginary author or villain of their satires.[12] Then, in October 1712, two young Whigs began to plan a satirical attack upon Robert Harley, Earl of Oxford, the leader of the Tory Government. They were Thomas Burnet, son of the eminent Bishop of Salisbury, a young man about town, a debauchee, a rake, and one of the notorious Mohocks, and George Duckett, a country gentleman, ten years the senior, a Member of Parliament and a dabbler in literature. The letters from Burnet to Duckett have been preserved, and in their pages we may read the story of the genesis and publication of what came to be called *A Second Tale of a Tub, or the History of Robert Powel the Puppet-Show-Man.*[13]

This can now be understood only with the aid of a key; its scurrilous and largely unfair attack upon Harley as a traitor and the Queen as a dipsomaniac has now lost its sting. What interest it has for us to-day lies in the few items of unvarnished information about Powell that can be sifted from its satirical allusions, and in the often reproduced, but ever fascinating, frontispiece showing Powell standing in front of his stage. By the time the book appeared in print Powell's theatre in Covent Garden had been closed for nearly a year, and much of its point must have been lost.[14]

Powell's puppets were quite certainly marionettes: apart from several references to the puppets' legs and to dancing, the frontispiece to *A Second Tale of a Tub* is conclusive evidence on this point. If this engraving can be taken literally they look about two or three feet high, but they may have been smaller; they were made of wood, as a dozen comments would show,[15] and were moved by wires, presumably a thick wire like the iron rod described by Quadrio. Burnet, for instance, wrote of Powell that "his wires are perfectly invisible, his puppets well jointed, and very apt to follow the motions of his directing hand." The figure of Punch was fitted with a moving mouth; Steele declared that:

> I can look beyond his wires, and know very well the whole trick of his art; and that it is only by these wires that the eye of the spectator is cheated,

> and hindered from seeing that there is a thread on one of Punch's chops, which draws it up, and lets it fall at the discretion of the said Powell, who stands behind.[16]

The wires in this last passage, however, would appear to be the network of fine wire stretched across the proscenium opening, already described by Addison. No wires of any kind are shown in the *Second Tale of a Tub*

FRONTISPIECE TO "A SECOND TALE OF A TUB, OR THE HISTORY OF ROBERT POWEL THE PUPPET-SHOW-MAN," 1715

PORTRAIT OF ROBERT HARLEY, EARL OF OXFORD, AFTER SIR GODFREY KNELLER

By courtesy of the Director of the National Portrait Gallery

frontispiece, but this is obviously an idealized picture—like too many theatrical illustrations—of the effect that the spectator was *supposed* to see.

The stage itself was lit by footlights—this is one of the earliest illustrations of footlights known—and was mounted with side-wings, sky-pieces, and a backcloth, like the human theatre of the time; an effect of considerable distance was obtained. The "machines," which figured so prominently on the bills, were pieces of moving scenery and flying effects. The floor of the stage seems to have been grooved so that triumphal arches and set pieces could rise up from below, back scenes divided in the middle and drew aside to reveal further and further perspectives, while flying chariots and fairy cars descended from above. Many of these effects had been tried out by Inigo Jones in the Court masques of the previous century, and were a staple part of opera and pantomime; they did not always work smoothly in the big theatre, but they may have proved prettier and more effective in miniature.

An interesting feature of the engraving of Powell's theatre is that the sky-pieces do not run parallel with the footlights, but at a slight angle to them. This may, of course, merely be an error on the part of the illustrator, but it seems an unnatural mistake to have made, and I once worked out a detailed theory to explain it.[17] Briefly, this was that the "bridges," on which the operators stood while manipulating the puppets, ran above the stage, following the line of the sky-pieces, at a slight angle to the backcloth; the effect of this would be that the puppets were not confined to a narrow strip of stage parallel with the footlights, but were also permitted a certain amount of up-and-down stage movement, thus filling the whole acting area with characters and action.

Of Powell himself, we can only say that he may have been Welsh—Burnet refers to Harley as his "countryman and namesake"—and that he was probably a hunchback or a dwarf. The curious body represented in the *Second Tale's* frontispiece may be Powell's, though the face is certainly Harley's. There are several references in this book to his crooked body and his deformity, and he was sometimes announced as speaking a prologue "in the shape of a Punchanello, in which he satirises on no body but himself." Presumably he wrote his own plays. He must also have been a tolerable actor, for no doubt he spoke for many of his characters; indeed, Steele reported that all the parts were recited by one person.[18] There was a Restoration actor called Martin Powell, and a Georgian actor (the contemporary of the puppeteer) called George Powell, but there is no real evidence to connect Martin, the puppeteer, with either of these.

We have no information as to the number of assistants he employed, but he refers to his "servants," and there must have been several of them to support such elaborate productions. For two of them, at least, he allowed Benefit Performances, just as in the human theatre: Mrs Kent was given a benefit each season in London, and Betty Smith was given one in January 1713. He obviously needed women's voices, and his company probably had to sing as well as act; there must, too, have been some kind of an orchestra. Powell claimed to have contrived his own scenery, but we learn that he was assisted in the mechanism of his scenery and the construction of his puppets by a Frenchman known in later years as "old father Luke," who had been apprenticed to the Gobelins tapestry works as a boy, and who later assisted Devoto, the scene-painter, at Lincoln's Inn Fields. Father Luke was an ingenious craftsman and a ripe eccentric, about whom many stories were told in his old age.[19]

Punch was, of course, the star of the theatre, giving it its very name and appearing, apparently, in every play. There are many allusions to his character: he is described as "a profane, lewd jester," who "seldom leaves the company without calling son of a whore," who is guilty of "some indecencies towards the ladies," and of disturbing "a soft love scene with his ribaldry."[20] He is "the diversion of all the spectators . . . a roaring, lewd, rakish, empty fellow," but under Powell's guidance "he now speaks choice apothegms and sterling wit, to the amusement of the applauding audience both in pit and boxes."[21] As to his appearance, he is described as "making bows until his buttons touched the ground,"[22] and he is shown standing on the stage in the *Second Tale* frontispiece. Here he may be seen as of rather shorter height than normal, with a big belly, little arms and legs, and a moustache; he is dressed in a high brimless conical hat, with some curious trimming round it, a big Elizabethan ruff, a garment hanging down to his knees, with buttons in front, and belted below his belly, knee-breeches, stockings, and shoes. He has *not* got any conspicuous hump, nor is his nose hooked; but the remark that his head had once been "laid aside for a nutcracker"[23] suggests that the now familiar silhouette of nose meeting chin was beginning to take shape.

The character standing with Punch on the stage is, almost certainly, "his scolding wife," Joan,[24] dressed as a plain countrywoman. Joan does not figure by name on any of Powell's bills, but we know from other sources that she was by this time taking her place on the puppet stage.

We have already met references to the squeak of Powell's Punch, in which, of course, he merely preserved an established tradition. Burnet, however, gives an indication of how the squeak was produced:

> For as my puppets, when you hear them squeak,
> Are but the wooden tubes thro' which I speak.

This is a variant of the tin squeaker described by Ned Ward; the wood may have produced a slightly less shrill but more mellifluous note.

Powell was certainly successful, and he was said to have become rich: a contemporary complained that

> Mr Powell, by subscriptions and full house, has gathered such wealth as is ten times sufficient to buy all the poets in England; that he seldom goes out without his chair, and thrives on this incredible folly to that degree, that, were he a freeman, he might hope that some future puppet show might celebrate his being Lord Mayor, as he has done Sir Richard Whitton.[25]

Of his popularity and fame there are many witnesses, "for what man, woman or child, that lives within the verge of Covent Garden, or what Beau or Belle visitant at the Bath, knows not Mr Powell?"[26] We cannot be sure how serious these essayists were, but even a good joke must have had some foundation in fact.

As to the real merits of his performances, we may accept the contemporary verdict that it was an "incredible folly . . . so much below ridicule, that the bare recital is a satire upon all who frequent this fantastic and childish entertainment";[27] or we may excuse such attacks as the jealousy of unsuccessful playwrights, and try to recapture something of what it was that made Punch's Theatre the third playhouse in the town for three years. Charm, prettiness, *naïveté*, all these things belong to almost any puppet show. Powell displayed spectacular scenery, and he was fortunate in his publicity, but there must have been something more: there must have been genuine wit. Many years afterwards Lord Chesterfield recalled how

> at the latter end of Queen Anne's reign, there was a great number of fanatics, who said they had, and very possibly actually thought they had, the gift of prophecy. They used to assemble in Moorfields to exert that gift, and were attended by a vast number of idle and curious spectators. The then ministry, who loved a little persecution well enough, were however wise enough not to disturb these madmen, and only ordered one Powell, who was the master of a famous puppet-show, to make Punch turn prophet, which he did so well, that it soon put an end to the prophets and their prophecies.[28]

I suppose that this refers to the play called *The Town Rake, or Punch turned Quaker*; it is certainly an adequate tribute to the keenness of Powell's satire.

By origin Martin Powell was almost certainly no more than a showman of the fairs, but this astute little hunchback had an eye to the taste of Society and an ear for the follies of the day, and for five years he caught fashion on the wing. Lords and ladies sat in his boxes, and wits and writers put his name in books and poems.[29] Thanks to this he is still remembered to-day, and accorded a fame perhaps out of proportion to his actual achievements. Yet his genius must not be ignored. In an age when the English theatre had sunk, in an understandable reaction from

Restoration bawdiness, into a decline of sentimentality, and when the only new movement of any significance was Italian opera and Italianate pantomime, let us remember the little theatre in the Piazza where the wit of Punch, descended from a long line of English clowns, lit up the follies of his age; let us remember that not an eye was dry in the house as the robin redbreasts covered the poor starved Children in the Wood with leaves to bury them;[30] let us remember Signior Punchanella descending from the flies in a chariot and squawking an aria to Paris.

Martin Powell had died by 1725, and for a time his son carried on the show. In that year the "son of the late famous Powell, of merry memory," announced his return from France, where he had performed before the King and the whole Court at Paris, and his appearance at Southwark Fair with *The Constant Lovers*, one of his father's favourite pieces.[31] He was playing in some kind of a double programme with Fawkes, a noted conjuror, with whom he also shared the bill the next year for a season at the Old Tennis Court in James Street.[32] In 1725 a puppet showman called Yeates had issued a challenge to any other puppet player to show richer or more natural figures, or better painted scenery, for fifty guineas;[33] Young Powell offered to take him up for a hundred guineas. I do not know whether, or how, the dispute was decided, but the upshot of it was that the two rivals joined forces, and the next year they were in partnership at the London fairs, offering a joint challenge to all comers.[34] These challenges remained common form on puppet playbills for over a century, but I have never heard of any judicial procedure for deciding them.

No more is heard of Powell junior after this. He traded largely on his father's name, but he never seems to have lifted the show above the level of the fairground. The elegant puppets and the wonderful scenery that had once graced the Piazza gradually disintegrated in the rough traffic of the fairs, in garbled drolls sandwiched between the contortionists and the rope-dancers.

Charlotte Charke

Charlotte was the youngest child of Colley Cibber, a talented actor, tedious Poet Laureate, and the author of an excellent autobiography. From early years she had shown herself an unconventional, tomboyish sort of girl, and when still very young she rushed into a marriage with Richard Charke, a musician, who very soon deserted her. She now essayed a career upon the stage, but soon displayed the imprudence that was to mark her life, and in a fit of pique with the manager of Drury Lane she threw up her parts and published a satirical farce abusing the management of the theatre. Her father's influence secured her return, but she did not long remain at the Theatre Royal, and she resigned again in somewhat mysterious circumstances, which at the same time seem to have completely alienated her from her father. At about this time she began to wear men's clothes—a practice which she seems to have kept up for the best part of her life.[35]

After a short season at the theatre in the Haymarket she abandoned the stage and set up in trade as a grocer in Long Acre; but the business failed to show a profit because of her unbusinesslike methods, and she presently sold out and began to plan the formation of a grand puppet show. She claims to have spared no expense in making this the most elegant that was ever exhibited, with magnificent scenery and costumes; she even bought engravings of several eminent persons, from which she had the faces of the puppets carved. The total cost was nearly £500.

She seems to have enlisted technical help in this project from Yeates, at one time the partner of Powell's son.[36] Yeates was a regular exhibitor at the London fairs with large waxwork figures, and, father and son, they were to become quite important proprietors of fairground theatrical booths. With Yeates's technical skill and Charlotte Charke's artistic inspiration the new puppet show opened its doors to the public in March 1738. In accordance with the new Licensing Act it was duly provided with a licence from the Lord Chamberlain, which was claimed as a unique honour for a puppet show.[37] The theatre was above the old Tennis Court in James Street, off the Haymarket; tennis courts had often been adapted as playhouses since the mid-seventeenth century, for the long open hall was easily converted into an auditorium, but this was the last tennis court to continue in use as a theatre, and it was, indeed, only used by the lowest kind of strollers as "a slaughter house of dramatic poetry." Nevertheless Mrs Charke advertised that Punch's Theatre was newly fitted up, and announced for performance a double bill of Shakespeare's *King Henry the Eighth*, intermixed with a pastoral *Damon and Phillida* by her father, which was being acted the very same night at Drury Lane. She promised that the christening of the young Princess Elizabeth would be represented, with dancing by Punch and his wife, and a new ode, written by Mrs Charke to "music by an eminent hand," printed copies of which were to be distributed gratis. The performance began at the fashionable hour of six o'clock, and prices were boxes 3*s*., pit 2*s*., first gallery 1*s*., upper gallery 6*d*. (At Drury Lane prices for the same accommodation ranged from 5*s*. to 1*s*.)

Ten plays were presented during this season, at the rate of two every night. The most successful, with some twenty performances, was *The Mock Doctor*, a ballad opera by Henry Fielding, based on Molière, which had been first performed six years before; the part of the Mock Doctor was taken by Mr Punch. Two other plays by Fielding were in the repertory: *The Covent Garden Tragedy*, an amusing but coarse burlesque of the old-fashioned heroic drama, set in a Covent Garden brothel, in which Punch appeared as the *madame* of the house, "being the first time in petticoats"; and *The Old Debauchees*, a crude, robust comedy inspired by the notorious affair of Father Girard, a Jesuit, who was, of course, played "by Signor Punch from Italy."

Other plays on the bill were *The Unhappy Favourite*, a historical play about the Earl of Essex; Shakespeare's *Henry IV*, with Punch as Falstaff; *Richard III*, also presumably Shakespeare's; *The Miller of Mansfield*, a sentimental drama that had first appeared the year before and was to last a hundred years on the English stage; and *The Beggar's Wedding*, a ballad opera inspired by *The Beggar's Opera*, in which one of the puppets was modelled on Farinelli, a celebrated singer. As *divertissements* the audience were promised "a grand dance by Mr Punch in a full-bottom Perriwig, the Irish Trot by Punch's wife," and performances on the kettle-drums by Job Baker, an ex-Army drummer to the Duke of Marlborough. In April the comedy of *Amphitryon*, by Dryden, was announced as in preparation, but it never seems to have been performed: the season had run for only eight weeks when Mrs Charke, as she explains in her breathless autobiography, "through excessive fatigue . . . acquired a violent fever, which had like to have carried me off, and consequently gave a damp to the run I should otherwise have had." By the middle of May Punch's Theatre was dark. The plays selected for this season were all regularly acted in the human theatres, and it is obvious that they were chosen by some one with dramatic taste; Charlotte Charke seems to have aimed at creating the real theatre in miniature, and her lack of any previous experience with puppets may have limited her approach. The emphasis was, perhaps, too literary, and not sufficiently in the puppet tradition of folk-drama. But in her use of Punch Mrs Charke showed a nice wit, and a realization of genuine puppet values; Punch as Falstaff and Punch, in petticoats, as Mother Punch-bowl cannot easily have been forgotten by the audiences at the Tennis Court.

Few technical details are available about Charke's puppets, except that they were obviously marionettes. Her Punch spoke in the traditional way through a squeaker, and a contemporary pamphleteer repeats the by now stale joke about the *castrati*:

> 'Tis said she intends, by their artificial voices to cut out the Italians; for it has been found that Punch can hold his breath and quiver much better and longer than Farinelli; I wish this may be true, for then we may expect to have Italian songs at a moderate rate, without the use of a knife.[38]

After the collapse of the Tennis Court season Charlotte Charke rested quietly for some time, and then thought to put her puppets to some use by taking a show, like Powell, to a fashionable watering-place. In the summer of 1739 she transported the entire equipment to Tunbridge Wells, but when she got there she discovered—what a sensible preliminary visit would have told her—that a successful puppet theatre, managed by Lacon, had already been established there for many years. With the human operators she had brought with her they managed to put on a few thin dramas, and then made their way back to London, penniless and disappointed. She must have taken a company of at least four or five artists.

Mrs Charke apparently lacked either the energy or the funds to mount another season, and she now hired the show out to Mr Yeates, who presented it once again at the theatre above the Tennis Court.[39] It opened in December 1739, and ran for over three months, during which ten plays were produced, eight of them new. This year only one puppet play was performed each evening, preceded by Mr Yeates's Dexterity of Hand, and followed by a pantomime entertainment with human actors, a Musical Clock, and a Moving Picture. Prices were the same as before, but complaints of the wretched discomfort of this barnstormers' playhouse were met by the announcement that "the theatre is made very commodious and warm, for the better reception of gentlemen and ladies." But, then, one notices that some such statement was obligatory with every new lessee of what must have been a horrible little flea-pit! A plaque on the wall of what is now Orange Street marks the site of this curious theatre to-day.[40]

During this season *Damon and Phillida* and *The Mock Doctor* were revived, and the new productions included *King Philip of Spain*, with Princess Elizabeth's accession to the throne and Punch as Lord Judge of the Inquisition, which Yeates had performed with young Powell at Southwark Fair thirteen years before; *Friar Bacon and Friar Bungay*, an old puppet favourite, with Punch as the comic servant, Miles; and five contemporary ballad operas, *The Lover His Own Rival*, *The Gardener's*

Wedding, *The Honest Yorkshireman*, *The Generous Freemason*, and *The Rake's Progress*. The last of these was, of course, based on Hogarth's paintings, with Punch as the prison gaoler.

The repertory was rather more popular than in the previous season, with more ballads and less Shakespeare; to us the mixture of historical legend and intimate opera seems fresh and enchanting. But Yeates was a fairground showman, who knew how to judge the taste at Smithfield or Southwark, but who may have been rather out of his depth in catching the fancy of the West End. For one reason or another the success of the season was only moderate, and business failed to keep up to expectations. In the end Mrs Charke sold the figures and scenery, together with the Lord Chamberlain's licence and the use of her name, for only twenty guineas. To the end of her life she retained a bitter grudge against the man who had thus taken advantage of her necessity.

The purchaser at this knock-down price appears to have been Fawkes, the son of young Powell's late partner, the great conjurer, who was the proprietor of several phenomenally successful fairground shows. He did not wait long before putting his purchase to account, and at Bartholomew Fair in 1740 Fawkes, Pinchbeck, and Terwin presented *Britons strike Home*, an epic of English naval gallantry against the Spaniards, by Mr Punch's celebrated comedians "formerly Mrs Charke's from the Theatre in the Haymarket." Two years later the same company was presenting Fielding's *Covent Garden Tragedy* as "the most comical and whimsical tragedy that was ever tragedized by any tragical company of comedians," and no doubt they played in booths up and down the country for many years, a sad and pale reflection amid the violent fairground drolls of Charlotte Charke's elegant and ill-fated enterprise.[41]

After the failure of Yeates's season, and the disastrous forced sale of the puppets, troubles came thick and fast. Charlotte was secretly married a second time to a worthy gentleman,[42] who died very soon afterwards, leaving her in debt up to her eyes. She was arrested by a bailiff, and only escaped imprisonment by the traditionally golden-hearted ladies of Covent Garden who subscribed to bail out "poor Sir Charles." Her bizarre, poverty-stricken figure, in gentleman's clothes and silver-laced hat, must by now have become affectionately notorious. She went on dragging out a precarious existence, spurned by her family, dogged by the bailiffs, barnstorming at the Tennis Court, and strolling in the provinces; an heiress fell in love with her, she turned valet to a gentleman, she sold sausages in the street, she worked as a waiter, till the landlady too fell in love with the slim, handsome young gentleman; she got some one to set her up as an innkeeper in Drury Lane, till she lost or was cheated of all the profit; and then at last, in 1745, she got a good job at a puppet show, managed by Mr Russel, representing Italian opera at Hickford's Great Room. She understood the language, and the manipulation of the figures, and was hired at a guinea a day to move Punch in particular.

According to Mrs Charke, this was a very elegant affair, with subscription tickets and an orchestra of ten talented musicians. Some of the female puppets "were ornamented with real diamonds, lent for that purpose by several persons of the first quality." Unfortunately it was short-lived: Mr Russel went bankrupt, and was confined in Newgate as a debtor, where he lost his reason and died within a few weeks. A subscription for his benefit, to which many of the nobility had contributed, was purloined by the person responsible for collecting it. Mrs Charke hoped to obtain Russel's figures for her own use, but the landlord valued them at sixty guineas, which was quite beyond her means. She describes them as very small.

Mr Hickford's Great Room had been opened in Brewer Street, near Golden Square, in 1739, and had been the scene of many elegant concerts given by leading musicians of the day; some years later Mozart and his sister, as young children, gave a recital here. The building was still standing as late as the nineteen-twenties at the back of a fine old Georgian house. The room measured fifty feet long by thirty wide, and was lofty with a coved ceiling and decorated mouldings and cornices; it was lighted by a large window at one end, below which stood a small low platform; at the other end of the room was the door, with a gallery over it; its acoustics were excellent.[43] The attraction of Russel's Italian puppet opera must have been largely musical, but unfortunately no details of its repertory can be gleaned from the newspapers of the day. Horace Walpole wrote rather severely of it—that "one Russel, a mimic, has a puppet-show to ridicule operas; I hear very dull, not to mention its being twenty years too late; it consists of three acts, with foolish Italian songs burlesqued in Italian."[44] Powell had, in fact, been doing just this sort of thing over thirty years before.

In our portrait gallery of puppeteers Charlotte Charke takes an obvious and important place for her eccentricity. She has, too, provided us with the unique documentation of her autobiography. This fascinating book is neither literature nor history, but the inconsequent and madly egocentric memories of an aging and desperate woman, a glimpse into a twisted and distraught human soul. Modern psycho-analysis would, no doubt, neatly label Mrs Charke as a psychopathic lesbian, but we need not here peer too far into the deep well of loneliness from which this unhappy woman drew her inspiration. We may remember her as a plucky girl in her early twenties, who found in her company of wooden players a loyalty and devotion that she could never command from human actors; and we may salute her as a puppet showman of unusual intelligence, taste, and courage.

Madame de la Nash

Charlotte Charke had been able to secure a licence for her puppet theatre, but another lady puppet producer was less successful, and in order to evade the Licensing Act of 1737 was forced to resort to a legal fiction. "Madame de la Nash," the advertisements announced on March 25, 1748, "will open her large Breakfast Room for the nobility and gentry in Panton Street, near the Haymarket . . . where she will give the very best of Tea, Coffee, Chocolate and Jellies. At the same time she will entertain the Company gratis with that excellent old English entertainment, called a Puppet Show."[45]

The idea was not new. As the law stood, only the two patent theatres were permitted to play legitimate straight drama; but all sorts of devices had been conjured up to disguise a theatrical performance as the rehearsal of a dramatic academy, as an interlude to a concert, or—as Samuel Foote had phrased it at the little Haymarket Theatre the year before—a gratuitous exhibition while the audience took a dish of tea! The fairground booths seem to have escaped without interference, but for anyone to open an unlicensed theatre in the streets of London was to invite trouble.

Madame de la Nash aimed at the cream of Society. "The House is fitted up in the most elegant manner," she announced; "ladies may take places by the Boxes at the Coffee Room in the passage to the Large Room, and footmen will be admitted to keep them." (Physical occupation was the only form of reservation accepted at any theatre in the eighteenth century.) Performances were at twelve and seven daily, and prices were boxes 3*s.*, pit 2*s.*, gallery 1*s.*

She opened her season with the lamentable *Tragedy of Bateman*, who died for love, with the comical humours of Punch and his wife, Joan. This ran for three weeks, a very long run for those days, and was followed by *Fair Rosamond*, the story of Henry II's lover, for another three weeks, Fielding's *The Covent Garden Tragedy* for one week, and *Whittington and His Cat* for a fortnight. On May the 30th prices were reduced to 2*s.*,

1s., and *6d.*, and the last advertisement appeared on June the 2nd. The entire season had lasted a little over two months; the reduction in prices suggests that business was falling off, but it is possible that the Lord Chamberlain forced the closure of the thinly disguised theatre.

The plot of *Whittington* was described in some detail, and it seems to have followed closely the Powell version; a complete set of bells and bell-ringers was a special feature. Punch himself played the part of Whittington, and there was shown his arrival at the Court of Morocco, his aptness in learning the Moorish salutations from a welcoming Bashaw, his humorous conversation with an English merchant at the Court, the curious account of his travels given on his return, and the procession of wagons loaded with treasure brought home in exchange for his cat. The play ended with his becoming Lord Mayor and being received by Henry V on his return from the conquest of France. There was a prologue by Punch and an epilogue by Joan. It all seems very traditional.

In one important respect, however, Madame de la Nash broke with tradition. Towards the end of the season she announced that "as the squeaking of the puppets has been thought disagreeable that objection is now removed, by their speaking by natural voices in this Puppet Show." The squeaker was to continue in use for centuries, until to-day, with popular puppet shows, but this is, I think, the first sign of the emancipation of the fashionable puppet from its shrill tyranny. What may well have been an ear-splitting but entertaining 'voice' for the re-telling of folk-dramas, that every one in the audience already knew backward, must have become a tedious irritation in a polite assembly, who wanted to hear the words.

There is something very curious about this short season. It was announced with a good deal of publicity, it solicited the custom of a fashionable and elegant audience, but of the four plays presented three were old traditional folk-stories that had been played for a hundred years as fairground drolls, and the fourth was a coarse and vulgar parody. This repertory would have been ideal at Bartholomew Fair, but it sounds an unlikely selection for a polite West End theatre. Madame de la Nash may, simply, have misjudged her public, but one cannot help wondering whether the whole thing wasn't a blind to cover up a political satire. There are a few not easily explained passages in her bills, references to

> the comical humours of the town, as drums, routs, riots, hurricanes, hoops, plaid waistcoats, criticizing, whisk-learning, mussel-boxing, mimicking, etc. in the characters of Sir Trusty Punch the Pimp, Lady Joan Punch the Drum Major, Miss Punch the Maid of Honour, and Master Jacky Punch the Critic.

What on earth does all that mean? And there are obscure references to the execution of Mr Puppet Fut, Esq., grocer and mimic, and to a "pacifick dance between Somebody and Nobody." It does not need an exceptionally sensitive nose to smell a political rat somewhere behind all this.

The allusion to Mr Puppet Fut, however, can at least be solved. This obviously refers to Samuel Foote, who was presenting a similarly illegal theatrical entertainment in the Haymarket, thrown in with grocery wares like tea and coffee. Foote replied to the puppets within a fortnight by printing at the head of his advertisement some verses from Fielding's *The Author's Farce* warning Punch to look out for himself. Somebody and Nobody were stock figures of popular legend—the one caricatured as all head, legs, and arms, and the other just the reverse; they must have lent themselves to interpretation by puppets.

In the absence of any texts it is difficult to carry identifications very much further, although I feel sure that an exhaustive study of political and theatrical gossip in 1748 would bring more clues to light. Of Madame de la Nash we can, indeed, only say that she brought the popular puppet theatre for a brief spell to the west end of the town, and that under her direction the puppets, in England as so often elsewhere, were not behindhand in the fight for liberty and free speech.

Samuel Foote

Samuel Foote is an interesting figure in the history of the English theatre. An actor and dramatist of minor and limited talents, he was nevertheless a mimic of genius; for thirty years he kept the Little Theatre in the Haymarket open with a series of plays and entertainments written by himself, in which no small part of the attraction lay in his impersonations of well-known actors and personalities of the day—to the delight of his audiences and the chagrin of his victims. At first he was in constant trouble with the Lord Chamberlain for performing without a licence, but in 1766 his difficulties were solved in a curious manner. He was then the guest of some titled gentlemen at a country-house party, among whom the Duke of York was included, and, although he was no horseman, he boasted of his skill in riding. Some of the gentlemen, including the Duke, egged him on to mount a particularly unmanageable animal, who threw him to the ground, breaking his leg, which had to be amputated. The Duke felt some compunction at this incident, and tried to make amends by arranging a special personal patent for Foote at the

Haymarket Theatre, for the duration of his life. Henceforth Foote could perform legally what he had hitherto done by subterfuge. He accepted the loss of his leg philsophically, and, indeed, jokes and business with his cork leg now provided him with an added source of humour.[46]

Foote's entertainments were presented with a very small company of actors, of whom only Tate Wilkinson, who later became a considerable actor-manager in the North of England, was of any comparable standing. No kind of spectacular display was possible, and it must have been difficult sometimes even to find enough bodies for a simple domestic farce. In these circumstances Foote seems to have turned, quite early, to puppets as a cheap means of augmenting his company. One of the sketches in which puppets were used has, fortunately, been preserved: it is entitled *Tragedy a-la-Mode*, and was presented at a special season at Drury Lane in 1758 and at the Haymarket in 1763.[47] The whole thing is a burlesque of the then rather old-fashioned heroic tragedy in blank verse, and is cast in the popular form of a rehearsal. An author (played by Foote) describes his new idea for a drama to the manager of a theatre; of the cast only the Prince was played by a living actor, the remainder—Princess, King, guards, and so on—by mute puppets. The burlesque drama, spoken throughout by the one character, contains some happy lines of parody, and is worth reviving. The puppets used were described as pasteboard figures, and as they played alongside a human actor they were probably life-size flat figures, cut out of thick cardboard, and pushed on from the wings; arm and head gestures could be conveyed by strings and pulleys. Tate Wilkinson says that the use of puppets in this play was a failure, but that when they were replaced by dumb human actors the effect was highly successful. However this may be, Foote certainly continued to make use of puppets in various ways in his entertainments, though the exact details have not always been preserved.[48]

Of his most ambitious puppet production, however, we have ample and very interesting information.[49] This was in 1773, towards the close of his career, when he announced "The Primitive Puppet Show" for performance at his theatre in the Haymarket. This aroused intense interest, and an hour before the performance was due to commence the Haymarket was impassable from the crowds waiting to get into the theatre; finally the doors were broken down, and many entered without paying; three ladies fainted, and a girl had her arm broken in the crush. Owing to the great crowd the orchestra pit and the upper gallery—which it was not intended to use—were occupied by spectators, and the fiddlers had to scrape away behind the scenes. The opening of the stage had been reduced by a false proscenium to accommodate the puppet theatre, on either side of which were painted the representations of Harlequin and of Punch. At length Mr Foote stepped before the curtain, and spoke the Exordium, or Prologue.

"I have the honour, gentlemen," he announced,

SAMUEL FOOTE WITH CHARACTERS FROM "PIETY IN PATTENS"
From *The Macaroni and Theatrical Magazine*, February 1773.

> to produce to you that species of the drama, which, from the corruption of its original principles, and the inability of its latter professors, has sunk into disrepute. . . . It is an exhibition at which few of you have been present since your emancipation from the nursery; and to so low a state has it been reduced, that, like the Thespian comedy, it has been carried about in carts to harvest-homes, wakes and country fairs; or if it has approached our capital cities, it has appeared in no nobler place than a neglected garret, or a dilapidated suburbian stable. . . . You will perceive, gentlemen, by this exordium, that my intention this evening is to produce, or rather restore to the present age, the pure, the primitive Puppet Show.

Foote then went on to refer to the ancient Roman theatre, with its masked actors, as in effect a great puppet show, and he stressed the adaptability of puppets to every language. Pointing to Harlequin, he declared that he had banished

> that offspring of an incestuous marriage between Folly and Extravagance. Nor will we suffer [pointing to Punch] that facetious gentleman, who was unquestionably one of the personages of the ancient drama, to sully our scenes. Indeed, his manners are too rude and licentious for the chastity of the present times.

Foote went on to refer to the kinds of wood from which his puppets were made, with analogies from each, compared the present stage, with its artificial dramas, to a puppet show, and announced for immediate presentation *The Handsome Housemaid, or Piety in Pattens.* "The curtain was then drawn up, and a puppet, admirably well made and dressed, was discovered bowing to the audience, who, according to the usual contrivance at a puppet show, spoke a humorous prologue."

The Handsome Housemaid was intended as a burlesque of sentimental comedy, a type of drama then highly fashionable, in the same way that *Tragedy a-la-Mode* had burlesqued the old heroic tragedy. The play describes a servant-girl whose master tried to seduce her; fortified by the butler, Thomas, she remained chaste, whereupon her master, impressed by her honest principles, offered to marry her. She asked that the butler might be present to hear her answer, and then bestowed her hand upon him in gratitude for his good advice. The master, overcome by such goodness, gives his consent, upon which the maid, in gratitude to them both, and lest either should be offended, resolved to marry neither and remain single all her life. To such sentiments had the drama ascended within a century of the Restoration!

Just at the end of the play a constable (a human actor) entered, and took the troupe, with Foote as their manager, before a magistrate as common vagrants. At the trial it was proved that neither whippings nor a diet of bread and water would have any effect upon the puppets, and as for Foote, he was three-quarters a man but one-quarter (his wooden leg) a puppet, so it would be impossible for the court to deal with him unless they could catch the body without the leg, or the leg without the body.

This entertainment met with a mixed reception. It was rather short, the comedy (as intended) extremely insipid, and the spectators in the upper gallery (who should never have been allowed there) were unable to see the puppets properly, owing to the sight-lines of the small stage. The gallery, who had expected a real modern puppet show with Punch and Joan, were disappointed and booed, but the boxes, who appreciated the subtlety of the satire, applauded warmly. On its revival the piece was lengthened by the addition of a scene after the trial in which Punch complained of Foote's interfering in his province, and maintained that he could manage affairs much better; he insisted upon being engaged as principal performer, and gave imitations of the leading actors of the day. He also demanded the engagement of his wife, Joan, cracking jokes about the deformity of her face and body; but Foote, imitating Garrick in his most managerial vein, positively refused to engage her. This "Primitive Puppet Show" was played nineteen times that year, and was revived for occasional performances during the next twenty years, but usually with an all-human cast.

"Foote has a great deal of humour," said Boswell to Johnson.

"Yes, sir."

"He has a singular talent of exhibiting character."

"Sir, it is not a talent; it is a vice."

In that talent, or vice, the puppets played their part. Exactly how expert a puppeteer Foote was we cannot now say. It is enough for our requirements here that this gifted and versatile man of the theatre saw the possibilities for satire, for parody, and for burlesque in the inscrutable mask of the marionette.[50]

Charles Dibdin

Two years later Foote repeated his famous Exordium all over again, but this time he was a puppet himself. This was in 1775, at the Grand Saloon over Exeter Change, where Charles Dibdin was presenting a puppet show called *The Comic Mirror.*

Dibdin, who was later to achieve immortality as the composer of so many fine sailors' songs, including *Tom Bowling*, had already made a mark for himself in the London theatre with pleasant ballad operas like *The Waterman*, and was employed by Garrick as the resident composer at Drury Lane.

At just this time, however, he lost his job because Garrick objected to the way he had deserted the actress he was living with and should have been supporting, and Dibdin, who was never at a loss for an idea or a speculation, looked round for something to do and hit on *The Comic Mirror, or the World as it Wags.*[51]

This was an entertainment very similar to Foote's, and would be described to-day as an intimate revue; the impersonations were probably not so clever, but the music must have been very attractive. It included *The Milkmaid*, a pretty serenata with a blacksmith; a Green Room scene introducing a musician, a scene-painter, and a prompter; a little burlesque on the Catch Club, a society of aristocratic musical amateurs; a skit on

Italian opera; an impersonation of Macklin as Shylock; and a spectacular view of the Ranelagh Regatta, which had just been the success of the London season, with a procession of boats up the Thames and a grand illuminated Temple of Neptune in the Gardens.

On the first night the elegant little theatre, which had been painted pink and white and adorned with lustres, was crowded with a fashionable audience, although there were complaints that the staircase leading up to the theatre from the pavement had been left unlit. All seems to have gone well until the last act, when, as a critic reported,

> a confusion arose between the scene-shifters, wire-workers etc. which destroyed the intended effect, and left us even without a single idea of what it might mean; the confusion at last became so general that voices, music and all sunk before it, and thus deprived us for the evening of what may prove hereafter a very striking part of the entertainment.

The audience seem to have made charitable allowances for first-night difficulties, but back-stage accidents continued to occur, and on a later occasion the procession of boats "stuck fast in the river, and they were obliged to drop the curtain on them in that situation." This was not to be the last time that a literary gentleman, who fancied puppets would be so "amusing," was to discover the wilful obstinacy and crass perversity of which these inanimate creatures are capable until their tricks have been mastered by strict discipline and long rehearsal.

Dibdin's puppets were quite large, about two feet six high, and were said to have been "admirably constructed and characteristically worked," which may imply that they moved like puppets and not like humans. The scenery was well designed, but a critic complained that it needed twice as much light, and the manager was recommended to strengthen his band and to ensure greater audibility for his actors, whose words could not be heard at the back of the theatre.

The Comic Mirror ran for three months, from June to September, and was by no means a failure; in Dibdin's own words, "it was full of whim." Performances were given at 7.30 three times a week, and the entertainment was over in time for other places of amusement to be visited. Admission was 5*s*. to boxes and 3*s*. elsewhere. (The Haymarket Theatre charged 5*s*. boxes, 3*s*. pit, 2*s*. gallery, and 1*s*. upper gallery.)

In February the next year the theatre was reopened. The programme was basically the same, but there were a few additions—*The Recruiting Serjeant*, an operatic interlude; an Auction Room scene; an amateur dramatic society or Spouting Club, introducing theatrical impersonations; the *Levée of Aristophanes*, which was a satire on Foote; and a rehearsal at Drury Lane, with Garrick laying down the law. Dibdin says this puppet was "a remarkable good likeness of the little man"; he had planned a more bitter attack on Garrick, accusing him of stealing one of Dibdin's plays, but this was never performed. Although his imitation of Garrick's voice was poor, he was said to have hit off his literary vanity, his managerial economies, his hesitations in speaking, and his hysterical laugh with fair success.

This second season does not seem to have lasted for very long, but in May the whole outfit was transferred to the Marylebone Gardens, where a grand puppet show entitled "The World in Miniature" incorporated the most popular items in *The Comic Mirror* with Foote's *Piety in Pattens*, a puppet orchestra, and a Naval Review. This ran until September.[52]

By this time Dibdin had gone abroad, probably to escape his creditors, and the puppets were purchased by Dr Samuel Arnold, a composer of some eminence in his day and a recent unfortunate lessee of the Marylebone Gardens. They eventually found a home in the Apollo Gardens, in the Westminster Bridge Road. Here, in these pleasure gardens of eighteenth-century London, the puppets seem to play in a congenial setting: looking back through the centuries, in grandiloquent bills and softly mezzotinted engravings, it seems always to have been summer evening, with a cool breeze lapping down the Thames after the hot, sultry day; the watermen are plying their fares across the river, and the lamps are out in the ornamental walks; we wander down the garden paths as the strains of Handel, or Arne, or Carey float softly across the air; and the fountains play, and the transparencies beckon us to the end of the artificial vista; we eat supper alfresco, and sip our wine upon the terrace; and it never rains. But there were other dangers: Sir Roger de Coverley at Vauxhall had asked for more nightingales and fewer strumpets, and the Temple of Apollo, despite the chaste example of its marionettes, became the haunt of thieves and prostitutes; in about 1793 it was closed down by the magistrates. The gaily stuccoed pavilions fell into disrepair and ruin, and buried in their general devastation the elegant and satirical puppets of Dibdin's *Comic Mirror*.[53]

Dibdin returned once more to puppets. In 1780 an entertainment called *Pasquin's Budget* was put on at the Little Theatre in the Haymarket —Foote's old playhouse. This was a mixture of puppets and shadows, with a satirical motif; one of the items was called *Reasonable Animals*, and it showed various characters of the day as the type of animal which they resembled—for instance, a lawyer became a wolf, an alderman a hog, and an Irishman a bull; each animal had a special little song to sing.

Then there were skits on classical legends brought up to date—Pandora, Ulysses, and the Siege of Troy; the Catch Club was revived, and there was a sketch of a Debating Club called *The Bear Garden.* Very large marionettes were used, and the idea of this entertainment seems to have been interesting and witty, but its execution was faulty. Although the Bannisters, who had appeared at Exeter Change, were singing behind the scenes, with Decastro and other creditable performers, it was impossible to hear a single syllable in the auditorium owing to the thickness of the canvas proscenium masking the puppet stage; and Dibdin hints darkly, and libellously, that the Italian shadow-show performer was bribed by Astley, a rival impresario, to ruin everything he put on.[54]

The evening was a frightful fiasco. The entertainment was hissed off the stage, and was never repeated; but later many of the individual items were played with success by human actors. It goes to show, what quite recent experiments in London theatres have corroborated, that puppets cannot be seen, or heard, to advantage in even a small orthodox playhouse. The dimensions of the figures, and the sight-lines of the little stage, call for an auditorium specially designed to their requirements.

Ten years later Dibdin included an impersonation of "a puppet showman" in his one-man entertainment called *The Oddities*, but he does not seem to have made any further use of puppets; they were only an interlude, but a significant one, in his active and busy career. He never seems to have really mastered their technique, but his fertile brain provided some interesting uses for their limited talent.

Dibdin's contemporary satires are lost to us, and we would not understand them if we could read them now; but his ballads still retain their freshness. Their straightforward, innocent approach lies well within the simple compass of a marionette's emotions, and we might well revive some of these little operas on our puppet stages to-day.[55]

The Patagonian Theatre

A few months after Dibdin's last season at Exeter Change another puppet show had established itself in the same building. In October 1776 "the beautiful Patagonian Theatre from Dublin" opened its doors, carefully disclaiming any connexion with the performances here "some time ago." The programme opened with a double bill of *Midas* and a new pantomime, *The Enchanter*, concluding with "a superb piece of Perspective Architecture, being a copy of the magnificent Altar erected in the Jesuit's church at Rome, as designed by Poppo."

This season ran for eight months, playing three times a week, and presenting eleven productions; it closed for the summer months (like all the chief London theatres), but reopened in December for a second winter season of six months, with fourteen productions, six of which were new. The third season presented sixteen productions, eight of them new; the fourth season twelve productions, three new; and the fifth season of 1780–1781 nineteen productions, of which eleven had not been seen before. This is a remarkable record. The Patagonian Theatre kept its doors open for five years, presenting about forty productions as well as numerous interludes and scenic displays. This far outstrips Powell's record of twenty plays in three years. The Patagonian Theatre is almost unknown, while Powell is lauded in every article on puppets that has ever been written, but it achieved one of the longest runs that a permanent puppet theatre has ever maintained in London, and we may well examine its repertory, disinterred at last from the original advertisements, with a peculiar interest.[56]

Of the forty plays performed here, about half had previously appeared in the human theatre. The great majority of these were ballad operas—Gay's *Beggar's Opera*, Dibdin's *The Waterman*, Bickerstaffe's *The Padlock*, *The Recruiting Serjeant*, and *Thomas and Sally*, and Carey's *True Blue*. The plots of these are often very slight, and a few examples will suffice. In *Thomas and Sally* we have all the budding elements of a Victorian melodrama: a fox-hunting squire with designs upon Sally, the village maiden; a wicked old woman who urges her to enjoy herself while she can; and her lover, home from the sea, who arrives just in time to rescue her from the squire's embraces. *The Recruiting Serjeant* is just a village episode of a countryman who pretends to enlist in order to shock his shrewish wife into affection. *The Waterman* tells how a gallant young Thames waterman wins the race for Doggett's coat and badge, and is able to marry the girl he loves with the prize-money. Simple songs, sung in a straightforward manner to the tunes of popular ballads, gave these unambitious anecdotes a quality of freshness and charm and virility; as we have seen, they had found a place upon the puppet stage already.

Parodies of the Italian opera had played a big part in Powell's repertory, and they were no less popular at the Patagonian. The most successful of these was *Midas*, by Kane O'Hara. This is said to be an extremely clever musical burlesque, and some of the incidents are peculiarly suited to puppetry. The play opens with the heathen deities seated amid the clouds in full council; Apollo has given offence, and Jupiter darts a thunderbolt at him and casts him from Olympus; the gods all ascend together to the rolling of thunder. Meanwhile the clouds part to reveal the earth, with a scene of "a champaign country with a distant village"; shepherds sleeping in the field are roused by a violent thunderstorm, and run away frightened; "Apollo is seen whirling in the air, as if cast from heaven; he falls to earth with a rude shock, and lies for a while stunned; at length he begins to move, rises, advances, and looking upwards, speaks." This play was given over seventy performances.

Burlesque of heroic tragedy had already been tried by Foote, and an extremely popular item in the Patagonian repertory, with over fifty performances, was *Chrononhotonthologos*, by Henry Carey. This tells how the King of Queerummania, Chrononhot(etc.), leads his people in victory against an invasion from the Antipodes; the Antipodean monarch—walking always upside down—is brought home captive in a Grand Triumph, but the Queen of Queerummania falls in love with him. Meanwhile at the victory banquet Chrononhotonthologos kills the cook for insolence, and is killed by his general in a brawl; the general kills the doctor who can't bring the King to life again, and then kills himself. The Queen, surveying the gory scene, is left free to marry the captive Antipodean. Two extracts will give an idea of the quality of the burlesque:

QUEEN.
Day's curtain's drawn, the morn begins to rise,
And waking nature rubs her sleepy eyes;
The pretty little fleecy bleating flocks
In baas harmonious warble thro' the rocks;
Night gathers up her shades in sable shrouds,
And whispering osiers tattle to the clouds.
What think you, ladies, if an hour we kill
At basset, ombre, picquet or quadrille?

And later:

GENERAL.
Ha! What have I done?
Go call a coach, and let a coach be called;
And let the man that calls it be the caller;
And in his calling, let him nothing call,
But Coach! Coach! Coach! Oh, for a coach, ye gods!

Delivered in the oratond tones of some popular heavy tragedian, this must have been very funny indeed.

A few fairly straight stage comedies, such as Garrick's *The Irish Widow*, found their way into the Patagonian repertory, but they did not usually achieve many performances, and it is doubtful if plays demanding so much individual characterization can be adequately performed by puppets. A little trifle, on the other hand, by Garrick called *Linco's Travels* proved immensely popular. This is almost a monologue in which Linco returns from his travels to his home and friends in Arcadia, and describes the strange country that he has visited, England.

> So furious are they to be free,
> Nothing so common as to see
> Britons dead-drunk for liberty.

The most curious piece ever performed at the Patagonian Theatre—and there were some very curious pieces—was undoubtedly a masque, taken from Shakespeare and Dryden, called *The Shipwreck*. The scene-painter had evidently visited the Mediterranean during the previous summer, and Prospero's enchanted island was the scene of some very remarkable vistas. In Act I we have drop-scenes of a moonlit and barren heath, a fine view of a cave, a view of Marson Dale, in Derbyshire, and a scene "in relief" of Mount Vesuvius in eruption, "as it appeared last August," with a thunderstorm and shipwreck. Act II introduced drop-scenes of mountainous country, a beautiful view of broken ruins, a fine view of the Gulf of Messina, and a relief of a rocky landscape, with water, and a land storm. Act III gives us a drop of a sea-coast, with a storm blowing over, and reliefs of Dovedale, in Derbyshire, inside a Gothic-formed cavern, with a cascade of water, and concludes with an extensive view of the Bay of Naples, with Vesuvius quiet, different Neapolitan vessels sailing into port, and the rising of the Sea Gods from the sea in a chorus. If we can forget all about *The Tempest* we can appreciate the skill and invention of this musical revue: we have here, in its very quintescence, the first stirrings of the Romantic Revival. Wild scenery, awful chasms, and Gothic caves were a new-found titillation for eighteenth-century Society.

Almost every performance included a pantomime. *The Emperor of the Moon*, which was apparently the earliest "dialogue pantomime" on the English stage, introduced "the descent of the Moon to the earth, with its increase to the full, and a fabulous idea of the inside of the same"; *Hecate* levied tribute once again from the long-suffering Shakespeare with the choruses from *Macbeth*; and so on. The dramatic critic of *The Morning Chronicle* reported that the

> pantomime, in point of music and scenery, is equal to any we ever saw; in point of absurdity, superior. What it meant we don't pretend to know, but that there were many exceeding beautiful scenes exhibited in the course of it

we fairly acknowledge. The last architectural assemblage is really a curious and grand exhibition; whether the town will be content merely with a feast for their eyes and ears, we won't take upon us to determine.

But there was something more than scenery and nonsense: as at the Little Piazza seventy years before, there was caricature and wit. Many of the plays that seem to have been specially written for the Patagonian Theatre were satires, to judge from their titles, full of contemporary allusions. The court-martial, and acquittal, of Admiral Keppel was followed within a few weeks by *The British Admiral, or the City in an Uproar*, in which the triumphant progress of the Admiral's coach through the illuminated streets of London, accompanied by a vociferous mob, was graphically represented. The strange medical practices of Dr Graham at the Temple of Health in the Adelphi were satirized in *Doctor Adelphi*; and Sheridan's memorial Monody to the Memory of David Garrick, spoken at Drury Lane after his funeral, was parodied in *The Apotheosis of Punch*, to be spoken by Melpomene, the Tragic Muse. This little squib, which we should consider in rather bad taste to-day, was described as "malignant without merit"; it drew the town, however, for twenty-five performances, and was published in book form. The author was Leonard Macnally, an Irish barrister and playwright.[57]

Between the main pieces of the evening's entertainment, and between the acts, there would be interludes of dancing, a hornpipe, a country dance, or a crutch dance; songs like "The soldier tired of War's alarms," by Thomas Arne, "Let the bright seraphim," from Handel's oratorio of *Sampson*, or "The lads of the village," from Dibdin's *Quaker*; or short scenes from popular comedies—*Taste*, or *The Devil upon Two Sticks*, or *The Minor*. The elaborate scenery must have required some time to change, and the Patagonian Theatre knew how necessary it was not to keep the audience yawning through lengthy intervals; there is a lesson here for some puppet shows to-day. The evening's entertainment always concluded with some magnificent scenic set piece. There was "a grand representation of the Doge of Venice going to wed the Adriatic"; "a superb scene of the Temple of the Sun, as formerly in the famous city of Palmira, with a grand chorus of the priests of Apollo"; and—another souvenir of the Mediterranean holiday—three scenes representing the victories of Admiral Rodney over the Spanish fleet, with a beautiful and extensive prospect of a naval engagement, a view of the Rock of Gibraltar and the coast of Barbary, with the Spanish men-of-war "entering the bay under convoy of the British Fleet, and an emblematical scene descending in the clouds in honour of Prince William and the brave Admiral, in the course of which will be introduced 'Britons strike Home,' 'God save the King,' and 'Rule, Britannia.'" After this stirring finale it is a sad anti-climax to read in a later advertisement that "on account of the unavoidable delays caused by the complication of the machinery in exhibiting such extensive scenes . . . immediately after each other . . . the first scene represented on Monday . . . will be omitted."

The Patagonian Theatre closed every summer from about May to November; performances were given, normally, three times a week, at about seven in the evening, and prices ranged from five shillings to one. The theatre was provided with pit and gallery, and after the second season the house was refitted with side and front boxes. The theatre seems to have been well patronized by the nobility and gentry, but ladies who came to gossip taxed the patience of the proprietor, who humbly requested "those ladies who honour him with their company to take off their hats and keep their seats during the performance, as, by adhering to these rules, he flatters himself every one will have an opportunity of viewing the scenery, which he has spared no pains or expense to render elegant and agreeable." Books of the play were on sale at the theatre, and refreshments were available, including tea, coffee, chocolate, jellies orgent, capillaire, lemonade, and plumb. The "band of music" included "a capital organ," which sometimes gave solo recitals. Members of the audience were strictly forbidden admission behind the scenes. There are several references to the excellent vocal performers engaged by the proprietor, and benefit performances were given every season. Members of the company included Mr and Mrs Mapples, Mr Hutton, Mr Chapman, Mr Costellow, Mr Louin, and Mrs Child. The proprietor of the theatre was the scene-painter, and he undertook "to instruct a few ladies and gentlemen on the art of drawing and painting in perspective" during the summer months.

In February 1781 the proprietor announced that he, "going to be much engaged in private business, will dispose of this theatre, with all the scenes, machinery, etc. Any person or persons willing to purchase either the public or private entertainments, may be fully instructed in the method of conducting it." The last advertisement for the fifth season was inserted on the 27th of April. After a fortnight's silence a new, and previously unheard-of, Summer Patagonian Season was announced, but it was billed for only five days. By the end of May 1781 the Patagonian Theatre was dark; it is said to have changed hands, to have run a few hundred pounds into debt, and to have been sold up at the demand of importunate creditors. Its whimsical name—a droll antonym to the obvious Lilliputian puppet theatres—had been adopted by a few fairground booths, but there is no record of any further authentic public performances.

Exeter Change was a large bazaar-like building on the north side of the Strand; the ground floor was taken up by a number of small traders' stalls, and the large room above was let out for all kinds of purposes. Ten years after the closing of the Patagonian Theatre it was taken over as a menagerie of wild beasts, which flourished until the building was demolished in 1830. The room, so far as one can tell from later illustrations,[58] was about seventy feet long; at one end the roof had been raised to allow the erection of a gallery. It is described as "a neat little theatre," holding about two hundred persons.[59] Once again, the "large room," with some theatrical fittings, proved itself the most suitable theatre for the marionettes.

The stage is said to have been about six feet wide, and the marionettes not more than eleven inches high. The puppets themselves are never described in the advertisements, and this suggests that their rôle in the productions was a subsidiary one; certainly the great attraction of this theatre must have been the beautiful and romantic scenery. The scenic display, however, was never allowed to submerge the drama; serious tragedy was never played here—nor for that matter in any of these fashionable puppet theatres—but light comedy, light opera, dramatic and musical burlesque, and contemporary satire all provided a solid dramatic vehicle for the scene-painter's fancy. The whole entertainment was presented with the support of pleasant music and at least adequate singing and speaking.

Who ran the Patagonian Theatre? It is curious that so little is known about the ownership of this fashionable and successful entertainment. It came, however, from Dublin. There, early in 1774, an amateur marionette theatre known as Mr Punch's Patagonian Theatre had been established at a house in Abbey Street, with seats for about 120 people; it was the fancy of Kane O'Hara, the well-known dramatist and wit. To assist him he had a delicate young man called Nick Marsh, a much-loved humorist whose fondness for company and the bottle brought him to an early grave, and a scene-painter called John Ellis; Michael Kelly, the famous tenor, sang in some of the productions here as a boy soprano. Admission to the theatre was by invitation, and it became quite the rage among all the people of fashion; occasional performances were given at high prices for charity. Here *Midas* was played, and O'Hara's burlesque opera *Tom Thumb* received its first performance.[60]

When the show was brought to London in 1776 it would appear that

Ellis came with it as manager. He had been apprenticed to a cabinet-maker in Dublin, but abandoned this to train as an artist. He is said to have possessed a remarkable skill in perspective, and his scenery at the Patagonian Theatre was so greatly admired that he was awarded a silver palette by the Dublin Society in recognition of it; this must be the only example in British history of an academic award being given for puppet-theatre scenery! He married the daughter of a Dublin grocer, against the wishes of both sets of parents, and the outlawed lovers took refuge in London; no doubt he brought the marionettes with him as a means of livelihood. On the death of his wife's father he returned to Dublin, and by 1790 had opened a shop in Mary Street, where he organized exhibitions of the works of Irish artists; he died soon after 1812. His son is said to have enjoyed a not unsuccessful career in England as a prolific forger of Canalettos. Between the bare bones of his biography there may be glimpsed the portrait of an ingenious craftsman, a clever artist, and something of a showman.[61]

Assisting him at Exeter Change in speaking for the puppets as well as making them was Mick Stoppelaer, a low Irish comedian who had played the first gravedigger at Drury Lane, and who possessed some skill as a caricaturist. The money-taker and box-keeper was a Mr Thomson, whose brother kept a bookstall in the bazaar below.[62] The theatre always retained a strong Irish connexion, with pieces by O'Hara, Bickerstaffe, and Macnally well to the fore. Kane O'Hara was described by one who knew him as "a first-rate wit, and in manners what was formerly called a fine gentleman"; Leonard Macnally was "a sprightly boy" with a passion for private theatricals, who "excelled all his contemporaries in keen and sarcastic wit," but his comparative failure as a dramatist for the human theatre seems to have soured him, and he has gone down to infamy in Irish history as a political informer;[63] Isaac Bickerstaffe was a fluent writer and charming companion, the friend of Garrick, until a homosexual scandal drove him into exile abroad. These eighteenth-century "toadies of the Ascendancy" may not stand in great honour in the Ireland of to-day, but the English theatre owes much to the work of Irish writers, and to the long score of our indebtedness we must now add the Patagonian Theatre, the Irish artists who designed it, and the Irish wits who wrote for it.

Stretch of Dublin

Dublin had known other puppet theatres before the Patagonian. The most famous of these was contemporary with Powell, and was already famous by 1721;[64] it was run by a man called Stretch. At this time the newly appointed Master of the Revels in Ireland tried to extort large fees for licences from the Irish theatres: the Smock Alley Theatre was expected to pay £300 a year, and £50 seems to have been demanded from Stretch. This inspired a satirical verse called *Punch's Petition to the Ladies*, written in 1724. The "fair ones who do all hearts command" were begged to intercede for their favourite Punch, with the Master of the Revels:

> Wh'invades without pretence or right,
> Or any law but that of might,
> Our Pigmy land—and treats our kings
> Like paltry idle wooden things;
> Has beat our dancers out of doors,
> And called our chasest virgins whores;
> He has not left our Queen a rag on,
> Has forced away our George and Dragon,
> Has broke our wires, nor was he civil
> To Doctor Faustus nor the devil;
> E'en us he hurried with full rage,
> Most hoarsely squalling off the stage.[65]

The success of the puppets inspired Thomas Sheridan to write a comedy burlesquing them called *Punch turned Schoolmaster*, in which the actors appeared as puppets going to school under the charge of Punch. Apparently it was not very amusing, but the prologue gives us a little further information:

> We found this House was almost empty grown
> From the first moment Stretch appeared in town.
> What could we do but learn to squeek and hoop it;
> Each actor change into his favourite puppet? . . .
> I now proceed to beg our Punch may meet
> As much applause as he in Capel Street.[66]

Stretch's puppet theatre was, therefore, certainly established in Capel Street by 1721, and it remained a great attraction for many years; in the sixties the manager was a James Harvey, but long after the founder's death in 1744 it continued to be known as Stretch's Show. Anything that was absurd or nonsensical came to be described in Dublin slang as "more of Stretch's Show." The proprietor used to sit in a box up against the wall, among the audience, presumably the stage box; and the story of the puppet play was carried on with the help of question and repartee between the showman and Punch. An amusing piece of regular business was provided by a small child who was trained to play with toys and marbles in the audience, and at the right cue to waddle up to Mr Punch, clasp him in his arms, and carry him completely off the stage. The performance was always concluded with a beautiful scene of Cupid's paradise. The theatre was very small, but the stage was deep and the auditorium had pit, boxes, and galleries. Towards the end of its existence, however, it fell into decay and was described as a wretched hovel. The theatre was at last closed in about 1765; it was refurnished and opened with human actors, with great success, in 1770.[67]

A satirical pamphlet of 1756 gives an interesting list of the supposed contents of the Capel Street theatre's wardrobe: heads, arms, crowns, truncheons, tinsel, suits of flock-paper—*i.e.*, wallpaper sized and coated with wool refuse—a suit of armour for the Dancing Hog, a pair of castanets for the dancing Blackamoor Lady, the Queen of Sheba's robe, Cupid's Paradise, King Solomon, a shower of imitation snow, the Serpent in the Grove, Adam and Eve (the fig-leaf wanting), Joan's ladle, and so on.[68] Even without the documentation of advertisements it is easy to reconstruct Stretch's repertory; it was a typical old-fashioned puppet show, very like many that flourished in England at the beginning of the eighteenth century, with Biblical stories and folk-tales, interspersed with the comical humours of Mr Punch. The puppets were marionettes, the speakers spoke through a squeaker, and the use of the showman as 'interpreter' on the front of the stage brings back memories of the Elizabethan motions.

Stretch's repertory was probably largely traditional; but farces and pantomimes were billed from time to time, and impecunious young Irish wits are said to have written for this theatre in the twenties—like the hunchbacked schoolmaster Charles Coffey and the future doctor of divinity William Dunkin. It would be fascinating to discover to what degree "the diversion in Capel Street" acquired a specifically Irish character. Its phenomenally long life of over forty years constitutes a remarkable record; London never achieved anything like this.

Stretch's show and O'Hara's Patagonian Theatre were by no means the only puppet theatres to flourish in Dublin. A cabinet-maker, Francis Whetstone, had played in rivalry to Stretch in 1748; and in 1775 John Cartwright, an ex-equestrian and maestro on the musical glasses, seems to have introduced an elegant display of Fantoccini to Irish society, to be followed by several others during the next decade. In 1779 an unsuccessful attempt was made to revive the glories of the Patagonian Theatre at the theatre in Fishamble Street; but during the next two years an extremely elegant and fashionable entertainment known as the Microcosm drew the world of fashion to its performances in Drury Lane. In 1792 an ex-drum major called Spencer Woffington appropriated the famous name of the Patagonian Theatre for his touring puppet booth; Fantoccini were playing in Capel Street regularly during the first decade of the nineteenth century; and a Lilliputian Theatre appeared in 1813. There was to be much more to chronicle as the century progressed.[69]

The history of the Irish puppet theatre calls for more detailed treatment than is possible here. Perhaps one day an Irishman will bring the whole rich and absorbing story to light.

Eidophusikon

The miniature scenic displays developed so successfully at the Patagonian Theatre were carried a stage further by Philip de Loutherbourg, an Alsatian artist, who had been brought to England by Garrick to paint the scenery at Drury Lane. During his five years at this theatre he revolutionized the art of scene-painting with a series of spectacular productions; for some of these he drew inspiration from the picturesque scenery of the Peak district, and his work may be set beside that of Horace Walpole in the first stirrings of the Romantic movement. After Garrick's death he quarrelled with his successor over the payment of his salary, and left the theatre for good. His taste for scenic design, however, found expression in the construction of what he called the Eidophusikon.[70]

This was really an elaborate model theatre, about six feet wide and eight feet deep. The scenes were not painted on flat canvas in the normal theatrical convention, but were built up in many rows of flat cut-out pasteboard. For instance, the first scene shown at its exhibition was the view across London from Greenwich Park, and here the foreground was actually built up from tiny pieces of cork and lichen, the trees of the park were each separately cut out, then came the sails of the shipping in the river, then the dome of St Paul's and the City spires, then the hills of Highgate and Hampstead, and at the back of it all clouds, painted in semi-transparent colours on linen, were wound across the stage in a diagonal direction, giving the effect of clouds rising above the horizon and passing overhead. The effect of distance was said to have been uncanny.

The lighting of the stage was effected by argand lamps—that is, oil-lamps with circular wicks—which were placed *above* the stage. De Loutherbourg was far ahead of his time in abolishing footlights, but then he had no actors whose faces needed to be well lit! The lamps were placed at the back of the stage as well as the front, so that their light shining through the translucent clouds lent them a luminosity. Before each lamp he had coloured slides of stained glass, which he could vary, as he could the strength of the flame; and he ran through the whole range of Nature's lighting effects with dawn breaking over London, noon at the port of Tangier, sunset near Naples, and moonlight in the Mediterranean. All this, which is accepted as commonplace to-day, was an exciting discovery in the eighteenth century.

Another very effective scene was that of a storm at sea, showing the loss of the Halsewell East Indiaman, whose wreck off Purbeck in 1786 had been a sensation of the day. For this he had every wave separately carved in soft wood and highly varnished, revolving on its own axis in the opposite direction to that next to it. The whole apparatus was controlled by turning one handle, which could be rotated at varying speeds, and foam was flung up here and there as the choppy seas boiled round the sinking ship. The exhibition was accompanied by a completely realistic accompaniment of noises: the sound of rain was counterfeited by shaking seed in a box, hail by beads, waves by peas, thunder by shaking a copper sheet, and the distress gun by striking a stretched parchment skin with a sponge on a whalebone spring. A grand final effect was a scene from Milton's *Paradise Lost*, with Satan arraying his troops on the banks of the fiery lake, and the rising of the Palace of Pendemonium from the waters.

The Eidophusikon was first shown in 1781 at the artist's house in Leicester Street, where a large room seating 130 people was most tastefully decorated for the purpose, and then in 1786 at Exeter Change, the old home of the Patagonian Theatre. No plays were performed and no puppets were used; the attraction of the exhibition was strictly pictorial, but there was music on the harpsichord by Mr Arne or English readings by Mr Creswick during the intervals. For a time the display was very successful, warranting a 5*s.* admission charge, but the public for such an exhibition was limited, and after two seasons it could not attract enough audience to pay even for lighting the theatre.

A successor to de Loutherbourg, the New Eidophusikon, was exhibited in Dublin in the nineties and opened in Panton Street in 1799. It was the work of a Mr Chapman, husband of an actress at Covent Garden, said to have been de Loutherbourg's original assistant. The scenes shown included a view near Cork at dawn, moonlight falling upon a lighthouse, sunset in Dublin Bay, and a storm and shipwreck at sea; later a representation of an eclipse of the moon was added, which was "extremely beautiful, and yields only, in effect, to nature itself." Chapman was perhaps an Irishman, like Ellis. The display was accompanied by recitations, comic songs, a learned dog, and Mr Wilkinson's performance on the musical glasses. The exhibition ended tragically: in March 1800 a fire broke out in a brothel opposite the Tennis Court in James Street, Charlotte Charke's old theatre, and spread to the Eidophusikon, which was probably in Hickford's Great Room, completely destroying it.[71]

A few years later, in 1819, what was described as "the remains of Loutherbourg's Eidophusikon" were exhibited at the Theatre of Arts, an exhibition room in Spring Gardens. The performance included mechanical and picturesque views of foreign cities, the Midnight Sun at the North Pole, and our old friend the Storm at Sea. This show was seen by Edmund Kean, who wanted the storm effects copied for his production of *King Lear* at Drury Lane in 1820, and Elliston was reluctantly put to vast expense in making trees with separate boughs and leaves rustling in the wind. In the event the storm stole the show, and Kean's own performance was comparatively ineffective.[72]

The Eidophusikon was described by a contemporary as "superior to any other scenic display that the world has yet seen." It was, perhaps, hardly a puppet show, but it would be a pity to lose this opportunity of referring to this contribution by the model theatre to the development of scene design. The puppet theatre is usually the repository of long-forgotten conventions of the human stage, but here, in the scenic displays of the Patagonian Theatre and the Eidophusikon, it foreshadowed theatre developments a century before their time.

Italian Fantoccini

When Foote pretended to revive the "Primitive Puppet Show" in 1773 he lamented the sad decadence into which this once flourishing art had fallen; even if we take his rhetoric with a pinch of salt there seems little doubt that the elegant and artistic marionettes of the Restoration and Queen Anne periods had by this time lapsed into disrepute. Yet the twenty years between 1770 and 1790 were one of the most brilliant and prolific in the whole history of English puppetry. Valuable though Foote's and Dibdin's initiative must have been, much of the credit for this revival must be attributed to the arrival of the Fantoccini, which is the Italian word for marionettes.

On October 4, 1770, the Italian Fantoccini of Mr Carlo Perico opened their season at the Great Room in Panton Street.[73] This had previously been Hickford's Music Room, and stretched between Panton Street and James Street, with a narrow frontage and a depth of about 100 feet, where the Comedy Theatre now stands. Mr Perico claimed to have performed already before the reigning monarchs of Sardinia, France, Orange, and Great Britain. Performances were, at first, given twice daily, at seven and nine, and thus cannot have lasted longer than an hour and a half; admission was at the flat rate of half a crown; each play was given a week's clear run—a modern conception of repertory, like Powell's, and quite unlike any contemporary theatre practice. The Fantoccini here ran, without any break for the summer months, right through 1771, and the season did not close until July 14, 1772; this unbroken run of nearly twenty-one months was (with the possible exception of Devoto) the longest run ever attained by a London puppet theatre, and set up a record that has yet to be broken.

This repertory was sustained with only thirteen pieces. The first, and most popular, went under the all-embracing title of *Harlequin Chimney Sweep*, *Bass-Viol*, *Astrologer*, *Skeleton*, *Child*, *Statue*, *and at last a Parrot*; nearly as popular were *Harlequin King of the Enchanted Island*, *Harlequin Great Sorcerer*, *The Enchantress Circe*, and *The Magical Combat between Pantaloon and Harlequin*. No descriptions of these plays have come down, but they were evidently in the tradition of the Italian Comedy, with Harlequin usurping the position once held by Pulcinella. They made a great feature of magic, and there must have been many spectacular spells cast, visions conjured up, and transformations. These transformations, or metamorphoses, were apparently the great feature of the Fantoccini, and the *Harlequin Chimney Sweep* play probably showed Harlequin, having gained possession of some magic spell, transforming himself into one object after another to escape pursuit from an indignant Pantaloon. These tricks are, of course, comfortably within the power of a skilful puppeteer.[74] The language used was, apparently, a mixture of French and Italian—perhaps the dialogue was in French and the songs in Italian. A few months after the opening of the theatre an English lady wrote to her son that "I was much pleased with the 'Fantocini' I saw last night. The novelty of an entertainment in French and Italian amused us all. My ears not being accustomed to a French *petite pièce*, I doubted whether I should comprehend, but I did perfectly well, and very droll it was."[75]

Between the acts there were always special tricks and interludes. A shepherdess played on a mandolina, while a shepherd accompanied her with the violin; a black balanced a spontoon; there were dances by the

Dwarf Giant, the Savages, a Spanish lady, and a tumbler; a rope-dancer performed; a hussar took off his cap and cloak, Harlequin came and stole them away (a complicated little trick, when everything is on strings), and a battle ensued sword in hand. There was a pantomime by a family of Pierrots, and Harlequin ate a dish of macaroni. This must have been funny, and quite easy to do; one can almost see each long coil of spaghetti disappearing through Harlequin's mouth with a 'plop,' as the wily Italian showman pulled his lattice-work of strings up above.

Everybody went to see the puppets at Panton Street—Dr Johnson, Sir Joshua Reynolds, Oliver Goldsmith, Burke, and so on. There is a nice story of how Johnson exclaimed, after seeing the show, "How the little fellow brandished his spontoon!" Goldsmith, who was supposed to be absurdly jealous, exclaimed, "There is nothing in it; I can do it as well myself," and then bruised his shins in trying to show the company how a puppet jumped over a stick.[76] A spontoon was a kind of short pike, carried by infantry officers. The mechanical skill of these puppets aroused admiration on every side; people exclaimed at the way they "were made to walk the stage, draw a chair to the table, sit down, and write a letter"; there is nothing very remarkable in any of these actions, and one feels that Powell must have presented a show quite as dexterous as this, but that was forty-five years earlier, and it was over twenty years since the last puppet show of any elegance, Madame de la Nash's, had been seen in Town, in this very same room. Carlo Perico's puppets came like a new discovery.

News of the success of Perico's puppets must have spread to Italy, and four years later another troupe of Fantoccini arrived in London.[77] These described themselves as "entirely different from all such as have appeared before in this metropolis. They belonged to a late king in Italy, and used to perform at his court. Their motions and feats of activity are so wonderful, and at the same time so natural, that in Italy they were commonly styled 'Wooden Magicians.'" This company opened in November 1776 at the Little Theatre in the Haymarket with *The Judgement of Pluto in favour of Harlequin*, but the first night seems to have been disastrous, as they were soon apologizing that "the scenes not being rightly disposed, and two boards of the little stage giving way in the first act, the new Fantoccini could not exert themselves in their usual surprising manner." The managers earnestly begged that they might be favoured with a second trial.

The season lasted under two months, and cannot have been very successful. Perhaps the acoustics and sight-lines of the Haymarket

Theatre defeated the Italian puppets, as they were later to defeat Dibdin. Fourteen plays were performed, many of them for only one performance; they were billed under their Italian titles, though sometimes with laughably ridiculous translations: the managers of this troupe evidently knew little English. At least four of these pieces had been given by Perico in his previous season, and the remainder drew upon the same mythological fairyland peopled by the masks of the Commedia dell' Arte.

This company was to run into still further difficulties in the course of its unfortunate visit to British shores. It had been brought over from Venice as a speculation by Signor Cardarelli, a burletta singer then resident in England, but after the Haymarket season he transferred his interest in the company to a Mr Briochi, a London merchant, who sent the troupe on a visit to Dublin with his clerk as their manager. They opened in Dublin at the Capel Street theatre, with matinée performances only, in April 1777, but they failed to attract, their manager abandoned them, Mr Briochi refused to pay their bills, and by the autumn of that year six or seven Italian puppeteers were still stranded in Dublin, destitute and starving. In October the manager of the Capel Street theatre generously offered them the use of it free of charge for a few nights, and the sympathetic patronage of the Dublin public enabled them to set out for England, with the expectation of a return season at the Haymarket that never seems to have materialized.[78]

Two years later another troupe of Fantoccini appeared in London, again at the Great Room in Panton Street, opening in January 1779.[79] Much the same repertory was again repeated, the most popular piece being *Harlequin Great Sorcerer*, *or the Birth of Harlequin from an Egg*. This had provided a highly successful pantomime theme for Rich at Covent Garden earlier in the century, and was to figure in the bills of every troupe of Italian Fantoccini. Other old favourites like *The Judgement of Pluto* and *The Enchantress Circe* made up the nine pieces presented.

The interludes between the acts introduced Harlequin and his little horse, a Turk with his wife in a basket on his back, a drunken sailor with a pot of beer in his hand, and a Spaniard with a spontoon. Harlequin ate a plate of macaroni again, and also drank a glass of wine to the company's health—I think he must have done this through a straw, or perhaps with a trick cup. There were some spectacular tricks in *Circe and Atlas*, with "the rival magicians exhibiting a beautiful transformation of a shepherdess into a flower-pot, and then into a fountain. Diana descends to the assistance of Harlequin and Cloras in an illuminated temple." The sensation of this season, however, was the "one figure transformed into six out of each arm, legs, head and body . . . after which the same figure will dance a Cotillon, the like as never was attempted before in this metropolis." This seems to be the earliest appearance in England of the trick now known as the Grand Turk.

The dialogue of the plays was still in Italian, or perhaps French, but an explanation was given in English at the end of every act. Prices were 3*s.* pit and 2*s.* gallery, and towards the end of the season the seats were reduced to 2*s.* and 1*s.* A private performance was offered for six guineas, with every person exceeding twelve five shillings extra. This company of Italian and French artists finally set out for abroad at the end of May after a four-month season.

Within less than a year, in January 1780, yet another troupe of Italian Fantoccini—the fourth in ten years—arrived to make their fortune out of the English.[80] This theatre is described as just imported from Italy, and as being "in a small compass the exact model of the superb Teatro Nuovo at Bologna," with scenery painted by "the celebrated Bibbiena"; it was under the management of Signor Micheli, and was presented at a room at 22 Piccadilly, which—as almost always in these advertisements—"was neatly fitted up, kept warm, and illuminated with wax." The alternative, and cheaper, lighting was, of course, smelly oil-lamps or tallow candles.

Several old favourites reappear in these programmes—*The Judgement of Pluto*, *The Transformations of Harlequin*, *Harlequin's Birth from an Egg-shell*, and so on—and for the first time an attempt was made to perform part of the repertory in English. Alongside these some quite ambitious operas were presented, like *La Serva Padrona* and *Fair Nancy at Court*, with music by Pergolesi, which had been the subject of a grand ballet at the Opera House.

Each evening there was a double bill of a comic opera and a pantomime, with the usual interludes, concluding with a grand climax when Harlequin launched himself from the stage and flew round the room, which was 60 feet long by 40 feet wide, "in a manner truly surprising and never before exhibited in Europe." Not content with this feat, he was presently joined by Columbine, who flew beside him, distributing printed prologues on their way. This is an effect that seems to have been forgotten by puppeteers to-day, but it is not difficult to work out the way in which it was probably done. It would be necessary to prepare the room beforehand, with strings running from the back of the audience through the opening of the stage curtain, and with a confederate in a gallery. If these strings were threaded through hooks on the puppet's shoulders he could be pulled to and fro along them, as if on a pair of railway-lines. The principle, though complicated, could be improved with many little subtleties, and the audience perhaps did not notice the threads stretched above their heads in the flickering light of the wax candles.[81]

Thirteen pieces were presented here during a four-month season, with tickets at 5*s.* each, reduced at the end of the season to 3*s.* and 2*s.* The theatre closed for the summer at the end of May, but was open again in December. Subscription tickets for one guinea admitted one person six, and later ten, times. During the second season the back seats were reduced to 2*s.* 6*d.*, and children were admitted to the front seats at half-price—a concession that had been anticipated by Powell, but which was still unusual. Signor Micheli claimed to have engaged the best performers, both vocal and musical, and the chief machinist and manipulator was Joseph Martinelli.

The most interesting addition to the repertory for the second season was Piccinni's popular opera *La Buona Figliuola*; Harlequin still flew round the room, holding, for full measure, a light in his hand. Attempts to cap this trick with something even more startling do not seem to have been successful: Micheli tried out a warrior who fell into pieces, and out of whose head issued a beautiful figure, and also a machine like a catherine-wheel revolving in the air, but everything else must have seemed an anticlimax. Eight pieces, four of which were new, were performed in the second season, which ran for five months; the theatre finally closed in May 1781.

The success of the Italian Fantoccini was by this time inspiring all sorts of shows to assume the title, and Micheli was continually advertising his claim to have the only original Fantoccini, which he "himself imported from Italy last year at a very great expense . . . and the figures moved by Italians engaged for that purpose only." There is an entertaining story, however, that has been handed down by tradition through several generations, that throws a little light on Micheli's expensive importation. According to this, the theatre was originally made for the amusement of a young prince in Bologna, who lost interest in it and put it aside after his marriage. His servant, hearing of the success of the puppets in London, smuggled the whole outfit away and sent it to an Italian friend in England. This friend was Micheli, an opera singer, who held the post of copyist at the Opera House at the time. But before he could get his hands on it to exploit it there was a period of excruciating suspense while the theatre was detained by the English customs, until the duty was paid.

None of the conspirators had enough cash to clear it through the customs! But then fate intervened, Micheli won a prize in the lottery, paid the customs, and set up in Piccadilly.[82]

Nine years later, in January 1790, what must have been the most elegant and socially successful season ever presented by the Italian Fantoccini opened at the little theatre in Savile Row, adapted from Squibb's Auction Rooms, under the direction of Mr Carnevale, who had recently been assistant manager of the Opera House, and thus a colleague of Micheli's.[83] The room was converted "into a very pretty theatre, with a pit and two rows of boxes, beautifully decorated with arabesque paintings, as it should seem, by Rebecca." Biagio Rebecca was an Italian painter who worked in England at the end of the eighteenth century; some of his work may still be seen in the great houses he decorated for Wyatt, at Heaton Hall, in Manchester, and at Hevingham Hall, in Suffolk. To know that this gifted artist's delicate brush once ornamented a London puppet theatre is a revelation for us in the converted attics and cellars that serve as puppet theatres to-day.

Carnevale had somehow obtained the interest of fashionable Society, and on the opening performance the boxes were occupied by the following parties: the Prince of Wales (later the Prince Regent), the Duke of Orleans, the Duke of Cumberland, the Duke of Bedford, Lord Salisbury, Lord Shaftesbury, Lord M. Churchill, Lord Malmesbury, Lord Cadogan, Lord Mornington, Lord Cholmondeley, and Mr Thompson. What a first night! The entertainment was so successful that every seat was taken up by subscriptions for the season, and no money was accepted at the door; a subscription of four guineas entitled the holder to attend twelve performances. Later, at the end of the season, individual seats were sold for 10*s.* 6*d.*—the equivalent of several guineas to-day! Performances were given at eight o'clock on only two nights a week. At these prices the fortunate performers could well afford to take life easily!

Twelve pieces were performed during the three-month season, ten in French and two in Italian; of these only one had appeared in the earlier Fantoccini seasons. There were *Les Deux Jumeaux*, *Les Trois Recettes*, *Les Deux Chasseurs et la Laitière*, *l'Erreur du Moment*, and so on, comedies and light operas by contemporary French authors, popular in their day. The Commedia dell' Arte tradition was less evident, but was preserved in pieces like *Les Fourberies d'Arlequin*; and the whole programme was interspersed with airs selected, and apparently sometimes specially written, by leading composers of the period, and played by a band of Italian musicians.

The charm of the *décor* and the quality of the light operatic music must have had a great deal to do with the appeal of this entertainment to the aristocracy. Of the puppets themselves there is no mention of any particularly startling new tricks, though a metamorphosis play was on the programme and the *entracte* turns included a hornpipe and feats on the tight rope. According to a contemporary critic, the puppets were "the public's old acquaintance in Panton Street," in which case they may have been the identical figures used by Perico in the season of 1770.

In March 1790 Mr Carnevale announced that he had disposed of the Fantoccini, and the season finally ended on April the 9th, with expressions of warmest thanks to the nobility and gentry "for the very kind patronage with which the entertainments had been received." Like a wise investor, Carnevale had sold out at 'at the top.'[84] The purchaser was, apparently, Lord Barrymore, a wealthy and eccentric English nobleman, with a passion for horse-racing, boxing, and amateur theatricals; he had already built himself a private theatre at Wargrave, and he seems to have been seized with a sudden passion to have a theatre in town. The stage was altered to admit human performers, and every one who mattered was invited on July 22, 1790, to the opening performance of *The Beaux Stratagem*, in which Barrymore and other notable amateurs appeared. The prologue referred to the puppets that had lately occupied the theatre:

No more their mimic action shall delight
Of Fashion's full-grown babes, the fickle sight . . .
But shall the ladies grieve for pleasure past,
And mourn the Fantoccini could not last,
We'll share each weeping fair one's grief, and then
Instead of puppets, we will give them—Men!

This was apparently the only performance given by Lord Barrymore in the theatre, upon the purchase of which he is said to have expended nearly £1500. He was already running into debt, and by February the next year another season of the Fantoccini was being presented. It is not certain whether Barrymore actually owned the Fantoccini at this time, or had merely surrendered his lease of the theatre. The second Fantoccini season at Savile Row ran for four months, and introduced fifteen pieces, nine of which had been played the year before. Two old Panton Street favourites were brought back—*Harlequin Chimney Sweep* and *The Birth of Harlequin*—and the most interesting of the additions to the repertory was Rousseau's *Le Devin du Village*; this pastoral operetta had been played before the Court at Fontainebleau twenty years before, and had already been parodied by the youthful Mozart. Admission was reduced to five shillings, and performances were now given four times a week.

The manager for this second season was said to be Thomas Robinson, the dissolute husband of the beautiful "Perdita," the solicitor's clerk who had climbed into Society on his wife's shoulders and who had been abandoned by her for the more alluring attentions of the young Prince of Wales. The most important new development this season was the engagement of Martinelli, who had manipulated the puppets in Piccadilly ten years earlier. He introduced his old effects of Harlequin flying round the room, and eating and drinking on the stage, with various other feats and tricks, and *The Times* gave its opinion that "the puppets are much better managed than in Carnivalle's time." The scenery was by Rebecca, Bibiena, and Capon. Bibiena, who had painted the scenery for the Piccadilly Fantoccini too, is, of course, a name of international reputation; he must have been one of the later generations of this brilliant family. Capon became scenic artist to Drury Lane under Kemble in 1794, and played a great part in introducing correct Gothic architectural scene paintings into the English theatre. That these three artists, perhaps the leading scenic painters of the day, could work for a puppet theatre is, indeed, a striking indication of the social and economic status of these Italian puppet theatres in late-eighteenth-century London.

The second Savile Row season closed for the summer after four months. The theatre was opened again in November 1791 for its third season under the title *Théâtre des Variétés Amusantes*, which was the name of an actual theatre of the *opéra comique* type in Paris;[85] prices were still further reduced to 5*s.* boxes and 3*s.* pit, and—as had always been the custom here—three or four plays a night made up what must have been a very full programme. Martinelli was again machinist, and the proprietor now was, apparently, Edward Iliff. This man was the son of a clergyman, who had served in the Navy as a midshipman, but who gave up a safe job at India House to go on the stage; he had appeared at the Little Theatre in the Haymarket as Douglas three years before, but failed to make any great mark in his profession.[86] In later life he became a Dissenter, and wrote some outspoken books attacking the State and the Church; his liberal political opinions drove his wife—an ex-actress—to leave him. Iliff seems an unexpected character to join our portrait gallery of puppet showmen; even at Savile Row he took life seriously, and a contemporary gossip writer reported that "his exertions and character merit protection."

Iliff certainly worked hard to make the Fantoccini a success, and a newspaper reported that he "bid fair to raise the Theatre to the same fashionable consequence that Carnevale did"; one evening in December the programme went over so well that several parties in the boxes demanded a repeat performance two days later. In this third season nineteen pieces were played, of which nine were entirely new. There were all the old favourites, French comedies and operettas, an intriguing piece described merely as "a new comedy taken from the MS. of the deceased Mirabeau," and a lone example of English light opera in Dibdin's *The Widow in Tears*, of which this is the only recorded performance. The *entractes* included a Pas de Deux in imitation of Vestris and Hillisberg, the two reigning male ballet stars of the day, and tumbling by a beautiful Spanish lady and a French clown. The music was selected from a wide range of the most eminent masters.[87]

Haydn himself, on his first visit to London, was invited to this theatre on November 13, 1791; he noted in his diary that "the figures were well manipulated, the singers bad, but the orchestra pretty good." Marionettes were no novelty to Haydn, who had written special puppet operas for the theatre at Esterház; his criticism was that of an expert.[88]

The third Savile Row season lasted three months; the last advertisement appeared on February 10, 1792, and after that no more is heard. Some time later Squibbs advertised the entire theatrical fittings of the room for sale, and this—the last of London's old puppet theatres to have survived—was destroyed in the recent War.[89] Mr Carnevale's Fantoccini appeared again in the great Rotunda at Ranelagh during the summer of 1796 and 1797; here they presented three of their old favourite comedies, and Harlequin flew round the Rotunda. Considering that this had a circumference of 440 feet, it was certainly no mean flight. A contemporary critic wrote that

> the performers, and in particular Harlequin, went through their parts in a manner that astonished every spectator; the action of the puppets being so very correct, and so well suited to the words. The dialogue is light and vivacious, as is usual with all the French works; the airs pretty, and the scenery and machinery of the whole admirably executed.[90]

During the winter Martinelli appeared with the Fantoccini in pantomime and burletta at several London theatres,[91] and finally the show is said to have been purchased by Astley, for his Amphitheatre across the river, but never used.

To assess the Savile Row Fantoccini fully would entail a detailed consideration of the French originals from which their plays were drawn, and of the musical works that embellished them. Our story is that of the

English puppets, and we must resist the temptation to be led too far into a side-issue. The Savile Row theatre stands in a class by itself; the other Fantoccini drew largely upon mythological themes, expressed by Commedia dell' Arte characters, and seem to have been principally Italian in inspiration, but at Carnevale's and Iliff's theatre, although the puppeteers and singers may have been Italian, the dramas were almost exclusively French. The entertainment here was literary and musical rather than traditional; here, alone in London, were to be seen the *comédies à ariettes* which were all the rage in a Paris already on the brink of revolution; here in the operettas of Sedaine, Favart, Duni, and many another could be caught the dreamlike atmosphere of Arcadia; here innocent shepherds and shepherdesses played out their pastoral loves; here tinkling music lulled jaded appetites with visions of fresh fields; this was the artificial state of nature in which Marie Antoinette had played at being a dairymaid. It must have been a type of drama in which the marionettes found themselves very much at home.

The invasion of the Italian Fantoccini was contained in a period of little over twenty years, in which five distinct companies can be recognized; between them they seem to have produced over sixty separate plays. Many of these pieces had been originally performed by the Commedia dell' Arte troupes of the seventeenth century, and—with Pulcinella instead of Harlequin as their comic hero—they had probably figured in the repertory of Bologna and Devoto when they played in Restoration London a century before. There had been invasions of Italian puppets before, in the 1570's and the 1660's, and there were to be other invasions since; they seem to recur every hundred years. No doubt there was much to admire in these Fantoccini of the 1770's, but the Englishman attaches a snob value to foreign puppets, like singers and —until recently—dancers. Were these Fantoccini really so much more clever than the puppets of Powell and the Patagonian Theatre? We cannot now say; and we must certainly record with pleasure and pride that London audiences, who so recently had hissed the greatest dancers of Europe off the stage because they were French, extended so warm a welcome to the Italian puppets. Their mythological playlets had no influence here, and Harlequin, who reigned upon their puppet boards, was powerless to usurp the throne of Punch; but the ingenious tricks they brought with them were copied by English showmen, and to this day, when we see the pole-balancer toss his spar from hand to foot, or the Grand Turk dismember himself into his numerous progeny, the Italian Fantoccini live on upon our puppet stages.

Of the Italian marionettes of the eighteenth century we fortunately possess some real knowledge; a number of them have been preserved, and we are no longer in the realm of deduction from inadequate evidence. In the Museo Civico in Venice are to be seen over thirty marionettes, probably Venetian and certainly of the eighteenth century;[92] they seem all to belong to one troupe. There are four recognizable masks—Harlequin, Pantaloon, Scaramouch (or perhaps the Doctor), and the Captain—and the remainder represent ladies and gentlemen, both grand and lowly, in contemporary costume; there is one very grand Moorish gentleman, and two dogs. In the Victoria and Albert Museum, unfortunately not on view at the time of writing, there is a superb marionette theatre of the same period and style. The stage is provided with two scenes painted on canvas, and mounted on wooden frames; one represents the Piazza San Marco in Venice and the other an elegant interior, with practical furniture. Accompanying this—and now on display—are twelve marionettes, including the same four masks as at Venice; but these fine figures have unfortunately had their original controls removed.

These Italian marionettes are about two feet high, beautifully dressed and carefully carved in a naturalistic technique, very different from the exaggerated and grotesque manner of the German school. They are manipulated by a strong wire to the top of their heads, and, normally, by four threads to the legs and hands. The wire terminates in a wooden 'turnip,' which can be grasped by the operator, to which are attached small strips of leather leading to the various threads; this constitutes the 'control.' This method of manipulation would be considered very crude by present-day puppeteers, but it is neat and simple, and must have been effective. The wire to the head cannot fail to have been visible, but it provides a firm articulation of the marionette's movements that cannot be entirely equalled by any other arrangement of strings.

The puppet theatre at the Victoria and Albert Museum stands thirteen feet high, and incorporates a door on either side of the proscenium leading back-stage; there is no trace of any wire mesh or grid in front of the stage, as described several times earlier in the century. This lovely theatre awaits critical examination by a technical expert, and may still hold some secrets for the puppeteer; it is tempting to believe that this very stage may have been brought over by the Italian puppet players when all London was flocking to see their Fantoccini.

A Venetian Marionette Stage and Figures of the Late Eighteenth Century

Ombres Chinoises

Five years after the first appearance of the Fantoccini another foreign intruder invaded our puppet stages. On December 5, 1775, Messrs Ambroise and Brunn announced that the Ombres Chinoises, invented by Mr Ambroise, would be performed daily at what was already London's favourite puppet theatre, the Great Room in Panton Street. "This spectacle is entirely new," we are informed, "it having been represented the first time on the 27th of February last before his most Christian Majesty, Louis XVI and the Royal Family, with uncommon success, and lately before his serene highness the Prince d'Orange and the whole court with an approbation very flattering to the performer." Brunn, who was a Saxon, provided feats of agility as part of the show. Admission was 5*s.*; this was evidently a smart entertainment.[93]

The Chinese Shadows was a shadow show. As we have seen, this type of entertainment was known in England in Jacobean times, and it never entirely disappeared from the repertoire of European showmen;[94] travellers returning from the East with descriptions of Oriental shadow plays must have provided the inspiration for this late-eighteenth-century revival of an ancient art. Shadow shows are common to this day in Java and Bali, where the puppets are opaque figures cut from leather, and are still known in China, where translucent coloured figures are used. Somewhat decadent types of the Chinese shadow puppets spread through the Near East to Persia, Turkey, and into Greece, where they can still be seen. Ambroise was, of course, not the inventor, though he may have perfected a certain type of control or mechanism. The European "Ombres Chinoises" of the seventeen-seventies were opaque puppets, forming a black-and-white silhouette picture upon the screen, and thus are—if anything—more like Javanese than Chinese shadows. But these little entertainments belonged happily enough to the spirit of *chinoiserie*.

The entertainment provided by Ambroise, who was apparently an Italian originally called Ambrogio, consisted of short incidents and sketches, with an orchestral accompaniment. Seventeen of these turns are mentioned in the advertisements, and they included *The Metamorphosis of a Magician*, *Duck Hunting*, a *Scene in the Gardens of Paris*, an *African Lion Hunt*, a *Storm at Sea*, and the *Escape of a Highwayman from Prison.* In February the back seats were reduced to half a crown, but the season was very successful, running for nearly five months until the end of April.

A year later a rival company directed by Braville and Meniucci, calling themselves the New Ombres Chinoises, arrived in London, and opened at the Great Room in St Albans Street, off Pall Mall, at the end of December 1776. The commentary was given in English, Italian, and French, and the programme included several items from the Panton Street season, with the addition of *The Broken Bridge* and a view of the *Dockyard in Venice*. A fortnight later Ambroise and Brunn were back in London at Panton Street, billing themselves as the Original Ombres Chinoises, and presenting almost identically the same programme as

THE OMBRES CHINOISES IN BERLIN
From an engraving by Wilhelm Chcdowiecki, *c.* 1785
By courtesy of the Curator of the Harvard Theatre Collection

their rivals in St Albans Street. For three months the two companies went at it, the Original and the New, hammer and tongs, and Londoners could indeed pay their money and take their choice; prices were cut to 3*s*. and 2*s*., and in the end the New cracked first. By the end of April 1777 their season had come to an end, though they seem to have been transferred themselves for a time to the Temple of Apollo, the last home of Dibdin's *Comic Mirror*.

The Original Ombres Chinoises went on to complete a six months' season, closing in July. Ambroise seems to have left the company for a time, and Philip Astley, the ex-sergeant showman, took over the management during his absence. Gallery prices dropped to as little as 1*s*. at one time, and private performances were offered for three guineas, half the price of the Fantoccini. The shadow show was helped along with conjuring, a performing horse, slack-wire balancing, and concerts of Italian music. A great attraction was a display of "elegant Fireworks without powder, noise, smell or smoke."[95]

In January 1778 yet another company of Italian and French shadows sought their fortune in friendly London; this was directed by Messrs Gabriel, Antonio, and Ballarini, and also described themselves, confusingly, as the New Ombres Chinoises. The Great Room in Panton Street was vacant, and they played here, with the now familiar repertory, until May. The novelty of the shadow show had now worn off, and the best prices they could get were 3*s.*, with the gallery down to 1*s.* 6*d.*; but the season ran over three months, and there must still have been a good public for this kind of entertainment.

In November this year Astley, who had already made one venture as a shadow-show impresario, opened an entertainment at 22 Piccadilly which included the Ombres Chinoises, along with the learned dog and horse, conjuring and imitating birds' cries. He probably bought up one of the Italian shows, and we know that he employed an Italian as manipulator, but he made an attempt to render the entertainment less foreign, and the songs and dialogue were given in English. This ran until March 1779, when Astley's Amphitheatre Riding House was reopened over the river, near the end of Westminster Bridge, with an entertainment of human and equine tricks, rather like a modern circus. The Chinese Shadows, or Lilliputian World, reappeared here during the summer, "the whole being adapted to the place of exhibition." Astley's Amphitheatre by this time was roofed over, and it incorporated a small stage adjoining the circus ring on which the shadow show was no doubt set up.

The Chinese Shadows remained a fairly regular feature in the repertory at Astley's for ten years; their last appearance seems to have been in the summer of 1790. During this decade shadow shows appeared irregularly at other entertainments all over London and in the provinces; we have already seen that they were featured in Dibdin's disastrous *Pasquin's Budget* at the Haymarket in 1780, when Astley provided the show; Micheli, the promotor of the Italian Fantoccini at Astley's old room in Piccadilly, offered "a new invented edifice of Ombres Chinoises" for sale in the same year; the Chinese Academy in Tooley Street presented shadows in March 1781; and the summer entertainment at Sadler's Wells in 1785 included a pantomime with "the celebrated large Italian Shadows." By 1781 at least one Italian showman, Manuelli, was touring the West of England with an entertainment of Fantoccini and Ombres Chinoises. As a fashionable novelty the Ombres Chinoises caught the fancy of the town only for some five or ten years, but we shall see later how they were absorbed into the popular tradition of English puppetry.

The repertory of the Ombres Chinoises remained surprisingly constant: several of the pieces performed in Ambroise's opening season were still being played at Astley's. Some nine or ten little playlets were featured in nearly every one of the six main London seasons. Of these the most popular was *The Storm at Sea*, which sometimes included a fight between sharks or whales, and must have lent itself to very spectacular effects; there was also *Duck Hunting*, which showed a sportsman with a rifle bringing down flying birds with a, no doubt, miraculous dexterity; *The Cat's Escape with the Dinner* out of the stewpot, while the poor cobbler's wife attended to her squealing child; and any number of character dances, hornpipes, and rope-dancing.

An effective item must have been *The Metamorphosis of a Magician*, and of this a single speech from the English text has, by a lucky chance, been preserved. The scene represented the grotto of a magician, who spoke as follows:

> For thirty years, with magic powers invested, have I reigned supreme of this mossy cave, where, assisted by invisible agents, awful daemons, and nightly sprites, I have transposed and metamorphosed, by my power, into different shapes these shelly walls; yet fain would I my utmost power know, and please mine eye with yet new wonders. Bring forth the huge and bulky elephant! [*The shadow of an elephant appears upon the screen.*] 'Tis well. Of life and flesh do I thee deprive, and nought but skeleton bones appear! [*The shape of the elephant is instantly replaced by that of its skeleton.*]

And so on, with who knows what wonders next! At the conclusion of this piece letters forming the word FINIS appeared upon the screen.[96]

Perhaps the most popular of all the playlets of the Ombres Chinoises was *The Broken Bridge*, which was mimed to the accompaniment of a French song. The scene shows a bridge across a river, broken in the middle, with a workman repairing it with rhythmical strokes of a pick-axe; at the opposite bank there enters a traveller who calls out "Heh! Friend, where does the road lead to?" The peasant sings back, to a catchy little tune,

> The road will lead to the city, tra-la, tra-la, tra-la, the road will lead to the city, tra-la tra-la tra-la.
>
> Can one cross the river?

The ducks swim over it, tra-la, tra-la, tra-la.
Is the river deep?
The gravel touches the bottom, tra-la, tra-la, tra-la.

And so on, until the infuriated traveller declares, "If I was the other side of the river I'd give you tra-la, tra-la, tra-la," finds a boat, rows across, and gives the workman the beating he deserves. The music for this and other popular shadow-show pieces was published in London and found a ready sale.[97]

The shadow puppets of the Ombres Chinoises were probably merely cut from cardboard, loosely jointed, and articulated by thin wire rods from below; the figures themselves were about six inches high, and were held close against the screen by their base. The screen was made of some tightly stretched translucent material, and the one used at Tooley Street was fourteen feet long; this would allow scope for wonderfully effective processions and panoramas, and is a great deal larger than most modern reconstructions. The shadow show maintained its popularity in France longer than it did in England, especially in the famous theatre of Séraphin in the Palais Royal. Many of Séraphin's figures have been preserved,[98] and from them we can reconstruct with fair accuracy the kind of figure, and the method of manipulation, used by Ambroise when he introduced the Ombres Chinoises to London in 1775.

The shadow show might be described as the moving picture of the eighteenth century, but despite its accidental resemblance to the film screen its opportunity really lies in fantasy and exaggeration. It is doubtful if the shadow puppet can venture into the realm of naturalistic drama, but in the light, amusing diversions chosen by these French and Italian showmen of the seventeen-seventies we find material well suited to the evanescent art of their black-and-white silhouettes. To this, the most delicate and artificial of all types of puppet show, London gave a warm welcome.

These fashionable puppet theatres of the late eighteenth century reveal certain marked changes from the earlier shows of Powell and Charlotte Charke. The Fantoccini and the Ombres Chinoises belong to a Continental tradition that never struck deep roots here, but even at the English puppet theatres the plays are now drawn from literary or theatrical sources, and the old folk-tales and traditional ballads that once made up so much of the puppet repertory would have been out of place among the sophistications of Johnson's London. The squeaker, already dispensed with by Madame de la Nash, is quite outmoded; most important of all,

Punch has almost disappeared, and if he appears at all it is only to speak an occasional prologue or epilogue. Foote, Dibdin, O'Hara, and Ellis must have brought much wit, delicacy, beauty, and charm to the English puppet theatre, but there was perhaps lacking in their artistic performances the rough-and-ready virility of Punch and Joan, and the uncouth but deep tradition of the old folk-dramas. The seventeen-seventies were, indeed, a golden age for Society puppet showmen:[99] in January 1777 no less than four different puppet theatres were playing at the same time in the West End of London; and the low tricks of Punch were banished to fairs and villages, to the "neglected garret or delapidated suburbian stable." The artists and the wits made a significant contribution to the history of the English puppet theatre, but in the end Punch has outlived them all.

Chapter VII

ENGLISH PUNCH: THE POPULAR PUPPET SHOW OF THE EIGHTEENTH CENTURY

The Showmen

WHILE the fashion for puppets waxed and waned in the West End of London, the popular traditional puppet show continued to be performed at fairs and country wakes in very much the same way as during the seventeenth century. The great London festivals of May Fair at the beginning of May, Tottenham Court Fair in early August, Bartholomew Fair at the end of August, and Southwark Fair in September attracted vast numbers of showmen of every kind. Stalls were set up for selling gingerbread and toys; freaks and curiosities and performing animals were displayed; swings, roundabouts, and an early form of Giant Wheel called the Up and Downs began to evolve; there were Music Booths where you could be entertained by a cabaret of dancing while you sat drinking; and there were innumerable booths for rope-dancing, conjuring, drolls acted by human players, peepshows, and puppets.[1]

Many vivid descriptions have been left of Bartholomew Fair in Smithfield, the greatest of them all; of the long lines of wooden booths, of the glaring lamps, of the vast crowds squeezing and swaying, of the indescribable din of shrieks and laughter and penny whistles; of the showmen bawling from the balconies outside their booths, and the parades of flashy kings and queens and heroes; of the crude gabbled drolls inside, which developed during the eighteenth century into quite decent theatrical shows; of the pickpockets who reaped a golden harvest, of the gambling-rooms, of the whores, and the servant-girls waiting to be picked up. We hear of the crowds rioting down the alleys, and then of a platoon of soldiers clearing the way as the Prince of Wales strolls round the fair between the flaunting rows of gawdy showcloths.

Besides these there were a host of suburban fairs all through the summer—at Brook Green, Camberwell, Peckham, Greenwich, Croydon,

Edmonton, Bow, Chiswick, Ham, Harlow Bush, Wandsworth, Parson's Green, Edgware, Tothill Fields, Fairlop Oak, the Horn Fair at Charlton,

MAY FAIR IN 1716

Detail from a contemporary engraving showing the pictorial showcloth of a puppet performance of *The Creation of the World.*

West End Fair at Hampstead, and many another at places now familiar on the map of London's Underground, but then neat villages half a day's walk across the fields from the great city. And beyond these the great circuits of provincial fairs, some, like Stourbridge Fair near Cambridge, larger than anything seen in London. At all of these the puppets found a place.

Then there were the simple country wakes held in every village in the land, at which a few pedlars would show their wares, a mountebank doctor extol his medicines, and the country-folk themselves would make up their amusements with sack-races and donkey-races for a new smock, and a ladies' race for a clean shift; the yokels would laugh as one of their number grinned through a horse-collar, gape at the man eating fire, and chance their pennies for a love token by "pricking the garter." Here the living theatrical booths might not penetrate, but the puppet shows were often to be found.

We cannot chronicle the story of these itinerant showmen in the same detail as was possible for the London theatres; nor is it necessary. But from a handful of old playbills and chance allusions we can build up a clear enough picture of the eighteenth-century puppet showmen as they made their way up and down the country, hiring rooms in inns or country barns as they went. A contemporary writer, indeed, pays them a more graceful tribute than we might dare to do ourselves. "These portable stages," wrote James Ralph in 1728, "are of infinite advantage to most country towns, where playhouses cannot be maintained, and, in my mind, superior to any company of strollers. The amusement is innocent and instructive, the expense is moderate, and the whole equipage easily carried about."[2] These travelling showmen did, indeed, a great deal to bring the tradition of theatre to the English provinces; here are some glimpses into the lives of four of them.

In 1723 John Harris, a puppet showman of Southwark, failed to pay the bill he owed to a carrier in Oxford, and on the orders of the Chancellor's Court his goods were confiscated. The inventory provides a good picture of the structure and accessories of a marionette theatre. It consisted of ten boxes, containing forty dressed and eight undressed figures, pieces of broken figures, "scenes and machines," "show cloths and lumber," and "twelve panels of painted boards." These last, I should guess, were for the proscenium arch and facia of the stage; the "machines" were probably flying chariots and moving bits of scenery; "sconces," which are bracket candlesticks fixed to the wall, are also listed. The whole property was valued at twenty pounds.[3]

There seems to have been no portable booth or tent in Harris's property, but he is known to have performed in open spaces like Tower Hill and at Bartholomew Fair. One of his Bartholomew Fair playbills has been preserved; it announces the popular story of *Fair Rosamond*,

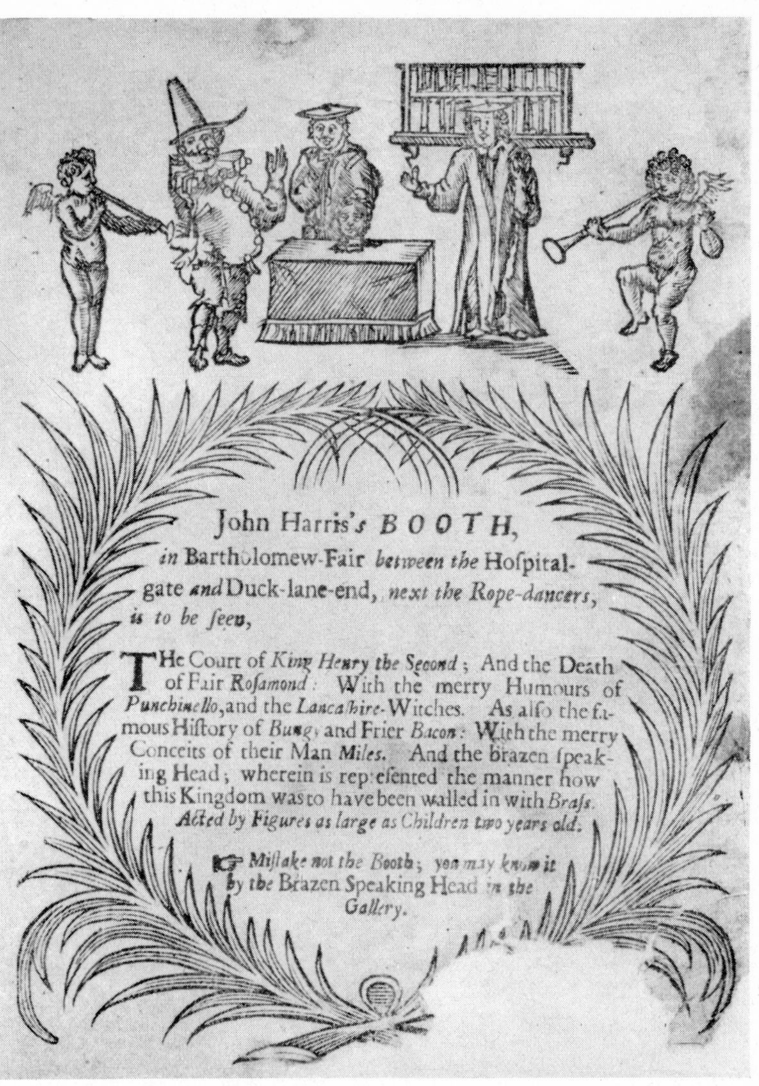

John Harris's *BOOTH*,

in Bartholomew-Fair *between the* Hoſpital-gate *and* Duck-lane-end, *next the Rope-dancers, is to be ſeen,*

THe Court of *King Henry the Second*; And the Death of Fair *Roſamond*: With the merry Humours of *Punchinello*, and the *Lancaſhire*-Witches. As alſo the famous Hiſtory of *Bungy* and Frier *Bacon*: With the merry Conceits of their Man *Miles*. And the brazen ſpeaking Head; wherein is repreſented the manner how this Kingdom was to have been walled in with *Braſs*. *Acted by Figures as large as Children two years old.*

☞ *Miſtake not the Booth; you may know it by the* Brazen Speaking Head *in the Gallery.*

A Playbill for John Harris at Bartholomew Fair, c. 1700

By courtesy of the Curator of the Harvard Theatre Collection followed by *Friar Bacon and Friar Bungay*, both popular legends of English history that had been played by puppets in the seventeenth century. The merry humours of Punchinello diversified the entertainment, and there is a vigorous illustration of this gentleman on the bill with his conical hat, large ruff, and big buttons down the front of his prominent belly; like Powell's Punch, with whom this illustration should be compared, he appears to have large moustachios, but no hunchback or grotesquely hooked nose. A very important piece of information is provided by the announcement that the figures are "as large as children two years old"—that is, about two feet six inches high.[4]

On September 8, 1727, a puppet showman named Robert Shepheard, with his wife, young daughter, and two manservants, stabled his two horses in one part of a barn that he had hired at Burwell, in Cambridgeshire, and set up his show in the adjoining portion. As an introduction to the performance one of the company performed some conjuring tricks in front of the curtain on an oval gatelegged table, which was then folded up and put out of the way in front of the only door into the barn. In the plays that followed Shepheard and his wife acted a scene of a lover wooing a coy lady, and there then was introduced the famous battle between St George and the Dragon, who seemed to spout real fire out of his mouth, with a noise like thunder and lightning.

While this was going on an ostler employed by the owner of the barn came to feed the horses at about nine o'clock in the evening. He seems to have expected to have been admitted free to see the performance, but when the modest admission of one penny was demanded he went back into the stable and, climbing on to some bales of oat straw, clambered over a low partition wall into the main section of the barn, where he could see the show for nothing. In the process the candle he was carrying was upset, set fire to the straw, and in a very short time the entire roof of the barn was ablaze. The audience rushed in panic towards the door, which was completely blocked by the table and—anyhow—opened inward. In the dreadful scene of confusion the only exit from the barn was jammed tight by the panic-stricken, hysterical mob, and the blazing roof fell down upon their heads. Out of about 140 persons present at the show, 80 lost their lives.[5]

Our third example is more entertaining. In Tyburn Road, London, there lived a puppet showman called Mr Griffin. One day in about 1745 he sent his Jack Pudding, gaily attired and accompanied by trumpets and drums, out into the streets of St Giles's to announce a performance of *Jane Shore*, with the comical humours of Mr Punch and his wife, Joan, at the King's Head tavern in Oxford Market. While promenading through the streets the Jack Pudding picked up an acquaintance with a fourteen-year-old girl who had run away from home, named Nancy Dawson; he took her back to the show and made her his mistress, until Mr Griffin himself fancied that he would take her under his own protection. One evening before a show the Jack Pudding observed Mr Griffin lay down his crowd (fiddle) in the orchestra, where he was playing "Over the Water to Charlie," and slip away with Nancy to a quiet spot behind the scenes; in jealousy he straightaway went to tell the showman's wife, who was seated at the door taking the three pennies for admission to the performance. Mrs Griffin rose up in her wrath, stalked behind the scenes, and, catching the two of them together, forthwith began hitting her husband over the head with his own fiddle. In retaliation he snatched up the puppet-show drum, while Jack Pudding took the opportunity to give Nancy a good beating, and she fought and scratched back for all she was worth. The audience were at first mystified by these sounds of screams and bastinadoes, till an arch wag, "laying hold of a string that hung over the side scenes, soon explained the matter by drawing up the curtain and exposing the combatants to view."

After this Mr Griffin parted company with his wife and went along with Nancy. Seeing that she had a good figure, he taught her to dance and tumble, "and in two months she got him more money by her feats of activity in that way than all his wooden equipage did in half a year." She went round performing in taverns, till she met a dancer from Sadler's Wells, who persuaded her to come and dance there. With her later notorious career in the London theatres we are not concerned here. Mr Griffin was left to his solitary puppets.[6]

For the fourth of these puppet-show masters we can produce a full life's biography. Harry Rowe was born in Nottingham in 1726; his father was a schoolmaster, and he was intended for the Church, but owing to his wild habits in youth this career was abandoned, and he eventually ran away to join the Army, where he became trumpeter of the Light Horse and fought at Culloden. On his discharge he made his way to London, where he worked as a "groaner," or fake patient, to various quack doctors, including the famous Orator Henley. When London became too hot to hold his master's dubious business methods he ran away again, and presently married and set up a Matrimonial Agency in Coventry. On the death of his wife, however, the "Wedding Shop" closed down.

Rowe now heard that a widow, who was the proprietor of a puppet show, wanted an assistant to travel with it from town to town, and he obtained the position. He is said to have displayed great skill in manipulating the puppets, which were dressed in an expensive and elaborate style. On arriving at a town he would hire a large room in a well-to-do working-class district, and distribute a few hundred small handbills giving details of the programmes. At the door would be placed a large oil-lamp with two spouts, which gave a bright light as well as a most offensive smell, and the interior of the room would be lit by tin candlesticks, shaped to hang from nails in the wall. There would be candle footlights in front of the drop-curtain, and an orchestra of one or two violins. The programme usually consisted of a tragedy and farce, between which there would always be a short concert. Among his most popular songs were the sentimental "The Rose of Allendale" and a comic ballad known as "Chorus Tommy." Ordinary performances took fully two hours, but at fairs the time was cut to twenty or thirty minutes; the whole show is said to have been very amusing, and to have made good use of local jokes. His mistress spoke for and worked the female puppets, he the male, and they did the entire show with one assistant. Before the performance Harry Rowe would stand outside inviting people in, and his mistress took the money; admission was a penny and threepence.

After a time they decided that it would be more profitable to work a regular circuit than to travel without any settled system, and they set upon York as their centre, visiting the surrounding market towns, such as Malton, Thirsk, and Tadcaster. The boxes of puppets were probably transported by carrier cart or perhaps pulled by a string of dogs. Harry Rowe eventually married the proprietress, and continued master of the puppets till his wife's death in 1796. Shortly after this he sold the show, and retired to York. He is said to have made money easily during his career, but to have spent it freely, and in 1798 he entered the city workhouse, where he died in the next year at the age of seventy-four.

As well as puppet showman, Harry Rowe held the post of Trumpeter to the High Sheriff of Yorkshire, and twice every year for forty-five years he attended the Assizes in this capacity. He seems to have been a genial man, fond of company and with a wealth of good stories. He often took the trumpet part in Handel's *Messiah*, and was fond of boasting of his superiority over the trumpet-blowers of St Stephen's Chapel, whose performance he held in the utmost contempt. Towards the end of his days he must have been a well-loved character of York society, and—very much in the same way as with Martin Powell—a couple of books were 'fathered' on him. The first of these was an edition of Shakespeare's

Macbeth, published in York in 1797 with emendations said to be based on a very old manuscript in the possession of Rowe's prompter, one of whose ancestors was rush-spreader and candle-snuffer at the Globe. It is hardly necessary to add that this was a completely bogus production, actually prepared for the press, it would appear, by Mr John Croft, a York wine-merchant and amateur Shakespearean scholar. This little literary joke was sold to provide a little money for Rowe in his declining years, but unfortunately generations of puppet historians have copied one another in paying tribute to the learned puppet showman who included Shakespeare in his repertory! Similarly, in 1797 a play satirizing the medical profession called *No Cure No Pay* was published, ostensibly by Harry Rowe, but actually by Dr Alexander Hunter, the editor of Evelyn and a well-known local physician.

"Here lies the body of Harry Rowe," reads the epitaph on his tombstone in St Olave's Church,

> . . . during his whole life he was never known to give a blast that tended to the dishonour of his King and Country; his favourite airs being "God save the King" and "Rule, Britannia." . . . Though a man weary of the disastrous tugs with fortune, he preserved his integrity to the last moment of his life, bequeathing to posterity this useful memento: That breath spent in the abuse of our King and Country is most unworthily employed. 1799.[7]

To complete this picture of the eighteenth-century puppet showmen something must be said about a few of the masters of the profession, the men who owned the elaborate theatrical booths at the great London fairs. Here much more factual information is available, but we lack the racy anecdote that can bring the picture to life. Once again I shall select four representative figures.

One of the most successful showmen of the century was a conjuror called Isaac Fawkes; he is first met at Bartholomew Fair in the early twenties, and when he died in 1731 he was said to be worth £10,000.[8] He gave several seasons at the old Tennis Court Theatre in James Street; his programmes included dexterity of hand, a posture-master, and almost always a Moving Picture or Musical Clock made by Mr Pinchbeck. These Moving Pictures were composed of cut-out flat pictures of coaches, ships and so on, made to move across a landscape by clockwork machinery; they are frequently referred to by contemporary writers and are sometimes confused with puppet shows, but the principle is entirely different, and we cannot examine them in detail here. Beside all this, Fawkes sometimes added genuine puppets to his programme. We have already met him in some kind of partnership with Powell junior at Southwark Fair in

1725, and at James Street the next year. There may have been other similar occasions, but Fawkes does not seem to have been a puppet showman himself: he merely occasionally engaged a puppet act for his show. His son, however, who succeeded to the show in 1731, seems to have been a keen puppeteer: during his father's lifetime he appears to have worked independently in Bath, the West Country, and Tunbridge Wells, exhibiting moving waxwork figures five feet high. In 1732 these were shown in the Opera Room in the Haymarket, and two years later at James Street, when they were said to "have all the just motions and gestures of human life." They presented *The Beggar's Wedding*, a popular Irish ballad opera, Fielding's *Tragedy of Tragedies, or Tom Thumb*, and a pantomime version of *Faustus*; prices were 2*s.* 6*d.* and 1*s.*

In 1740, it will be recalled, Fawkes junior purchased Mrs Charke's puppets at a knock-down price and presented them that year at Bartholomew Fair, and two years later at the James Street theatre. Meanwhile the younger Fawkes continued to show conjuring, tumbling, a perpetual-motion machine, and other such variety turns; our last record of him is in 1746 with a human theatrical booth.

Powell junior, it will be remembered, also went into partnership with Yeates. The earliest mention of this showman that I have noted is at Bartholomew Fair in 1725, when his puppet booth was patronized by the Prince of Wales. At Southwark Fair that year he was presenting the *History of St George for England*, with his conquest over the Egyptian dragon. That was the fair at which Powell junior made his first appearance, in Fawkes's booth, and at Southwark the next year Yeates and Powell junior were in partnership with *The Princess Elizabeth, or the Rise of Judge Punch*, "concluding with a glorious piece of machinery after the Italian manner, representing Cupid's Paradise, breaking into double and triple Prospects, quite different from those in common puppet shows." This may have been some old machinery from the Covent Garden Piazza Theatre.

From now on Yeates began to develop a medley of entertainments, including very often a puppet play, a posture-master, conjuring, and a Moving Picture or some similar automaton. As early as 1728 we begin to hear of Yeates junior, sometimes in partnership with his father and sometimes on his own, and it is often extremely difficult to determine which is which. It would appear, however, that the father was the puppet showman and the son principally a conjuror, thus reversing the test that distinguishes the two Fawkeses. The Yeateses were to be found at all the London fairs, year after year, and by 1728 they had begun experimenting with very large puppets four feet high; these were almost certainly wax figures, for a wooden figure of that size is really too heavy to be manipulated. In that year a challenge of a hundred guineas was again issued to "any one in England to show so lively and so rich figures, or such fine painting in the scenes and other decorations." By 1737 the height of the "artificial moving waxwork" had increased to five feet; I don't know whether new figures had been made, or whether the old ones had grown overnight in response to Fawkes junior, who had presented his five-foot moving waxworks in London a few years earlier.

The plays presented by Yeates's puppets during these years included *The Town Rake*, which had been in Powell's repertory and was presumably brought into the show by his son; *The Harlot's Progress*, a dramatization of Hogarth's narrative paintings; *Punch's Oratory, or the Pleasures of the Town*, Fielding's mock-puppet satire on the literary and theatrical follies of the day; *The Lover His Own Rival*, a recent ballad opera; and Henry Carey's burlesque opera *The Dragon of Wantley*. This is an extraordinarily good list of plays, of real literary and dramatic quality, and very different from the usual run of historical legends and Biblical stories that made up the repertory at most fairground puppet booths. Yeates was evidently a man of some taste.

No doubt that was the reason why Charlotte Charke got him to make her puppets for her in 1738. We have already traced the tragi-comedy of that enterprise, and seen how Yeates himself took over the management of her second season. In the years that followed, Yeates's career may be traced right up to the fifties as a manager of human theatrical booths and as the proprietor of the New Wells, but there is little indication of further interest in puppets. The waxwork figures may have been touring Kent in the forties, and in 1752 they were at Bartholomew Fair and at the Tennis Court in James Street, which here makes its last appearance in our chronicle.

Charlotte Charke, who had worked with him and knew him well, wrote of the elder Yeates that "as we are both equally odd, in separate lights, neither of us can ever be surprised or offended at what the other says or does." Coming from such a quarter this is, perhaps, a doubtful compliment, but with its vivid phrase it casts a sudden revealing light upon the hidden character of this impresario of the pleasure gardens, of the fairs, and of the puppets.

One of the leading puppet showmen of the second half of the eighteenth century was Jobson. He originally bought up Lacon's puppets, which Charlotte Charke had encountered at Tunbridge Wells in 1739, and his earliest public appearance that has come to light was in 1759 at Canterbury, where he presented a Grand Medley of Entertainments that included "operatical moving figures" showing Mr Punch and his merry family in *The Necromancer* (probably the Faust story), as well as eight Lilliputians in a country dance and six figures ringing bells by clockwork—a trick that had been shown by Crawley fifty years earlier. No doubt he toured the provinces regularly, but nothing further can be recorded till 1778, when he is reported at Bartholomew Fair.

The next year he was at Bartholomew Fair again, announcing that he was from the Theatre Royal, Covent Garden, and styling his booth "The Patagonian Puppet Show," in imitation of Ellis's theatre at Exeter Change, then at the height of its popularity. His programme consisted of *Julius Cæsar, or Punch being Emperor of Rome*, Little Ben dancing a hornpipe, a posture-master (or—as we should now say—an acrobat), four country girls dancing a country dance, a hornpipe by Master Jobson (apparently a child dancing on the puppet stage), a display of moving waxwork figures five feet high representing a foreign Court, and, to conclude, a scene between Punch and his wife, Joan. Prices for this entertainment were 1*s.*, 6*d.*, and 3*d.*, and he offered to give private performances for 10*s.* 6*d.*, plus 1*s.* for each person above ten. The next year much the same bill was presented, but it was concluded with a battle between Punch and the Devil. By 1790 the play's title had changed to *The Rival Brothers, or the Death of Cæsar*, but every play that he presented during fifteen years at the fairs was some variation on the Cæsar theme, and it really looks as if the only set of puppets he possessed must have been dressed in Roman costume.

Jobson attended the fairs regularly through the eighties and nineties; his last appearance at Bartholomew Fair was in 1794. Although an occasional provincial appearance with rope-dancers, tumblers, and human drolls has been recorded, he seems to have been first and foremost a puppet showman, and evidently one of the old school who showed no desire ever to vary his performance. He is said to have been indebted to his wife for what little celebrity he did acquire, and to have died at a very advanced age in a provincial workhouse in the eighteen-twenties. Jobson was sometimes moved to add little verses to his playbills, and these crude and halting compositions perhaps reveal to us a shadowy picture of the unlettered conservative old puppet-master, whose heart was nevertheless touched with poetry:

> Come neighbours, come; let us to Jobson's go,
> And see his grand and famous Puppet Show.[9]

A contemporary of Jobson, but a more eminent master of the puppets, was Flockton. We first hear of him in the seventeen-sixties in what appear to have been a couple of brief seasons at Hickford's Great Room in Panton Street, later to become famous as the *venue* of the Italian Fantoccini and Ombres Chinoises. Here he presented a performing monkey, pole-tossing by a five-year-old child, conjuring, a piece of mechanical automata containing 900 figures in motion, and some puppets. "The figures are the most surprising ever seen in England," he announced:

Flockton proposes, on just grounds,
To match his figures for five hundred pounds.
For charming actions and for graceful air
With many living actors they'll compare.

The challenge stakes were certainly being raised, and I do not think this figure was ever exceeded. By 1776 a poem on Bartholomew Fair could refer to him as "the noted Flockton," and for twenty years this "old servant of the public" was "rewarded with the most flattering marks of applause" at all the London and suburban fairs.

His puppets presented *The Padlock*, Dibdin's light opera that had been performed at the Patagonian Theatre, for which he obtained the services of two Italian singers; but for the most part his plays were quite unknown little comedies such as *The Sailor's Return*, *The Ghost*, or *The Conjuror*. *The Rival Queens, or the Death of Alexander the Great* seems to have been his only incursion into history. The great attraction of his show, however, was the trick figures, or, as he called them—borrowing the title from the Italians—the Fantoccini; his Italian rope-dancer, especially, is said to have been "an exquisite piece of mechanism." A popular piece of business that Flockton introduced was to have a trained Newfoundland dog to fight his puppet devil, and when he had mastered him to run off with him in his mouth. Since Powell had brought a live pig on to his stage other showmen had developed the idea, and a puppet-master called Williams, for instance, who lost his reason after a terrible accident to his show at Chester in 1773, when seventy-five people were killed or injured, had had a dog with a saddle on its back, on which Punch used to ride across the stage.[10]

As at most of the fairground booths, Flockton's prices ranged from threepence to a shilling; on the day after Bartholomew Fair he was in the habit of holding a "private night," attended by "a highly respectable audience embracing the city marshals and, not infrequently, some of the aldermen." At Smithfield he usually performed in a room at the George

Inn, while Jobson favoured the Greyhound, but both these performers certainly also owned portable booths for other open-air fairs.

Flockton was well described as "the prince of puppet-showmen." He is said to have died at Peckham in 1784, where he resided during the winter "in a respectable way," and to have left a fortune of five thousand pounds. He had no children, and this sum was divided among the members of his company. The puppet show was bequeathed to two members of his troupe—Mrs Flint, a widow, and a man called Gyngell.[11]

The widow Flint and Gyngell continued in partnership, appearing at the fairs and pleasure gardens, until 1804; after this Gyngell remained as sole proprietor. He seems to have been principally a conjuror himself, and he trained his children to be extremely clever circus performers on the slack and tight rope. Puppets figured only occasionally in his programmes, but he did bring out Flockton's old Fantoccini during his season at the little Harmonic Theatre in Catherine Street in 1816. He is said to have been a handsome fellow, "the Apollo of servant-maids," and in his old age "a quiet gentlemanly man"; he died in 1836, and is buried in the churchyard at Camberwell. His death marks the final extinction of Flockton's puppets; it was the end of an era.

An interesting point revealed by a study of provincial advertisements is that the Italian invasion of the seventies seems to have been preceded in the provinces by one or two immigrants from Germany: in the seventeen-thirties Henry Collyer, a popular traveller in Kent, was billing his show as "the Saxonian Novels," in the forties the High German Puppets were touring in Kent, and in the sixties an English showman called Thompson advertised a Prussian Punch, and a Prussian Puppet Show was touring in Yorkshire. One further ingredient was now added to the tradition of English puppetry, that was already intermingled with Italian and French blood.

The licensing system for travelling showmen that had been administered by the Master of the Revels during the seventeenth century continued into the eighteenth, but the showmen themselves seem to have ignored its provisions, and after a few plaintive and familiar complaints from Charles Killigrew he seems to have abandoned the unequal struggle with so elusive a prey. There was to hand, however, a rival authority who hunted and harried the showmen of England for well over a century in the pursuit of his legally entitled fees. This was the Sergeant Trumpeter of England, an office in the gift of the Lord Chamberlain, who had already crossed swords with Devoto just after the Restoration. This man was empowered to issue a licence at the cost of 25*s*. a year entitling the holder to sound a trumpet, drum, or fife "at any plays, dumb-shows, models, rope-dancers, mountebanks or prizes." Local authorities were authorized to collect a fine of one shilling a day from any showman not in possession of this licence. As every showman, and especially every puppet showman, found it essential to advertise his show by some kind of trumpet-calls or drum-rollings, he could not avoid liability to the Sergeant Trumpeter, and this functionary (who probably paid a rent to the Lord Chamberlain for his privilege) continued to claim his rights at intervals throughout the eighteenth century and up to at least as recently as 1809.[12]

Innumerable examples of the use of drums, trumpets, and flags by puppet-masters could be quoted, and two must suffice. In 1745 Tom Jones and his friend are walking through the English countryside when they see flying in the air in front of them what they at first take to be the colours of the enemy (the Jacobites), but which turns out to be the sign of a puppet show, whose drum they had heard beating shortly before; and Horace Walpole reports a parson who commented on the wagering mania of the upper classes that "I protest, they are such an impious set of people that if the last trumpet were to sound, they would bet puppet-show against judgement."[13] The story of puppets is full of age-old customs, and we cannot fail to remember here Perrinet Sanson collecting his little audience with a drum and trumpet in the France of 1400 or Lantern Leatherhead running up his flag and sounding his drum in the London of 1600.

The Puppets

What, then, were the kinds of puppets used in these popular shows? There is no doubt that they were marionettes: the type of figure made popular by the Italians after the Restoration was the accepted media for puppet shows throughout the eighteenth century, whether in Panton Street or at a provincial fair. One can, indeed, continually notice how quick the fairground showmen were to imitate the latest novelties from town: Punchinello was at Bartholomew Fair five years after his first appearance at Covent Garden; the Patagonian Theatre, the Primitive Puppet Show, the Fantoccini, the Ombres Chinoises, were all billed at the fairs within a few years of their first nights in the West End.

Of the size of the marionettes we have a little information. Harris's were two foot six—a very satisfactory height for a marionette, though larger than those usually found convenient in England to-day; but during this century there was a most curious popularity for the very large wax-work figures four or five feet high—if we can believe the playbills—as shown by Fawkes junior, Yeates, and several others. For the most part these almost life-size puppets seem to have presented scenes of Courts—Great Britain, France, Hungary, and Prussia were all represented—and it may well have looked very impressive to the town sluts and rustic wenches as the great figures passed slowly before their eyes, loaded with tinsel finery and paste jewels, in the elementary evolution of a State procession.[14] But a number of real dramatic plays were undoubtedly performed by these wax puppets, and it is very difficult to understand how such unwieldy figures could possibly be manipulated in the quick action and movement that such plays demand. It is not, indeed, certain that these five-foot puppets were worked like ordinary marionettes at all, for such large figures impose unusual problems upon stage and bridge construction and the sight-lines of the proscenium opening. It is possible that they were manipulated in the manner invented by Bartolommeo Neri and described by Quadrio.

In fact, Quadrio, writing in Italian in 1744, appears to have known of and to describe this very type of puppet. "But the English," he writes,

> with their ingenious skill have to-day developed this invention [of Neri's] to perfection. Without departing from its primary principle, by which the effect of movement is obtained—not too successfully—by the simple use of counterweights, they have introduced a type of puppet which is still more worthy of playing spectacles before the eyes of a Court even more cultured than that of France. Figures about four feet high and finely dressed are made to appear upon a fairly high stage, before which a net has been drawn; a great many threads are attached to all the limbs of each puppet, and these threads, handled from somewhere out of sight, control the hands, the feet, the mouth, and even the eyes, so as to give to each figure the natural movements and gestures of a living person.

Quadrio's exact meaning is tantalizingly elusive, and his description should be compared with that already quoted in Chapter II. Did he mean that these very large figures were supported from above by one strong wire counterweighted in the wings, with several threads (or wires—the Italian word *fila* can mean either) for the articulation of their limbs? The use of the wire net across the stage opening—the optical 'baffle' of which we have already found many descriptions in the course of our story—certainly suggests overhead manipulation. Or did he mean that the figures were slid along grooves in the stage floor with the aid of under-stage counterweights, and their movements controlled by threads passing up *inside* their bodies? Such a method of manipulation is technically feasible, though the resulting gestures are much limited in scope.

Some ten years earlier the Abbé Prevost, describing life in England, had reported that "marionettes of human size had been seen for several years past performing entire tragedies with great success . . . , with dress, gestures, walk, and moving lips and eyes, in every way resembling human beings," and that in 1734 a new invention had been announced by which they would enact an opera, "singing, dancing, and carrying out all the business of the theatre without the means by which they were supported being visible." This description suggests that some form of interior control, invisible to the audience, had been perfected, and this is confirmed by another French report of an Englishman, a contemporary of Brioché, "who discovered the secret of making the puppets move by springs and without strings."[15]

There is, I am afraid, no doubt that this ingenious method of manipulation—if I have reconstructed it accurately—would have proved cumbersome, unwieldy, and undramatic in practice; but it is at least clear that the English puppet-masters had achieved a signal development in technique, the fame of which spread throughout Europe. In 1731 a German showman was advertising performances "with large English marionettes,"[16] and it is above all pleasant to have in Quadrio's description this tribute from an Italian. An American too made a claim for his adopted countrymen that is seldom heard now. "The mechanical genius of the English is obvious . . . ," wrote James Ralph, "but in none more properly than in the contrivance and conduct of our puppet shows, the improvement of which is certainly owing to us, if not the invention."[17] The secret of these almost life-sized puppets—veritable *Übermarionetten*—has now been lost, and perhaps they died, like the dinosaur, from lack of movement; but let us remember that in their day these English puppet showmen led the world.

The craze for very large puppets may well have lead to a stultification of puppet drama, and there are welcome signs of a healthy reaction. Henry Collyer, who toured in Kent with great success in the thirties, made a special point of announcing his Lilliputian figures, which were exactly eighteen inches high. He claimed to show fifty to sixty figures in one night, and fifteen to twenty on the stage at the same time, "which is as many as three common puppet shows have in all." Lilliputian figures were also billed by Jobson and other showmen, and this is a size very popular with puppeteers to-day. The eighteenth century seems to have seen a fascinating technical competition between large and small puppets for the favour of the public.

The basic control of the orthodox marionette continued to be by a stout wire to the crown of the head, with subsidiary strings to the hands and feet; whether they met in a wooden control of the "turnip" shape adopted by the Italians of the period we do not know, as, unfortunately, no English specimens from this century have survived. Among dozens of similar allusions, Foote, in his prologue to *Piety in Pattens*, spoke of the "hands that were employed in moving wires and strings" behind the curtain; and Edward Popham's Latin poem describing an eighteenth-century touring puppet show tells us that not only the arms, legs, and head, but also the eyes, of the puppets were moved—like the Punch immortalized by Addison; but he goes on to observe that "the threads which control their limbs and govern their movements may be easily seen by sharp eyes."[18] Perhaps the network threaded across the stage opening was not always very effective in hiding the puppets' strings, or perhaps it had already, by the seventies, been abandoned; we cannot be sure quite how general its use ever was.

Until somebody reconstructs a puppet stage of the eighteenth century it is difficult to visualize exactly what the effect of this grid would be; quite apart from its primary purpose in concealing the marionette's controlling wires, it may well have lent an air of remoteness and mystery to the performance, and have placed the strangely moving puppets in another world of enchantment behind the narrow bars of their magic stage.

Writing at the end of the century, Joseph Strutt recalled the puppets of his younger days, and commented acidly that

> in my memory, these shows consisted of a wretched display of wooden figures, barbarously formed and decorated, without the least degree of taste or propriety; the wires that communicated the motion to them appeared at the tops of their heads, and the manner in which they were made to move evinced the ignorance and inattention of the managers; the dialogues were mere jumbles of absurdity and nonsense, intermixed with low immoral discourses passing between Punch and the fiddler, for the orchestra rarely admitted of more than one minstrel; and these flashes of merriment were made offensive to decency by the actions of the puppets.[19]

This old antiquary's severe comment has little validity for a generation that has discovered the charm of the English tradition in Popular Art, but his picture of artistic and dramatic decadence requires investigation. There is, indeed, no doubt that, despite the fashionable revival of the seventies, the English puppet show had seriously declined by the end of the eighteenth century. Throughout the century the popular puppet theatres continued to play the old historical legends and Biblical stories that had provided its repertory ever since the sixteen-hundreds. We find titles like *Whittington*, *Faustus*, *Queen Elizabeth*, or *Arden of Faversham* recurring time and again, and among the Biblical stories *The Creation of the World* still led the field, closely followed by *Solomon and the Queen of Sheba* and *Jephthah's Rash Vow*. These puppets drew their plots from the chapbooks and ballads of the people, and only occasionally did an original dramatic play from the human theatre find its way upon their humble boards. This traditional conservatism is indeed the chief pride and glory of the puppet stage, and it is a remarkable tribute to the power of popular tradition that the temptation of Eve and the sacrifice of Jephthah's daughter were still being enacted to public audiences in England as the Age of Reason was being proclaimed by the intellectuals of London and Paris.

Towards the end of the century, however, there are signs that this Elizabethan and medieval tradition had at last had its day. The robust folk-dramas suffered first, perhaps, from the slowing down of their lively action imposed by the large waxwork figures, and, secondly, certainly, by the craze for trick turns introduced by the Italian Fantoccini: before an invasion of rope-dancers and posture-masters the simple fables of the puppet stage degenerated into vulgarity and nonsense. A fair indication of the development of the popular puppet show during this period may be obtained by comparing performances at Bartholomew Fair at the beginning and the end of the century.

In 1701 an anonymous scribbler recorded his visit to the fair: he visited the booths of the strong man, the rope-dancers, a Medley, and two puppet shows—one presenting *Jephthah's Rash Vow* and the other *The Creation of the World*. Unfortunately he was more interested in the pretty girls he sat next to than in the progress of the show, and the booths seem, indeed, to have been regarded as a social amenity not dissimilar to the cinema to-day by providing an opportunity for quiet love-making in the dark. Looking around, he saw "the old game going forward all over the booth . . . so that nothing but love's harmony could be seen from one side of the booth to the other." Before an audience, then, of "females of all sorts and sizes," interspersed with spooning couples, a little opera called the old *Creation of the World* was newly revived.[20]

The play opened in the Garden of Eden with the awakening of Adam and Eve; Lucifer appeared, tempted Eve to take an apple, and the two humans were expelled from Paradise; Cain was then seen ploughing, Abel driving sheep, and then Cain murdering his brother; this was followed by the incident of Abraham sacrificing Isaac. We then move to the New

Testament with a scene of the Nativity of Christ, with the visit of the Wise Men, Joseph and Mary fleeing on an ass, and the massacre of the innocents with King Herod's "men's spears laden with children." The final incident shows Dives at table and Lazarus begging at his gate, with dogs licking his sores, Dives is taken sick and dies and is buried with great solemnity, while Death claims Lazarus, who is pleaded for by the Good Angel. As the stage was emptied the scenery began to draw apart revealing deep vistas of far perspective; one—in the lower part of the stage—showed the flames of hell amid which Dives lay in agony, while in the upper portion a shining throne descended, guarded by choirs of angels, upon which Lazarus sat in glory, while behind him the clouds parted to draw the eyes to yet more distant prospects of the Palace of the Sun.

These Paradises or Prospects were a great feature of the puppet shows, and we have already seen how they were utilized by Powell. On these little stages the scenery and machinery of the Jacobean Court Masques were displayed for many generations before a humbler audience.

After the grand "transformation scene," the performance concluded with several dances, and was completed by a comic scene between Sir John Spendall, presumably a bankrupt *roué* of the time, and our old friend Punchanello.

This elaborate yet unsophisticated Biblical revue may be compared with the entertainment at Punch's Puppet Show in 1772, of which we possess a unique pictorial record.[21] Outside the booth two Merry Andrews are distributing playbills advertising "Punch's Opera" and beating a drum; on the parade balcony another blows a trumpet, a Harlequin orates to the crowd below, and a human Punch chucks a human Joan under the chin; a crowd gathers and begins to mount the steps up to the booth. When the spectators have seated themselves upon benches, the first turn presented is by a human conjuror seated at a table in the "pit" of the theatre, where there seems traditionally to have been an open acting area. The curtains then draw aside, revealing a puppet stage illuminated by a hoop of candles, with the King and Queen of France seated in majesty upon a throne, surrounded by their courtiers.

Into this scene of majestic elegance there enters Punch trundling his wife, Joan, on a wheelbarrow; no doubt he upsets her on to the ground and has to suffer the lash of her tongue as she scolds and nags him round the stage. The Court of France has, by this time, disappeared, while Harlequin and Scaramouch dance on, and the backcloth then changes to the representation of a naval combat while little Ben the Sailor dances a hornpipe with grace and agility. The scene changes again to show a baker crossing the stage with a basket full of loaves of bread, when there suddenly enters the Devil himself, with horns and a tail; the Merry Andrews in the orchestra throw themselves on the ground in terror at this apparition, while the Devil tugs at the baker's substantial money-bags.

For the last scene Punch comes on once more, belabouring his wife with a pair of bellows while she hits back with a ladle; the Devil appears

OUTSIDE AND INSIDE A PUPPET BOOTH AT BARTHOLOMEW FAIR, 1772
From *Punch's Puppet Show*, a "turn up" published by Robert Sayer.

again, comes to Joan's assistance, and after a fierce tussle flies away with them both in his arms:

> Here's a sad sight, Poor Punch is going
> To pay for all his former doing.

The band of music at this crude little entertainment consisted of an old blind fiddler, a bumbass or "string and bladder," the outside trumpeter, and Harlequin playing "the salt-box," a hollow wooden box upon which a spoon was drummed, much in favour at the time as an elementary percussion instrument. We have already noted Griffin's and Rowe's violins;

the dulcimer—a kind of hand piano—which Pepys had noticed at Bologna's theatre in 1662, was said in 1740 to be still in use at puppet shows, though not much heard elsewhere.[22] It is certain that there always was a little orchestra at the puppets, however crude it may sometimes have been.

The curiously unrelated incidents that were flung together to make up this fairground show of the seventies represent the leavings of a hundred years of puppet dramas; all idea of continuity and dramatic structure has been lost; all that remains are certain characters and certain situations, but none of them were peculiar to this performance, and they may all be traced in their development across the years.

Punch himself had assumed a distinctive English character, as the successor of the Elizabethan stage clown, before the end of the seventeenth century; during the eighteenth there was little significant change. The most revealing summary of his personality is provided in a poem by Swift:[23]

Observe, the audience is in pain,
While Punch is hid behind the scene;
But when they hear his rusty voice,
With what impatience they rejoice!
And then they value not two straws,
How Solomon decides the cause,
Which the true mother, which pretender,
Nor listen to the witch of Endor;
Should Faustus, with the Devil behind him,
Enter the stage, they never mind him;
If Punch, to stir their fancy, shows
In at the door his monstrous nose,
Then sudden draws it back again;
O what a pleasure mixed with pain!
You every moment think an age,
Till he appears upon the stage;
And first his bum you see him clap
Upon the queen of Sheba's lap:
The duke of Lorraine drew his sword;
Punch roaring ran, and running roared,
Reviles all people in his jargon,
And sells the King of Spain a bargain;[24]
St George himself he plays the wag on,
And mounts astride upon the dragon;
He gets a thousand thumps and kicks,
Yet cannot leave his roguish tricks;

In every action thrusts his nose;
The reason why, no mortal knows;
In doleful scenes that break our heart
Punch comes, like you, and lets a f—t.
There's not a puppet made of wood,
But what would hang him, if they could;
While, teasing all, by all he's teased,
How well are the spectators pleased!
Who in the motion have no share,
But purely come to hear and stare;
Have no concern for Sabra's sake,
Which gets the better, saint or snake,
Provided Punch (for there's the jest)
Be soundly mauled, and plague the rest.

This vivid description may be compared with that of Addison thirty years earlier, and of Popham fifty years later. "See," Popham wrote,

> a little man advances with a ridiculous face, a humpback and a vast belly; Punch is his name, and there is none more impudent; he is always intruding into serious scenes, putting everything in disorder with his chattering and his jokes. Often, turning towards a tightly packed bench of girls he sits himself down near to them; My beautiful ones, he says, winking roguishly, here's a girl friend come to join you! His double-meanings, hinting at gross indecencies, bring a blush to every modest cheek and broad smiles to the rows of men and boys.[25]

There is really little to add. The interfering buffoon has reached the climax of his glory; he is so much funnier than the other characters among whom he struts that they have ceased to matter, and the plays into which he intruded are now much less important than himself. The folk-dramas of the puppet booths are no more than a background to his vulgar and robust vitality. Soon even the background could be shed away.

As the century went on Joan grew more and more like her husband. It is clear that she was a nagging shrew, and that Punch's battles with her were partly in self-defence.

Joan you are the plague of my life,
A rope would be welcomer than such a wife

he sings in desperation;

Joan, Joan, Joan, has a thundering tongue,
And Joan, Joan, Joan, is a bold one.
How happy is he,
Who from wedlock is free;
For who'd have a wife to scold one?

To which she replies with a good taste of her tongue:

Punch, Punch, Punch, prythee think of your hunch,
Prythee look at your great strutting belly;
    Sirrah, if you done
War with me [to] declare,
I will beat your fat guts to a jelly.[26]

The joke of a hen-pecked husband is older than Mrs Noah, and always up-to-date.

The eighteenth-century Punch, in fact, was not at all the kind of person that he is usually imagined to have been. "Being but a timid and weak fellow [he] is always thrashed by the other puppet-actors in the show; yet always boasts of victory after they are gone, as feeble cowards are apt to do, bragging that they have gotten the better of those by whom they were soundly bastinadoed,"wrote Baretti in 1786.[27] In fact, he was a comedian not a villain, a hen-pecked husband not a wife-beater, the receiver of slaps not the dealer of blows, the author of puerile vulgarities not a Don Juan, a naughty and mischievous wag not an insensate and indiscriminate assassin.

The hunchback and strutting belly are now well-established ingredients of his shape, and the nose and chin become more markedly hooked as the century progresses. A human Punch, dancing at Sadler's Wells in 1730, described himself thus:[28]

My cap is like to a sugar loaf,
And round my collar I wear a ruff;
I'd strip and show you my shapes in buff,
But fear the ladies would flout me.
My rising back and distorted breast,
Where e'er I show him, become a jest;
And as for what is below my waist,
No lady need ever doubt me.

Indeed, it must have been his barely veiled hints of what lay "below his waist" that endeared him to the servants and apprentices at his booths, and drew upon him the severe censure of the visiting antiquary, who—true to his kind—could only appreciate bawdy humour when it was a hundred years old.

We have a handful of pictorial illustrations for this century, and Punch's costume, with its ruff round the neck, big buttons, and high hat is now easily recognized; he was, too, a common character in masquerades at Ranelagh or Carlisle House. By about the middle of the century he had discarded his plain white Italian costume and was beginning to wear the red-and-yellow motley of the English jester that has distinguished him ever since. His goggling eyes still caught attention, and a rhymster of 1763 could invite us

> . . . to see the puppet show;
> Here swaggering Punch, with eyes agog and stare
> Shall, more than Garrick, please the country fair;
> Here sticks and rags delight a village-town,
> And the dull smutty jest goes glibly down.

In his relations with the Devil Punch fulfilled the role of the Vice in the old morality plays, who was sometimes carried off to hell at the end of the play. The function of the Devil in the show was, indeed, purely medieval; as the landlady in *Tom Jones* complained, "I remember when puppet shows were made of good scripture stories . . . and when wicked people were carried away by the devil"; it was not only Punch who suffered this fate, for Faustus, Mother Shipton, Bateman's perjured bride, and Friar Bacon's comic servant were all carted off to hell at the end of their respective plays, and Punch's fate should perhaps be seen in comparison with these incidents rather than as a direct derivation from the Middle Ages. Whatever play was being performed, the accepted conclusion of the eighteenth-century puppet show was normally for the Devil to carry Punch off: in 1741, for instance, an epilogue could apologize that

> . . . our catastrophe
> Does not with puppet rules agree;
> Vengeance for Punch's crimes should catch him,
> And at the last the Devil fetch him,[29]

and in 1801 Strutt recorded that "in compliance with the old custom, Punch, the genuine descendant of the Iniquity, is constantly taken away from the stage by the Devil at the end of the puppet show."

For the rest, the elements of the show were gathered from many quarters. The Baker was perhaps the baker who left penny loaves on the ground for Jane Shore to pick up, as she wandered the streets in disgrace;[30] *Jane Shore* was, of course, an ever-green favourite of the puppet booths. Bakers were an unpopular trade, as they were often suspected of giving short weight in their loaves, and the spectacle of the Devil catching one of them out must have satisfied the audience's sense of justice. It was from this feature in the puppet show that the phrase "Pull devil, pull baker" probably originated.[31]

Wheelbarrows were often wheeled on ropes by the rope-dancers, and

Punch may well have emulated them; a well-known seller of gingerbread at May Fair used to cry out that "it will melt in your mouth like a red-hot brick-bat, and rumble in your inside like Punch and his wheelbarrow." Little Ben the Sailor, who was so popular a turn, had appeared by the fifties;[32] a hornpipe is a dance that suits very effectively the vertical movements of a marionette, but other dances were also popular, especially jigs and country dances; sarabands were often danced by a Moor, "to the time of a pair of castanets, which he rattles in each hand."[33]

Besides the more or less 'straight' variety acts, a couple of trick turns are recorded in the popular puppet shows of this century. After the Jacobite Rebellion, when many of the ringleaders were executed, there were two shows in the same year at May Fair exhibiting the beheading of puppets. It is a quite feasible, though finicky, trick for a marionette executioner to strike off the head of a puppet victim on the block and then hold the dismembered head up in his hand to the admiration of the bystanders; perhaps that little effect was, in fact, achieved. And the famous trick of the Dissecting Skeleton, which had been shown in the Restoration Theatre, was certainly exhibited by Parsloe at Southwark Fair in 1752 when he announced "a moving skeleton, which dances a jig upon the stage, and in the middle of his dance falls all to pieces, bone from bone, joint from joint, all parts of his body separate from one another; and in the twinkling of an eye up in his proper proportion, and dances as in the beginning."[34] Perhaps the play called *Harlequin Conjurer, or Pantaloon Dissected*, presented by Hill in 1754, indicates use of the same effect.

Continuing references to "puppets squeaking" confirm that those who spoke for them still did so through a squeaker, though this was perhaps reserved for Punch alone. In 1786 we have an early description of this instrument:

> Punchinello . . . as you well know, speaks with a squeaking voice that seems to come out at his nose, because the fellow, who in a puppet-show manages the puppet called Punchinello, or Punch (as English folks abbreviate it), speaks with a tin whistle in his mouth, which makes him emit that comical kind of voice.[35]

By the end of the century we find this squeaker, whose existence we have traced so assiduously through so many centuries and in so many countries, acquiring an English name: in 1790 Jobson concluded his "Primitive Puppet Show" at Bartholomew Fair with "a sparring match between those celebrated pugilists Mr Swatchel (alias Punch) and his wife Joaney." The origin of the word is obscure, but the "swatchel," or "swazzle," is—to this day—the term used by puppet showmen for their Punch "squeakers."

The device of the 'interpreter,' which we have traced from Elizabethan times, was also still employed within these little theatres in which time seemed to stand still. Perhaps the clearest examples of how he participated in the show are provided by the puppet shows that were introduced into a couple of contemporary plays in the human theatre. Fielding's *The Author's Farce* of 1730 tells the story of a penniless author whose plays lie unread in the bookshops, and who conceives the idea of presenting a puppet show that will satirize the literary and theatrical follies of the day. At its production in the theatre the puppets were represented by humans, and we need not concern ourselves here with the story they enacted, but it is very clear that the author stood in front of the puppet stage and introduced each character with a few words of explanation as it appeared; the dialogue was then taken up by the puppets.

Similarly, *The Rehearsal at Gotham*, by John Gay, of 1754, presents the puppet-show incident from *Don Quixote* transferred to English surroundings; the actual puppet play is interrupted before it can be performed, but the showman's fool clearly stands before the curtain to describe the action of the drama as it takes place.

Finally, in the written script of a tavern entertainment that was performed by George Alexander Stevens, the celebrated lecturer on Heads, we have an amusing and—I suspect—a graphic impression of how these 'interpreters' actually introduced their shows:

> The first figure, Gemmen and Ladies, I represent you with, is St George and the Dragon. Observe and take notice of the richness of his dress, the lance in his hand, the rolling of the Dragon's eyes, and the sting in his tail. This figure, Gemmen, is the wonder of the world; it has been shown before the 'Riol Siety,' and those learned scholars could not tell what to make of it; for some said it was a sea-monster, and some said it was a land-monster, and some said it was no monster, only a monstrosity; and some said it was a griffin, and some said it had ne'er a fin, and so at last they all agreed that it was neither one thing nor another.
>
> The next figure I shall show ye, is Adam and Eve a going to be created. Why don't you bring them out?
>
> (Here he changed his voice, as if answered by a companion.) They ain't ready yet, but there's the two Babes in the Wood; show them; anything will do now-a-days . . .[36]

This, of course, is the decadence of a long tradition. But there is a certain inherent incongruity in the voice of a man issuing from the—

usually immobile—lips of a marionette, and the device of the puppets miming their action while their story is told for them provides an artistic unity of presentation that might well be revived more often in the puppet theatres of to-day. The swazzle and the interpreter were both ancient devices to lend to the dialogue of the puppet actors that un-human timbre and un-naturalistic way of speech that is their birthright.

Besides the marionettes and the moving waxworks, shadow shows made brief appearances in the eighteenth-century fairs. In 1737 at Bartholomew Fair, Hallam, a well-known theatrical-booth proprietor, presented a Medley that included the Italian shadows, performed "by the best masters from Italy, and which have not been seen here these twenty years"; no doubt there were other short engagements, but it was not until the Ombres Chinoises appeared in the West End in seventy-five that this type of show attracted much popularity. In 1779 a troupe of Ombres Chinoises was showing at Bartholomew Fair, describing themselves as "the grandest that ever was exhibited in Europe," with an impressive list of command performances before European monarchs; ladies and gentlemen could purchase the Ombres, and be taught the method of playing them. Their somewhat subtle and delicate appeal, however, was perhaps not really suited to the rough-and-tumble of the fairs; Gyngell brought them out for his season at Catherine Street, but they played—in this century—only a small part in the story of popular entertainment.

In these closing years of the eighteenth century, a century in which the puppet theatre had attained an elegance and prosperity it had never known before, it must have seemed that the wheel had turned full circle. The fashionable craze for Fantoccini had burnt itself out, and the humble puppet theatre of the people, which for so long had told the simple legends of their history, had fallen into disrepute and decay. Ambitious showmen were at pains to disassociate their puppets from the sordid level of the common puppet show. "Mr Yates begs leave to acquaint the public," reads an announcement of 1779,

> that though it goes under the mean appellation of a Puppet Show, yet its performances are singular . . . diverting and rational. Here the chaste ear will not be offended, as is usual with people in the profession, to amuse by low and obscene language, for grovelling mortals to laugh at. Harmony, fine music, and good taste are our greatest fortifications.

Mr Yates's grammar may be uncertain, but his meaning is not. The puppet shows, wrote Strutt in 1801, "still continue to be exhibited in

Smithfield at Bartholomew-tide, though with very little traces of their former greatness; indeed, of late years, they have become unpopular, and are frequented only by children." The official records of Bartholomew Fair confirm this gloomy story; out of an average attendance of over one hundred shows of all kinds at the fair the following figures record the number of puppet shows each year:

1790	.. 9	1798	.. 2	1806	.. 0
1791	.. 5	1799	.. 5	1807	.. 0
1792	.. 11	1800	.. 6	1808	.. 0
1793	.. 5	1801	.. 3	1809	.. 0
1794	.. 7	1802	.. 1	1810	.. 1
1795	.. 3	1803	.. 1	1811	.. 0
1796	.. 8	1804	.. 2	1812	.. 0
1797	.. 3	1805	.. 0	1813	.. 0

It seems, indeed, like the end of a story. Surveying the scene at the dawn of the nineteenth century, we might well be pardoned for writing FINIS beneath the story of Punch and of the English puppet theatre.

Chapter VIII

PUNCH AND JUDY

The Submerged Tradition

AT the moment when Punch and all his tradition was in danger of disappearing he found new roots in the old despised glove-puppet show that had once enjoyed so lively a supremacy. We have seen how the puppets of Jonson's *Bartholomew Fair* and the whole of that vigorous Jacobean era had been glove puppets, and how their simple stage had been ousted by the marionette theatres of the Italians. By the end of the seventeenth century the glove-puppet booth was almost extinct. Almost, but not quite; the tradition was too old and vigorous, the dramatic power of the hand puppet too powerful, for it ever to disappear entirely.

An obscure hint here and there makes it certain that glove-puppet shows played some small but enduring part in the popular entertainments of the eighteenth century. Ned Ward, whose lively pen has already brightened our history, makes a curious reference to a puppet show at Bartholomew Fair in 1705:[1]

A booth diminutive there stood,
Where pigmy actors, made of wood,
Were leaning o'er a canvas clout
And squeaking to the rabble rout.
As the two puppets thus were sporting,
Guided by hands behind the curtain,
Young Coridon, from country farm,
With Phillis hanging on his arm. . . .
Were gazing round to feast their eyes
With the fair's tempting rarities . . .
But Roger jogging of his Dolly,
And pointing up, to show his folly,
Cried out "Wolaw! there's little folk
Ads heart! how prettily they talk . . .
Look, look, Joan, how the Vezons fight!
Who'd think they were so full of spite?
What woundy pelts one gives the other?
Nouns, how he marks his little brother"!

The country girl takes them for real elves and hurries away in fright, and the show goes on with a battle between a real man on a hobby-horse and a pasteboard dragon on a long pole; but the interest of the passage lies in its first few lines. Here, without any possibility of doubt, is a glove-puppet show, with the fights at which it excels, for all the passers-by of the fair to see.

SOUTHWARK FAIR, BY WILLIAM HOGARTH, 1733

Detail from the engraving, showing glove puppets and humans performing outside a puppet booth.

A few years later, in 1713, Swift, another keen observer of the puppets, gives us the explanation of how these outside glove puppets were used.[2]

> I have seen the same sort of management [advance puffing] at a puppet show. Some puppets of little or no consequence appeared several times at the window to allure the boys and the rabble; the trumpeter sounded often, and the door-keeper cried a hundred times till he was hoarse, that they were

just going to begin; yet after all, we were sometimes forced to wait an hour before Punch himself in person made his entry.

Apparently the hand puppets "at the window" were used as a kind of outside attraction, or 'barker,' to gather a crowd and entice people into the booth for the marionettes within.

Exactly this use of glove puppets can, in fact, be seen in Hogarth's famous painting of Southwark Fair of 1733; here, next to Lee and Harper's theatrical booth presenting *The Siege of Troy*, may be seen "Punch's Opera," with a showcloth representing Adam and Eve (evidently the play was *The Creation of the World*) and Punch trundling his famous wheelbarrow, with Joan in it, up to the flaming jaws of hell. On the balcony a human hobby-horse is nibbling a Harlequin, and beside them, in a shabby open booth, two hand puppets cross sticks against the sky. This fascinating detail, from a picture crowded with details, portrays so much better than words the outside appearance of the fairground booths; the pictorial showcloth, painted in two sections, seems to have been in a style common with puppet shows of the period.[3] The representation of Hell's Mouth, in which Punch no doubt wanted to deposit his wife, is a striking link with the medieval mystery plays.

Finally, *The Morning Chronicle*, describing Bartholomew Fair of 1784, comments that "the walking French puppet-show had hired an apartment, with additional performers; Punch and the Devil, in his little moving theatre, were performing without doors, to invite the company into the grand theatre."[4] Here is a clear distinction between the "walking" puppets, or marionettes, which played in a room hired for the purpose, and the "little moving theatre" out of doors—evidently a hand-puppet booth—which advertised the big show. The description of the marionettes as French is interesting; and the information that the glove-puppet characters included Punch and the Devil confirms beyond question that the traditional figures of the popular marionette stage were also established in the hand-puppet booths.

By this time the portable glove-puppet show began to appear not only in the fairs, but in the streets. We do not know when this first happened. We can only assume from the absence of any reference to these shows in the many early-eighteenth-century books that describe the streets of London—Gay's *Trivia*, for instance—that their earlier appearance in the streets was unknown; but in 1785, when George III and Queen Charlotte drove through the streets of Deptford to inspect a man-of-war, Thomas Rowlandson was present with his inimitable brush to record the crowds that swarmed in the Broadway, the sights and shows that had gathered to entertain them, and—set up at the side of the street—a glove-puppet booth, with a blue check cover, in which Punch in red-and-yellow costume delivers a sound spanking to the bare bottom of a struggling figure held across the playboard, who, I fear, must have

PROBABLY THE EARLIEST ILLUSTRATION OF A PUNCH STREET SHOW
Detail from a watercolour by Thomas Rowlandson showing George III and Queen Charlotte driving to Deptford Dockyard, 1785.
By courtesy of Minto Wilson, Esq.

been his wife. In the same year an engraving by Samuel Collings of "the Italian Puppet Show" was published by Carington Bowles, showing a glove-puppet booth set up at a street corner, with the gentry, the crossing-sweepers, and the fishwives looking on, while a puppet-lady, dressed in the contemporary Georgian fashion, threatens Punch with a stick. Here, in these illustrations of 1785, for the first time in history, Punch and his now familiar theatre may be seen in the streets of London.

Ten years later, in 1795, we have another illustration of a street show, published by Laurie and Whittle. This provides a few more details: a man is playing a hand-organ, a girl is passing the hat round and picking pockets as she goes, a couple of performing dogs and a monkey are sporting themselves. The "Italian" Punch of 1785 wore a curious high stiff "topper," but Rowlandson and the print of 1795 both illustrate the familiar floppy jester's cap; in every case the hooked nose and chin are unmistakable; despite differences of detail, this is the authentic English Punch.

"In the present day," wrote Strutt in 1801,

> the puppet-show man travels about the streets when the weather will permit, and carries his motions, with the theatre itself, upon his back! The exhibition takes place in the open air; and the precarious income of the miserable itinerant depends entirely on the voluntary contributions of the spectators, which, as far as one may judge from the squalid appearance he usually makes, is very trifling.[5]

There was, inevitably, a period of transition. For the first decade of the nineteenth century Punch could still be found occasionally at the fairs, both as a marionette and as a hand puppet outside the show; but this did not last for long; Punch was, literally, thrown on to the streets. From about the year 1800 he had no other existence than that of a glove puppet.

The cause of this complete change of technique was economic. A marionette theatre is not an easy show to transport, nor is it a cheap show to run; four or five operators and assistants are really needed for a smooth performance, and a cart was essential. As the popularity of puppets declined at the end of the eighteenth century admission charges were reduced to a few pence, and the standards of production must have become shoddier and shoddier; eventually the receipts cannot have justified even the use of a horse and cart. At this stage the only course for the showmen, who made their living at the game, was to reduce their overheads still further by doing the whole show single-handed and by carrying it on their backs. We must always remember that the high-flown literary and historical derivations of the Punch show that are so often adduced have had far less influence upon its development than the compelling economic necessity of making the thing pay.

There was not much scope for a free open-air show at the fairs, when there was no larger theatre to attract people into; and so the puppet showmen were reduced to performing where and when they could in the streets, wherever people passed and could be induced to linger. No longer could they charge even a penny for the show, but they must make what they could by passing the hat round; the essential assistant to the performer was now a collector, or—as he is still called in showman's slang—a 'bottler.'

But the puppet-masters had stumbled unawares upon the recipe for success: people would linger and place a coin in the hat who would never have paid to enter a booth, and despite Strutt's slighting observations

"Punch's Puppet Shew," probably by Isaac Cruikshank
Published by Laurie and Whittle, 1795.

there can be little doubt that the first showmen who took to the streets found there in the great metropolis the vast unhurried audience that will still gather and stare at any new thing.

The street shows proved successful not only financially, but also artistically. In the rapid movements of the glove puppet, in its direct projection of the performer's dramatic skill, in its suitability for backchat and repartee, in its easy handling of little properties, Punch found his soul once again. The show blossomed anew, shaped by the practical requirements of its little stage.

In the last quarter of the eighteenth century Punch first established himself in the London streets, and during the first quarter of the nineteenth century he increasingly made himself at home there. He was welcomed as the darling of the people; by 1825 he could be lauded as "the most popular performer in the world."

The Evolution of the Drama

The Punch show of the streets is the direct descendant of the Punch show of the fairs; Punch the glove puppet is the same person as Punch the marionette; but in the process of evolution his character and his drama have undergone modifications. Nevertheless there was a continuity of tradition, and to imagine—as is sometimes suggested—that the street show was 'introduced' by some visiting Italian is surely to ignore the whole of the long story of puppets in England that we have already traced.

To appreciate the modifications that the show underwent one must understand the physical structure of a glove-puppet booth, in which one man stands inside the frame, holding the puppets on his hands above his head. To keep the action going, and avoid leaving the stage empty, it is useful for the chief character to remain in sight of the audience for most of the time, usually on the operator's right hand, while a succession of other characters is introduced in turn on his left; it is not possible to have more than two figures in view at a time. There are, it is true, larger booths in which several operators can work, which permit much more ambitious productions, but as the whole merit of the glove puppet at this period lay in its economy in permitting one man to present a show single-handed, these need not detain us here.

It is obvious that the hero of the show is Punch, and therefore he must occupy the operator's right hand. In the eighteenth-century marionette shows, Punch would keep popping in upon one scene after another. Here this is not technically easy, and instead one character after another keeps popping in upon Punch. It is this simple but fundamental reversal of procedure that explains the dissimilarity between the Punch shows of the eighteenth and nineteenth centuries.

Moreover, the plot that can be conveyed in the glove-puppet show is limited by its conventions; and when the show is being presented in the open air, before a shifting, casual audience, with all the noises of the street in competition, any subtlety of incident is wasted. The show must be lively in action, it must compel the attention of passers-by, and it must utilize the natural movements of a hand puppet, which are the natural movements of the human hand.

We have seen that the glove-puppet shows of the eighteenth-century fairs introduced Punch and the Devil, and puppets fighting. It is certain that the personages represented in these shows outside the booths were a few of the more popular characters to be seen upon the marionette stages within. Punch, Joan, and the Devil were certainly there, perhaps the Baker and some others; it is doubtful if they ever attempted to tell a story —that was not their function. When the glove-puppet booth was transferred to the street the showmen merely repeated the kind of performance that they had been giving in the fairs; no story was told, none was required; it was merely a bit of knock-about fun. Early in the nineteenth century we are told that no more than four characters were ever introduced into the street shows—Punch, his wife, the Devil, and a Doctor or a Constable.[6] Gradually upon this foundation a regular order of incidents grew up and new characters appeared; gradually an accepted 'drama' was adopted by all the showmen: a drama that has no author, for—as every puppeteer knows—the puppets have a way of imposing their actions and their own personalities upon the performance; a drama that did not vary like the earlier marionette plays in which Punch had lorded, but which assumed an unchangeable traditional form; a drama that is substantially still performed and still loved to-day.

Seen in this light, the curious course of the traditional street show may be understood. It is like the trailer of a film that has become detached from its parent, and has then been expanded by any number of extraneous additions. It is like a story compiled in a parlour game of Consequences. The show should, indeed, not be regarded as a story at all, but as a succession of encounters, dictated by the conventions of its medium. The plot cannot be measured by any considerations of cause and effect, and to try to extract a 'meaning' from Punch's incoherent progress is to seek for the impossible.

So far from hiding a recondite moral, the whole thing is almost too simple for a twentieth-century mind to comprehend; it was never written or even planned—it just happened. It was shaped by the fingers of hungry showmen, it was born from the traditions that ran in their blood, it was moulded from the laughter of street urchins.

The play, then, should be considered not in the outline of its plot, but in the enumeration of the different characters who enter one after another to share the stage with Punch. Some of them we have already met, some of them will be new, but they one and all repeat the familiar pattern of blows which had already marked Punch's encounters with his wife and with the Devil. There *was* a reason for Punch beating his wife —she was a shrew; there *was* a reason for Punch fighting the Devil—he didn't want to be carried off to hell; there is no reason for the combats that mark his encounters with the rest of them—except that they repeat a bit of business that made people laugh. Punch the glove puppet wields

"Mr Punch in all his Glory," by Robert Cruikshank
From *The English Spy*, 1825.

a stick because glove puppets are good at handling little properties; Punch the marionette cocked up his legs and sat on ladies' laps because that is the sort of action marionettes do well. Punch merely adapted his 'business' to the conventions of his new stage.

Approached historically in this way, Punch will be seen not as an inhuman monster who goes through life striking and murdering every one who crosses his path, but as the old comedian whose footsteps we have been following for so many centuries already, who only murders each new character brought up before him as the quickest way of ending *that* scene and getting on with the next.

Perhaps that is the fundamental reason why we laugh at Punch, and are not horrified. Without knowing any of the history that I have so laboriously uncovered here, we have sensed with a sure instinct that the beatings and the killings are only a convention with no relation to reality, and that behind his wooden victories there lies the arch-type of "he who gets slapped," the primitive and eternal clown.

The Texts

By the third decade of the nineteenth century the humble street performance of Punch had become sufficiently a part of the London scene and sufficiently fond a youthful memory of men now approaching middle age for it to find a place in the essays and journalism of the day. In 1821 a nostalgic article in *The Literary Speculum* untimelily lamented Punch's absence from the streets, and in 1825 Blackmantle's *The English Spy*—one of the many imitations of Pierce Egan's *Tom and Jerry*—contained the earliest description of a Punch street show that really gives a clear idea of the action of the play. Here, too, was an excellent illustration by Robert Cruikshank, and for the first time we find that Punch's wife has changed her name to Judy. Poems about Punch had appeared in the literary magazines, in 1824 hailing him as

> Thou lignum-vitæ Roscius, who
> Dost the old vagrant stage renew,
> Peerless, inimitable Punchinello . . . ,

and in 1826 recalling his combats with Judy:

> And now they hug—now fight—now part—now meet
> While unextinguished laughter shakes the street.

Antiquarians too were turning their attention to this vulgar popular entertainment, and discussing its origins; in 1823 William Hone had referred to the show as a relic of the medieval mystery plays, and in 1826 a correspondent to *The Every-Day Book*—that fascinating bran-tub of antiquarian lore—had developed this theme further. Interest in this quaint little entertainment of the streets was fully aroused, and the time was ripe for the publication of the complete text of the play.

This important event in our history took place in 1828 when Mr Septimus Prowett, an enterprising but short-lived publisher, commissioned George Cruikshank to execute a number of sketches of a street performance. He fixed upon the show given by an old Italian named Piccini, who had been playing in the London streets for a great many years, and arranged for a special performance, at which he sketched the incidents and characters of the drama as it progressed. For the text Mr Prowett turned to John Payne Collier, an ambitious young student of the English drama who had been editing a new edition of *Dodsley's Old Plays* during the past two years. Payne Collier had, apparently, noted down the text of a Punch show that he used to follow round the streets of Brighton when he was a boy in about 1805, and this he combined with Piccini's version into a "correct" and definitive text. Collier was also persuaded to write an introduction, sketching the history of puppets; he complained later that he was allowed only three weeks in which to write this, and as he did not believe that he could produce anything good enough to satisfy himself at such short notice he stipulated that his name should not appear on the book. However, spurred on by the offer of a £50 fee, Payne Collier set to work with enthusiasm, and by the appointed date the material was ready.[7]

Punch and Judy was an immediate success. It was reprinted in 1828, and for the second edition Collier added a great deal of new information that he had discovered. The book was reprinted again in 1832, in 1844, in 1859, in 1870, in 1873, in 1881, and so on; two editions were published in America. Shorn of Collier's introduction, it is still in print to this day.[8]

Cruikshank's illustrations are so well known that there is no need to say much of them here. Not only are they fine examples of this great artist's work, but they have captured in a rare and delightful manner the quality of 'woodenness' in the figures. So many artists who have drawn or painted puppet shows have romanticized their pictures in a hopelessly unrealistic manner, but these figures really do look like puppets, and really do strike the attitudes that are natural to glove puppets. Yet, without compromising the fidelity of his vision, Cruikshank has subtly indicated the changing expressions that appear, in the spectator's fancy, to flit across the immobile mask of the puppets during the action of the play.

For Collier's text and introduction we must modify our enthusiasm. The text itself was, admittedly, a composite production; it reads to-day with a slightly literary flavour, and seems too wordy for the conditions of a single street performance. Although it undoubtedly introduces the characters and situations of the Punch and Judy shows of its time, with a great deal of the authentic dialogue, I cannot help suspecting that part of it was written by Collier himself. We must indeed be grateful for what we have, but an unvarnished shorthand transcript, without literary improvements, would have been even more valuable.

Collier's historical introduction has provided the basic foundation for every history of puppets in England that has been written since—including this one. It was an extraordinary feat to have collected so much information in three weeks (if this really was the time limit), and for many years it stood unchallenged. Despite many omissions—and in particular the failure to record Punch's appearance in England at the Restoration—it must still be regarded as a fine piece of original research for its period. Before examining it more closely, however, it would be well to glance at the remainder of Payne Collier's literary career.

BACKSTAGE, BY GEORGE CRUIKSHANK
From *Punch and Judy*, 1828.

Three years later a *History of English Dramatic Poetry* by Collier was published, containing a vast amount of erudite investigation into the medieval and Elizabethan drama. Collier continued his researches for many years, publishing the results in the transactions of learned societies, and in 1852 he startled the literary world by revealing a number of annotations in a Shakespearean Second Folio in his possession. But already suspicions had been aroused, and even before his death in 1883 various scholars had cast doubt on his honesty. When his papers were examined after his death it was proved conclusively that this brilliant literary student had been forging annotations, altering documents even in the State Papers, and inventing entire literary works and passing them off throughout his lifetime as his own discoveries. *The History of English Dramatic Poetry* as early as 1831 contains a great deal of forged and spurious matter. What of *Punch and Judy* of 1828?[9]

Punch and Judy was begun half as a joke. I do not imagine that Mr Prowett really expected a serious historical introduction, and Payne Collier treated the whole thing, with its pompous array of footnotes and literary comparisons, as something of a satire on literary scholarship. It is quite clear, however, that what may have started as a joke soon became a serious study. But it was an anonymous production, and evidently Collier felt it quite excusable to embellish the rather bare bones of his history with a mock-ballad which he pretended to have discovered in an eighteenth-century scrapbook, with an "allegorical" version of the play said to be "extracted" from a newspaper of 1813, and with a Sonnet to Punch that he hinted came from the pen of Byron. Nobody queried these at the time; "Byron's" sonnet is still quoted to this day in puppet histories; and the ridiculous theories of the imaginary newspaper correspondent have received the imprimatur of respectability in Brewer's *Phrase and Fable*. It was all so easy.[10]

There is, I think, no doubt that with *Punch and Judy* Collier first experimented with the forgery of literary evidence. It was nothing very serious; puppets were, perhaps, hardly important enough to matter; but he saw how easy it was, and an intoxicating sense of power and importance swept over him; he turned to his next work as a *creative* artist.

Payne Collier was not a dishonest man in any legal sense or in his personal relationships, and he was an enthusiastic explorer into literary history; but the gross intellectual dishonesty of which he was guilty, the mental aberration that distorted his literary scholarship, makes it impossible to accept *anything* he writes as true, unless it can be independently verified. The full list of his forgeries has not yet been reckoned, and the myths he propagated are still being repeated. *Punch and Judy* is to be warmly welcomed as the first history of puppets in England, but it is also to be sadly examined as the first experiment of a literary criminal.

About twenty-five years later we find preserved in the wonderful canvas of Mayhew's *London Labour and the London Poor* a truly verbatim text of a Punch and Judy show. To the very great interest of the interview with the showman recorded by Mayhew I shall allude later, but the text of the play is of enormous value itself, and with its cockney humour and grammatical errors it is clearly a genuine product of the streets. This text of the eighteen-fifties undoubtedly provides a more authentic script for Punch and Judy than that of Payne Collier, which has so often been reprinted.

During the second half of the nineteenth century innumerable texts of Punch and Judy were published, mostly in the form of children's picture-books, and the story begins to take on an independent existence as a nursery classic. How closely these children's books reflect the actual performances currently given in the streets we cannot be sure, but their evidence helps to build up the general picture of the continuing tradition of the show. The many reprints of the Payne Collier edition certainly tended to establish an 'official' text, but the scripts of a few other actual performers have been independently recorded, and these enable us to compare the versions of different showmen and to trace the evolution of the drama through the years.

In the summary that follows I have principally relied upon eight main texts. All except one of these are based upon the performance of an actual known showman, and all seem to be quite independent personal versions, that are not copied from one another. Here is a list of them—shabby, cheap little booklets, many undated, the despair of the bibliographer, but here they are in all their glory:

1828. *Punch and Judy*, edited by John Payne Collier from the performance of Piccini, with illustrations by George Cruikshank.

1854. *The Wonderful Drama of Punch and Judy . . .* by Papernose Woodensconce, Esq. (Robert Brough), with illustrations by "The Owl."[11] (Although this was published as a text for juvenile performers, it is so racy and instinct with the vocabulary of the street, and so completely different from Collier's text, that I feel sure it substantially reproduces a genuine street performance.)

1856. In Henry Mayhew, *London Labour and the London Poor*, vol. iii. (The text was taken down in about 1850. It has been reprinted in Peter Quennell, *Mayhew's London* (1949), and in P. J. Stead, *Mr Punch* (1950).)

1887. In *The Pall Mall Gazette* of June 15th. (An interview with Mr Mowbray of Notting Hill.)

(*c.* 1926.) *The Book of Punch and Judy*, containing the original dialogue . . . by the late Professor Smith of London. (A crude but authentic text of a decadent period in Punch's history.)

1937. *The Story of Punch and Judy*, by P. F. Tickner. (The script used by a contemporary showman.)

(1938.) *Punch and Judy*, by Arthur Hambling. (An intelligent text, traditional, but with literary influences.)

(1939.) *How to do Punch and Judy*, by Sidney de Hempsey. (A typical modern showman's script.)

In all these versions—and in the many others with which they have been compared[12]—there is a general similarity of incidents, though not of the order in which they occur; there is a basic core of characters common to all texts, but with many individual additions and substitutions; but there is *no* exact similarity of verbal dialogue, except in certain catch-phrases that tend to be passed on, with minor corruptions, from showman to showman down the century. The Punch and Judy show is, in fact, the last example of the Commedia dell' Arte tradition of extempore dialogue; the situations are fixed, but the words are left to the instinct and invention of each individual performer.

A few examples will illustrate this in practice. Punch's remarks on Judy's first appearance are recorded as follows:

1828. What a pretty creature! A'nt she one beauty?

1854. Ain't she a beauty? There's a nose!

1856. What a sweet creature! What a handsome nose and chin!

1887. Oh, what beautiful lips!

1926. Oh! You little beauty! Oh! You little bit of jam!

1937. Hullo, my girl.

1938. Come up here, my beauty.

1939. Oh! you little darling!

Here is an example of a famous joke that disappeared from some of the later texts. The officer of the law has just arrived:

1828. OFFICER. I'm come to take you up.
PUNCH. And I'm come to take you down.

1854. I am under the necessity of taking you up.
And I am under the necessity of knocking you down.

1856. I've a special order in my pocket to take you up.
And I've a special order to knock you down.

1937. I have come to lock you up.
And I've come to knock you down.

And here, on the other hand, is a joke that did not appear in Collier's text, but has crept into almost every subsequent version. On the death of the Hangman Punch's remarks are:

1828. Huzza! Huzza!

1854. Here's a man tumbled into a ditch, and hung himself up to dry.

1856. He got wet through, and I hung him up to dry.

1926. Why, the poor fellow fell in the water and I have hung him up to dry.

1938. Fallen in the water—so you have hung him out to dry.

1939. He fell in the river and I am hanging him out to dry.

Examples like these—and I could quote several others—suggest considerable verbal similarity between the various texts, but it must be emphasized that these are quoted as exceptional cases; in general, there is *no* verbal similarity at all between the various versions. To indicate this more clearly I quote, quite at random, Punch's final remark as he dispatches Judy:

1828. To lose a wife is to get a fortune.

1854. Root-to-to-to-to-oo-it.

1856. Get out of the way.

1887. Take that! Get up then and down then.

1937. That's the way to give it 'em.

1938. Wallop!

1939. Everybody's doing it.

And so one could go on, if it were not tedious; but I need hardly urge that these texts have absolutely no literary value. There are occasional references to the miserable puns and rather coarse jokes of the entertainment, and in its early days Punch is said to have sworn dreadfully; but the words are nothing. The dialogue was certainly not always intelligible through the swazzle, and the play does not depend in any way upon its verbal wit. It is the characters and their actions that give life to the performance, and it is by examining the characters one by one that we can best sense the development and the spirit of the extraordinary drama in which they play their parts.

The Characters of the Drama

There are eleven basic human characters and three animals in the Punch street drama; the complete set of fourteen figures are, however, never all found together in one show. In addition there are some dozen or more characters who make a fleeting appearance in only one or two allusions. The largest cast recorded was sixteen in 1828, the smallest seven in 1895; many humble shows, which never got into print, no doubt managed—and still do to-day—with even less.

Judy. Punch's wife changed her name from Joan to Judy at about the same time that she changed from a marionette to a glove puppet. The last use of Joan that I have noted and the first of Judy, are in 1818.[13] It is not at all easy to understand why there was any change at all; she is clearly the same person. Perhaps the name became familiarized and corrupted: in 1790 Jobson was referring to her as "Joaney"; spoken through the swazzle this must have sounded very like "Judy." Joan was the most popular girls' Christian name among the lower orders during the sixteenth and seventeenth centuries, and was used almost as a synonym for a domestic; so it was right and proper that Punchinello should take to himself an English Joan as his wife. Perhaps there was some verbal descent from a Dame Gigone, the companion of Polichinelle, but that lady was noted for her prolific fertility rather than for her tongue, and there are no other points of resemblance.[14] A "Judy" in the nineteenth century was a slang term for a tramp's woman, and this connotation may well have seemed appropriate to the early-nineteenth-century street shows.

Collier's Judy was still a shrew, like the eighteenth-century Joan. When Punch praised her beauty (she was, of course, as facially distorted as he was) and asked for a kiss she slapped his face: "Take that then: how do you like my kisses? Will you have another?" In later texts it was usually Punch who struck the first blow, and the whole character of Judy became lost. There is now no rhyme or reason in Punch's treatment of his wife, but at one time he must have expressed the subconscious desires of many suffering husbands in his audience.

Judy traditionally wears a Georgian mob-cap. Normally she is the only woman in the play, and showmen did not think it necessary to talk in a falsetto voice for her; she usually speaks nowadays like a pantomime dame. Her rôle in the drama is to dance and squabble with Punch at the beginning, to bring him the Baby, to return with fury after its disappearance, and to fall the first victim to Punch's stick.

Ghost of Judy. Judy usually returned as a ghost to haunt Punch. She was doing this as early as 1823, and there is a suggestion that this business was current in the eighteenth-century marionette shows.[15] With the exception of Collier's text, the Ghost appears in every nineteenth-century version that I have seen, but she began to be discarded during this century, and is now rarely introduced.

The Baby. There are occasional references to Punch's children in the eighteenth century, but the well-known business with the Baby seems to be a nineteenth-century addition—though a very obvious one as soon as the glove puppets found that they could nurse and fondle a baby satisfactorily. Punch, of course, is left with the Baby, who cries, and when he can't quieten it he throws it out of the window. I don't know of any 'origin' for this business, and I imagine it probably started accidentally one day when Punch did drop the Baby, and got a big laugh. This atrocious act brings to the surface the momentary emotions of *every* parent of a howling baby! These three characters—Punch, Judy, and the Baby—are unchanged and unchangeable in every version of the drama.

Doctor. A doctor appears in twelve out of fourteen versions that I have analysed. Sometimes he comes to Punch's assistance after a fall from a horse, sometimes after his fright from the Ghost. There are various traditional funny lines and bits of business while he prods the body for bruises and feels his pulse; Punch usually pretends he is dead—and says so! Eventually the Doctor always decides that Punch is shamming and produces his physic—a stick; sometimes the physic is called a stick of liquorice. In the end Punch always gives the Doctor a dose of his own medicine.

It would be nice to trace a 'descent' from the Doctor in the mummers' play,[16] but there is no suggestion of bringing anybody to life again. Alternatively we can look to the *dottore* of the Italian Comedy—but he was a doctor of law. We should rather regard the Doctor as a typical stock character of the English scene, a not unnatural choice as a new figure to be introduced into the Punch shows of the streets as their popularity began to demand an increased cast.

Nigger. There has almost always been a black man in the Punch drama. From 1825 to 1939 he appears in eleven out of fourteen versions. In the early years he was a Negro servant—a figure then still familiar in English society—who was sent by his master to tell Punch to stop ringing a bell. There was a lot of funny business with Punch pretending that it was an organ or a fiddle or a drum or a trumpet, and forcing the unfortunate domestic to agree with him.

Sometimes the black man was a foreigner, usually with a bristling beard, who could utter only one word—"Shallaballa." In the fifties the popularity of the nigger minstrels transformed the black man into a "Jim Crow"—from the title of a popular song first sung in London by Thomas Rice in 1836; and Jim Crow he has remained until the present day, though he is no longer seen as frequently as he once was.

Beadle. This is an essential character. Sometimes he is a beadle, sometimes a charley, sometimes a constable, and sometimes a policeman, but there must always be some officer of the law to come and arrest Punch, and often there are several of them in succession. A beadle was an official of the parish with multifarious duties—which were sometimes recited at length—and some authority for the punishment of minor local misdemeanours; he had appeared in the eighteenth-century marionette plays. As Punch's murders multiplied the presence of the Beadle became essential.

Hangman. Eventually Punch is captured and taken to be hanged. Often there is a last dying speech, dictated by the Hangman, with Punch getting the words all wrong—

> HANGMAN. I have been a very bad and wicked man.
> PUNCH. I want a slice of bread and jam.

and so on—the identical business of the morality *Like Will to Like*! Then Punch pretends that he can't understand how to put his head into the noose of the gallows, and the Hangman demonstrates how to do it, and Punch pulls the noose tight and hangs the Hangman. It is an enchanting and evergreen bit of business, and I wish I knew where it originated. It is certain, however, that Punch had long been familiar with the gallows. We need not rely on the occasions when the Vice was led off to be hanged, for we have a description of a genuine bit of puppet business from the mid-eighteenth century: in the popular play *Jane Shore* Robert Southey has recalled that

> the beadle in this piece, after proclaiming in obvious and opprobrious rhyme the offence which had drawn upon Mistress Shore this public punishment, prohibited all persons from relieving her on pain of death, and turned her out, according to the common story, to die of hunger in the streets. The only person who ventured to disobey this prohibition was Punch the Baker; and the reader may judge of the dialogue of these pieces by this Baker's words, when he stole behind her, and nudging her furtively, while he spake, offered her a loaf, saying, "Tak it, Jenny, tak it!" for which act so little consonant with his general character, Punch died a martyr to humanity by the hangman's hands.[17]

As late as 1824 a description of the show tells us that Punch *was* hung by the Hangman, and I suggest that we may not be very far from the truth if we believe that the hanging of Punch was an occasional alternative ending to the marionette plays of the seventeenth and eighteenth centuries, and that the stroke of genius which placed the Hangman in the noose was introduced into the show at the beginning of the nineteenth century, at the time that the figures became glove puppets and Joan became Judy.

The Hangman was usually called Jack Ketch, after a real public executioner, but after the eighties he sometimes changed his name, with the times, to Mister Marwood. He is an essential character in every version of the play, though sometimes—on grounds of economy—the Policeman or the Beadle will undertake his duties. The Hangman took his place very easily in the show in a city where public hangings attracted vast crowds all night before an execution, and where the last dying speeches of executed criminals were hawked everywhere upon the pavements.

The Devil. As we have seen, there have been devils in English puppet shows ever since the seventeenth century, and the business of the Devil carrying Punch off to hell was the traditional finale of the eighteenth-century marionette plays. But even in the eighteenth century there seems to have been a feeling that Punch should remain master of the field to the last, and some showmen allowed him to conquer the Devil, for no less an observer than Dr Johnson remarked in 1765 that "in rustic puppet plays I have seen the Devil very lustily belaboured by Punch" and "in modern puppet shows, which seem to be copied from the old farces, Punch sometimes fights the devil and always overcomes him."[18] Popham supports this unexpected testimony with another racy description:

> But now there interrupts the scene one fitted for vengeance. See, the instrument of punishment, the Devil, stands forth, horrid in shape, deformed, monstrous and black. Nearer he approaches with tremendous shrieks, and as he stretches out his muscular arms the battle begins. The Hero [Punch] wages his more than human struggle with unequal strength; the fierce din of their contest is heard by his wife, a woman worthy of her husband in every feature. . . . She promptly joins his side, for (wonderfully) she loves him. The enemy is attacked with nails, hands and feet; he rushes at each adversary in turn, as from either side they belabour him with alternate blows. Suddenly, however, he flees from this double embrace and, thinly shrieking, vanishes in the air.[19]

At the time of his change from marionette to glove puppet Punch's victory seems to have become generally accepted, but the medieval and eighteenth-century tradition took some time to die, and there are several references to show that during the eighteen-twenties Punch was still often borne away to the infernal regions by his ancient horned adversary. Payne Collier recalled "a showman, on one occasion, not merely receiving little or no money, but getting lamentably pelted with mud, because, from some scruple or other, he refused to allow the victory over the Devil to

Punch," and as late as 1922 Maurice Baring reported seeing a show in Tottenham Court Road in which "Punch . . . finally met with the doom of Doctor Faustus. Terrified, he went into the night, crying out the Cockney equivalent for *O lente, lente, currite, noctis equi.*"[20]

These were exceptional cases, and the normal ending, as noted by Collier and almost every other observer, was for Punch to conquer even the Devil; sometimes he hung him on the gallows. Orthodoxy and justice may have demanded that Punch should suffer for his crimes, but those who know and love him will feel that Punch is, somehow, immortal, and that even the Prince of Darkness cannot touch him. In this reversal of the accepted tradition Punch has shown himself to be something more than a quaint relic of the medieval drama: he has established his authority as an original creative personality.

As the Regency gave way to the morality of the Victorian Age this relic of medieval buffoonery was looked at askance. Some folks, lamented Mayhew's showman, "won't have no ghost, no coffin, and no devil; and that's what I call spiling the preformance entirely. . . . It's the march of hintellect wot's a doing all this, it is, sir." When the Devil did appear he was sometimes disguised as Spring-heeled Jack (a notorious highwayman) or (at the time of the Crimean War) the Russian Bear; sometimes his battle with Punch was omitted, and he carried off the body of the Hangman in mistake for Punch's; eventually he almost disappeared from the show, and after the eighteen-fifties the performance usually ended with some funny business with the Hangman's coffin. In the absence of the Devil there is no very obvious place at which to end the play, and not the least useful feature of his introduction was that his combat with Punch, whichever was the victor, provided a logical culmination to the drama. In the nineties Professor Jesson gave it as his opinion that the Devil was then never represented because "it was apt to harrow the feelings of the little ones and give them bad dreams." Parents who paid the bill at children's parties and clergymen who commissioned performances for Sunday Schools no doubt objected to his irreverent intrusion, and his appearances in the show are to-day very rare indeed, but it would be a pity for the Devil to be banished for ever from a drama that he has graced for so many centuries.

Clown. Punch always has a merry companion; he may be Scaramouch or Clown or Joey or Mr Merryman, but one or the other is an essential member of the cast. Scaramouch in 1828 had his head knocked clean off his shoulders, but in later versions the Clown has usually been Joey—after Joey Grimaldi—and it is a tradition that he alone of Punch's adversaries does not get killed. He usually helps Punch dispose of the Hangman's corpse, and in the last half-century a very effective bit of business has been built up with Clown confusing Punch while he is counting the number of dead bodies by continually inserting himself, or taking one away.

Toby. In the print of a Punch street show in 1795, which we have already noticed, a couple of performing dogs, with a monkey, are seen taking part in the entertainment; and in 1826 a writer complained that "apes and dressed up dogs" were being added to the Punch and Judy show. Probably these animals were originally quite separate turns on the pavement, but one day a showman trained his dog to perform with the puppets in the booth, and this soon became incorporated as a very popular feature of the show. There was no novelty in having dogs and other animals to act with the puppets, and—as we have seen—they made several such appearances in the marionette plays of the eighteenth century.

The dog in Piccini's show was a puppet, but a live Toby had been recorded in the twenties; the showman whom Mayhew interviewed claimed to remember the first introduction of a live dog into the play, though the idea was perhaps older than he imagined. "And a great hit it were," he said; "it made a grand alteration in the hexibition, for now the performance is called Punch and Toby *as well.* There is one Punch about the streets at present that tries it on with three dogs, but that ain't much of a go—too much of a good thing I calls it."

I do not know why the dog was called Toby; but the Tobit's Dog was an inn-sign of the time (named after the story in the Apocrypha), and this may have led to a very natural corruption; it is an easy name to speak through the squeaker (like Judy), and Toby he has remained to this day. His function is to sit on the playboard, with a ruff round his neck, and to bite Punch's nose on the right cues; sometimes he was trained to 'smoke' a pipe. For a century Toby was considered essential to a Punch and Judy show, but in recent years many showmen have dispensed with him; the R.S.P.C.A. inspectors, I have been told, used to "make a nuisance of themselves," and it wasn't worth all the bother. No doubt some dog Tobys went through rough times, like their masters. A live dog has a wonderful sales appeal for the British public, but from the strictly dramatic point of view his introduction tends to slow down the speed and to limit the gusto that a good Punch show should always possess.

Mr Jones. When there is a Toby he usually has a master. In 1828 this was Scaramouch, but by 1854 "a respectable tradesman" named Mr Jones had appeared, and a dispute with Punch over the ownership of the dog is featured in four of the versions I have examined. This contains some of the best verbal lines of the play:

JONES. I lost the dog three weeks ago to-day.
PUNCH. I found the dog three weeks ago to-day.
JONES. That shows the dog is mine.
PUNCH. No, that shows the dog is mine.
JONES. How can the dog be yours, when I lost it?
PUNCH. How can the dog be yours, when I found it?
JONES. You found the dog before it was lost.
PUNCH. You lost it before it was found.

This exchange, from Smith's text of 1926, is a pleasant foretaste of ITMA.

Hector. A horse named Hector is occasionally introduced into the show. Men on hobby-horses used to parade outside the fairground puppet booths, so the idea was a familiar one. Hector appears in only four out of our fourteen versions, but he was known as early as 1825; he seems to have been discarded quite soon afterwards. His only function is to enable Punch to gallop round the stage and get thrown off. Occasionally he seems to have been replaced by a donkey.

Crocodile. A dragon, and later a crocodile, made its appearance in the show in the sixties, and took over the business formerly associated with the Devil. It usually appears towards the end of the play, and Punch's battle with it is a very exciting affair, though Punch always wins in the end. A reptilian glove puppet can roll his body and snap his jaws in a most effective manner; it is a terrible moment when the Crocodile swallows Punch's stick. All the twentieth-century versions include the Crocodile, and purists should regard it as the Devil in disguise.

These, then, are the fourteen basic characters. It would be impossible to list every additional character that has ever appeared in a Punch and Judy Show: every contemporary event introduces a new hero or a new villain, and the list stretches from Nelson to Winston Churchill, from Paul Pry to Hitler. Punch's eighteenth-century notoriety for amorous by-play was supported for some years early in the nineteenth century by a girl called Polly; she figures as a mute object of adoration in Collier's text, and in the same year people in Scotland were referring to puppet shows as "Punch and Polly";[21] but nothing is heard of her after this. There was sometimes a Neighbour or a Publican to complain at Punch's bell-ringing, instead of the Negro servant. A pair of Undertakers occasionally stuffed the Hangman's body into his coffin; we have references to a Judge, an Irishman, a Blind Man, and a Sailor. There have also sometimes been introduced into the show variety turns with no connexion whatever with the play: Piccini had a Courtier or a "Nobody"[22] who could take his hat off with his hand and whose neck stretched up to the top of the stage; jugglers occasionally presented a turn, and in the fifties we first hear of the boxers, who can still sometimes be seen in shows to-day. The boxers' act is a very good one when well performed, but it must inevitably interrupt the course of the play, and in the main Punch and Judy showmen have wisely avoided introducing extraneous material into the breathless and incoherent progress of their little drama.

Punch. Of the central character, the hero of the drama, there remains little that can usefully be added. The magic of his popularity lies in the gay abandon of his character, in the piercing chuckles with which he wields his stick, in the mock contrition of his repentance. Why do we laugh? We do not know. This is a mystery of the human soul. Perhaps the spectacle of his fierce assaults releases from our inner consciousness aggressive primitive hidden repressions; and the devils issue out of our lips in gales of laughter. Certain it is that Punch fulfils some deep-seated instinct of human nature, that his little drama has always acted as a cathartic agent upon society. The man who laughs at Punch beating Judy is all the less likely to beat his own wife, and the child who laughs at Punch killing the constable is all the less likely to trouble the policeman round the corner.

The Professors

The Punch and Judy men did not issue playbills, they never advertised in the papers, and the story of their lives, and even most of their names, are lost to us for ever. They belong to that great army of beloved vagabonds stretching from the mimes beside the Ionian Sea to the pierrots upon the sands of the English Channel, whose only memorial is the laughter of children and the memories of the aged. A rare personal reminiscence is all that we can trace to-day of these showmen of the streets.

Piccini, the Italian performer who 'sat' for George Cruikshank, seems to have been a familiar character of the London streets at the turn of the century. By 1821 his show had not been seen in the streets for many years, but he was remembered as

> a little thick-set man, with a red humorous-looking countenance. He had lost one eye, but the other made up for the loss of its fellow by a shrewdness of expression sufficient for both. He always wore an oilskin hat, and a rough

green coat. At his back he carried a deal box, containing the *dramatis personæ* of his little theatre; and in his hand, the trumpet, at whose glad summons hundreds of merry, laughter-loving faces flocked around him, with gaping mouths and anxious looks, all eager to renew their acquaintance with their old friend and favourite, Punch. The theatre itself was carried by a tall man, who seemed a sort of sleeping partner in the concern, or mere dumb-waiter on the other's operations.

In 1827, when Cruikshank's *Punch and Judy* was being drawn, Piccini was already eighty-two years old, and lived at the King's Arms, a low public house off Drury Lane, where he gave a command performance for the author and illustrator. Collier recalled the interview as a very droll one:

> I never had a more amusing morning, for Piccini himself was a strange character; the dirt, darkness and uncouthness of his abode, together with the forbiddingness of the appearance of Mrs P., I shall never forget. She was an Irishwoman, and he an Italian, and the jumble of language in their discourse was in itself highly entertaining.

A few years later Piccini sold his theatre and figures for thirty-five shillings to the anonymous Punch man interviewed by Mayhew. His successor recalled that

> every one in London knowed him; lords, dukes, princes, squires and wagabonds—all used to stop to laugh at his performance, and a funny old fellow he was . . . he always carried a rum-bottle in his pocket, and drinked out of this unbeknown behind the baize afore he went into the frame, so that it should lay in his power to give the audience a most excellent performance. . . . I've heard tell he used to take very often as much as £10 a day . . . and he used to sit down to his fowls and wine, and the very best of luxuriousness, like the first nobleman in the world. . . . At last he reduced himself to want, and died in the workhouse. . . . He was past performing when I bought my show of him, and werry poor. . . . He had spent all he had got in drink, and in treating friends. . . . Ah, poor fellow! he oughtn't to have been allowed to die where he did, after amusing the public for so many years.

Piccini died in St Giles's Workhouse in 1835.[23] Thanks to the genius of Cruikshank and the industry of Mayhew, he has acquired a posthumous fame granted to few puppet showmen.

Piccini's apprentice was a man called Pike. Mayhew was told that "he is handed down as a most clever exhibitor of Punch. . . . He exhibited the performance for many years . . . the most noted showman as ever was. . . . He was the first inventor of the live dog called Toby, and a great invention it was." Pike's booth and vigorously carved figures were used as models by Benjamin Robert Haydon in 1828 for his painting called "Punch or May Day," which is now in the Tate Gallery. With this oil-painting Punch's iconography grows again, to be constantly increased during the next fifty years with a succession of *genre* paintings and prints, but the character and spirit given to his effigy by Rowlandson, Cruikshank, and Haydon were never equalled by the artists who followed

DETAIL FROM "PUNCH" BY BENJAMIN ROBERT HAYDON, 1828

The inscription above the stage opening reads "Pike. Original Punchinello."

Reproduced by courtesy of the Trustees of the Tate Gallery, London

them.[24] Pike was a showman of many parts; he exhibited at Bartholomew Fair between 1812 and 1831 with conjuring, rope-dancing, and tumbling, and travelled the country with a portable fit-up; but in the end, like his master, he too "at last came to decay, and died in the workhouse . . . their names is handed down to posterity among the noblemen and footmen of the land."

The showman whose cockney idiom and philosophy Mayhew has so faithfully preserved was originally a footman in a gentleman's family;

he had heard of the good money to be made by showing Punch from a friend in the business, but for a long time he felt it beneath his dignity to descend to performing in the streets. But after his master had gone abroad he was out of a position for five months, and at last he began to think "that the Punch-and-Judy business was better than starving after all," and in 1825 he enrolled himself as an apprentice-partner to a Punch showman.

> He was to give me twelve shillings a week and my keep for two years certain, till I could get my own show things together, and for that I was to carry the show, and go round and collect.... I used to stand outside and patter to the figures. My dignity was hurt at being hobligated to take to the streets for a living. At first I fought shy, and used to feel queer somehow, you don't know how like, whenever the people used to look at me. I remember werry well the first street as ever I performed in. It was off Gray's Inn, one of them quiet, genteel streets, and when the mob began to gather round I felt all-overish, and I turned my head to the frame instead of the people. We hadn't had no rehearsals aforehand, and I did the patter quite permiscuous. There was not much talk, to be sure, required then; and what little there was, consisted merely in calling out the names of the figures as they came up, and these my master prompted me with from inside the frame. But little as there was for me to do, I know I never could have done it, if it hadn't been for the spirits—the false spirits you see (a little drop of gin), as my master got me in the morning. The first time as ever I made my appearance in public, I collected as much as eight shillings, and my master said, after the performance was over, "You'll do!" You see I was partly in livery, and looked a little bit decent like.

At the end of two years he had saved enough money to buy Piccini's old outfit.

> I bought it cheap, you see, for it was thrown on one side, and was of no use to any one but such as myself. . . . When I made my first appearance as a regular performer of Punch on my own account, I did feel uncommon nervous, to be sure . . . it was as much as hever I could do to get the words out, and keep the figures from shaking. When I struck up the first song, my voice trembled so as I thought I never should be able to get to the hend of the first hact. I soon, however, got over that there, and at present I'd play before the whole bench of bishops as cool as a cowcumber.
>
> It's a pretty play Punch is, when preformed well, and one of the greatest novelties in the world; and most ancient; handed down, too, for many hundred years. . . . You can pick out a good many Punch preformers, without getting one so well versed as I am in it; they in general makes such a muffing concern of it.

We could linger long with the rambling memories of this old troubadour of the streets; his story should be read in its entirety. As we pass into the last half of the nineteenth century we find the first traces of the families who have provided generations of Punch showmen right down to the present day—the Codmans, the Staddons, the Smiths, the Davises, the Jessons; but to trace the genealogies of the Punch men of the twentieth century is a task beyond the scope of this volume—a quest that deserves a volume to itself. Here we must only select an anecdote here and there to highlight the characters of our story—the showmen who at about this time, the seventies and eighties of the nineteenth century, began to describe themselves as "professors" of Punch and Judy.[25]

The art of Punch and Judy, with the secrets of its presentation,was for the most part handed down from father to son among a very few families, drawn from the small-part players of the circus and the music-hall, nigger minstrels, seaside pierrots, and street buskers; there is an old tradition that there has never been a Jew in the business. Paul Herring, the famous clown, is said to have been an excellent Punch and Judy performer, but only rarely has an actor from the legitimate stage sunk as low as Punch; yet the performance of the show demands dramatic ability of a high order, a strong and adaptable voice, an ability to gag in the true Commedia dell' Arte tradition, perfect timing of minute finger movements, and considerable physical toughness, for the strain of holding one's arms above one's head for half an hour and of throwing one's body about during the fights is most exhausting. No actor need feel ashamed of interpreting Punch's immortal drama.

It was not all quaint gambols on the village green. There was, for instance, old Jim Body, of whom a gipsy who used to nobble for him told this story:[26]

> Old Jim was shy about it, like; he couldn't do it reglar, and as soon as he got a few shilluns he had to go and spend it on beer in the pub. And then we did have a time of it! When he was boozed he used to start swearin' if he couldn't git the dolls up quick enough. He used to swear something 'orrible —and all the people outside could hear him. I used to have to bang the curtains and say, "Ere you shut up—we can hear everything you're saying inside." And then he used to start banging about and nearly knock the show over. It used to rock about, and there was me 'olding on to it and 'im inside a-cussing 'orrible, shouting out that the dashed dolls wouldn't keep still, and talking to 'em, and telling 'em to keep still as if they was alive. And when he was like that he used to make Punch hit the dog too hard, and then Toby would up and bite his hand what was inside the Punch, and Jim would

git that mad, I've seen him slosh the Toby right out of the show among the crowd. Cor, we did 'ave a time of it.

And so the line runs out in poverty and drunkenness, but somehow always shining through there is the spirit of showmanship and the gusto of Punch; these bedraggled professors of the pavement, with their aspirated dialogue and tawdry fit-up, shaped and preserved something greater than themselves, something more ancient and profound than they knew. The story is told of Professor Davis, who trained his Toby to hide in a sack as soon as he called "Guard," and thus avoided paying fares for him on the railways, that his second son at first refused to work Punch, but when the old man was dying he sent for his son, and there and then insisted on his learning the business before his eyes as he lay on his deathbed. This son was working the Leicester Square pitch in 1940.

And in the end the public turned to the last representatives of this old school of showmen with gratitude and sympathy. When Professor Codman needed a new booth for his site outside Lime Street Station at Liverpool, where Punch had been shown since at least the seventies, the local society of artists, the Sandon Studios Society, clubbed together to make one for him, which was solemnly unveiled at a civic ceremony in 1923. When Professor Hayes, said to be the oldest Punch and Judy performer in the country, died at Folkestone in 1931 a seat given in his memory was placed on the Leas, near the spot where he had performed; it bears the inscription:

Of simple piety he hitched his Waggon to a star.

We have some idea of the earnings made by Punch showmen. The ten pounds a day that Piccini is said to have earned is probably a legend, but in 1828 Payne Collier estimated that two to four shillings was often collected at each performance, and with ten performances on a summer's day this worked out at the quite satisfactory figure of thirty shillings a day to be shared between the two partners in the show. We have seen how Mayhew's Punch man took up eight shillings at his first collection, and he says that when he started on his own in 1830 his takings were regularly over a pound a day, and he averaged five pounds a week all through the year. At this time he had his wife to collect for him, and without any necessity to split his takings this was quite good money for those days: "You can see Punch has been good work—a money-making business—and beat all mechanics right out." For a private performance in a gentleman's house he never had less than one pound, and for an "order"—that is, a special performance on the street outside a gentleman's windows—he would be given at least half a crown. But during the next twenty years business declined terribly, and in the eighteen-fifties his collections often amounted to only a few coppers, and he was lucky

"The Punch and Judy Show," by Frederick Barnard, 1887

Reproduced by permission of the Proprietors of "Punch"

if he collected five shillings all day: "the business gets slacker and slacker every season . . . people ain't getting tired with our performances, but they're stingier; everybody looks twice at their money now afore they parts with it." With a weekly income of twelve and six this old Punch-man could indeed look forward to nothing but the workhouse at the end of his days.

A pleasant feature of the economics of Punch and Judy is the co-operative partnership between the performer and the collector. "It's the common practice," Mayhew was told,

> for the man what performs Punch to share with the one wot plays the drum and pipes—each has half wot is collected; but if the pardner can't play the drum and pipes, and only carries the frame, and collects, then his share is but a third of what is taken till he learns how to perform himself.

The performer must trust the collector; there is an old joke that the only 'bottler' you can trust is a one-armed man, the box hanging round his neck, and five flies in his only hand, liable to instant dismissal if one of the flies is dead after the show! Occasionally a 'bottler' will bring round a locked collecting-box, but it has been well said that "where there's no trust there's no business," and Sidney de Hempsey in his lively book of memoirs proudly recalls that he has always used an open bag, trusted his collector completely, and never had cause to regret it. The manner and personality of the 'bottler' is, indeed, a factor of prime importance when the hat goes round.

Happily the decay of Punch was arrested in the second half of the nineteenth century. In 1887 Professor Mowbray estimated his earnings at about three pounds a week, and in 1897 Professor Jesson claimed that the revival dated from about thirty years previously. "People then began to write about the show," he said, "and that led to its becoming more popular, and being taken up by the rich; and its popularity grows year by year." But, as we have seen, people had been writing about Punch for a long time before the sixties, and a more probable reason is a social one: the garden-parties, the receptions, and the children's parties of Victorian Society could all make use of a modest, light-hearted entertainment, and from this time on the party engagements of the Punch and Judy man became more and more important, and the street shows increasingly occupied a secondary place.

Some of the street shows, indeed, were in very low water in the early decades of the twentieth century, and sometimes little more than an excuse for begging. One old showman actually never bothered to perform at all, but used to put his frame up with a puppet in position, and then sit outside with a cap, waiting for pennies. This melancholy picture might have been the end of our long story, but—as so often before—Punch has risen like a phœnix from the brink of disappearance and decay.

Punch by Night, 1898

There are a few calculations of the numbers of Punch and Judy performers to be gleaned from our records. In 1856 Mayhew's informant estimated that there were sixteen Punch frames in the country—eight in London and eight in the country.

> We are all acquainted with one another; are all sociable together, and know where each other is, and what they are doing on. When one comes home, another goes out; that's the way we proceed through life. . . . The principal part of the showmen are to be found about Lisson Grove. In this neighbourhood there is a house of call, where they all assembles in the evening.

In 1887 there was little significant change, and Mowbray thought that there were only about "fifteen of us left"; in 1904 Professor Davis estimated that six Punch men were then earning their living in London.[27] Perhaps there never were more than ten performers at any one time playing the London streets. In such few hands there rested the destiny of Punch; but they did not fail him.

The Production of the Drama

The glove puppet is essentially an actor's medium; the speech and the movements of the hands are a direct projection of the performer's dramatic sense, and the show stands or falls by the personality of the man inside. There is little scope for scenic elaboration. The booth consists of a simple frame of four vertical poles, providing enough room for one man to stand; the stage opening will come just above his head, and a shelf will run along the bottom edge of it—called the play-board; inside there will be a row of pegs from which the puppets can hang, another shelf for properties. The performer sometimes stood on the ground, but it helped the sight-lines of a standing audience if he was slightly raised on a footboard.

In the earlier years the frame was usually covered with a pleasantly patterned blue-check cover; often with a green baize beneath. In the latter part of the nineteenth century the declining standards of Victorian taste were reflected in the Punch and Judy show with heavy velvet curtains and draped tassels; the Punch booth of the end of the century was, indeed, one of the more unpleasant examples of tawdry Victoriana. In recent years there has been a welcome return to gaily striped red-and-yellow designs.

The proscenium opening was sometimes painted on a wooden surround. Piccini had the Prince of Wales's feathers painted above his booth

—no doubt he considered the Prince Regent a suitable patron—and from quite early in the century the tradition grew up of inscribing the royal coat of arms above the show: "we can have them up when we like, cos we are sanctioned, and I've played afore the rile princes," Mayhew was told. There was probably some old tradition of Charles II's patronage for puppets handed down by oral tradition among the puppet showmen, and, indeed, a garbled version of this is still handed out to-day by one of our traditional Punch showmen to inquiring journalists in exchange for a pint at the local pub; but the frequently printed story of the ancestor who was granted a licence by Charles II to perform on the beaches of England need not be taken seriously. In this century many Punch performers have been privileged to play before members of the royal family, and the show is still often proudly entitled the Royal Punch and Judy. The name of the show was sometimes lettered on the proscenium arch, too. We find "Pike's Original Punchinello" and "The Dominion of Fancy, or Punch's Opera." There is a very old tradition that Punch's show was called an opera, which persisted from the Restoration to the middle of the nineteenth century.[28]

The scenery was very simple. Piccini used a formal garden scene as his background, which rolled up towards the end of the play to show a prison with cut-out windows revealing Punch behind the bars. After the middle of the century the change of scene seems to have been dispensed with, and the play is always now played straight through in one set. This usually now represents a street scene, with a preference for half-timbered Elizabethan houses in the background. Wings are sometimes fitted, and Mayhew was told that they were convenient for exits, but most performers would regard them as rather a nuisance, and it is a well-established tradition that the characters can enter out of the floor.

The size of a glove puppet is largely controlled by the size of the human hand, and little variation is possible; about twelve inches should normally be seen above the playboard. Punch is usually provided with legs, which he swings over the playboard when he wants to sit down, and they are often made so that the operator can slip two fingers inside them and move them about; this is how Punch kicks the Doctor in the eye when he is being examined. The Hangman too, who has to be shown full-length swinging from the gibbet, will usually have dummy legs, but for the rest only a wooden face and arms are required, with a dress fitted over a hollow cloth body. The accepted English tradition of manipulation is for the first finger to be placed in the puppet's neck, and the second finger and thumb in its arms. Other systems, such as the Catalan, with three middle fingers in the shoulder-piece, or the French, with three outside fingers in the armpiece, enable the puppet to 'bulk' larger on the hand, but the English method best permits the firm handling of little properties, such as the stick, which play such an important part in the show.[29]

In general, some of the old figures were carved from ash, which is a good wood for carving, but very heavy. The strain of holding heavy figures above one's head throughout a performance is very considerable, and everything must be done to reduce their weight; willow is sometimes recommended as a strong light wood. A few performers use *papier-mâché* heads, but, though this is very light, it is not really strong enough for the hard knocks it must receive.

Payne Collier claimed that Piccini's puppets were "much better carved, the features having a more marked and comic expression, than those of his rivals. He brought most of them over with him from Italy, and he complains that in England he has not been able to find any workman capable" of replacing a lost or broken figure. Mayhew, however, was told that

> there was at that time, and is now, a real carver for the Punch business. He was dear, but werry good and hexcellent. His Punch's head was the best as I ever seed. The nose and chin used to meet quite close together. A set of new figures, dressed and all, would come to about fifteen pounds. Each head costs five shillings for the bare carving alone, and every figure that we has takes at least a yard of cloth to dress him, besides ornaments and things that comes werry expensive.

Most Punch men have probably made their own puppets, but there have always been carvers to the profession. Mr A. Quisto, who, I believe, is still at work, has been supplying Punches and ventriloquists' dolls since about 1900, and in 1943 I bought a set of *papier-mâché* heads from Professor Bourne, who has been making them to the same design since 1895. The advertisement columns of *The World's Fair*, that fascinating weekly paper for showmen, sometimes carry advertisements of Punch and Judy shows, a recent one offering a complete set of nine new dressed puppets, with props., for £12 10*s*. 0*d*. This is less than the price asked a hundred years ago.

Whether Piccini's puppets came from Italy or not, there is no doubt that the carving of the figures used by most of the old showmen in recent years represents a sad decline from the vigorous effigies represented by Cruikshank and Haydon. Yet, however dirty, tawdry, and uncouth some of these puppets may have become in their decadence, they still hold the seed of Punch's grotesque and lovable character within them, and the characters of the Punch and Judy show must take their place alongside the figureheads of ships and the flamboyant horses of fairground roundabouts in the gallery of English popular art.

By the sixties instructions on how to make a Punch and Judy show at home were beginning to appear in boys' books, and in 1879 Hamley's were offering sets of figures at their famous toy-shop at prices ranging from fifteen shillings to five guineas a set. Home performances of Punch have continued ever since, and there has always been a steady trade in the necessary figures and apparatus.

In the time of Piccini the show was announced by sounding a trumpet, as it had been for many centuries before; but early in the nineteenth century a new instrument was introduced to accompany the drum outside the show. This was the panpipes, an arrangement of half a dozen or so pipes of varying lengths bound by a stock round the musician's neck in such a way that he could produce a rudimentary musical noise by turning his head to and fro and blowing down their openings. At the same time he kept both hands free for beating the drum suspended from his shoulders. This archaic music, the flute-like call of the panpipes mingling with the heavy beating of the drum, became inseparably linked with the Punch and Judy show in the memories of Victorian Londoners.

The "pardner," who played the drum and pipes before the show, carried the frame from pitch to pitch, and took up the collection, also filled the ancient role of "interpreter." By tradition he wore a white top hat, and he had to engage Punch in conversation during the show, and generally "interpret" the action in the manner described to Mayhew that has already been quoted. In another description of 1827 we learn that the interpreter, looking down into the booth and pretending to watch Punch dressing inside, would ask him why he put on his waistcoat before his shirt, to be told that it was because he had no shirt. The text of 1854 is particularly valuable for the dialogue between Punch and the showman that it provides:

PROPRIETOR. Mr Punch, you are in prison!
PUNCH. What for?
PROPRIETOR. For having broken the laws of your country.
PUNCH. Why, I never touched 'em.

And a great deal more rubbish in the same strain. But what memories of *Bartholomew Fair*!

Although a collector is often still needed in Punch and Judy shows to-day, the drum and pipes, the white top hat, and the repartee with the puppets have almost all disappeared in the twentieth century. They are, perhaps, incidentals to the show, unnecessary in the polite air of drawing-rooms and children's parties; but with the last showman who called up "I never know'd as 'ow you was married, Mister Punch," we may hear the whisper across the centuries of Hamlet's bitter jest, "I could interpret between you and your love, if I could see the puppets dallying."

Punch's voice, whose shrill tones had provoked so many comparisons with the *castrati* at the opera a century earlier, continued to rend the air in the theatres of the street; but it was now, quite certainly, reserved for Punch alone. "Our speaking instrument," Mayhew was told,

> is an unknown secret, cos it's an 'unknown tongue,' that's known to none except those in our profession. It's a hinstrument, like this which I has in my hand, and it's tuned to music. We has two or three kinds, one for out-doors, one for in-doors, one for speaking, one for singing, and one that's good for nothing, except selling on the cheap. They ain't whistles, but 'calls' or 'unknown tongues'; and with them in the mouth we can pronounce each word as plain as a parson.

Mayhew describes the call as "a small flat instrument, made of two curved pieces of metal about the size of a knee-buckle, bound together with black thread. Between these was a plate of some substance (apparently silk), which he said was a secret."

In 1866 Frank Bellew was, I think, the first writer to expose the full secret of the "swazzle" and to give exact instructions in print on how to make it. He complained that "it was not until after two years' hunting and inquiry, and the employment of agents to hunt up performers of Punch and Judy, that we discovered an expert who, for a handsome fee, explained the matter." The instrument he described, however, was made of wood, like Powell's. This is not the usual material, and most performers recommend pewter or silver: one old showman used to beat out two half-crowns for the purpose. A few years later Professor Hoffmann described the swazzle as made of tin, but this is poisonous, and—perhaps fortunately—the professor admitted that his attempts to talk through it had not been very successful, and recommended his young readers to rely on their natural voices. The substance placed between the two elliptical pieces of metal is actually nothing more romantic than ordinary tape, which is then twisted round the outside of the instrument, and the whole tied fast with cotton. The swazzle is soaked in water, and held in the mouth between the tongue and the upper palate. Speaking through it produces the familiar shrill overtones that have rung through our history during so many centuries.

Variation in pitch can be obtained by tightening or slackening the tape; and it is important that the metal should comfortably fit into the roof of the mouth. Alternating between using the swazzle and an ordinary voice is purely a matter of practice, but most Punch men have swallowed the swazzle at one time or another, though—despite rumours to the contrary—never, I believe with serious results. The recommended treatment is plenty of plum-pudding!

Making or buying a swazzle is only the beginning of the art of using it, and of very few Punch performers to-day could it be said that they pronounce each word "as plain as a parson." Too often the sound that issues forth is a quite unintelligible gibber. To overcome the difficulty of understanding what Punch says a useful convention has grown up—though this too is as old as *Bartholomew Fair*—of another puppet, or the showman, repeating all Punch's remarks after him.

For many centuries the squeaker has been the most closely guarded of all the puppet showman's secrets; it is only within quite recent years that the mystery of the swazzle has been at all widely published, and many Punch men still refuse to discuss how they are made. Mayhew was told that the performers of a hundred years ago used to carry special dud calls, to sell to gentlemen for a sovereign each; but those days are over, and I have bought excellent swazzles from a contemporary Punch man for half a crown. The squeaker is a secret no longer, but the sense of mystery, the un-human timbre, the unearthly tone, the intrinsically 'puppet' voice, remain. We remember the squeaking puppets of eighteenth-century England, the "quaile pipe voice" of the Elizabethan motions, the French *pratique*, the Italian *pivetta*; it may be that in Punch's almost incoherent squeak we can hear the authentic tones of the antique comedy.

And so this was the drama, these were its performers, and this is how it was acted in the streets of early-nineteenth-century London. These streets swarmed with entertainers and with kerbside sellers, with colour and life and vivacity; with postmen and soldiers in scarlet coats, and rifle volunteers in green, and beadles in canary-yellow breeches, and milkmen in country smocks; with Jewish old-clo' men, gipsies selling brushes and pegs, Tyrolese peasant-girls with brooms, and Italian boys with images; with muffin-men, chimney-sweeps, lamplighters, crossing-sweepers, shoeblacks, mutes, and beggars. And as the pale spring sunlight played upon the squares of Bloomsbury and Belgravia, or the autumn fogs drifted slowly round the crescents of Kensington and Marylebone, there came down the cobbled streets the music of the barrel-organ, or the scraping of a hurdy-gurdy, or the high call of the Pandean pipes.

It might, at the beginning of the century, be a dancing bear; or stilt-walkers, or acrobats, or a sword-swallower, or a fire-eater, or a conjuror; it might be a "happy family" of little animals in a cage, or performing dogs, or a monkey on a stick; it might be a band of Ethiopian serenaders, or ballad-singers, or the whistling man; it might be a peepshow, or automatic figures, or Chinese Shades, or jigging puppets, or Fantoccini; it might be Punch and Judy.

And the children in the street would run up and follow the show for miles; the children in the houses would press their noses against the nursery window-panes, and their father would send out a servant to "order" a performance on the pavement outside; and passers-by would gather, as they still do, from nowhere, the draymen and the errand-boys crowding up, and the respectable pedestrians holding aloof, but hoping to see the show without being seen themselves.

"Ladies and gents," says the man with the drum and pipes,

> I'm now going to exhibit a preformance worthy of your notice, and far superior to anythink you hever had a hopportunity of witnessing of before. This is the original preformance of Punch, ladies and gents; and it will always gain esteem. . . . The preformance will continue for upwards of one hour—*provising as we meets with sufficient encouragement*. . . . Now, boys, look up your ha'pence! Who's got a farden or a ha'penny?

If the pennies come in well, or if the footman comes out with an order from a house, the performance will run right through all the characters and take half an hour or longer; but if the crowd produces, as it may, a total of threepence-halfpenny the drama will be brought to an abrupt conclusion—for it is capable of infinite compression or expansion—and the panpipe man will hoist the frame on his shoulders while the performer slings the flat box of puppets round his neck, and the two pardners will tramp a quarter of an hour to another and, they hope, more appreciative neighbourhood.

> We in generally walks from twelve to twenty mile every day, and carries the show, which weighs a good half-hundred, at the least. Arter great exertion, our woice werry often fails us; for speaking all day through the 'call' is werry trying, 'specially when we are chirruping up so as to bring the children to the vinders.

In the summer the London Punch men went into the country, wheeling the frame in front of them, playing—like Codlin and Short—in every village through which they passed, and eventually reaching the coast. At the beginning of the century the visitors to the seaside consisted only of gentry taking the sea-water cure, but the middle classes followed the quality to the resorts that were springing up all along the coast, and by the middle of the century Punch was a familiar entertainment on the beaches. Here he has struck deep roots, and as the holiday by the sea has become more and more a feature of English life, Punch and Judy on the sands has taken its place with the donkey-rides, the buckets and spades, the high fish teas, and the pierrots on the pier, in the pattern of the Englishman's summer holiday.

Punch's audience has gradually changed. In the first prints of his appearance in the streets his audience is composed of adults, mainly of the labouring class, with a few children; this seems to have been the composition of the marionette-show audiences at the eighteenth-century fairs. But by the middle of the nineteenth century the children outnumbered the adults, and by the end of the century they practically composed the entire audience. Punch was not originally an entertainment only—or even especially—for children; but he has always spoken to the simple-hearted and to the unsophisticated; as with so much else of nursery literature, the children have inherited the folklore of peasants. Here, in the streets, on the beaches, in the drawing-rooms, at the end of the long Victorian Age, with the little children gathered round, Punch might seem to have run his course, to have reached his second childhood, and to have had his say.

Punch and Judy To-day

Punch and Judy, like any other drama, can be acted well or badly. Tribute has already been paid to the fine band of old showmen who kept the tradition of Punch alive, but it does no service to the art whose history we have followed for so far in these pages to allow a romantic enthusiasm to cloud a critical judgment. Literary essayists who fall into raptures of stylistic quaintery over a shabby Punch at the street corner would be better employed in writing that the show was terrible, and in looking out for a performance that could be praised on its merits. It must be said that some of the performances put over in the first few decades of the twentieth century by "traditional" Punch and Judy performers were sadly incompetent.

People have always been prophesying the disappearance of Punch. It seemed inevitable in 1800; it seemed very near in 1850; it must have seemed certain in 1920. But Punch is not dead, and, so far from being nearly extinct, the Punch and Judy show is to-day probably more prosperous, with more showmen making a living from it, than ever before. More important, the quality of the performances has enormously improved; some of the traditional families still produce good performers, but it is probably fair to say that the best performances come from men who have brought new blood into the profession from the music-hall. Exactly what has led to the renaissance of Punch and Judy is not easy to answer—even though we have seen it happening under our very eyes. Perhaps the slump and the cinema have driven good men from the boards to the beach, and it is certain that a few performers have shown that a really well-acted presentation will draw a delighted response from a public that still retains a deep affection for Punch and Judy.

In one sphere, however, Punch has, indeed, almost disappeared. The show is now very seldom to be seen in the streets of London, and Liverpool is, I believe, the only provincial town to boast a street performance at all. As early as 1839 the New Police Act gave power to the police to clear the streets of a large number of the traders that were infesting them, and it was thought at the time that this might spell the death of Punch.[30] In practice Punch and Judy shows have been allowed to continue wherever they do not cause a serious obstruction, but as the streets have grown more and more crowded with traffic, the scope for street performances has become increasingly restricted. We can never expect to see again the street shows of Victorian London, but it will be a sad day if Punch vanishes for ever from the streets which nurtured him for so long; at the date of writing at least one show pitches regularly every Sunday morning near Hampstead Heath.

But if Punch has declined in the streets his position is secure on the sands; the latest returns indicate that there are seasonal shows at over sixty seaside resorts and holiday camps round the coast of Great Britain.[31] I cannot claim to have seen anything like all of these, but I can vouch that many of them provide excellent performances. It is well worth taking a day ticket to see Tom Kemp play at Brighton, or Joe Barnes at Southend; in the West of England members of the Staddon family will be found at Bournemouth and Weston-super-Mare, and in the North members of the Codman family at Colwyn Bay and Llandudno.

The usual arrangement is for the Punch performer to pay a rent to the local council for the right to perform on the beach; the rent may range from about ten pounds up to forty pounds a season. Sometimes a pitch is put up for tender. In these cases the performer relies on collecting from the crowds who watch. In recent years, however, there has been a tendency for Punch men to avoid pitches on which they have to pass a hat round like a street busker; they like to think of themselves as entertainers at least as good as the concert-party on the pier, and they prefer the dignity of a railed enclosure, perhaps with a covered theatre, and with a proper admission charge made for entrance. Sometimes, as at Hastings and Southend, the Punch show is part of a complete Children's Theatre, with comedy conjuring, competitions, and all the rest. In all this Punch is merely adopting the spirit of the age; but there is something very appealing in the gratuitous performance of the show in the open air, and Punch showmen will probably be wise never entirely to forsake this well-tried mode of exhibition.

During the summer Punch and Judy may also be seen in many city parks, engaged by the local authorities. Percy Press has a permanent theatre at the Festival Pleasure Gardens, and the L.C.C. issues a most convenient list of their holiday attractions, with the help of which the inveterate Punch and Judy follower may be able to run down three or four different performances in the course of a week. As one who has contributed himself towards these programmes, I can assure any student of the drama that the art of handling, subduing, and—where necessary—exciting the vast crowds of children that flock to these shows calls for a quality of skill, dramatic sense, and pure personality compared with which the making of points to a West End theatre audience is mere child's play.

All in all, it is probably true to say that a hundred men are professionally performing Punch and Judy in Great Britain during the summer. During the winter, and especially at Christmas-time, there is a lively demand for their services at children's parties, where many of the Punch men combine their show with ventriloquism, conjuring, paper-tearing, hand-bell ringing, chapeauography, and similar feats. Every English child has some memory of the entertainer who produced eggs from behind his ear, who poured lemonade out of a top hat, and who missed the stool when he sat down at the piano. In these memories Punch and Judy find a place.

As an incurable collector of Punch shows, I have seen dozens of different performances, and no two are identical; a good performance is worth going miles to see. The *aficionado* of Punch will compare Bruce Macleod's Clown counting the corpses with Le Fay's boxing-match, or Francis Keep's Crocodile with Stan Quigley's sausages, or Paul Capser's jugglers with Sam Corry's Toby, as ardently as any balletomane matches Fonteyn against Shearer.

Punch and Judy is not only a quaint survival from the past, but it is still genuinely funny. The details of the show may change in the future, as they have changed in the past, but there seems no reason for it to disappear. Punch is part of the English tradition, and although an occasional educationist or town councillor objects to him, his place is secure in our affections. His features appear on hundreds of different articles—chocolates, match-boxes, tooth-paste, socks, playing-cards, notepaper, transfers, Easter eggs, Christmas cards, and cigars. He will live long into the future. Let us hope that in time the Minister of Works will find a permanent home for his little theatre in Kensington Gardens; and meanwhile let us remember that a little practical assistance is worth a great deal of goodwill, and when the bottler comes round—if the show has been a good one—do not hesitate to put a little silver in the bag.

The Origin of the Drama

And so, at last, this long story has been told. Can we now answer the question that has posed itself inescapably in our minds? What is the origin of Punch and Judy?

Collier provides a definite answer; "Piccini's exhibition was, in the first instance, purely Italian, and such colloquies as he introduced were in the language of that country; he soon learnt a little broken English, and adapted his show more to the taste of English audiences." Mayhew was told the same story:

> The history or origination of Punch . . . is taken from Italy, and brought over to England by Porsini, and exhibited in the streets of London for the first time from sixty to seventy years ago [from 1850]: though he was not the first man who exhibited, for there was a female here before him, but not to perform at all in public—name unknown, but handed down to prosperity. She brought the figures and frame over with her, but never showed 'em—keeping it an unknown secret.

Philip John Stead, in what is by far the soundest modern study of Punch, accepts this story; he knows, as did Collier, but not Mayhew's informant, something about the eighteenth-century development of Punch in England, but even with that background he still argues the claim of "Piccini as the man who first brought the street show to England" in what amounted to a second Italian introduction of the character.[32]

There are other witnesses to urge the Italian origin of the show. It appears Piccini may not have been the only Italian puppet showman on the London streets: the print of 1785 by Samuel Collings is entitled "The Italian Puppet Show"; at the beginning of the nineteenth century Isaac D'Israeli noted that "perhaps there never was an Italian in a foreign country, however deep in trouble, but would drop all remembrance of his sorrows should one of his countrymen present himself with the paraphernalia of Punch at the corner of a street";[33] and at about the same date Mrs C. Maxwell wrote that

> it must be acknowledged that the Italians, who go about with puppet shows in the streets, galanta shows, etc. are extremely imaginative, and contrive their puppets with great neatness and accuracy, and well deserve the precarious encouragement they meet with for their trouble and invention.

The dialogue of the show seems often to have been delivered in a foreign accent; and according to Collier, "the performers of Punch and Judy, who are natives of Great Britain, generally endeavour to imitate an outlandish dialect." This tradition may go back a long way, however, for in a political pamphlet of 1741 the master of a puppet show is supposed to talk like Chico Marx: "Don't dey know dat I hold de strings dat move dem about on de stage? Dat it is I speak what you squeak out?"[34]

But this will not do. Are the English puppet-masters to be allowed no hand at all in shaping their destiny? Blackmantle agreed in 1825 that, despite Punch's "foreign, funny dialogue . . . and Italian origin, he has been so long domiciled in England, that he may now be considered naturalized by common consent"; and Prince Pückler-Muskaw wrote home in 1826 that "the hero of this drama is Punch—the English Punch—perfectly different from the Italian Pulcinella . . . the most godless droll that ever I met with . . . a little, too, the type of the nation he represents."

There is no question that Punch is ultimately derived from the Pulcinella introduced by the Italians into England after the Restoration; but a far more debatable question is whether the Punch and Judy drama, as we know it to-day, was the product of native development, or was brought to England by another Italian showman a century later.

Without doubt, an Italian named Piccini was showing Punch in the London streets at the end of the eighteenth century; and, no doubt, he liked to claim that he was the originator of the show. But before we accept his claim we must bear in mind the evidence I have produced for the existence of the glove-puppet Punch show in the English fairs ever since the beginning of the eighteenth century, with traditions going back much further. We cannot actually disprove Piccini's claim to be the first performer in the streets, but his witnesses are suspect: Collier is a proved liar, and the showman Mayhew interviewed could only repeat the legends that he had been told; he even made the ridiculous claim that "Porsini brought the calls into this country with him from Italy," as if English puppet players had never known the use of such things before. His reference to the earlier "female" is intriguing; perhaps there was a half-forgotten memory of Charlotte Charke or Madame de la Nash handed down among the English puppet players; but his whole well-meaning incursion into history is an eloquent example of the dubious value of oral tradition.

We know the names of scores of puppet showmen who played in England during the late eighteenth and early nineteenth centuries; they are listed in full in the Appendix. Apart from the distinct group of Fantoccini performers, who can have had little influence on the Punch drama, there are not more than a couple of Italian or foreign names among them: Appleby, Bannister, Blower, Carter, Catchpole, Gregory, Holmes, Robust, White, Wilson—the Anglo-Saxon roll-call of Smithfield tenants proves decisively that, as always, the overwhelming majority of puppet players in England were Englishmen.

In my analysis of the fourteen basic characters of the Punch and Judy show there is not a single one that cannot reasonably claim an English eighteenth- or nineteenth-century ancestry. Punch and Clown are, in fact, the only two traditional figures of the English Punch show that are known to have an Italian origin—and in each case they were introduced into England in the seventeenth century, and had long been fully naturalized Englishmen. Of the fourteen basic characters of the drama, ten are known to have appeared in the English eighteenth-century marionette shows—Punch, his wife, the Baby, the Clown, the Beadle, the Ghost, the Hangman, the Devil, the dog, and the hobby-horse. Of the remaining four characters, the Crocodile replaced the Devil in the middle of the nineteenth century, and so can owe nothing to Piccini or any other Italian contemporary of his; Mr Jones is surely a solid enough Englishman; the Doctor is a natural native addition; and, in fact, the only foreigner in the entire show is "the distinguished foreigner," the cryptic utterer of "Shallaballa," the Negro servant or the nigger minstrel—in every case a typical foreigner resident in England. Judged in the light of history, the characters of the Punch and Judy show are of unquestioned English descent.

The action of the drama tells the same story. The character of Punch, with his droll aggressiveness, was shaped in England; so was the shrewishness of his wife; the combat with the Devil is a very ancient English tradition. Of the chief actions in the play, the only two that cannot be traced in the eighteenth century are the scenes with the Baby and the Hangman; as has been shown, both of these might have been very natural spontaneous English growths at the turn of the century.

There is—and this is the most important paragraph in this book—there is a clear case for claiming a purely English origin for Punch and Judy.

Nevertheless, to complete our investigation into the origin of the drama, we should now proceed to compare Punch and Judy with the roughly similar glove-puppet shows of Italy. Unfortunately that is impossible. As far as I have been able to discover, the text of the Italian street show has never been printed. It is, indeed, probable that there never has been one single street puppet play in Italy, as there was in England. The full story still needs to be told, but it is clear that puppets never lost their popularity with the Italians, and that in every province there flourished regional puppet heroes and clowns—at Rome Cassandrino, at Turin Gianduja, at Milan Gerolamo, at Florence Stenterello, at Naples Pulcinella, and so on with many another. The traditions of the Italian Comedy have lived on for two centuries in the puppet theatres, after their disappearance from any but the humblest human stages.[35]

The marionettes and the glove puppets seem to have flourished side by side in Italy throughout the eighteenth century, and the repertory of the glove-puppet shows was drawn from hundreds of skeleton plots, embroidered in the traditional manner with extempore dialogue. Perhaps gradually some kind of simplified pattern imposed itself upon the drama of the streets, but it would be a task beyond the scope of this volume to try to reconstruct the plot of the Italian puppet shows from the allusions and descriptions buried in a hundred books of travel.

A list of the chief characters of the Italian puppet stage was provided by P. C. Ferrigni in the eighteen-eighties;[36] they are almost all drawn from the Commedia dell' Arte—Arlecchino, Brighella, Stenterello, Meneghino, Gianduja, il Dottore, Gerolamo, Tartaglia, Rugantino, Pulcinella, Carciafo (the artichoke—a modern Neapolitan character), a policeman, and the Devil. This list should be compared with that of typical *burattini* given by Carlo Racca in about 1921[37]—the King, the Queen, the Devil, the Old Woman, the Young Man, Death, the Carabiniere, the Sailor, the Brigand, the Magician, the Ogre, and so on, alongside the familiar traditional masks. From these lists it is clear that no close comparison is possible between the characters of the Punch drama and of the Italian puppet plays; Pulcinella, the Devil, and the Policeman are the only figures common to both countries.

There is a suggestion that the trick of Punch hanging the Hangman originated in Italy, for in 1840 F. Mercey described seeing what he called this "well-known" incident performed by a human Pulcinella at the Teatro San Carlino at Naples in a Commedia dell' Arte playlet entitled *Pulcinella Brigand Chief*;[38] but there is no trace of a hangman in any of the puppet casts or descriptions, and this late appearance of the business in a human performance in Italy may quite possibly have been derived from England. To establish its Italian origin a much earlier reference must be discovered, but early written allusions to what every one assumes to be a very old traditional stage trick are not easily come by.

In character there certainly does seem to be some resemblance between Pulcinella and Punch. Benedetto Croce wrote in 1899 that

> the Pulcinella of the puppets deserves a special study. It is singular that in this performance he usually appears as a wicked villain, similar to the French Polichinelle, who beats and kills people for nothing at all. But the little assassin, in his white blouse, with the black half mask . . . and the false little voice, the 'Pullecenelluzzo' who gathers upon his head so many comic answers, still makes the passers by laugh so much that they treat him with the tenderness shown to capricious children.

This is a very familiar comment, but surely the truth is not that Punch and Pulcinella are necessarily exactly the same character, but that they are both street glove puppets, and that the same knock-about slapstick buffoonery comes naturally to each. English travellers are always recording that they have seen "Punch and Judy" in Italy, or Persia, or China, but a South Sea Islander might say in just the same way that he had seen "a play" in Paris, London, and New York. The fact of the matter is that one glove-puppet show looks very like another glove-puppet show to the inexpert eye.

In the absence of any better description, we can only turn to the numerous paintings and prints of the Pulcinella street show for further information regarding the manner of its performance.[39] I have examined some two dozen of these illustrations, dating from about 1700 to 1850, and their evidence is surprisingly consistent. The booth is, of course, similar to that used in England, but it is usually placed on some kind of trestles or platform, raising it considerably higher above the street than is usual here; it is normally covered with a drab cloth cover, and never with the distinctive Regency check pattern. The cover almost always has two flaps in the front—an arrangement that was scarcely

A Pulcinella Street Show, after Morner, c. 1830

known in England. Pulcinella is invariably dressed in white, and almost invariably wears a black half-mask; the nose of his mask is hooked, but not his chin; his hunchback, if visible at all, is very slight, and there is no protruding belly. Contrary to general opinion, there is very little physical resemblance between the Pulcinella of nineteenth-century Italy and the Punch of nineteenth-century England. The Pulcinella of these prints is the Punchinello who came to England in 1660, but it is almost impossible to believe that the Punch drawn by Cruikshank ever came from Italy at all.

The characters shown sharing the stage with Pulcinella are limited in number. There is often a woman, with unexaggerated features and contemporary costume; sometimes a man, dressed like Pulcinella in white, with an immensely long nose sticking straight out of his face; once what may be a moor in a turban, a gentleman in a tricorn, and a grenadier in a busby. The incident with the Baby is never represented, nor the Hangman, nor the Ghost. There are, nevertheless, some familiar features. Pulcinella, of course, often holds a stick; a live dog appears occasionally, though not on the stage; the sheep-bell is illustrated twice.

Visitors to Italy to-day report that the Pulcinella glove-puppet show may be seen regularly in the Pincio Gardens in Rome on Sundays. Pulcinella wears the traditional black mask and is dressed in white, he is partnered by a female, and fights a Policeman, Death—in the guise of a skeleton—and the Devil. There is no gallows and no Hangman. Pulcinella speaks through a *pivetta*, but the dialogue is in some dialect that an English visitor finds impossible to understand. The action consists entirely of knock-about business with the stick, of a very crude character, but the show appears to be well patronized.

Summarizing this brief, and perhaps inadequate, survey of Italian glove puppets, the resemblances between the Pulcinella and the Punch street performances may be narrowed down to the manner, but not the costume or appearance, of Punch himself, the Policeman, the Devil, the dog, and the bell. As to Punch, I have already suggested the danger of arguing any closer relationship than the possession of a common ancestor and the mastery of the same kind of stage; the Policeman is an almost essential ingredient in this kind of show, wherever it happens; the Devil descends both in Italy and in England from the medieval religious mysteries, and the English puppet tradition is as old as the Italian; the dog too has a respectable English ancestry; the business with the bell—which has now disappeared from the English performance, but which was certainly featured by Piccini—we may, I think, gladly give to the Italians. For the rest, despite a superficial resemblance, there is no evidence whatever to derive a single character or incident of the English Punch and Judy from the Pulcinella show of the Italian streets.

The Italians carried the Pulcinella puppet all over Europe during the seventeenth century. It was one of the most extraordinary invasions in history, and to trace its progress, even in broad outline, would require a book as long as this one; but perhaps the story of the development of Pulcinella in other European countries may throw some light on his career in England. We have already recorded his introduction in France, and the modifications his appearance and character underwent in his transformation into the Gallic Polichinelle. The history of French puppets seems to have been largely parallel to that of the English: in France also Polichinelle appeared as the clown of hundreds of different plays in the theatres of the fairs during the eighteenth century; in France also he seems to have disappeared from the marionette stage at about the beginning of the nineteenth century; in France also he was to be seen at that time in the glove-puppet booths of the streets. In France also a text of *Polichinelle* was published in 1836.

But when we examine this text it is only to discover that it is an almost word-for-word translation from Payne Collier, illustrated with Cruikshank's engravings! Two more versions were published during the next sixty-five years, both also translated from the English.[40] Does this mean that the English and French street puppet shows were identical? And if so, was Punch brought from France, or was Polichinelle brought from England?

The many excellent French historians of puppets are strangely silent upon this question, and in the absence of an authentic native text we must once again, as in Italy, turn to descriptions and illustrations to give an idea of the nature of Polichinelle's performance. The earliest allusion to what might be termed the stock characters of the Polichinelle theatre seems to be provided in 1811 by J. B. Gouriet, who listed them as follows: Polichinelle, Cassandre, Commissaire (a police superintendent or magistrate), a Blind Man, a moustachioed Suisse (beadle), Scaramouch, Mother Simone, Dame Gigogne, an Apothecary, Archers (constables of the watch), and Devils.[41] This is an extremely interesting list, with many affinities to Punch and Judy across the water. Gouriet was a rather unreliable antiquary, but he can hardly have imagined the characters he lists. Later descriptions are all after 1836, and therefore are probably influenced by the English text of that year; here, again, I must refrain from plumbing the story deeply, but three authorities may be quoted.

A fictional biography of Polichinelle by Eugénie Foa, placed in 1838, includes a short text of the performance; the dialogue resembles, but is in no way exactly copied from, the translated text of two years earlier.[42] The characters introduced are Polichinelle, a Publican, his wife, the Magistrate, the Gendarme, the Hangman, and the Devil; all the earlier characters are beaten by Polichinelle's stick, he hangs the Hangman, and is finally carried off to hell by the Devil. This may be the nearest we have to an independent French text of the drama. In 1892 Lemercier de Neuville wrote that, "like our Polichinelle, Punch beats his wife, his children, his friends and his enemies, is imprisoned, and kills the hangman and the devil," and he goes on to refer to Mère Gigogne, Pierrot, Arlequin, and Cassandre as well-known characters in the show, and "when I have told you that the judge is always biased, the policeman always hated and the hangman always hanged, I shall have told you nothing new. There is, however, a character who plays no part in any play, but nevertheless appears in all. . . . I mean the cat."[43]

A live cat had made an appearance on the playboard of the stage before the middle of the nineteenth century, and for some time he fought mimic battles with Polichinelle in much the same way that Toby did with Punch. He found a place in the list of characters given by Ernest Maindron in 1901, along with Polichinelle, his wife, his neighbour, the Gendarme, the Apothecary, the Magistrate, the Hangman, and the Devil.[44]

From nineteenth-century illustrations we can see that the booth of Polichinelle resembled the English one rather than the Italian; it stood on the ground, and it was often covered with a check-patterned cloth, without flaps. Polichinelle himself is closer to Punch than to Pulcinella: he has no mask, but he does display a very exaggerated hump and belly, hooked nose and chin, and a bright red-and-yellow costume. He can be distinguished from Punch most clearly by his hat, which is totally different from our familiar sugar-loaf shape, and provides a curious combination of the bicorne *chapeau à la Suisse* with a primitive *jockey*, or top hat, rising out of it.[45]

As in Italy, Polichinelle probably originally figured as the hero of many different farces on his glove-puppet stage, but, as in England, these seem to have been eventually simplified into one basic plot. The four sources that I have referred to combine to provide a cast of fifteen basic characters, all of whom—except two—have a clear equivalent in the English drama: Polichinelle is our Punch; Scaramouch, Arlequin or Pierrot are our Scaramouch or Clown; the Apothecary is our Doctor; the Neighbour or Publican (we recall that Polichinelle had had a com-

A Polichinelle Street Show, by A. G. Descamps, c. 1850

The Italianate nature of the crowd and background must be set down to gratuitous artistic licence. The Polichinelle, with the cat on the playboard, is purely French.

Victoria and Albert Museum. Crown copyright

panion called Voisin in the seventeenth century) is our Neighbour or Publican; the Blind Man (who was a traditional character in the French popular theatre) is the Blind Man who figured in Piccini's performance; the Gendarme is our Constable; the Suisse is our Beadle; the Archers are our Policemen; the Commissaire is the Magistrate or Judge to whom there are occasional English allusions; the Hangman is our Hangman; the Devil is our Devil; the cat is our dog; Mère Gigogne is our Judy. The only two characters that we cannot pair are Cassandre, an elderly foolish gentleman, who comes from the Italians, and Mère Simone, who was perhaps an alternative to Mère Gigogne.

What is the meaning of this extraordinary correspondence? Did the two shows grow up together, on either side of the English Channel, with almost identical characters? Or did one country borrow the show from the other, for, as we have seen, neither could have got it from Italy? And if so, who borrowed from whom? At least as far as the printed text went we already know the answer: France borrowed from England. Did Polichinelle copy his drama from Punch?

Charles Magnin, never backward in championing the claim of French puppets, who hotly disputed any Italian share in the formation of Polichinelle, waived aside any claim for France in this matter. "However, Mr Payne Collier," he wrote,

> without misunderstanding certain truly British traits in the character of his hero . . . is none the less disposed to hand to France (through pure jesting courtesy) the principal honour for this unedifying creation. I assuredly do not deny the extensive influence that belongs to us in this popular and to-day European character; that is his gaiety. But I feel bound, and without any thought of epigrammatic reciprocation, to restore to England a considerable part of this legend. The rights of our neighbours in this regard are ancient and real.[46]

So be it. It is to my mind an inescapable conclusion that the drama of Punch, his wife, the Hangman, and the Devil was carried either from France to England or from England to France. Clear evidence in either direction is almost non-existent: there is no record of any French showmen playing in England at the turn of the century; I do not know of any English showmen who visited France. The two countries were at war. But perhaps there is a clue in the fact that the French Judy is said, to this day, to be called "Darling."[47]

If Frenchmen wish to claim the honour of originating the Punch drama it is for them to state their case; we shall await their argument with interest. Meanwhile their most distinguished advocate has virtually abandoned his brief. On the other hand, we have here built up a purely English case-history for every character in the drama. With all reserve, and subject to further investigation, I now—for the first time—put forward the claim that the Polichinelle drama of the streets was directly derived from the English Punch and Judy.

Polichinelle has to-day almost disappeared from the French puppet stage. At the end of the eighteenth century the character of Guignol, based on the silk-weaving *canut* of Lyons, was created by a local puppet showman, and his popularity gradually spread throughout the country, reducing Polichinelle to a mere prologue. To-day Guignol is the lovable and amusing hero of a wide repertory of plays in the many puppet booths of the Paris parks; Polichinelle is a name and a legend.

Of Pulcinella's history elsewhere in Europe I lack both the evidence and the space to write here. Whether the English Punch extended his influence beyond France cannot be determined without much further research; what is certain is that a common pattern of development ran through European history in which national puppet heroes, one after another, ousted the Italian from the supremacy of their booths during the revolutionary fervour of the dawn of the nineteenth century. In France he has been replaced by Guignol, in Spain by Christovita, in Germany and Austria by Kasperl, in Holland by Jan Klaasen; in Russia Petroushka survived until the Soviet revolution; in England alone of the countries colonized by Pulcinella does he still rule unchallenged. Like the British monarchy, Punch has ridden out all storms; but, also like the monarchy, though he once came from abroad, Punch has been long absorbed into the English tradition.

In the last analysis, there is perhaps not so wide a gulf as might appear between the orthodox derivation of the Punch and Judy show, as set out by P. J. Stead, and the derivation I have traced here. We both agree that Punch and Judy is the product of an amalgamation between English and Continental influences; but we do differ—and differ fundamentally—upon the weight to be given to each of these sources. To Mr Stead, Punch and Judy is an Italian, or perhaps a French, puppet play, "worked upon by the native tradition"; in my view it is an essentially English show, to which Italian and perhaps French showmen have brought quite minor and incidental accretions. In a detailed analysis of Collier's text I should assign only the business with the bell to Italy, and the introduction of the Blind Man to France. But we cannot expect to delimit these matters with precision; and after we have had our argument we can both join in laughing at the show together.

There are two main lines of development from which Punch has sprung, both of which have been traced in this volume. His Italian ancestry is self-evident, though its extent may sometimes be exaggerated; his English ancestry, from the Elizabethan stage clown and the Renaissance Vice, was first, I believe, propounded by Dr Johnson in the mid-eighteenth century,[48] and although his theory has not gone unchallenged, it is, I feel sure, substantially sound. The mystery of Punch's origin has, however, always attracted the imaginative speculations of romantic antiquaries and amateur philologists, and we cannot conclude this chapter without a brief glance at their well-meaning flights of fancy.

Punch, then, means a little flea, because he skips and jumps; or is derived from Paunch, after his belly; or from *pantch*, the Hindustani word for 'five,' from which the drink takes its name, because it is the play of five characters; or from Pontius Pilate, with Judy from Judas Iscariot or *giudei*, meaning the Jews. And if we go back to his Italian name he is derived from *pollicena*, meaning a turkey-cock, or *pulcino*, meaning a hen-chicken, or from all sorts of people named Puccio d'Aniello or Paolo Cinella or what you will. And farther back still perhaps he comes from the Greek *polu kineo*, meaning 'I move much,' or from *polynices*, meaning 'the man of many quarrels.'[49]

Perhaps there is a germ of truth somewhere in all this, but the game must not be taken too seriously. Not a single one of these derivations really explains Punch, and most of them—notably Pontius Pilate—are complete rubbish; but Punch does extend in character, if not in name, back to the religious plays of medieval England, and to the improvised farces of the Italian comedians, and to the folk festivals of pagan Greece. He draws from these deep roots the accidents of his appearance and his costume, the primeval quality of his character, his Englishness, and his universality.

Perhaps, now that we have traced the road all the way, the whole long saga can most clearly be expressed in the form of a genealogical tree. This, of course, is far too neat, far too simplified, but it will at least serve to refresh our memories after the journey.

THE ANCESTRY OF PUNCH

Continental Sources | *English Sources*

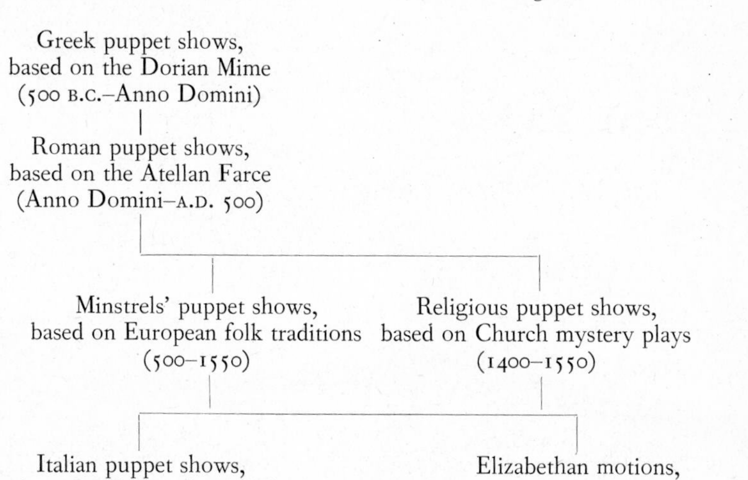

Italian puppet shows,
based on the Commedia dell' Arte
(1550–1600)

Pulcinella and Polichinelle,
the hero of the puppet stage
(1600–60)

Elizabethan motions,
based on folk traditions
(1550–1640)

The Commonwealth,
the puppet show the only theatre
(1640–60)

Punchinello,
introduced into the English puppet show
(1660–1700)

Punch,
the clown of every puppet play
(1700–1800)

Punch and Judy,
the glove-puppet drama of the streets
(1800–)

Chapter IX

MARIONETTES OF THE NINETEENTH CENTURY

At the Fairs

IT remains only to chronicle the story of the marionettes of the nineteenth and twentieth centuries. When we left them in 1800 their theatres were deserted and their art abandoned; puppetry seemed to live only in the glove puppets of the streets; a newspaper commented that "although motions and puppet-shows are still favourites on the continent they have had their day in England, the exhibition of Punch being the only relic we have left of them." Descriptions of Bartholomew Fair in 1817, in 1825, in 1832, and in 1833 all record the absence of puppet shows from the fair in which they had once flourished.[1]

Yet this limited and complicated art was not to disappear; there was at least one showman who continued to tour an elaborate marionette theatre during the first half of the nineteenth century. In 1831 Middleton's Royal Automaton Figures appeared at Bartholomew Fair in a domestic comic opera entitled *The Election, or the Choice of a Husband*, followed by a selection of *divertissements*; three years later he was back again, this time without the opera, and for this year an observer has recorded a most valuable factual description of his performance. "This commenced," we are told,

> with four dancing girls; then a tumbler (which was well managed); a female danced a hornpipe; our old friend Joey Grimaldi; a school boy 'creeping like snail unwillingly to school,' on his back a label with the ominous word 'dunce,' he lays down, falls asleep, is awoke by a butterfly, which he tries to catch without success, goes to sleep again, and a snake crawls along the ground, and coils round his neck; then came the moral, which was told us by the attendant, to beware of loitering on the way. An excellent figure of Mahomet the Turk, which after dancing a short time, the limbs fall off and become perfect figures; the head is divided into two, and formed Somebody and Nobody. But the great novelty of the show was a capital model of an Elephant, which displayed great ingenuity; the figure performed a variety of singular tricks very dexterously, amongst others, it fetched a carrot and swallowed it,

> kneeled down, etc. This was one of the best displays in the fair. On the outside were many well-dressed characters for a pantomime, and a remnant of the ancient May game, a hobby horse. The charge here was the first day, twopence [in 1831 it had been *6d.* and 1*s.*]; but the proprietor found he was obliged on the second day to yield to the times, and reduce his terms to one penny; he then did well, having 28 performances daily to crowded houses.[2]

They cannot have lasted more than a bare quarter of an hour.

A few further items from Middleton's repertory can be gleaned from his bills. There was a Scaramouch "with no head and afterwards all head"; a clown balancing a bottle on his hands, feet, and head; and "the Yorkshire Hag, who will light and smoke her pipe." Punch no longer appeared in the performance at all, but a resident clown seems to have been provided by a character called Old Caleb Comical, who introduced his drolleries.

The marionettes used in the plays were very large; they are described as being four feet high and made of wax, and "apparently speaking, moving and acting with a fidelity equal to life, dressed in strict costume according to their respective character"; the variety tricks, on the other hand, were performed by the small Lilliputian figures. The illuminated pavilion was provided with "a private entrance at the side of the theatre for parties to the Front Circle . . . who may feel an objection to crossing the stage."

There was a tradition in the family that Middleton's marionettes had been founded in 1711, and in 1830 he boasted that his show had "been established upwards of 100 years," but I have unfortunately been unable to discover any earlier written record of it. It toured in the South of England, and had been "patronised by the Royal Family at Brighton, and by most of the nobility and gentry in Kent, Sussex and Hampshire." In 1838, when it was at the Coronation Fair in Hyde Park, the show was put up for sale, but I do not think a purchaser was found. After Middleton's death it was carried on by his widow, Frisby, herself a puppet-showman's daughter.

Middleton provides a link between the eighteenth century and to-day; there are relics of the old English tradition in his use of the hobby-horse outside the show, and in the "attendant," or interpreter, inside. He borrowed some of the best tricks from the Italian Fantoccini, like the Grand Turk, and he was perhaps the first man to present this come-to-pieces puppet in Turkish costume. In essentials he established a tradition of puppet variety acts that is still alive to-day.

Middleton's was the last puppet theatre at Smithfield. By progressively raising the rents the City authorities at last succeeded in stifling Bartholomew Fair, and in 1855 a sad remnant of its former glory was proclaimed for the last time. The Smithfield revels had gone the way of Southwark and Mayfair, and the puppets must search for another home.

On the Streets

Marionette showmen, reduced to playing for a penny admission in such fairs as still remained, must have cast envious glances at Punch's popularity on the streets, and it was not long before an attempt was made to present marionette shows too in a portable street booth.

The first man to introduce the street Fantoccini was said to have been a Scotsman called Grey, in the eighteen-twenties. He had a booth about the size of an ordinary Punch frame, with small marionettes nine inches high which he dangled from the top; the strings must have been extremely short, and the position of the manipulator very uncomfortable. Grey went on to enjoy a colourful career: he was engaged at the Rotunda, Vauxhall Gardens, at ten pounds a week in 1823, and appeared at Sadler's Wells and Covent Garden in an hour's programme, with no turn lasting more than two or three minutes, "done as quick as lightning." For these engagements he used figures two feet high, with a cut cloth let down to form his stage opening. At about this time he was on tour, in partnership with a lady pyrotechnist named Madame Angler, from whom he parted in Preston and joined forces with Billy Purvis, a booth proprietor who has left us a racy autobiography. Grey tried to keep the secret of how he worked his figures even from his partner, but Billy Purvis made a hole in the green curtain surrounding the stage and learnt to "slang,"[3] or work the figures, for himself—which was just as well, for at North Shields the Scotsman decamped with all the takings. The last we hear of this Fantoccini performer, who did so well that he sported diamond rings on his fingers, is that he arrived in New York with his puppets in 1832, and entertained the Americans for some years.[4] Later street performers seem to have considerably increased the size of their booths, and a Fantoccini man interviewed by Mayhew in about 1852 said that he had a theatre ten feet high by six feet wide, with a four-foot-wide opening, and puppets two feet high; but it was always a one-man show—apart from the panpipe player and bottler outside—and at the best he cannot have had much room to manœuvre in. When first introduced the street Fantoccini were a great success, taking four or five pounds a day. "Where Punch took a shilling we've taken a pound," Mayhew was told, but "the crowd was always a great annoyance to us. They'd follow us for miles, and the moment we pitched up they'd come and gather about, and almost choke us. What was their hapence to us when we were taking our half crowns?"

But the novelty wore off—at least among the half-crown customers, who ordered private performances outside their windows. In the fifties there were only two street shows on the go, and the profit might be about

CANDLER'S STREET FANTOCCINI

From Hone's *Every-Day Book*, 1825.

two pounds a week. The Fantoccini lacked the drama and vigour of Punch, and the virtues of the marionette must have been much circumscribed on so small a stage. They did not survive long into the second half of the century.[5]

The turns presented in the street shows were evidently derived from the performances of Flockton and Middleton. In 1825 Hone recorded the following programme, as performed by Candler in the streets of Pentonville—a tumbler, a dissecting skeleton, a neck-stretching Scaramouch, a chair-balancer, a sailor dancing the hornpipe, an Indian juggler, and Billy Waters, the one-legged nigger fiddler, who was a well-known character in the London streets.[6] By the fifties the programme, as told to Mayhew, consisted of—a female hornpipe dancer, four ladies dancing a quadrille (no gentlemen, as this would need an extra operator), Grimaldi catching a butterfly, the enchanted Turk, an old lady whose arms drop off and turn into figures and whose body turns into a balloon in which the figures fly away, a tight-rope dancer, an Indian juggler, a sailor's hornpipe, the Italian Scaramouch with extending neck, a chair-balancer, dancing and dissecting skeletons, Judy Callaghan with six figures jumping out of her pockets, a countryman on a comic donkey, the Nondescript who juggles with his head, a flower ballet girl, a Scotsman dancing the Highland fling, and Tom and Jerry flooring the watchman.

The Fantoccini too found their way—like Punch and Judy—into the pleasure gardens. Puppets had found a congenial home in the pleasure gardens of eighteenth-century London, and they continued to entertain in the modest tea-gardens of the Regency. In 1826, for instance, at the New Bagnigge Wells in Bayswater, "the celebrated Jackson" presented a programme of popular items—a man balancing on a ladder, a comic old man, the animated skeleton, Joseph Grimaldi, the Indian juggler, the tight-rope Polander, the enchanted Turk, and Tom and Jerry flooring a Charley.[7] This was the staple fare of the street Fantoccini. At Vauxhall, at the Chalk Farm Tea Gardens, at the St Helena Gardens, Rotherhithe, or on the back lawn of many another suburban public house, the unpretentious tricks of the marionettes provided a pleasant summer entertainment.

It will be seen that a traditional repertory of trick figures had by this time been well established: of the eighteen turns presented in the fifties, six had been played by Candler, six by Jackson, and six by Middleton. The dissecting skeleton was a traditional English trick from the Restoration theatre; the hornpipes and the quadrilles and the rope-dancers had been popular in the shows of the eighteenth century; the Grand Turk and the polander had been brought by the Italian Fantoccini; the Indian juggler was based on the famous Ramo Samee, who had appeared in London by 1820. Gradually new characters were introduced, but on this, the most conservative of all Western stages, the old effects were never discarded.

The Fantoccini and Punch were not the only types of puppet show to invade the London streets. At night-time many a Punch and Judy performer fitted a sheet of calico across the proscenium of his stage, with three candles burning behind it, and moved some flat cut-out figures across the screen in the manner of the Ombres Chinoises. This entertainment came to be known as the Galanty Show. An old Punch man called Tom Paris was said to have been the first to try this out, and he was followed by Paul Herring, the famous clown, "who did it for a lark; he was hard up for money, and got it"; when it was a novelty he took up to two pounds a night at it. By the fifties, when Mayhew recorded yet another of his invaluable interviews, the takings had gone down to five shillings a night, and that had to be divided between two men.[8]

The plays presented were a few of those introduced by the Italians in the seventeen-seventies. *The Broken Bridge*, *The Enraged Cobbler*, and *Kitty boiling the Pot* seem to have been the favourites; Mayhew has preserved a fascinating account of the plot of *Kitty*. "The shadow of the fireplace is seen with the fire alight, and the smoke is made to go up by mechanism," he was told; the woodcutter's wife has put a leg of mutton in the pot, and tells her daughter Kitty to watch it. "Then mother says, 'Kitty, bring up the broom to sweep up the room'; and Kitty replies, 'Yes, mummy, I'll bring up the room to sweep up the broom.' It's regular stage business and cross-questions, you see—comic business." Then Kitty works the bellows and makes the sparks fly and blows the fire right out; and the cat steals the meat out of the pot; then the mother comes back, and "you see her with the child on her knee correcting of her. Then the woodchopper comes in and wants his supper, after chopping wood all the days of his life. 'Where's supper?' . . . Passionate directly you see; and then comes a fight. . . . It's a beautiful performance."

The Galanty Show was still being performed in London streets up to the end of the century. The audience was rather more adult than for Punch and Judy, and perhaps in consequence the dialogue became somewhat coarse; it was a far cry from the Georgian Society ladies fanning themselves in Hickford's Great Room to the Victorian swells in Regent Street lounging on the pavements around the flickering shadows, but the play and the puppets were the same; the vicissitudes of the traveller on the broken bridge had become part of the English folk drama.

A Galanty Show was also sometimes the name given to a magic-lantern entertainment, and I think this was its earlier use. During the early part of the nineteenth century there were many of these shows being presented in private houses during the winter by Italians, with glass slides painted with various scenes and characters. Their subject-matter was often akin to that of the puppets, but their history lies outside the scope of this book.[9]

The entertainments of the pavements were enriched yet more by the jigging puppets, with an almond-eyed Savoyard boy playing his pipe as the little figures danced upon their narrow plank. These had been drawn by Hogarth at Southwark Fair in 1733, and a whole gallery of *genre* sketches records the travels of these Italian showmen and their dancing dolls to every street corner in Europe.[10] The accidental jerks of these simple puppets possess a charm that the most elaborately articulated marionettes seem to have lost. They are not often seen now, but as these

"THE LITTLE SAVOYARDS," 1826

Jigging puppets in the streets of London.

pages were being written I was able to purchase a delightful example for one shilling from a demonstrator in the Charing Cross Road.

The theatres of the street are, alas, to-day little more than a memory; but even now we may at times catch a faint echo of the tumultuous cries with which the puppets transformed the pavements of London into their stage.

In the West End

The Italian invasion of the seventeen-seventies was not repeated on anything like the same scale in the next century, but three seasons presented by foreign marionettes in London theatres call for special mention.

The first of these was billed as the French Théâtre du Petit Lazary of Messrs Maffey, from Paris; it announced that it had already appeared in the different capitals of Europe, and after a provincial tour visiting Dublin, Edinburgh, Glasgow, Liverpool, Manchester, Bristol, Birmingham, Hull, York, Nottingham, and Bath, it opened at the Argyll Rooms, the small concert-hall in Regent Street, in September 1828.[11] Although it was a French company—one suspects the proprietors were born as the MM. Matthieu—the repertory was very similar to that of the Italian Fantoccini of the eighteenth century. The season opened with *Harlequin Prince by Magic*, which had been played half a century before at Panton Street, the Haymarket, and Savile Row, and included a great many Harlequin plays in the tradition of the Commedia dell' Arte—*Arlequin Juge et Partie*, *Harlequin of All Work*, *Arlequin President*, *Harlequin swallowed by a Whale*, and so on.

The plays were performed in a mixture of French and English, but *The Times* considered that the dialogue was untranslatable, and that "it is quite delightful as they give it . . . Arlequin talks most eloquently, and although his discourse is as parti-coloured as his dress, it is perfectly intelligible. . . . The whole of the entertainment is very clever, very amusing, and well deserving of encouragement."

The plays themselves were little more than a vehicle to display mechanical tricks and effects; the transformations effected by Harlequin's magic wand were said to be remarkably ingenious—especially when a table changed into a flying dragon—and he repeated his traditional business of eating macaroni, drinking a bottle of wine, and—a new trick—lighting two candles. The marionettes were two feet high, and the costumes and scenery were exquisite.

Like the Théâtre des Variétés Amusantes at Savile Row, the Messrs Maffey introduced a few current successes from the Parisian human theatres. The burlesque operatical extravaganza of *The Danaides, or the Ninety-nine Victims* had been performed for 300 nights at the Porte Saint-Martin, and *The Attack of the Convoy* was a grand military melodrama, showing a battle with bandits in a romantic defile of the Appenines, which had been played for 200 nights at Franconi's.

Each play ran for one week, and in addition every programme included ballets and an animated view of famous sieges or battles. The season was a great success, running for nearly eight months until May 1829, during which eighteen different plays were presented. Tickets cost from 1*s.* to

3*s*., and performances were at 7.30 nightly; the experiment of giving two matinées each week was not successful. At the beginning of June the company played for a week at the Surrey.

Twenty-five years later, in 1852, the Adelaide Gallery, off the Lowther Arcade in the Strand, which had existed for some years as a scientific and semi-educational exhibition room, was reopened as the Royal Marionette Theatre. The puppets were Italian ones "from the theatres at Naples, Rome, Milan, Genoa, etc.," directed by Signor Brigaldi. They brought their own orchestra, "selected from the two Italian Opera Houses."[12]

This visit, again, caused great excitement in the town. Each programme consisted of about three items. First there came a prologue from the puppet manager, Mr Albany Brown, who then proceeded to interview a number of applicants for engagements in the theatre. This gave an excuse to introduce some of the stock marionette turns, like the warbling tenor, the zephyrine ballet-dancer, the horn-pipe dancing sailor, and "the bust of ——," which turned out to be an actress who busted into two pieces. Similarly, the programme concluded with a ballet, of which the most popular was *Arlechino Fortunato*, introducing the grotesque frolics of the regional Italian mimes.

The principal item in the programme usually consisted of a burlesque or parody, recalling the satirical puppet plays of the eighteenth century. The season opened with *Bombastes Furioso*, a popular burlesque of classical tragedy then some forty years old; this was followed by the famous melodrama of *The Bottle Imp*; a *vaudeville* called *The Swiss Cottage*; *The Sixth Act of Romeo and Juliet*, a Shakespearean parody; *Aladdin and the Wonderful Lamp*, an Oriental extravaganza; and so on. Of particular interest were a number of political satires: *The United Services*, a rhyming squib directed against the recent *coup d'état* of Louis Napoleon in France; *Poll Practice*, "exposing the corruption of electioneering and urging parliamentary reform"; and *The Arcadian Brothers*, a burlesque on *The Corsican Brothers*, attacking the censorship of the Press under the Second Empire, "in which Charivari is killed in Paris under Napoleon, but is revenged by his twin-brother, Punch, from London, who gallantly opposing the pen to the sword mortally wounds the oppressor." *Charivari* was a Parisian newspaper that had been suppressed by Napoleon. These satirical pieces, being presented by puppets, did not require the Lord Chamberlain's licence—which would certainly not have been granted—and Londoners had a brief opportunity to enjoy the outspoken saliency and wit of an uncensored theatre. Not since Madame de la Nash had anything of the kind been known in England.

These political playlets, however, did not figure largely in the programme, which mainly relied on the managers' interviews, *Aladdin*, the ballets, and the Ebony Marionettes, a grand Ethiopian musical entertainment in imitation of the American minstrel troupes which were just becoming all the rage. The season ran for six months until July 1852, during which eighteen pieces were represented, with a weekly change of bill. Prices ranged from 1*s*. to 3*s*., and performances began at eight

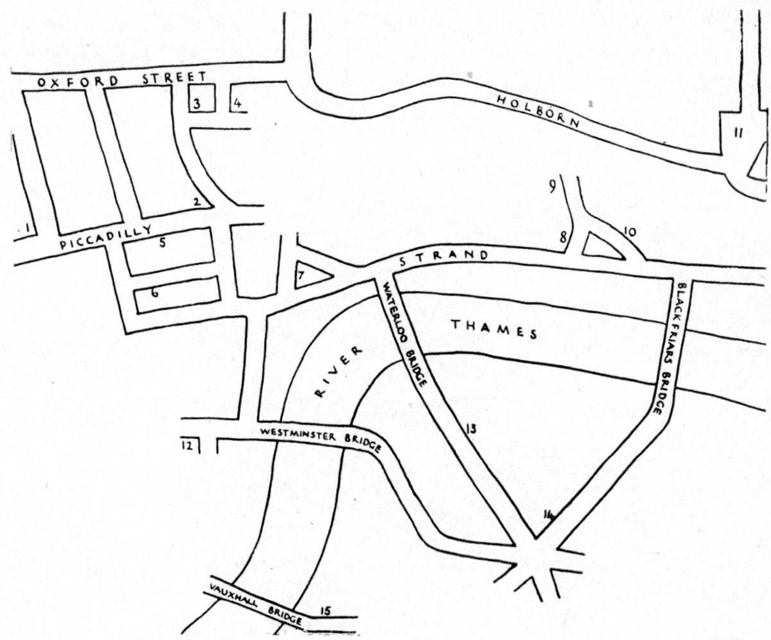

PLAN OF LONDON SHOWING PLACES WHERE PUPPET SHOWS WERE PERFORMED IN THE NINETEENTH CENTURY

1. Hyde Park Coronation Fair; 2. St James's Hall; 3. Argyll Rooms, Regent Street; 4. Hengler's Cirque; 5. Egyptian Hall; 6. St James's Theatre; 7. Adelaide Gallery, Lowther Arcade; 8. Little Theatre, Catherine Street; 9. Covent Garden Theatre; 10. Olympic Theatre; 11. Bartholomew Fair, Smithfield; 12. Westminster Aquarium; 13. Royal Victoria Hall; 14. Surrey Theatre; 15. Vauxhall Gardens. *Off the Map.* New Bagnigge Wells, Bayswater Road; Chalk Farm Tea Gardens, Primrose Hill; Cremorne Gardens, Chelsea; Earl's Court Exhibition; Sadler's Wells Theatre; Agricultural Hall, Islington; Westbourne Hall, Bayswater; Crystal Palace, Sydenham; Alexandra Palace, Wood Green; Albert Palace, Battersea; Olympia.

Music halls where puppet acts were presented are not listed. Probably every variety house in London could qualify under this heading.

Q

o'clock, with "morning performances" at three o'clock on two days of the week.

Brigaldi's company of marionettes numbered about 150; they were between two and three feet high, with heads modelled from *papier mâché* and with cork and wood bodies, and their consequent lightness lent them a tendency to "float" in the air which was commented upon adversely by the critics. They were manipulated from a high bridge, and were fitted with moving mouths—and one character at least with elevating eyebrows—but it was remarked that "the means of communicating these motions to them from above are a little too visible." Complaint was also made of the orchestra being too noisy, and that the performance was rather slow. An English marionette performer, who worked for this company and provided his own figure of a sailor, told Mayhew that "it was a passable exhibition, but nothing out of the way. When I had finished performing [my puppet] I took good care to whip it into a bag, so that they should not see how I arranged the strings, for they was very backward in their knowledge." But the critics were the exception; the general comment was that "the performance is irresistibly comic and certainly deserves patronage."

This season of the Royal Marionette Theatre had a considerable influence in its day. It certainly was largely responsible for the popularizing of the word 'marionette' in the English language, in which it previously had not gained much currency. For some years afterwards the Adelaide Gallery retained the name of the Royal Marionette Theatre, even when used by human performers; it was eventually converted into Gatti's restaurant, and is now the Nuffield Services Centre. This season also inspired the formation of a troupe of children who mimed plays to the accompaniment of voices 'off,' under the title of the Royal Living Marionette Theatre; they moved their mouths, like Brigaldi's puppets, and it was thought a great advantage that there were "no ugly strings to destroy the illusion"!

After their season at the Adelaide Gallery the Royal Marionettes undertook a provincial tour, playing for three months at Manchester and two at Liverpool; they were back in London at the St James's Theatre for Christmas, made a limited reappearance at the Adelaide Gallery, and were eventually established at Cremorne Gardens in 1857 in a magnificent Marionette Theatre, with an imposing Italianate façade, capable of seating a thousand people, which had been specially built for them.[13] Here, with Mr Albany Brown, their manager, and Hugo Vamp, their author, they played nightly at nine o'clock for several years, charging from *6d.* to *2s.*, in a further selection of pantomimical extravaganzas. Eventually, in the early sixties, perhaps handicapped by their large and un-intimate theatre, the Royal Marionettes disappeared from a Cremorne whose increasingly

THE ROYAL MARIONETTE THEATRE

From *The Illustrated London News*, January 17, 1852.

raffish and dissolute clientele may have failed to appreciate the whimsicality and charm of their innocent *travesties*.

We should like to know more of the men behind the Royal Marionette Theatre. Of the puppets themselves it seems that these much vaunted

Italians contributed nothing new to the technique of the marionette as it was known in England, but the dramatic material used by them was cleverly adapted to the English scene. Who was the "gentleman of considerable literary eminence," with liberal sympathies, who was rumoured to have contributed—under the *nom de plume* of Hugo Vamp—the highly barbed sketches to its repertory? Evidently there was a keen wit somewhere behind the scenes, who appreciated the puppet's gift for satire, though Henry Morley, in an interesting criticism, made the point that the puppet, who is a burlesque actor in himself, should not perform burlesque plays, but should rather, more whimsically, contrast "intense gravity in the subject with helpless absurdity in the actor."

Something, though not much, of the background to this enterprise can now be revealed. The impresario responsible for bringing the company to England was Thomas Bartlett Simpson, who had once been the head waiter at a theatrical tavern opposite Drury Lane, and who had recently bought Cremorne Gardens; a shrewd, kindly, and generous gentleman, who made a fortune from his enterprising management of Cremorne. The manager and principal "voice" of the marionettes was a Jewish actor named Morris Barnett, described by G. A. Sala as "a remarkably clever man, with a pronounced musical faculty and extraordinary powers of mimicry." In his day he had been quite a well-known character actor, and was the author of a number of dramas and farces at the minor theatres, but he had abandoned the stage for journalism, and for many years had been a dramatic critic. In 1854 he sought his fortune, unsuccessfully, in America, and a note of mystery hangs round his memory; his widow spoke of him as a "celebrated and gifted, but misguided man." "Hugo Vamp," the mysterious author, has been identified as a certain J. R. O'Neill, a minor playwright and entertainer of the fifties; but exactly who O'Neill was, or how he, Barnett, and Simpson came to co-operate with Brigaldi is a question to which we shall probably never know the answer.[14]

There was to be one further sally upon London by the Italian marionettes during this century. In 1888 "Dagonet," the columnist of the popular sporting and theatrical Sunday newspaper *The Referee*, wrote a glowing description of the puppet shows he had seen in Naples. In particular he praised a company playing at the Teatro Mercadante; its programme consisted of a spectacular performance of *The Universal Deluge*, with Noah marshalling the animals into the Ark and the awful rainstorm and flood that covered the earth, followed by Manzotti's famous ballet of *Excelsior*, that had already been played at every opera house in Europe, celebrating the Genius of Science in its conquest of Darkness, with steamships, express trains, electric flashes, the Mont Cenis Tunnel, a dance of the telegraph messengers, and an apotheosis of glory for the present and future, science, progress, and fraternity of the nations! "Dagonet" concluded that "they would draw all London."[15]

The Italians did not fail to take the hint, and four months later, in May 1888, the Colla Company, describing themselves as the Royal Italian Opera and Grand Ballet Marionette Company opened a season at Hengler's in Argyll Street, under the management of J. Brett and Co., proudly quoting *The Referee's* eulogy in their advance publicity. Their repertory included the two pieces that had so impressed "Dagonet," together with Meyerbeer's *Roberto il Diavolo* and additional ballets, but the entertainment that had appeared so delightful in the warm, romantic Neapolitan night sadly failed to impress in London. One review roundly stated that

> in our opinion these puppets will *not* draw all London . . . and though the audience was evidently willing to be pleased it was evident that they were frequently bored. . . . It may be doubted whether a marionette performance can be made sufficiently attractive to successfully furnish a whole evening's entertainment, especially when what dialogue there is is delivered in a foreign tongue.

The next day the management desperately announced that in future the services of the Italian spokesmen would be dispensed with and the action carried on in pantomime, but an even greater trial lay ahead.[16]

Less than three weeks later the Italian Exhibition at West Brompton announced that the brothers Prandi would present their celebrated Italian marionettes at a theatre in the exhibition, with the very same performances of *The Universal Deluge* and *Excelsior* of which "Dagonet" had written "they will draw all London."[11]

What can have happened? One can only guess that Colla and the Prandis had been in partnership at Naples, that their partnership had been dissolved, and that each of them insisted upon visiting a London that they had been assured would fall at their feet. So they went at it, each presenting an identical repertory, twice daily; and once again the Londoners could pay their money (up to 5*s*. at Hengler's, 3*s*. at Brompton) and take their choice. There had been nothing like it since the first rush with the Ombres Chinoises.

But this time Colla gave up after a week of competition, and within a month of their arrival his grandiloquently titled company stole silently away from an unappreciative London and an inconsiderate rival. The

Prandis went on playing spectacles and ballets all through the summer at the exhibition until it closed at the end of October, and they were back in London once again at the Crystal Palace in 1893. It was said of them that "the family has been in this line for two or three generations, and possesses some secret as to the method of working [these marionettes] which its members jealously keep to themselves"; but that is a familiar Press agent's hand-out, and the English were not so easily impressed. One critic complained that though "the performance is certainly amusing . . . there is really no attempt to deceive, the thick black strings by which the figures are worked from above being quite visible."

The marionettes of the Maffeys and of Brigaldi had made a great impression upon London Society, and during the first seventy years of the century they stood almost alone; they kept the memory of the marionette alive through a particularly barren century in our history. But by the time that Colla and the Prandis had reached London marionettes were no longer a novelty, and English companies were playing regularly at half a dozen metropolitan halls. The enduring English tradition had been preserved at the fairs, at the pleasure gardens, and on the streets until in the fullness of time it reasserted itself, as we shall see, in the West End.

On the Road

Driven from the fairs, and never admitted to the theatres, the humble marionette showmen took to the road, with their carts and tents, like their fathers before them. It is a dark period, this first seventy years of the nineteenth century, with a bare name here and there to assure us that the art of the marionette was not, indeed, entirely extinct. But gradually, out of the obscurity, new names and new faces begin to appear, and by the seventies and eighties we pass into an age of which men still living twenty years ago could tell stories to men of our own generation. And we are in time, to-day, to garner these fleeting memories of oral tradition and give them here the immortality of print.[18]

The touring marionette shows of the nineteenth century were the successors of the eighteenth century, but the old Elizabethan tradition of the interpreter, the squeaker, and the folk-plays had disappeared. In their place we find the late Victorian marionette theatres announcing *Black-eyed Susan*, *Dick Turpin*, *East Lynne*, *Lady Audley's Secret*, *Maria Martin*, *The Miller and His Men*, *Sweeney Todd*, and *Uncle Tom's Cabin*; the marionettes had now taken over the melodramas of the theatres and of the strolling players. What had happened was, in fact, that the human theatre had in this century, for the first time, become the popular entertainment of the masses; that the human theatre of London performances and printed texts was now, for the first time, identical with the popular theatre of farce and melodrama that had always existed in fairs and villages; and that the puppets, who have always provided the best vehicle for folk-drama, could now take their themes not from chapbooks and ballads, but from the theatre itself.

Not more than two or three of the popular folk puppet plays of the eighteenth century survived into the latter half of the nineteenth century, but there was still a tenuous link to show that the tradition had not been entirely broken. *The Children in the Wood*, for instance, was regularly played as a drama, not as a pantomime, and concluded in the traditional way with the babes being borne to Heaven by angels, while the wicked uncle was carried off to Hell through the trap, with smoke and fireworks. In this play, too, the birds still covered the sleeping children with leaves in 1896, exactly as they had at Powell's theatre nearly two hundred years before.

In addition to the dramas, the marionettes usually presented a pantomime, often in a special afternoon performance for children, and we hear wonderful accounts of the grand transformation scenes with which they ended. At Wilding's theatre this contained six changes with gauzes, taking seven minutes to operate, and concluding with a waterfall, and he paid a scene-painter £200 for painting it. And before it there would, of course, be a genuine harlequinade.

The traditional Fantoccini tricks were still introduced, with songs and dances, and there was one little ballad that became a feature of almost all these marionette theatres. It is printed in some collections as "Oh, Cruel were my Parients," and is supposed to be sung by the old beggar-wife of a sailor, who has lost an eye and a leg in his country's service and is reduced to stumping round the country with a fiddle. Every verse, in the manner of such ballads, ends with a chorus of "too-rol-loo-rol-loos" in which the husband is supposed to join, and an amusing slant is given to the song by the old salt invariably missing his cue and by his wife fairly bawling into his ear "Chorus Tommy" on every occasion. From this bit of business the song came to be known in the puppet theatres as "Chorus Tommy."[19] It was in the repertoire of Harry Rowe, and provides one more of the few links between the marionette shows of the eighteenth and nineteenth centuries.

Punch no longer appeared in these nineteenth-century marionette theatres, but puppets need a clown in their dramas; we have seen how

Middleton tried to supply the lack, and before very long a character appeared who was adopted by almost every marionette troupe as its resident comedian. This was a slow-witted country bumpkin named Tim Bobbin, who had, nevertheless, some grains of cunning beneath his stupidity. The origin of this character may be traced to a certain John Collier, an itinerant schoolmaster and sign-painter in Lancashire during the mid-eighteenth century, who wrote a book about the misadventures of a typical yokel of his region, in a phonetic approximation to the Lancashire dialect, and published it over the pseudonym of "Tim Bobbin."[20] His story gained immense popularity and many imitators in the North of England, and his own pseudonym seems to have become attached to the hero, or clown, of whom he wrote. Some time near the middle of the nineteenth century he became a marionette.

Tim Bobbin is in the true line of universal clowns. In *Maria Martin*, where he appears as a foolish yokel courting Maria's sister, he is held up by a highwayman while taking the rent to the landlord. "Your money or your life," cries the highwayman, brandishing his pistol. "Nay, take my life and spare my money," answers Tim. Then, having handed everything over without the least resistance, he begs the highwayman as a favour to shoot through his hat and smock so as to suggest he had made a fight of it. The highwayman obliges, again and again, until he runs out of bullets, and Tim then bashes him on the head, collects his goods back, and marches him off to justice.[21]

Tim Bobbin might well be revived in the puppet theatres of to-day. Punch, although an adopted Englishman, is, after all, one part Italian; but Tim Bobbin is an authentic regional type, a worthy companion to Kasperl and Lafleur and Tchantches as the national English marionette clown.

The theatres in which these shows were presented were portable structures, with walls constructed from six-foot-wide wooden shutters and with a canvas roof. The front, which might extend from 30 to 100 feet, would be highly decorated in fairground rococo, and along it would stretch a parade platform on which performers might strut and from which one entered the theatre. The Jewell-Holden show had a uniformed band playing on the parade, and others boasted a Marenghi paper organ, perhaps with a kettle-drum and a great bronze bell. Admission charges ranged from 3*d.* to 1*s.*, with often a penny matinée for children, and the theatres might seat from 200 to 700 people on tiered rows of planks. In 1864 Calver claimed that his new monster portable pavilion could seat 1000. When the shows were pitched at fairs performances lasted only fifteen to thirty minutes, but when set up on their own at a village or small town, where they might stay two or three weeks playing a different bill every night, one or two hours' programme was usually given. For orchestra one show took a piano, and relied on finding a pianist, or "joger-ohmy," to play it at every stop, another travelled an harmonium, and another had a cornet-player, who played a wrong note to warn the

THE EXCELSIOR MARIONETTE BOOTH, WITH THE TILLER FAMILY OUTSIDE, C. 1900

From a photograph in the Gerald Morice Collection

operators if a figure was "flying" its feet off the ground; fiddles and dulcimers still accompanied the puppets, and the band, which might number up to half a dozen players, would promenade around the district to advertise the show. When it was time to move on to the next pitch the whole theatre was dismantled and loaded on wagons. The Tillers travelled three wagons, Testo five, and Wilding eleven wagon-loads and five living-vans for the performers.

The shows were run as family concerns, and the names of dynasties of puppet families creep into our story, each touring its own rural circuit. There was Grandfather Clowes, who worked in the Lancashire mills and was stood off during the Hungry Forties; he went busking with some mates playing the hand-bells, joined Simms's Marionettes as an instrumentalist, and brought his eldest son up in the business. This son founded his own show, with the help of the Tillers, two cousins, in 1873. The partners changed from time to time, each new branch of the family setting up on its own until the story becomes too complicated for words, with at one time five different branches of the Tiller family all running their own shows.

Then there was Clunn Lewis, an Irishman, who was taught by his father to play the harp and paint inn-signs, but who wanted to be a Catholic priest; but the call of the theatre proved too strong for him, and at sixteen he was playing Pantaloon, and at nineteen he married an actress. The young couple saved enough money to buy Middleton's Marionettes from one of the many descendants of that great family of puppet troupers, and they continued to tour the southern counties until living memory. Clunn Lewis became a familiar figure, wearing a top hat and pushing his theatre on a hand-barrow in front of him, as he wandered through the villages of Kent and Sussex. He remained an ardent Catholic all his life, and was in the habit of distributing the leaflets of the Catholic Truth Society as he went.[22]

And so one could tell the story of many another family of hard-working vagabond artists: of the Lawrences and the Testos and the Wildings, of bewildering inter-marriages between one dynasty and another, of family partnerships and family feuds, of the friendly welcome of the villagers on their annual visit, of carving new puppets and dressing them and reading new plays in Dick's Penny Editions; of rearing babies amid the clutter of the show; of bringing up the children in the mysteries of their art, and of the firm discipline of the father, the master of the show. One night one of the Clowes daughters, a girl of fifteen, failed to fit the white "ghost" smock over Maria Martin for the dream scene. As soon as the curtain came down her father called her to ask why it hadn't been done. "I forgot, Father," she confessed. "Let that teach you not to forget again," her father said, as he smacked her there and then in the wings.

Here and there a puppet theatre settled permanently. Seward, once an agile Harlequin, whose puppets had appeared at Bartholomew Fair, established a theatre at Cheltenham at the beginning of the nineteenth century, and his family flourished there for some forty or fifty years.[23] At Sunderland a marionette theatre kept its doors open from 1843 to about 1904, with a change of bill every night and a fantastically varied programme.[24] At Dublin, D'Arc's Marionettes and Waxworks were

An Entertainment for the Children at Arundel Castle
From *The Illustrated London News*, January 9, 1869.

Barnard's Harlequinade, c. 1890
By courtesy of Kenneth Barnard, Esq

shown at the Rotunda for long resident seasons during the last thirty-five years of the century, and then moved to Cardiff. At Hull[25] and Bristol, and who knows where else, penny theatres played nightly their seemingly inexhaustible repertory of marionette dramas to audiences of boisterous, wide-eyed boys.

All this vivid and lively activity was halted in its tracks at the dawn of the twentieth century by a new invention. The Bioscope, or the Kinema, swept the country; every fair was provided with its flickering moving pictures, and many a marionette showman laid his puppets aside and re-equipped his booth with a projector. A few shows struggled on till the Great War, but none long survived it. We are, once again, at the end of an epoch.

Clunn Lewis lived long enough into our own age to be written about by journalists and praised by Bernard Shaw. G. K. Chesterton wrote of him: "Your work . . . is the best of all that popular art that Englishmen used to have, and would have still, if they had not been cheated of it by pushing and showy people, who are not artists and often not Englishmen."[26]

On the Halls

New life had been stirring in the provincial marionette troupes since the sixties, and in 1872 an English company appeared in London. There had been no English marionettes in the West End—apart from the street Fantoccini—since 1780, nearly a century before.[27]

On July 23, W. J. Bullock's Royal Marionettes opened at the Great St James's Hall, behind the Quadrant between Regent Street and Piccadilly, with a programme of Fantoccini, the Christy Minstrels, and *Little Red Riding Hood*. The Fantoccini included "Chorus Tommy," Pat and Biddy in an Irish jig, the tight-rope walker, and so on. Of the pantomime it was announced that

> the most beautiful scenery works by a new system of mechanism never before equalled for splendour and rapidity. . . . The management can assert that nothing hitherto has been produced in London or on the Continent on so extensive a scale of magnificence as this exhibition; the space required for working being larger than the stages of many theatres. The automata are nearly all life size, and splendidly modelled in wax; the band and chorus number over 20 performers, and the staff of manipulators are the greatest artists in their profession.[28]

This show took the town by storm. *The Times*, in a typically scholarly review, commented that

A GROUP OF TILLER-CLOWES FIGURES
Tim Bobbin is the large white puppet on the right.
By courtesy of the Old-Time Marionettes

A GROUP OF BARNARD FIGURES
From the Collection of the Lanchester Marionette Theatre

> puppets, highly patronized in the days of Addison's Spectator, less favoured when revived at the Adelaide Gallery some 20 years ago, have, after a long oblivion, burst upon public notice in a state of perfection. . . . The arrangement of the stage cannot be too highly recommended. When we say that there are twelve scenes in the little pantomime, and that but one of these is in the first groove, all who can understand us will see that a difficult problem is solved.

One wonders whether Bullock's "new system of mechanism" was the flying of scenery instead of the sliding of flat scenes in grooves. Other reviews from a rave Press spoke of "a highly ingenious, thoroughly amusing, and wholly unimpeachable entertainment . . . a marvel of ingenuity . . . manipulated with wondrous skill . . . to make old and young weep with laughter . . . it is difficult to believe that they are not endowed with life."

The show had been announced as for a short summer season only, but it ran right through the autumn until November, when it had to vacate the St James's Hall and moved across the road to Albert Smith's room in the Egyptian Hall in Piccadilly, where it continued to play until the middle of March 1873. The season had lasted nine months, with over 400 performances, twice daily, at prices ranging from 1*s.* to 5*s.* At capacity the Great St James's Hall, which was the home of the Moore and Burgess Minstrels, could hold nearly 5000 persons.

On leaving London Mr Bullock announced that the Royal Marionettes would shortly open in New York, after a short provincial tour. In America most of the company deserted to another impresario, and Royal Marionette companies sprouted in every other state of the Union; but that is a story that we cannot pursue here.[29] It is sufficient for our purposes that Bullock had restored the marionette to London.

Very little is known of the early history of this man who must be hailed as one of the most important figures in our chronicle. He is said to have been originally a schoolmaster. Before coming to London his company had played for six months at the Queen's Hall in Liverpool, and before that for four years in Dublin. His heads were made of wax, as were those of D'Arc, and as D'Arc had had a theatre in Dublin from the sixties, where the ubiquitous Middletons had been engaged as operators, it is highly probable that Bullock learnt something of his art from this French modeller of waxworks who had worked for Madame Tussaud. Dublin had already enjoyed a fine reputation for its puppet theatres in the eighteenth century, and clearly this continued into the nineteenth. We are left more than ever eager to learn the full story. The renaissance of the English marionette seems to have sprung from Dublin.

After Bullock's success marionette companies began to follow one another thick and fast into London. They played in the bill at the newly rising music-halls, at the Holborn, the Bedford, the Metropolitan, the South London, and many another; but above all they found a congenial home in those partly educational and scientific exhibitions that were so

BLONDIN AND A JUGGLER FROM THE TILLER-CLOWES TROUPE
By courtesy of the Old-Time Marionettes

dear to the late Victorian middle class. At the Crystal Palace, the Alexandra Palace, the Albert Palace, Battersea, the Westbourne Hall, the Royal Victoria Hall (recently reclaimed from the gin and melodrama of the Coburg), or the Westminster Aquarium the marionettes provided an entertainment that was amusing, instructive, and unobjectionable; above all it was suitable for children. The puppet show, which for so many centuries had been accepted as an adult form of theatre, was now discovered to be an ideal entertainment for the juveniles, to whose special needs dressmakers, booksellers, and teachers were now beginning to devote so much attention. This development must not be exaggerated, for children had visited Powell's show at the beginning of the eighteenth century, and Middleton had advertised special school performances at the beginning of the nineteenth. It is certain that the puppet show had *always* been considered specially attractive for children; but it was not until towards the end of the nineteenth century that specialization in children's entertainment began to stamp the puppet as primarily—though not yet exclusively—a children's show.

A pantomime was usually the main feature of these entertainments, and *Beauty and the Beast*, *Red Riding Hood*, and *Blue Beard* were the most popular. The harlequinade that followed it was full of comic business: Clown chased a butterfly about the stage and kicked Pantaloon in the eye, they had a ride on a donkey-cart and were thrown out on to the ground, a bull tossed and gored them, Clown danced on a table laid for supper and smashed all the plates, the landlady called the policeman, the policeman chased them, but a dog caught his coat-tails and they escaped, they sailed away in a balloon, but the car fell off and they crashed to earth again, the policeman caught them in each hand, but they made off in opposite directions, and the policeman split in two down the middle![30]

To introduce the pantomime the Nigger Minstrels usually made an appearance; there might be an Aquarium scene, with pretty fishes swimming about and a crocodile eating them up at the end; and there would always be a selection of Fantoccini tricks. The old favourites of the street Fantoccini were still played—the Skeleton, the Grand Turk, the Indian Juggler, and so on—and contemporary sensational human performers were imitated. Every rope-walker became a Blondin, and an extraordinary leaping dance by J. H. Stead to a song called "The Perfect Cure," introduced at the Holborn in the sixties, was parodied and greatly improved by the marionettes with a pair of expanding and contracting figures still known as the two Cures. The neck-stretching Scaramouch was now provided with three heads, rising one out of the other; the Chinese Bell Ringers, who had perhaps been introduced by the Maffeys, seem to have supplanted the old English quadrilles and country dances. There was usually a stilt-walking clown who drank out of a bottle and became inebriated, an acrobat who balanced a large roll called a Tranka with his feet, and a balancer on the horizontal bar between two chairs. A full two hours' programme was always available.

At the head of these theatre and exhibition-hall companies were further dynasties of puppet showmen: Chester and Lee, founded in 1868 by one of the Christy Minstrels; Delvaine, founded in 1877 by the son of the organist at Dublin Cathedral, who had started by selling programmes when his father played the piano at Bullock's Dublin theatre; Cooper, Wycherley, and Pettigrove's Imperial Marionettes; Jewell, who married a Holden; Pettigrove, who issued a challenge in *The Era* for £200 to anyone who could prove himself a better puppet manipulator (Harry Wilding took this up, and nothing more was ever heard of it); and many another.

The shows these companies toured were large and elaborate. D'Arc claimed to possess over 300 figures, Delvaine over 500; Delvaine travelled a stage 14 feet wide by 8 feet deep, with a bridge 8 feet high; Bullock's stage covered over 500 square feet; Clowes's proscenium was 12 feet by 6 feet, and the stage 12 feet deep. The Imperial Marionettes took three tons of scenery and eighteen artists; Bullock some ten operators and over twenty artists in all; and D'Arc fifteen manipulators—with, it is said, another fifteen in reserve in case they got drunk!

Companies multiplied so fast in the last decades of the Victorian era that it was not unknown for three different troupes to be playing in a town like Birmingham at the same time, and Mr Wilding claimed to remember a week when no less than seven different marionette companies were all performing in Liverpool—and the proprietors used to meet at night in the American Bar under St George's Hall and compare business. Many of the larger of these shows toured Europe, America, and the Far East; during the eighties and nineties D'Arc travelled to Australia, India, China, and Japan; Holden to every country in Europe; the Imperial Marionettes to Russia. At this period English marionettes were acknowledged as the best in the world. At a time when English opera singers were adopting Italian names and English chefs French names, French marionette performers were adopting English pseudonyms as their *noms de théâtre*.[31]

Perhaps the greatest of all these English puppeteers was Thomas Holden. He was descended from a fairground family, and his father or grandfather had demonstrated glass-blowing at Bartholomew Fair in the twenties and thirties. In the early seventies he was stage manager to Bullock, and by 1877 he was touring in Europe, where his fame rapidly spread. There is no real evidence that Holden's marionettes were any more wonderful than those of his fellow English puppeteers, but they made an enormous impression in France: Edmond de Goncourt wrote that "these creatures of wood are a little disturbing; there was a ballerina pirouetting in the moonlight, like something out of *The Tales of Hoffman*, and a clown who gets into bed, snuggles down, and goes to sleep with all the movements of a flesh-and-blood human being." But there were

R

those who found his marionettes almost too perfect: Lemercier de Neuville gave his impression that they "were certainly marvels of precise workmanship, and I would by no means deny them their value, but they addressed themselves to the eyes and not to the heart. . . . One admired them but one did not laugh, they astonished but did not charm."[32]

Another fine performer was Richard Barnard. When he was only thirteen years old he ran away from home after a whipping and lived on his wits in the streets until his uncle, Charles Middleton, picked him up and taught him to slang the puppets in the family booth. He trouped all over England with a variety of small shows, playing wherever they could raise an audience, and earning 25*s*. a week when he was lucky enough to be paid. In 1874 he joined Bullock's as a figure-worker, visiting the larger provincial towns for four or five years and rising to a weekly salary of 35*s*., and then toured the Continent with Holden. In 1880 he formed his own company, and during the next ten years played in France, Belgium, Holland, Germany, Austria, Bohemia, Roumania, Hungary, Russia, and Spain. Back in England he built up a series of regular bookings at the Crystal Palace, the Westminster Aquarium, and the variety circuits. Barnard's was a comparatively modest company, employing usually only three operators, but his figures are among the finest that have survived; he carried the fame of the English marionettes through appalling difficulties to the remotest corners of Europe.[33]

One could fill a book—and I hope some one will one day—with the stories of these grand Victorian puppet-masters, of their alliances and their rivalries, of their world-wide travels, and of the secrets of their craft; with them English puppetry reached its apogee. But, as with the sailing-ship and the stage-coach, destruction was near at hand: these unsophisticated mysteries fell all too easily before the new wonders of the cinema. The music-hall provided their last haven, and one or two shows, notably Delvaine's, continued to appear, infrequently, on the smaller circuits up to the Second World War. But a show of this scale is expensive to travel, and we shall see no more of this old-time entertainment now.

These late Victorian marionettes carried the seed of decadence within them; as so often before in our history, the turns became stereotyped, every puppeteer imitated each other, and the tradition grew stagnant. The seventies and eighties had been a period of great new developments, but—as with the golden age of conjuring with which these marionettes may be paralleled—there was no further technical or artistic advance. And with the slackening of Victorian standards of parental control the

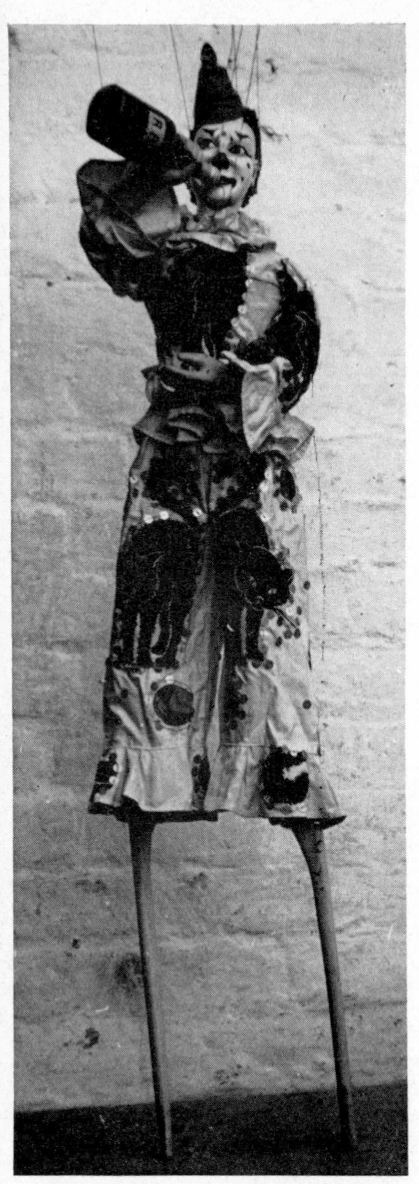

STILT-WALKING CLOWN AND FOUR-HEADED SCARAMOUCH FROM THE BARNARD TROUPE

From the Collection of the Lanchester Marionette Theatre

family partnerships broke up. Two or three decades sufficed for the virtual extinction of the great puppet companies of the nineteenth century. Yet in their day they had constituted the supreme English contribution to the art of the marionette.

At the Slangs

The construction of their marionettes was regarded by these showmen as a secret to be handed down from father to son and jealously guarded from outsiders. Holden insisted on having the back of his stage hidden behind a kind of tent, let down from the flies, when he was playing in a big theatre, so that not even the stage-hands should see how it was done; when he did once, unwillingly and after much bargaining, agree to sell a figure to a fellow-performer he carefully cut its strings off before allowing it out of his hands. The few descriptions of marionette-making that began to appear in later Victorian boys' books are hopelessly vague and impractical.

But as the great troupes were broken up their figures were left here and there, mouldering in barns and attics, to be discovered in our own day by puppet enthusiasts of a new generation. Now their secrets have been revealed in books, and their mysteries need bewilder us no longer.[34]

I was myself responsible for an attempt to revive one of these companies. Not many years ago, during the recent War, a friend of mine, Mr Gerald Morice, who has written a weekly puppet column for many years in the showman's paper *The World's Fair*, received a letter from an elderly lady in Lincolnshire saying that she possessed a number of old puppets and wished to sell them. I was home on leave at the time, and Mr Morice asked me to go up and have a look at them. When I finally reached the village where their owner lived, and opened the three large boxes where they were stored in a barn, I saw before me the entire troupe of one of the great Victorian marionette companies; harlequins and clowns, acrobats and jugglers, Tim Bobbin and Maria Martin, heroines and villains for any melodrama, lay jumbled before me, their paint still bright, their costumes faded but whole. It was the Tiller troupe that had been founded, in partnership with Clowes, in 1873. When the Great War broke out the men had gone off to fight, and the show had been stranded in this Lincolnshire village; the puppets had been put away in a barn, and there they had lain untouched for nearly thirty years.

The show was bought—there were some fifty figures and much painted scenery—and a few years later we set to work to make it ready for performance once again. For several months we washed the puppets and their clothes, repaired their joints and renewed their strings. As I worked with these figures in the romantic task of bringing them back to life I felt an excitement as intense as that of any archæologist delving among the ruins of Babylon or Troy. Finally we presented them—as "The Old-Time Marionettes"—in the lovely Riverside Theatre at the Festival Pleasure Gardens in a programme of old music-hall songs and tricks, with Tim Bobbin, "Chorus Tommy," and a harlequinade. It was an exciting and a rewarding experience. For a few brief months, during that memorable summer of 1951, before political prejudice and economic stringency had their way, Londoners could again drink beer and wine beneath the trees, and listen to the band, gaze at the fireworks down the fountain vista, and watch the puppets beside the flowing Thames.

Bullock's claim to have shown "life-size automata" can be ignored. The word 'automata' was often used by puppet showmen, incorrectly, to describe their figures in the hope of making a mystery of their manipulation, and in this period we find hybrids like Manikins and Fantoches frequently employed. It is also very unlikely that they were life-size; it is quite impossible for an audience to guess the true size of a marionette without a human figure to compare it with, and a claim like this was not likely to be contradicted. Bullock's company had split up in America, and many of its members had gone on to found their own shows; in this dispersal the Bullock tradition became widely spread over both continents. Enough figures have survived for us to be able to reconstruct the appearance and construction of the Victorian marionette.

The majority of Victorian marionettes were about 2 feet 6 inches or 3 feet high, though 18-inch or even 12-inch figures were used for drawing-room entertainments; their heads, arms, and legs were carved in wood, but to save weight the bulk of their trunks and their arms above the elbow were usually of cloth stuffed with straw. They were normally controlled by seven strings, which were coloured green, as this was believed to be the least visible colour. These were attached to two straight wooden sticks or controls, the two leg-strings to one stick and the two arm-, two head-, and back-strings to the other. Elaborate and trick figures would, of course, have more control sticks, and Barnard's Witch, out of whose pockets half a dozen small characters would jump, is said to have had fifty strings.

So that they could play their parts in the frequently varied repertory, the puppets were given costumes that could be easily changed without involving restringing the figures. With the Tiller-Clowes puppets there went a fascinating box full of every variety of costume in rich Victorian fabrics. Stockings, however, were usually stuck over the well-shaped calves of the marionettes, and you can often peel three or four layers off an old figure.

All the major Victorian companies fitted a high bridge above the stage, which allows for spectacular effects impossible when the bridge is no more than a low step behind the backcloth; and with half a dozen or more operators some very splendid productions must have been achieved. Holden once described graphically how his shirt would be soaked with perspiration during a performance, and how the true secret of his profession lay in one's ability

> to pull the strings, sometimes standing, sometimes kneeling and most often lying on one's stomach in positions often dangerous and always uncomfortable, sometimes hanging by a foot or clutching with an arm to an iron bar, rushing from right to left, up and down, singing, talking, shouting, according to the needs of the moment, without time even to take breath, changing one's voice according to the character presented to the public, and the whole time sweating as if in a Turkish Bath.[35]

These Victorian marionettes were, for the most part, made by the puppet showmen themselves, and dressed by their wives and daughters; they all conform to a common tradition, though their quality varies between different troupes, and there were many variations in detail. Some had painted eyes and some artificial glass eyes, some carved hair and some crêpe hair, moving mouths and *papier-mâché* heads were uncommon, and D'Arc and Bullock were, I think, the only puppet-makers to provide wax heads.

As we have seen, the marionettes of the eighteenth century—even of the end of the eighteenth century—were controlled by one firm wire to the centre of their heads, with subsidiary strings to their arms and legs, while the earliest English marionettes that have survived, dating probably from the eighteen-seventies,[36] are controlled—in the modern manner—by strings throughout. No more interesting problem is presented to the puppet historian than that of determining when and where this fundamental development of the disappearance of the wire took place. It has been stated that Holden was responsible for the change,[37] but though he may well have initiated it in Europe, there is no evidence that he introduced any revolutionary technical development in England. On the contrary, the street Fantoccini performer who told his story to Mayhew in 1852, and who found Brigaldi so backward in his knowledge, speaks continually of his strings, but never of his wires, and he learnt his craft

HEADS OF PUPPETS FROM THE BARNARD TROUPE

From the Collection of the Lanchester Marionette

from Seward, in the days of the Regency. It seems, indeed, that while the wire is a quite satisfactory control for orthodox figures, it can never have been used for trick marionettes like the Skeleton, the Grand Turk, or the neck-stretching Scaramouch. Probably the two systems worked side by side for some years, the wire for plays and the strings for tricks, but when the plays fell into disuse in the early nineteenth century puppeteers must have become increasingly familiar with all-stringed figures, and in the revival of the seventies this type became universally adopted. The abandonment of the wire was a significant step in the quest for perfect illusion, but a certain imprecision of the puppet's movement was the price that had to be paid. Although we cannot be sure how the Italians may have controlled the trick figures of their Fantoccini, it does seem that English puppeteers led the world in the general abandonment of the wire-controlled marionette,[38] and if any one puppet-master can claim the credit I feel that this may well be awarded to Bullock in the sixties. The whole subject, however, bristles with difficulties, and there is scope for much further research before a definite claim could be substantiated. One recalls the large English puppets of the seventeen-thirties, that were said to be moved without any visible form of control; were these, perhaps, manipulated by thin and almost invisible threads? It is tempting to speculate that it was Fawkes, the eighteenth-century conjuror, who first experimented with the use of the fully strung marionette.

Some visitors to the performances of the Old-Time Marionettes may have thought the movements of these Victorian figures somewhat stiff, but to my mind a certain monumental rheumatism in a marionette is greatly to be preferred to the incessant jigging to which so many modern puppets are liable, and the natural weight of the figures lends to their gestures an inherent force and authority that belongs rather to the puppet than to the manipulator above. At their best, these Victorian marionettes, with the primitive vigour of their carving and the theatrical *panache* of their costume, must be rated among the finest creations of English popular art, and their existence and interest are as yet all too little known.

As it is, a hundred or so survivals have been rescued from oblivion by the perseverance of a handful of enthusiasts, but English marionettes are preserved in only two provincial museums.[39] The great national museums contain puppets from the East and puppets from Italy, but not a single example of our own native marionette art. France, Germany, and Russia have their own puppet museums, and may the day not be far distant when England too can boast her own, as an annexe to that general Museum of the Theatre of which we stand in equal need.

Chapter X

THE TWENTIETH-CENTURY REVIVAL

AND so, once again, we seem at the end of our story. In the first decade of this century the puppet theatre in England was, indeed, on the verge of extinction. Yet once again this phœnix art has risen anew, and the voice that called it from the shadows was that of the artist.

In 1897 Arthur Symons wrote in an essay entitled "An Apology for Puppets" that

> I am inclined to ask myself why we require the intervention of any less perfect medium . . . this is nothing less than a fantastic, yet a direct, return to the masks of the Greeks . . . let the marionettes remind us that the art of the theatre should be beautiful first, and then indeed what you will afterwards . . . the appeal in what seems to you these childish manœuvres is to a finer, because to a more intimately poetic, sense of things than the merely rationalistic appeal of very modern plays.[1]

Ten years later, in the first volume of *The Mask*, a new journal of the art of the theatre, Edward Gordon Craig wrote on "The Actor and the *Übermarionette*." He never claimed, as has sometimes been thought, that all actors should be replaced by puppets; but he pleaded that the old style of realistic acting was played out, that a still older art of conventionalized gesture must be discovered, and that the actor must give way to the inanimate figure, the super-, the *Übermarionette*. And that this, the living actor "plus fire, minus egoism," might learn much from that other actor, the actor of wood.

> The marionette appears to me to be the last echo of some noble and beautiful art of a past civilization. But as with all art that has passed into fat and vulgar hands, the puppet has become a reproach. All puppets are now but low comedians. . . . 'Puppet' is a term of contempt, though there still remain some who find beauty in these little figures, degenerate though they have become. . . . And who knows whether the Puppet shall not once again become the faithful medium for the beautiful thoughts of the artist.[2]

In many countries of the sophisticated Western world artists and poets at this time began to discover the strange charm of the marionette, and to see the tawdry and debased puppet show with new eyes. In England, hesitantly and in a small way, a few amateur experiments were made. In 1908 J. A. Fuller Maitland, the editor of Grove's *Dictionary of Music*, converted a billiard-room in St John's Wood into a puppet theatre, where he gave private performances of *Interior*, the play that Maeterlinck had described as being "for marionettes," only because he felt sure that human players would never act it.[3] In 1910 the old German folk puppet play of *Doctor Faustus* was revived by Yorkshire amateurs.[4] In 1914 Gair Wilkinson was inspired by some toy Italian puppets to make some for himself, and toured England in a caravan, performing with them.[5]

The technical skill of these early revivals must have fallen far short of their inspiration; these new puppet players had to learn the hard way, from first principles, with little help from the old school of showmen; but their technique quickly improved, and in the years after the Great War some of these artist-puppeteers produced figures of the highest quality. There was William Simmonds, with a one-man marionette show of great charm, with exquisite animals, fauns, and woodland nymphs, carved with delicacy and moved with understanding, who brought his theatre on rare visits to London. There was Walter Wilkinson, who gave new life to the glove puppet with subtle mimes, simple ballads, and a pleasant revival of the old morality *Thersites*, who tramped all over Britain with his show and wrote a series of popular books about his travels. And there was Olive Blackham, who developed a marionette theatre of extraordinary interest, and explored the possibilities of puppet drama with Japanese Noh plays, medieval miracle plays, Shakespeare, Chekov, and Kreymborg. The work of these artist-puppeteers, and of the many others who might be mentioned, may sometimes have lacked the theatrical 'attack' of the born showman, but it was and is—for it still goes on—a little-known but significant contribution to the culture of our time.[6]

Springing from the same inspiration, educationists who were stirred by the new theories of child-art and self-expression in the school recognized in the puppet a medium of vast potentialities. From the early thirties onward puppet-making increasingly found a place in the school as a craft activity that led on to many stimulating adventures in drama, and that could enrich not only every subject in the curriculum, but the personality as well. To-day, largely guided by its own organization, the Educational Puppetry Association,[7] puppetry flourishes in a vast number of English schools, ranging from nursery classes to Eton College.

So rich and detailed is the story of the puppet revival of this century that I cannot do more than offer a mere sketch of the broad lines of its development. We are too close to see it in perspective, but there is no doubt that men have turned from the speed and mechanization of the age with relief and gratitude to the simple crafts of the hand; and among these crafts the puppets have found a place. I write now not of men who would call themselves 'artists' at all, but of craftsmen and simple men with a hobby. In 1923 the publication of a book called *Everybody's Theatre*, by H. W. Whanslaw, led to the creation of the British Puppet and Model Theatre Guild, which—largely due to the wise guidance of Mr Seymour Marks, its first secretary—has provided a friendly meeting-ground for many amateurs and professionals ever since.[8] At the Annual Exhibitions organized by the Guild the artistic standard of the puppets shown and of the performances given has not always been high, but with this widespread activity in many thousands of homes and workshops the puppet has indeed entered upon a new inheritance in this age of the common man.

No longer is the puppet a secret and a mystery: books on how to make puppets have followed each other year by year, and the puppeteers of this generation, working in the light and sharing their knowledge with each other, have produced figures that are better jointed, better strung, and in every way technically superior to those of the last century. But are they better actors? Too often, alas, the puppet-maker has had little idea of what to do with his figure when he has made it.

From the artists and the craftsmen a new generation of professional puppet showmen has arisen. To-day the marionettes of Waldo Lanchester, of Jan Bussell, or of John Wright may be seen on tour in the provinces, or in occasional London seasons; and the subtly differing features of their shows may be compared. Lanchester is the craftsman *par excellence*, his figures beautifully carved, painted, and dressed, his manipulation smooth and perfect. His repertory has included some interesting and out-of-the-way operas, but on second or third seeing his show sometimes seems to lack the dramatic punch necessary to put it over in a big theatre. Bussell, with his Hogarth Puppets, on the other hand, has made much cruder figures, that succeed nevertheless in getting across the footlights with some success; there is much hope for the future from his present policy of employing master-carvers and puppet-makers to make his figures while he is busy performing. To some minds his repertory, with the over-familiar circus and band, is lacking in interest, but if he was not chained by public demand to the antics of a performing mule he would certainly embark on more enterprising material. In some ways his most successful work has been his revival of the Shadow Show, in collaboration with the exquisite silhouettes of Lotte Reiniger. Wright assumes a rather more sophisticated taste in his audience than do most of his colleagues, and his *divertissements* come as a refreshing change after the traditional but now somewhat stale tricks of the Fantoccini. He also mounts longer and more elaborate plays than most puppeteers of this generation, with a welcome use of human readers, but the perfect synthesis between voice and puppet has perhaps yet to be found.[9]

There are others—many others. Perhaps half a dozen companies able to mount a full programme in a medium-sized theatre; perhaps ten or twenty able to fill a ten-minute spot in a music-hall; perhaps forty or fifty able to entertain a school or drawing-room party.[10] Few of these shows can afford more than three operators, and only one has an overhead bridge. The productions must be simple, and cannot compare with the elaborate spectacles mounted by their Victorian predecessors or by some contemporary Continental companies. The struggle to restore the puppet is a hard one, and though much progress has been made, much more is necessary before we can feel satisfied with our achievements. Above all, it must be recognized that the puppet show is *not* an easy and inexpensive way of carrying the theatre about, but that it is infinitely *more* difficult and *more* skilful, and almost as expensive, to present a theatrical show of quality with puppets than with human actors. It is a fine and delicate art in its own right, and one that is rarely mastered.

But though enthusiasts for the art of the puppet may complain, the public for puppets is growing, and it has been enormously increased by television. Puppets have proved themselves ideal performers on this medium, and the characters of Muffin the Mule, Andy Pandy, and many another have endeared themselves to millions of children. In what would seem a miraculous way to the showmen whose stories have been told in these pages their ancient art has been made new by one of the most amazing inventions of the twentieth century.

During this century too we have not failed to extend to Continental puppet showmen the ready welcome that has ever characterized the English. The visits of Podrecca's Teatro dei Piccoli in 1923, and on later occasions, made an enormous impression on the English public; one could wish that English puppeteers had imitated the verve and 'attack' of its presentation, rather than the brilliant pianist who has been palely reflected on so many of our puppet stages since. After the coming of Hitler we were proud to be able to offer hospitality to the fine Marionette Theatre of Munich Artists of Paul Brann, which played among us for several years; and in recent years, among many other visitors, it has been a great inspiration to see the delicate Salzburg Marionettes of Hermann Aicher, the witty Czech marionettes of Professor Skupa, the artistically integrated production of Harro Siegel, and the satirical Russian hand and rod puppets of Sergei Obraztsov. The influence of the American Bob Bromley, who plays without stage or scenery in a simple spot, has inspired many English puppeteers—who have not always shared his effective theatrical personality—to discard the bulky equipment of their puppet stages.

Puppeteers in England to-day ask for three things. They ask for a permanent puppet theatre in London, at which different companies may play short seasons, thus relieving them from the everlasting grind of touring and one-day stands all over the country. They ask for intelligent, informed, and constructive criticism of their performances. And they ask for the recognition that the puppet is an adult art, and not only an entertainment for children. To-day a puppet show is regarded almost universally as "a show for the kiddies," and puppeteers who try to present an adult or sophisticated programme find it difficult to obtain an audience. Yet the story that we have traced in these pages through many centuries should prove decisively that the puppet has an ancient and honourable history as a medium of drama and of satire, and that it has pleased artists and wits as well as peasants and nursemaids.

In the end, when we wonder how these moving dolls can engage the wonder and attention of human beings, we must understand that their secret lies in their ability to arouse the sympathetic imagination of their audience. We who watch must endow their cryptic masks with the emotion of the drama, and inhabit their cold bodies with the passion of the stage; and thus, as we lend them our pity, our laughter, and our tears, there is created that true union between the actor and the audience that is the heart and the soul of the theatre.

NOTES

I am a puppet showman, not a professional scholar, but I have tried to present this history with the elements of authority and scholarship. In general the following principles have been observed throughout.

No references are provided for statements of common historical knowledge. *General* references are given for statements regarding the history of the theatre. *Detailed* references to original sources are given for all statements regarding the history of puppets. These have all been checked by me personally, or, in rare cases, are vouched for by what I believe to be fully reliable authorities. Quotations in the text are given in English, and with modern spelling and punctuation; in cases of doubt the original is quoted in a note. (The exception to this rule is the name of Punch, in its many varieties of orthography, which is always quoted as originally spelt.) I am aware that this practice is frowned on by the most correct scholars, but I think that the idiosyncracies of seventeenth- and even eighteenth-century spelling provide an unnecessary barrier between the sense of the passage and the general reader, for whom this book is primarily intended. Where there are cases of confusion dates have been rendered according to the New Style.

In general, references are given in sufficient detail to enable an intelligent inquirer to locate them within a few minutes of taking up the necessary volume. I regret that the usefulness of *always* giving page or line references impressed itself upon me only when it was too late to apply this rule consistently; nevertheless a close reference (of at least act and scene in the cases of plays) has, I think, been provided in every case where the plan or index of the work referred to does not render this a labour of supererogation.

Finally, to scholars I would offer apologies for any shortcomings in the critical apparatus of this work; and to the general reader I would extend an invitation not to stop reading at this point, but to follow me through the succeeding pages to some of the books and manuscripts to which I refer, and to recapture the fascination, the fun, and the thrill of tracing the rich and varied history of puppets in the literature of eight languages through two thousand five hundred years of European history.

Abbreviations

The following books, to which frequent references are made in the notes, are referred to on all occasions after the first by abbreviations. Listed thus they provide a skeleton of a desirable library for the more extended study of our subject.

BASKERVILL: C. R. Baskervill, *The Elizabethan Jig* (Chicago, 1929).
BIEBER: Margarete Bieber, *The History of the Greek and Roman Theatre* (Princeton, 1939).
Biographica Dramatica: D. E. Baker, Isaac Reed, and S. Jones, *Biographia Dramatica* (third revised edition, 1812).
VON BOEHN: Max von Boehn, *Dolls and Puppets* (1932).
BRAGAGLIA: Anton Giulio Bragaglia, *Pulcinella* (Rome, 1953).
Cal. S.P. Dom.: *Calendar of State Papers, Domestic*, in the Public Record Office.
CHAMBERS: Robert Chambers, *The Book of Days* (1863–64).
E. K. CHAMBERS: Sir E. K. Chambers, *The Mediæval Stage* (1903).
CHESNAIS: Jacques Chesnais, *Histoire générale des marionnettes* (Paris, 1947).
COLLIER: *Punch and Judy*, with illustrations by George Cruikshank and introduction by John Payne Collier (1828).
CROCE: Benedetto Croce, *Pulcinella e il personaggio del Napoletano in Commedia* (Rome, 1899).
D.N.B.: *Dictionary of National Biography.*
DUCHARTRE: P. L. Duchartre, *The Italian Comedy* (1929).
FERRIGNI: "Yorrick" (P. C. Ferrigni), *Storia dei Burattini* (Florence, 1902).
FLÖGEL: *Flögel's Geschichte des Grotesk-Komischen*, neu bearbeitet von Friedrich W. Ebeling (Leipzig, 1862).
FROST: Thomas Frost, *The Old Showmen and the Old London Fairs* (1874).
HONE: William Hone, *The Every-Day Book* (1825–26).
JOSEPH: Helen Haiman Joseph, *A Book of Marionettes* (1922).
McKECHNIE: Samuel McKechnie, *Popular Entertainments through the Ages* (1931).
McPHARLIN: Paul McPharlin, *The Puppet Theatre in America* (New York, 1949).
MAGNIN: Charles Magnin, *Histoire des marionnettes en Europe* (Paris, 1852).
MAINDRON: Ernest Maindron, *Marionnettes et guignols* (Paris, 1901).
The Mask: E. Gordon Craig (editor), *The Mask: a Journal of the Art of the Theatre* (Florence, 1908–29).
MAYHEW: Henry Mayhew, *London Labour and the London Poor* (1861), vol. iii.
MORLEY: Henry Morley, *Memoirs of Bartholomew Fair* (1859).
DE NEUVILLE: Lemercier de Neuville, *Histoire anecdotique des marionnettes modernes* (Paris, 1892).
NICOLL: Allardyce Nicoll, *Masks, Mimes, and Miracles* (1931).
The Puppet Master: The Puppet Master, the Journal of the British Puppet and Model Theatre Guild, 1946– (in progress).

Puppetry: Paul McPharlin (editor), *Puppetry: a Yearbook of Puppets and Marionettes* (Birmingham (U.S.A.), 1930–47).

Revue d'Histoire du Théâtre: Revue de la Société d'Histoire du Théâtre (Paris, 1949; in progress).

SAND: Maurice Sand, *The History of the Harlequinade* (1915).

STEAD: P. J. Stead, *Mr Punch* (1950).

Theatre Notebook: Theatre Notebook, the Journal of the Society for Theatre Research (1945; in progress).

Chapter I

1. Richard Pischel, in *Der Heimat des Puppenspiels* (Halle, 1900), translated as *The Home of the Puppet Play* (1902), advanced the theory that "it is not improbable that the puppet-play is in reality everywhere the most ancient form of dramatic representation. Without doubt, this is the case in India, and there, too, we must look for its home." William Ridgeway, in *The Dramas and Dramatic Dances of Non-European Races* (1915), disputes this claim, and demonstrates that puppets did not originate in India, that their existence in Europe can be traced far earlier than in the East, and that "if there has been any borrowing, India rather than Europe has been the borrower." He finds that "the puppet-play is not the origin of the drama, but a cheap means of placing famous historical dramas within reach of the populace . . . and that when we come face to face with the historical facts relating to puppet-entertainment, we find their dates to be comparatively recent."

In this fundamental dispute I must place myself on the side of Professor Ridgeway.

2. The most valuable books on the Greek and Roman popular theatre are those which give illustrations from contemporary vases and statuettes; a careful study of these pictures reveals more than the most laborious description. Especially to be recommended for this reason are:

Allardyce Nicoll, *Masks, Mimes, and Miracles* (1931).

Margarete Bieber, *Denkmäler zum Theaterwesen in Altertum* (Leipzig, 1920).

Margarete Bieber, *The History of the Greek and Roman Theater* (Princeton, 1939).

Other important studies are:

A. E. Haigh, *The Attic Theatre* (1907).

A. W. Pickard-Cambridge, *Dithyramb Tragedy and Comedy* (1927).

W. Beare, *The Roman Stage* (1950).

The brief summary given here may oversimplify a difficult and obscure subject; its true origin is a matter of conjecture, and the connexion between the various forms of mime should not be accepted too literally without further reference to the authorities cited.

3. The standard study for this period is Sir E. K. Chambers, *The Mediæval Stage* (1903). A useful shorter survey is A. P. Rossiter, *English Drama from Early Times to the Elizabethans* (1950).

4. The literature on the Commedia dell' Arte is enormous. Nicoll is again invaluable. I have also used:

K. M. Lea, *Italian Popular Comedy* (1934).
Winifred Smith, *The Commedia dell' Arte* (New York, 1912).
P. L. Duchartre, *The Italian Comedy* (1929).
Maurice Sand, *The History of the Harlequinade* (1915).

Of these Sand and Duchartre take the derivation from the Atellan Farce for granted, Smith and Lea question it with reasoned arguments, and Nicoll replies with a more closely documented plea for the traditional romantic theory.

5. The history of Pulcinella is very well told in A. G. Bragaglia, *Pulcinella* (Rome, 1953); his derivation is discussed exhaustively in two monographs: Albert Dieterich, *Pulcinella: Pompejanische Wandbilder und Römische Satyrspiele* (Leipzig, 1897), and Benedetto Croce, *Pulcinella e il personaggio del Napoletano in Commedia* (Rome, 1899).

6. This consists of 156 leaves, most of which represent birds, but 44 illustrate musicians and actors of the Commedia dell' Arte. It is now in the library of McGill University, Montreal. This library also possesses one of the best puppet collections in North America.

7. *I Balli di Sfessania.*

8. A full selection is reproduced by Nicoll and Bieber.

9. Nicoll. See also N. M. Bernardin, *La Comédie Italienne en France* (Paris, 1902).

10. E. K. Chambers, *The Elizabethan Stage* (1923).

11. See note 40, Chapter II. An illustration of an entertainment given by a troupe of hunchbacked grotesques at the marriage of Henri IV with Marie de Medici is reproduced in Lucien Dubech, *Histoire générale illustrée du théâtre* (Paris, 1932). This was in 1600, probably at Avignon; see George Slocombe, *Henry of Navarre* (1931).

12. 104 drawings of Pulcinellas were made, probably in the 1790's, for a picture-book that was, however, never published. As late as 1921 the entire series was intact and exhibited in Paris, but it has now been split up, and examples are scattered among many museums and collections in Europe and America.

Chapter II

1. The definitions given here are those accepted by contemporary English and American puppeteers. The definitions given in dictionaries are often based

on literary and metaphorical usage and are extremely confusing for technical purposes. The French word *marionnette* should be translated as 'puppet' in English—a continual source of confusion for translators.

2. The earliest attempt to record the history of puppets in antiquity was by Father Antonio M. Lupi, S.J., in *Storia Litteraria della Sicilia* (*c.* 1720), vol. i. The standard work on the subject is still Charles Magnin, *Histoire des Marionnettes en Europe* (Paris, 1852). The period examined throughout this chapter is largely covered by his researches, to which students are referred for a fuller treatment, and more detailed references. A well-illustrated general survey of puppets throughout the world is Max von Boehn, *Puppen und Puppenspiele* (1929), translated as *Dolls and Puppets* (1932).

3. Herodotus, *Works*, 2, 48.

4. Xenophon, *Symposium*, 4, 55. Magnin did not quite get the sense of this passage, and later writers have completely distorted it.

5. Athenæus, *The Deinosophists*, I, 1, 19, E.

6. *Satires*, 2, VII, 82, "Duceris ut nervis alienis mobile lignum." It has been claimed that this phrase alludes to the whipping of a top, and not to puppets at all.

7. Philo, *On the Creation*, XL.

8. Apuleius, *De Mundo*, II, 351. This was freely translated from an earlier Greek work attributed to Aristotle, *Peri Kosmon*, but Aristotle's authorship is disputed by modern scholars. The original Greek, which was probably written in about A.D. 100, refers not to puppet showmen, but to "machinists," and the whole passage probably alludes to automata rather than ordinary puppets.

9. *Noctes Atticæ*, XIV, 1.

10. Marcus Aurelius Antonius, *De Se Ipso*, VII, 3.

11. Illustrated in von Boehn, Figs. 86, 87, 89, 90, 94, 95, 295 (Figs. 94 and 295, although described as Roman and Greek respectively, illustrate the same figure), and Helen Haiman Joseph, *A Book of Marionettes* (1922; U.S.A., 1920), p. 20. There are some examples in the British Museum.

12. Compare Xenophon, *Hellenica*, II, 1, 8; and Plato, *Phaedrus*, 230 B.

13. Johannes Philoponus, *Commentary on Aristotle "De Generatione animalium,"* 701, b, 1–32.

14. Eustathius, *Commentary on "Iliad,"* IV, 151.

15. This is the basic argument of Hermann Reich, *Der Mimus* (Berlin, 1903). According to some theories, Karageuz, the Turkish shadow puppet, is derived from a common original with Pulcinella.

16. Quoted from a manuscript source under "bastaxi" in Ducange, *Glossarium Mediæ et Infimæ Latinitatis.*

17. *Flamenca*, translated by H. F. M. Prescott (1930). The verse translation is my own.

18. See Ducange, under "bastaxi"; E. K. Chambers, p. 71; and Raynouard, *Léxique Roman*, under "bavastel."

19. Now destroyed by fire. Reproduced by Nicoll, Fig. 120, and Joseph, p. 55.

20. *Li romans du boin roi Alexandre* (MS. Bodl. 264, fol. 54*v* and 76*r*). The first modern reference to these seems to have been by T. O. Westwood, in *The Archeological Journal*, No. V, 1848, in which he claims that they are almost identical with Punch and Judy. They were rediscovered by J. J. Jusserand in *An English Miscellany presented to Dr Furnivall* (1901), where he claimed them as illustrations of pageants; but this is unlikely. The entire manuscript has been reproduced as *The Romance of Alexander*, with an introduction by M. R. James (1933). Both miniatures are reproduced by Jusserand and by Nicoll, Fig. 121. For a further discussion of these see Chapter IV.

21. *Guillaume de la Barre*, Roman d'aventures par Arnaut Vidal de Castelnaudari, edited by Paul Meyer, v. 3171.

22. This list is taken, with a few omissions, from the catalogue of stories told after the banquet in *Flamenca.*

23. For a full history see Archdale A. King, "The Holy Blood of Hayles," in *Pax* for Autumn 1943. There is a similar French figure in the Cluny Museum.

24. E. K. Chambers, p. 157.

25. See Nesta de Robeck, *The Christmas Crib* (1938).

26. Jacques Chesnais, *Histoire générale des marionnettes* (Paris, 1947), pp. 81, 88–94, 104, and *Illustration*, Christmas 1948.

27. All the examples given, unless otherwise mentioned, are taken from Karl Young, *The Drama of the Medieval Church* (1933).

28. At Dieppe, and elsewhere in Northern France. See *Blason des singularitez et excellences de la bonne ville de Dieppe*: "For at this beautiful display neither artificial strings nor an iron rod can be seen, but the movements are produced so subtly that it seems like magic." This developed into a regular raree-show until it was put a stop to by Louis XIV in 1647; see Vitet, *Histoire de Dieppe*, quoted by Chesnais, pp. 83–85. *Les Marionnettes chez les Augustins Déchaussés de Rouen* (1889) reprints an interesting Jansenist poem of 1678, but in this case (a tableau of the laying of Christ in the tomb set up in a church in Rouen) the figures seem to have been static dressed images, and not puppets.

29. *Synodus Oriolana* (1600), Cap. 14.

30. W. Lambarde, *Alphabetical Description of the Chief Places in England and Wales* (1730). This was written in about 1570.

31. Bragaglia has some valuable chapters on puppets in Italy, but the only general Italian history of puppets is "Yorick" (P. C. Ferrigni), *Storia dei Burattini* (Florence, 1902). An English translation was published in *The Mask* (Florence, 1912–15). For its early history this work—like so many others—is almost entirely dependent upon Magnin.

32. John Evelyn noted in his diary for December 24, 1644: "the puppetry in the church of the Minerva [at Rome] representing the Nativity." This must have been some kind of crib.

33. Described by Gerolamo Cardano, *De Vanitate Rerum* (1557), Book XIII, and Lorenzo Lippi, *Il Malmantile Racquistata*, edited by Paolo Minucci (Florence, 1688) (written in *c.* 1649), i, 34.

34. Gerolamo Cardano, *De Subtilate Rerum* (1551), Book XVIII.

35. *Storia e ragione d'ogni poesia* (Milan, 1744), vol. iii, Part 2, pp. 245–248. The bulk of this translation from an abominably obscure original is my own.

36. *Punch and Puppets*, published by J. and R. Maxwell (1885). The text is partly taken from Frank Bellew, *The Art of Amusing* (1866), and is almost certainly the work of this well-informed enthusiast.

37. Magnin describes yet another method of control of a puppet by which all the threads were led through the body into a hollow iron rod. He gives no authority for this, and the method is not technically feasible for anything more than the most elementary movements, but it is occasionally met with for limited purposes.

38. Lippi, *Malmantile Racquistato*, ii, 46.

39. Guastalla Baldi, Preface to a translation of Hero's *Automata* (1589).

40. Guillaume Bouchet, *Les Sérées*, XVIII (1608).

Except where otherwise stated, all references in this section are taken from Magnin, pp. 118–149.

41. Evelyn, *Diary*, February 3, 1644: "The front [of the Isle de Palais] looking on to the great bridge is possessed by mountebanks, operators, and puppet players."

42. The genealogy of the Briochés is the subject of some dispute. Magnin, a true patriot, makes him a Frenchman; Ferrigni pleads for his Italian origin with eloquence and conviction.

43. Colletet, *Le Tracas de Paris* (Paris, 1666). My translation.

44. Evelyn, *Diary*, March 1, 1644, and March 20, 1651.

45. Chesnais, p. 116. This arrangement of wires in front of the stage, the importance of which has hitherto scarcely been understood, is actually illustrated in an edition of *Don Quixote*, ii, 2, published in Brussels in 1706. I have unfortunately been unable to obtain a sight of this engraving by Harrevyn; it is referred to by Paul McPharlin in *The Puppet Theatre in America* (New York, 1949), p. 27. One might think that the illustrations to this chapter in early editions of *Don Quixote*, showing his combat with the puppets, would throw valuable light on contemporary puppet stages; but unfortunately they seem to be almost invariably drawn by artists with absolutely no technical knowledge of the construction of any kind of practical puppet. The editions of 1657 (Dordrecht) and 1687 (London) appear to illustrate a glove-puppet booth, but the puppets themselves look like marionettes. The popular eighteenth-century editions illustrated by Coypel (reproduced in *Puppetry*, 1939) and Hayman clearly indicate the use of marionettes.

46. Anthony Hamilton, *Œuvres* (Paris, 1812), iii, 72. My translation.

Chapter III

1. I have largely relied on Enid Welsford, *The Fool* (1935). There is a valuable chapter on "Clowns and Fools" in Francis Douce, *Illustrations of Shakespeare* (1839).

2. L. W. Cushman, *The Devil and the Vice in the English Dramatic Literature before Shakespeare* (Halle, 1900), treats the subject exhaustively. *The Three Estates*, as presented at the Edinburgh Festival, is one of the few successful revivals of a morality in recent years. The well-known *Everyman* has no Vice in its cast.

3. *A Declaration of Egregious Popish Impostures* (1603).

4. *Cf.* Ambidexter in *King Cambyses* (*c.* 1563).

5. *Defence of Poesie*. For this section I have drawn extensively on O. M. Busby, *Studies in the Development of the Fool in the Elizabethan Drama* (1923). On the jig see C. R. Baskervill, *The Elizabethan Jig* (1929), C. J. Sisson, *Lost Plays of Shakespeare's Age* (1936), and Eric Walter White, "A Note on the Reconstruction of Farce Jigs," in *Theatre Notebook*, VI (1952). On the costume of the stage clown see Leslie Hotson, *Shakespeare's Motley* (1952).

6. "On the underrated Genius of Dick Tarleton," in W. J. Lawrence, *Speeding up Shakespeare* (1937). He reproduces here a recently discovered portrait of Tarleton which shows an unmistakable humpback.

7. For the texts used in these drolls see Francis Kirkman, *The Wits, or Sport upon Sport* (1662, reprinted 1932). See also M. Willson Disher, *Clowns and Pantomimes* (1925). I understand that Miss Sybil Rosenfeld is working on this subject, and her study will be eagerly awaited.

8. William Hone, *The Table Book*, ii, 247.

9. Wakeman, "Rustic Stage Plays in Shropshire," in *Transactions of the Shropshire Archeological Society*, vii, 383.

10. See George Borrow, *Wild Wales*, Chapters 59 and 60, and T. J. R. Jones, "Welsh Interlude Players of the Eighteenth Century," in *Theatre Notebook*, II (1948).

11. My descriptions of these are drawn from those storehouses of antiquarian information—Hone's *Every-Day Book* (1825–26) and Chambers' *Book of Days* (1863–64).

12. E. K. Chambers, *The English Folk Play* (1933), p. 87. See also R. J. E. Tiddy, *The Mummers' Play* (1923).

Chapter IV

1. The quotations are from the Prologue to *Sir Thopas* and *The Miller's Tale*.

2. Lambarde describes it as having been performed "in the days of ceremonial religion"; this must have been earlier than about 1535. (See note 30, Chapter II.)

3. "A Note on the Chester Plays," by the Rev. Robert Rogers, written in 1609 (Harl. MS., 1944), quoted in *The Digby Plays*, Early English Text Society, Extra Series, LXX (1896). William Jordan, *The Creation of the World*, edited by William Stokes (1863).

4. Historical MSS. Commission, *Report* XIII, Appendix, Part VI (1893). In the same year the disapproving John Hall, in "A Marvellous Dream of the Author: anno 1561," printed in *The Court of Virtue* (1565), referred to the many lewd jugglers with apes, bears, performing horses, and "foolish puppet plays."

5. *The Pleasant and Stately Moral of the Three Lords and Three Ladies of London.*

6. *Anatomy of Melancholy.*

7. J. T. Murray, *English Dramatic Companies, 1558–1642* (1910). This work has been invaluable, and all the references to provincial puppet shows in this chapter are drawn from it.

8. *The Two Gentlemen of Verona*, Act II, Scene 1.

9. Jonson, *Every Man Out of His Humour*, Act II, Scene 1, and *Bartholomew Fair*, Act V, Scene 3. For a detailed description of the Perpetual Motion at Eltham, an automata of the movements of the heavens, see W. B. Rye, *England as seen by Foreigners in the Days of Elizabeth and James the First* (1865).

10. "A musical organ with divers strange and rare motions" was shown at Coventry in 1624 (see Murray).

11. William Gostlynge was licensed to show "the portraiture of the City of Jerusalem" in 1635 (see Murray). Davenant appears to refer to "Sodom and Gomorrah" as displayed in a peepshow (see note 29).

12. Cristóbal de Villalon, *Ingeniosa comparición entre lo antiguo y lo presente* (1539), and Sebastian Covarrubias, *Tesoro de la lengüa castellana* (1611), quoted in J. E. Varey, *Minor Dramatic Forms in Spain, with Special Reference to Puppets*, a Doctoral Dissertation in Cambridge University Library.

13. Privy Council Minutes, July 14 and 19, 1573. Quoted in E. K. Chambers *Elizabethan Stage* (1923).

14. J. Quincey Adams, *The Dramatic Records of Sir Henry Herbert* (Yale, 1917).

15. Acts III and IV.

16. Its opening lines parody Marlowe's *Hero and Leander* (1598).

17. In Dekker's *Satiromastrix* (1601), in which Jonson is satirized as Horace, he is called a "puppet teacher" and "old Cole."

18. Pye Corner, where Captain Pod hailed from, was a popular pitch at Smithfield (see note 40). For a more explicit reference see Jonson, *Volpone* (1605), Act V, Scene 2.

19. *Letters written by John Chamberlain during the Reign of Elizabeth* (1861), for August 23, 1599.

20. *Every Man Out of His Humour*, Act II, Scene I.

21. *Volpone*, Act V, Scene 2.

22. Thomas Randolph, *Hey for Honesty*, Act I, Scene 2.

23. Lupold von Wedel's original narrative is printed in *Baltische Studien*, vol. 45 (Stettin, 1895); his German is sometimes obscure and the translation printed in *Transactions of the Royal Historical Society*, second series, vol. ix (1895), and quoted in Chambers' *Elizabethan Stage*, does not quite convey the sense of the passage. See also Thomas Nashe, *Strange Newes* (1592).

T. Fairman Ordish, *Early London Theatres* (1894), states that puppets were shown at the Rose Playhouse between 1603 and 1622. I have been unable to find any authority for this, and it is doubtful if the Rose was even standing at that period.

24. Further confirmatory details may be found under Whiting and Bradshaw in G. E. Bentley, *The Jacobean and Caroline Stage* (1941).

25. Sir John Davies in *Epigrams* (*c.* 1596), "In Dacum," classes together the "poetry" spoken by the exhibitors of elephants, performing horses, and apes, the guide to the Westminster monuments, "and also him with puppets represents."

26. Jonson, *The Alchemist*, Act I,

> And blow up gamester after gamester,
> As they do crackers in a puppet play,

and *Bartholomew Fair*, Act V, Scene 3.

27. But attention should be drawn to the suggestion in Thomas Dekker's *Lanthorne and Candlelight* (1608), Chapters 5 and 6, that some motions were elegantly written out, with effusive dedications, to solicit patronage from country gentry. I am not sure what meaning of 'motion' is intended in this passage.

28. I was privileged to arrange and perform the puppet play in the Old Vic production of *Bartholomew Fair* at the Edinburgh Festival of 1950, and later in London. Many of the points discussed in this chapter were incorporated in that production. For further details see *The Puppet Master*, iv, 3 (1950).

29. This poem was first printed (not exactly in this form) in *Wit and Drollery* (1661). It refers, however, to the Globe Theatre, which was pulled down in 1642, so must have been written at least by that date.

30. Act III.

31. The nearest identification of a marionette that I have noted is a reference likening a man who fails to respond to a women's lovemaking to "dead motions moving upon wires" in Beaumont and Fletcher, *The Woman Hater* (*c.* 1606), Act III, Scene 1.

32. *The Silent Woman*, Act III, Scene 2. The same expression is used in Marmion, *A Fine Companion* (1633), Act II, Scene 6. William Sampson, *The Vow Breaker, or the Fair Maid of Clifton* (1636), Act V.

33. This reconstruction of the method of operation is, admittedly, conjectural, but it is practicable, as I once made a small model to try it out. The actual description given in the text, in case anyone can think of a better method, is as follows:

First I have fixed in the earth a Tub . . .
[and] this Tub I have capt with paper,
A fine oil'd Lanthorn paper that we use . . .
Which in it doth contain the light to the business;
And shall with the very vapour of the candle
Drive all the motions of our matter about,
As we present them.

34. This is suggested in a valuable pioneer article by W. J. Lawrence on "Elizabethan Motions," in *The Times Literary Supplement*, January 29, 1920, and also by Karl J. Holzknecht, "Puppet Plays in Shakespeare's Time," in *Puppetry* (1933).

35. *Jests to Make You Merry.*

36. J.D., *The Knave in Graine, New Vampt* (1640), Act V.

37. Thomas Nashe, *Pierce Penniless* (1592).

38. *The Wonderful Year* (1603).

39. See note 32.

40. *The Blind Beggar of Bethnal Green* (1600), Act IV; Jonson, *Every Man Out of His Humour* (1600), Act IV, Scene 4; Dekker, *Jests to Make You Merry* (1607); Jonson, *Bartholomew Fair* (1614), Act V, Scene 1.

41. Act IV, Scene 2.

42. *Bartholomew Fair*, Act V, Scene 3.

43. *Every Man Out of His Humour*, Act II, Scene 1. Referring to a new motion at Fleet Bridge, a character says, "I think there be such a thing, I saw the picture."

44. The remaining details are all drawn from *Bartholomew Fair*, Act V, Scene 1.

45. Nashe, *Terrors of Night* (1594).

46. Geoffrey Fenton, *A Form of Christian Policy* (1574), iii, 7.

47. *Every Man Out of His Humour*, in the list of characters, Sogliardo, country bumpkin but would-be gentleman, who "comes up every term to learn to take tobacco, and see new motions."

Cynthia's Revels, Act IV, Scene 1, "as a country gentlewoman, keep a good house, and come up to term to see motions." See also Gervase Markham and Lewis Machin, *The Dumb Knight* (1608), Act II, Scene 1.

48. Henry Farley, *St Paul's Church* (1621).

49. *Bartholomew Faire . . . with the several Enormities . . . which are there seen and acted* (1641). Quoted in Morley, a valuable pioneer work which has yet to be superseded. Collectors may like to be warned that a facsimile reprint of the 1641 pamphlet was issued in the nineteenth century.

50. Alluded to in a scurrilous and obscene verse entitled *The Dagonizing of Bartholomew Fair*, reprinted in Hyder E. Rollins, "A Contribution to the History of the English Commonwealth Drama," in *Studies in Philology* (July 1921). This reveals that the puppet booths still kept up the Elizabethan practice

of flying a flag outside the theatre, and that fireworks were still a common puppet stage effect. The Lord Mayor's objection seems to have been that the puppet booths started performing before the fair was officially opened, rather than to anything that they acted.

51. Printed in Tom D'Urfey, *Wit and Mirth, or Pills to purge Melancholy* (1719), vol. iv.

52. *The Lord Henry Cromwell's Speech in the House* (1659).

53. *Mercurius Democritus*, April 20–27, 1653. Quoted by Rollins.

Chapter V

1. Public Record Office: Office of Works Accounts (5/3 and 5/9) and Lord Chamberlain's Books (L.C.5/107). Quoted by Eleanore Boswell, *The Restoration Court Stage* (Harvard, 1932). See also Pepys' *Diary*, October 8, 1662.

2. Pepys' *Diary*, September 4, 1663.

3. *Calendar of State Papers*, *Domestic*, 1664, January.

4. In the Overseer's Books of St Martin-in-the-Fields, quoted in L.C.C. *Survey of London*, vol. xvi: "Charing Cross" (1935).

5. Herbert (see note 14, Chapter IV). This book throws valuable light on the licensing system of the Restoration.

6. *Cal. S. P. Dom.*, 1672, January 9; P.R.O., Entry Book 37, p. 16.

7. P.R.O., L.C. 5/140, p. 129. Quoted in Nicoll, *Restoration Drama* (1923).

8. P.R.O., S.P. 29, vol. 317, No. 187. This bill is undated, but is bound up in the Records Office volume for 1672; it is reproduced in George Speaight, "The Earliest Known English Playbill," *Theatre Notebook*, VI (1952).

9. Churchwardens' Accounts of St Martin-in-the-Fields, quoted in L.C.C. *Survey of London*: "Charing Cross."

10. Marvell, *The Statue at Charing Cross.*

11. *Diary*, August 21, 1667. Evelyn's *Diary* is less frequently quoted than Pepys's, owing to its inefficient index! There are about a dozen references to puppets in it, and here, for the record, are the dates I have noted: February 3, 1644; March 1, 1644; December 24, 1644; March 20, 1651; February 5, 1658; August 9, 1661; August 21, 1667; April 4, 1672; September 23, 1673; January 24, 1684; September 15, 1692.

12. An "Anthony Devoe" rented a fifty-foot frontage at Bartholomew Fair regularly between 1672 and 1677, for an annual rental of five pounds. This seems fairly certainly the puppeteer. A "John Divoe" also took space during this period. See the "Bartholomew Fair Account Books," 1670–87, in the Corporation of London Records Office.

13. "The Second Part of Bartholomew Fair," in Playford's *Second Book of the Pleasant Musical Companion* (1686 and later editions).

14. Evelyn, *Diary*, January 24.

15. Samuel Butler, *The Character of a Juggler*. This, together with many other fugitive pieces, was written *c.* 1670, but not printed until the publication of *Genuine Remains* in 1759.

16. *Cal. S.P. Dom.*, November 1660 and July 11, 1663. For a further attempt to include stage players in this authority see December 24, 1669, January 28, 1670, and February 17, 1670.

17. *A Play-house to be Let*, Act I.

18. Walter Rye, *Extracts from the Court Books of the City of Norwich, 1666–1688* (1905).

19. Sybil Rosenfeld, "The Players in Cambridge, 1662–1800," in *Studies in English Theatrical History*, for the Society for Theatre Research (1952).

20. Published in Tempest's *Cries of London* from drawings by M. Laroon, *c.* 1690. See *Theatre Notebook*, vols. viii and ix (1954–55). Grainger's identification of this Merry Andrew as Phillips in his *Biographical History* (1769) lacks confirmation. There is a fine watercolour by this artist in the British Museum (1852–2–14–412), showing a mountebank tooth-drawer standing on a trestle platform before a shabby booth, above which two glove puppets appear; the characters are male and female, but apart from a ruff round the gentleman's neck he possesses none of the characteristics associated with either Pulcinella or Punch. This important drawing, however—probably made in England in the last decade of the seventeenth century—confirms that here, as in Italy and France, glove puppets were used to gather a crowd for the sellers of medical nostrums.

21. Printed in Lord King, *Life of John Locke* (1830).

22. Epilogue to Sir Francis Fane, *Love in the Dark*.

23. Shadwell, *A Lenten Prologue refus'd by the Players* (1682).

24. "The French Dancing Master and the English Soldier" (*c.* 1665), in the Luttrell Collection of Ballads. Printed in John Ashton, *Humour, Wit and Satire of the Seventeenth Century* (1883).

25. Duke of Newcastle, *The Humorous Lovers* (1677), Act III.

26. Act I, Scene 1; III, 7; IV, 2; V, 2.

27. Playbill in the Archives Nationales, reproduced in *Revue d'Histoire du Théatre*, IV, 1950.

28. Sir Thomas Browne, *Works* (1931), vol. vi, p. 244.

29. *Diary*, May 2, 1668.

30. *Diary*, April 20 and April 30, 1669. See also E. Phillips, *The New World of Words* (edition of 1706), for the first appearance of Punch in an English dictionary.

31. Ned Ward, *The London Spy*, Parts VII and XI. This first appeared in parts in 1698–1700.

32. Butler, "Upon Critics" (see note 15).

33. Malagene in Act III.

34. Butler, "Satyr."

35. From a ballad in the Wood Collection, quoted by Baskervill.

36. Act III, Scene 2, and IV, 2.

37. "Machinæ Gesticulantes, anglice A Puppet Show" first appeared in the unauthorized *Examen Poeticum Duplex* (1698); it was reprinted with some alterations in *Musarum Anglicanarum Analecta*, vol. ii (1699), and then in numerous editions of Addison's works. The bibliography of the translations of this poem makes a fascinating study. Text A appeared in *Miscellaneous Translations from Bion, Ovid, Moschus and Mr Addison* (Oxford, 1716); the translator was anonymous. Text B appeared, with the Latin original, in *Poems on Several Occasions by Mr Addison* (E. Curll, 1719), and was reprinted in the fourth edition of *Miscellanies in Prose and Verse* (Dublin, 1721); the name of the translator is revealed in Curll's second edition of 1725 as Dr George Sewell. Text C appeared in *Miscellaneous Poems by Several Hands* (published by D. Lewis; vol. i, 1726); this was reprinted in *Poems on Several Occasions* (1733), where the translator's name is given as the Rev. Thomas Fitzgerald; another edition was published by the poet's grandson in 1781. Text D was printed in *The Gentleman's and London Magazine* (Dublin, February 1760). Text E would appear, from internal textual references, to have been written in about 1780; I have seen only a manuscript copy. Text F appeared in *Miscellanea*, by J.G. (James Glassford), privately published at Edinburgh in 1818.

Of these translations Text F is an almost literal, line-by-line version, useful but rather stiff, and Text E contains interesting additional matter of later date. In the extracts printed here I have drawn upon Texts A, B, and C, selecting whichever version gave the most accurate translation of Addison's words; they are all three pleasant examples of the eighteenth-century rhyming couplet. As we are not really concerned with the literary merit of these rival translations, I have not thought it necessary to identify the sources of my quotations more closely.

A quite different Latin poem on the same theme, entitled "Pupæ Gesticulantes," was included in Edward Popham, *Selecta Poemata Anglorum* (1774). This is discussed in Chapter VII, Section 2, and Chapter VIII, Section 4.

38. Addison:

> Tandem ubi subtrahitur velamen, lumina passim
> Angustos penetrant aditus, qua plurima visum
> Fila secant, ne, cum vacuo datur ore fenestra,
> Pervia fraus pateat:

Text F:

> At last the curtain slides; and straight, all eyes
> Fix on the box, where thread in many plies
> Crosses the window, lest the pervious space
> Betrayed the guile.

39. Addison: "Homuncio." Sometimes rendered as Hero or Manny, but there is really no doubt about who the character is.

Chapter VI

1. Nos. 1, 44, 45, 50, 77. See also a ballad, "The Bath Teazers," printed in Tom D'Urfey, *Wit and Mirth*, vol. vi (1720), alluding to "little Punch Powel."

2. No. 115.

3. Aaron Hill, "Prologue spoken by Mr Keen," printed in *Works* (1753), vol. iii. Aaron Hill was stage manager at Drury Lane in 1709–10.

4. The original playbill is preserved in the British Museum Library (816 m.19 (26)). It is reproduced in Chambers for August 21. See R. P. Bond, *Queen Anne's American Kings* (1952).

5. The greater part of the information in this section is derived from Powell's advertisements in *The Daily Courant* between January 27, 1711, and March 5, 1714, and in *The Spectator* between February 7 and December 2, 1712. Where no other reference is given it may be assumed that the source is a contemporary advertisement. For a more detailed analysis of Powell's repertory the reader is referred to a much expanded version of this chapter in *Studies in English Theatrical History*, for the Society for Theatre Research (1952).

6. *Venus and Adonis*, first performed in 1713. Copies of the text were on sale at the theatre, and a copy was recorded by Isaac Reed in the second edition of *Biographia Dramatica* (1782), but I have been unable to locate a copy anywhere to-day.

7. No. 14 (1711); compare No. 372 (1712).

8. *The Spectator*, No. 14. The pig is also referred to in *Punch turned Critick* (1712) (see note 12)—"so do I [combat] the great pig . . . on the stage"—and in Mrs Delany's *Autobiography*, where she recalls seeing "Powell's famous puppet show, in which Punch fought with a pig." Mrs Delany was maid of honour to Queen Anne from 1708 to 1714.

9. There is a plan of Covent Garden in about 1700 bound up in Pennant's *London*, vol. vi, No. 33, in the British Museum Print Room. The Little Piazza was the short stretch on the east side south of Russell Street. Powell was apparently a tenant, and not a ratepayer, but in one of the Rate Books for St Paul's for 1713 the name Powell has been entered against No. 20, and then erased. This seems to be the building that later became the Bedford Arms Tavern. All this part of the piazza was burnt down in 1769.

10. *Bartholomew Fair: an Heroi-Comical Poem* (1717), quoted in Stead, p. 55.

11. His son returned to England in 1725 after performing at the French Court (see note 31).

12. See *The Tatler*, Nos. 44, 45, 50, and 51, 1709, for a mock quarrel between Steele and Powell as a cover for his attack on Bishop Offspring Blackall in his controversy with Benjamin Hoadley, a long-forgotten dispute between a high-church bishop and a low-church divine. And *Punch turned Critick, in a Letter to the Honourable . . . Rector of Covent Garden* (1712), by "Seignioro Punchanello, from the corner of my Piazza in Covent Garden," a pamphlet attacking the Whig rector of St Paul's.

13. *The Letters of Thomas Burnet and George Duckett 1712–1722*, edited for the Roxburghe Club by David Nichol Smith (1914).

This was planned in imitation of Swift's *Tale of a Tub* of 1704; Powell's name was adopted probably because he was an adroit 'wire-puller,' but his Christian name was changed to Robert to make the target of the satire obvious. The book was finished by the end of 1712, but Burnet felt that it would be too dangerous to publish it at that time; then, quite suddenly, in July 1714 Harley was dismissed from office and the Queen died. The MS. was disinterred, brought up to date, and—although dated 1715—rushed into print by October; it was published, under the cover-name of J. Roberts, by Curll, the profits to be shared fifty-fifty between the publisher and the authors. By 1717 it had run into three editions, and its influence had perhaps helped towards the impeachment and imprisonment of Harley. What was far more important, it brought the authors well-paid jobs under the new Whig Ministry! Burnet became consul at Lisbon, and eventually a judge; Duckett was made Commissioner of Excise. Pope's bitter summing up of the joint authors, to whom contemporary scandal assigned a rather more intimate relationship, completes the story:

Like are their merits, like rewards they share;
That shines a consul, this commissioner.
(*The Dunciad*, Book III)

14. In later life Burnet is said to have been ashamed of his early political pamphlets, and especially of *A Second Tale of a Tub*, of which he purchased all the copies he could find, at considerable expense, to destroy them (*Biographia Britannica* (1784), vol. iii). The book is uncommon, but as the British Museum has two copies and I have two copies myself it cannot correctly be described as excessively rare.

The frontispiece was reprinted by Curll, for no better reason than that he had the plate in stock, in *A Key . . . upon the Travels of Lemuel Gulliver* (1726). A reversed, and inaccurate, copy, is reproduced in Duchartre; these two prints are compared in Richard Southern, *Changeable Scenery* (1952).

The same pair of authors once again made use of Powell's name in *Homerides, or a Letter to Mr Pope*, by "Sir Iliad Doggrel" (1715). This was an opening shot in the pamphlet campaign designed to discredit Pope's translation of Homer before it was even published. It was suggested that "that ingenious mechanic Robin Powell" should put on special performances of *The Siege of Troy* to advertise the forthcoming translation, and an Epilogue for Punch to speak after the puppet show was printed.

15. "I would not have you despise what I say because it comes out of a mouth of wood"—*Punch turned Critick*; "Actors of wood and wire . . ."—*Spectator*, No. 372; "'Twill make a wooden head a wise one too"—*Second Tale of a Tub*.

16. *The Tatler*, No. 44, 1709.

17. George Speaight, "A Reconstruction of Powel's Stage," in *Puppetry* (1944–45).

18. *The Tatler*, No. 45.
19. "Ephraim Hardcastle" (W. H. Pyne), *Wine and Walnuts* (1823).
20. *The Tatler*, Nos. 44 and 45.
21. *Second Tale of a Tub*.
22. *The Tatler*, No. 16, 1709.
23. *The Tatler*, No. 115, 1710.
24. *The Tatler*, No. 115. The earliest reference to Joan, by name, as Punch's wife seems to be in bills for Bartholomew and Southwark Fairs, of about 1700, preserved in the collection referred to in note 4, Chapter VII.
25. *Les Soupirs de la Grand Bretaigne, or the Groans of Great Britain* (1713), attributed to Defoe, but probably by Charles Gildon or perhaps Jean Dumont.
26. *Second Tale of a Tub*.
27. *Les Soupirs de la Grand Bretaigne*.
28. Letter to the Bishop of Waterford, January 26, 1766. In a letter to Captain Irwine on October 26, 1749, Lord Chesterfield adds the information that the fanatics were "French prophets."
29. Among the nobility recorded as visiting the theatre were Lord Bolingbroke, Sir Bevil Granville, Sir John and Lady Stanley (Mrs Delany, *Autobiography*), Lady Kerry and the children of Lord Shelbourne (Swift, *Journal to Stella*, Letter XI, December 1710). Among writers Addison, Steele, and Swift all wrote of the theatre from personal knowledge, as well as a host of lesser fry.
30. *Second Tale of a Tub*. This play does not appear in any of Powell's London advertisements, and was presumably performed at Bath.
31. Advertisement in *The Daily Post*, September 15, 1725.
32. Cutting in the Osborne Collection at the Guildhall Library; advertisement reproduced in *The Puppet Master*, II, 4 (1948).
33. *Parker's Penny Post*, September 8, 1725.
34. *The Daily Post*, September 13, 1726.
35. Almost all the information for the life of Charlotte Charke is derived from *A Narrative of the Life of Mrs Charlotte Charke*, written by herself (1755) this was reprinted in 1827 and 1929. The Tennis Court seasons were advertised in *The London Daily Post* from March 11 to May 9, 1738, and from December 15, 1739, to April 2, 1740. Except where otherwise noted, all statements in this chapter are based upon either of these two sources.
36. *Narrative*: after her return from Tunbridge Wells she let her "comedians out for hire to a man who was principally concerned in the formation of them." The lessee seems to have been Yeates; see below.
37. Charlotte's claim is substantiated by an entry in the Lord Chamberlain's Warrant Book for March 10, 1738 (L.C. 5/161, fol. 8).
38. *The Usefulness of the Stage* (1738). "Remarks upon Mrs C——'s new Licensed Figures," added to the second edition, April 18. The first edition had appeared on February 8 of the same year. This is confirmatory evidence that her season opened some time between February and April 1738.

39. Yeates's name is not billed as the promoter, but as he (or his son) was performing conjuring tricks and dancing in the pantomime at the Tennis Court, it is certain that he was intimately connected with it. The cast for the pantomime included Rosoman and Warner, who played at Yeates's booth at Bartholomew Fair in 1740, and were closely associated with him later at the New Wells.

40. A drawing of the exterior of this building is reproduced in L.C.C. *Survey of London*, vol. xx (1940), Plate 97.

41. Paul McPharlin's suggestion that Yeates was the purchaser of Charke's puppets is the exact opposite of what she meant to convey. Fawkes's advertisement for Bartholomew Fair, 1740, is reproduced by McPharlin, p. 28, but—curiously—he does not seem to have realized its significance. The bill for 1742 is quoted by Frost, p. 143.

42. Charlotte herself displayed an intense secrecy over this marriage, declaring "nor shall any motive whatever make me break that vow I made to the person, by a discovery of his name" (*Narrative*, p. 76). But an advertisement for the New Wells in *The General Advertiser*, June 3, 1746, promises "an occasional epilogue written and spoken by Mrs Sacheverel, late Mrs Charke." The mystery of her second marriage, equalled only by that of Dr Watson, is now revealed!

43. Grove's *Dictionary of Music and Musicians* (1879).

44. *Letters* to Horace Mann, March 29, 1745.

45. Madame de la Nash's season was advertised, almost daily, in *The General Advertiser* from March 25 to June 2, 1748.

The best study of the theatrical monopoly and of the causes and effects of the Licensing Act is Watson Nicholson, *The Struggle for a Free Stage in London* (1906).

46. Percy Fitzgerald, *Samuel Foote* (1910), is a readable popular biography. A more scholarly and documented study is Mary Megie Belden, *The Dramatic Work of Samuel Foote* (Yale, 1929).

47. Printed in Tate Wilkinson, *The Wandering Patentee* (1795), i, 286–290.

48. For instance, in an alternative second act to the *Diversions of the Morning*, printed by Wilkinson, *Wandering Patentee*, vol. iv, the proprietor of a dramatic academy boasts that his art includes even puppet shows, and offers to give a demonstration. "Here the puppets," reads the cryptic stage direction. "Upon my word . . . this is a masterpiece of invention," declares an admiring student. Similarly, Tate Wilkinson, in *Memoirs* (1790), ii, 27, refers to how Foote "did his puppets, etc.," during the Drury Lane season of 1758.

49. There is a very good account of this performance in *Biographia Dramatica*. I have checked this, and gleaned a few additional details, from the contemporary descriptions in *The Public Advertiser* and *The Gentleman's Magazine*, February 15, 1773, and *Town and Country Magazine*, 1773. A manuscript of *The Handsome Housemaid* is in the Larpent Collection of the Henry E. Huntingdon Library in California. It has never been printed.

50. For a useful study of theatrical burlesque during this period see V. C. Clinton-Baddeley, *The Burlesque Tradition in the English Theatre after 1660* (1952).

51. The first authority for the life of Dibdin is his own autobiography, *The Professional Life of Mr Dibdin* (1803). *The Comic Mirror* is described in the *Professional Life* (i, 153–154), and was advertised in *The Public Advertiser* from June 26 to September 23, 1775, and February 2–9, 1776. Some reviews of it are included in a book of cuttings on Exeter Change in the Enthoven Collection.

52. *The Public Advertiser*, May–September 1776.

53. Warwick Wroth, *The London Pleasure Gardens of the Eighteenth Century* (1896).

54. *The Professional Life* (ii, 65), *Memoirs of J. Decastro* (1824), E. W. Brayley, *Accounts of the Theatres of London* (1826), and *The Public Advertiser*, March 1–3, 1780.

55. A number of songs from Dibdin's puppet plays were printed separately, and in *The Professional Life* and in George Hogarth, *The Songs of Charles Dibdin* (1848). *The Recruiting Serjeant* and *The Milkmaid* were printed in their entirety, and so were *The Waterman* and *The Padlock* (see Appendix B); for details see E. Rimbault Dibdin, *A Charles Dibdin Bibliography* (1937). The Hogarth Puppets have recently introduced *The Waterman* into their repertory.

56. The Patagonian Theatre was advertised regularly from October 26, 1776, to May 23, 1781, in the London papers. Except where otherwise stated, all the information in this section is drawn from advertisements in *The Morning Chronicle*, *The Morning Post*, and *The Morning Herald*; many of these, with several valuable reviews, and the text of the prologue recited by a Hibernian Punchinello on the first night, are contained in the Exeter Change scrapbook in the Enthoven Collection.

57. Printed in 1779. It had forty-two pages, so must have been quite a long work; I have seen a description of the book, and it is noted in *Biographia Dramatica*, but I have been unable to locate an actual copy. *The Shipwreck* was printed in 1780, and has now also apparently disappeared.

58. There are two watercolours in the British Museum Print Room (Crace Collection), and a good collection of prints and drawings in the Exeter Change volume in the Enthoven Collection.

59. *Wine and Walnuts* (see note 19). Pyne's very interesting account of this theatre is confused by the fact that he fails to distinguish Dibdin's season here from the Patagonian Theatre proper. He says, "I remember the place well; it was a delightful exhibition," but as he was born in 1769 he would have been only six at the time of Dibdin's tenancy, and it is almost certain that he is describing the later Patagonian seasons. If Pyne's account can be accepted Dibdin continued his association with the theatre after the change of tenancy, but he was describing events of fifty years past, and there can be little doubt that his childhood memory was at fault. Unfortunately this account was copied

by Dutton Cook in *Art in England* (1869), and parts of it have found their way into standard reference books like Redgrave's *Dictionary of Artists* and Bryan's *Dictionary of Painters*.

60. The history of the Patagonian Theatre in Dublin has been revealed by W. J. Lawrence in *The Musical Quarterly*, vol. x (New York, 1924). See also the account in Michael Kelly, *Reminiscences* (1826), i, 1.

61. Walter G. Strickland, *A Dictionary of Irish Artists* (Dublin, 1913).

62. Strickland's *Dictionary* and Pyne's *Wine and Walnuts*. According to Pyne, "Hubert" Stoppelaer was Dibdin's partner at the Patagonian Theatre. If this refers to Herbert Stoppelaer it is difficult to see what assistance he can have given Dibdin in 1775, as he had died in 1772! Probably Pyne is thinking of Herbert's brother, Michael; but it seems more likely that he was associated with his fellow-Irish at Exeter Change, and had nothing to do with Dibdin. There is no mention of Stoppelaer in Dibdin's *Professional Life*.

63. According to *The Memoirs of J. Decastro* (1824), McNally was, at one time, unable to get his plays acted in the theatres, "and, therefore, had recourse to the assistance of two monied men, friends of his, of the names of 'Gaynes' and 'Sharpe,' who went to a great expense in building a very elegant theatre at the 'Cassino Rooms,' Great Marlborough Street, for the purpose of bringing forward some of them, through the aid of figures, to be styled the 'Wooden-headed Family.'" I have been unable to discover any other records of the Casino Rooms, and it is possible that there is some confusion here with the Patagonian Theatre.

64. "Powel and Stretch the hint pursue," from *The Puppet Show* (1721), attributed to, but probably not by, Swift.

65. Attributed, wrongly, to Jonathan Swift, and printed in Scott's edition, vol. x. See comments on this poem in the *Works* of Jonathan Swift, edited by Harold Williams.

66. Printed in *Miscellaneous Poems*, published by Mr Concanen (Dublin, 1724). The play had been performed in 1721.

67. For the history of this theatre see W. J. Lawrence, "A Famous Dublin Show," in *The Irish Independent*, August 19, 1905; "The Diversion in Capel Street," in *The Irish Rosary*, vol. xxiii (Dublin, 1919); and "Early Irish Ballad Opera and Comic Opera," in *The Musical Quarterly* (New York, July 1922). Contemporary references are to be found in John O'Keefe, *Recollections* (1826), i, 5; W. R. Chetwood, *A General History of the Stage* (1749); Thomas Amory, *The Life of John Buncle, Esq.* (1756–66), for May 1731; and quite a bundle of scarce ephemeral Dublin pamphlets.

68. *To the Honourable K . . . s, C . . . s, and B . . . s in P . . . t assembled, the humble petition of Thomas Punch Esq.* (Dublin, 1756). A satire on Sheridan's Memorial against the building of a new theatre in Crow Street. See also *Punch's Petition* (Dublin, 1758).

69. The only information on Dublin puppet theatres to have been recorded

systematically is to be found in the periodical articles of the late W. J. Lawrence. In addition to those already noted, reference should be made to *The Dublin Evening Mail*, October 17, 1908, and to *The Saturday Herald*, July 11, 1908, February 3, 1912, and October 11, 1913. It is greatly to be regretted that Dr Lawrence was not himself able to publish the complete study of this subject that he was so admirably qualified to write.

70. There are good descriptions of the Eidophusikon by Pyne (note 19) and in William T. Whitley, *Artists and Their Friends in England 1700–1799* (1928); and a biography of de Loutherbourg in Dutton Cook, *Art in England.* The dates of its performance are incorrectly given both by Cook and in the *D.N.B.* It was advertised in *The Morning Herald* and other London papers during the spring of 1781, and again in December, and from January to March 1786.

71. *The Monthly Mirror*, April 1799; February, March 1800.

72. Playbills in the Enthoven Collection and George Raymond, *Memoirs of Robert William Elliston* (1844–45), vol. ii, Chapter VIII.

73. Advertised in *The Public Advertiser*, October 4, 1770, to July 14, 1772. All information in this section, except where otherwise mentioned, is drawn from contemporary advertisements and theatrical notices. For a note on Perico in Paris see Chesnais, p. 124.

74. Compare the Metamorphosen der Puppenkomödie illustrated in Flögel, *Geschichte des Grotesk-Komischen* (1862).

75. From Mrs Harris, February 1771, in *Letters of Lord Malmesbury* (1870). See also *The Diary of Sylvas Neville*, edited by Basil Cozens-Hardy (1950), for September 23, 1771.

76. Arthur Murphy, *Essay on the Life and Genius of Samuel Johnson* (1792). More or less the same story is told in Boswell's *Life of Johnson* (1791), and in J. Cradock's *Memoirs* (1828). The often quoted remark attributed to Dr Johnson that *Macbeth* might well be acted by puppets is based on an unsupported note by George Steevens to the 1803 Variorum edition of Shakespeare, which was contradicted by Boswell's son in the 1821 edition. It is probably mythical.

77. *The Public Advertiser*, November 22, 1776, to January 17, 1777.

78. Letter from "Benevolus" in the *Freeman's Journal*, Dublin, October 11, 1777.

79. *The Public Advertiser*, January 25 to May 29, 1779.

80. *The Public Advertiser*, January 19 to May 20, 1780, and December 8, 1780, to May 2, 1781.

81. A similar effect was achieved with human performers by Kirby's Flying Ballet at Covent Garden in 1938. See *The Oxford Companion to the Theatre* (1951), under "English Playhouse: Machinery."

82. From a manuscript note "taken down in conversation with a member of the Lupino family in his 76th year," quoted in *The World's Fair*, August 24, 1940. This manuscript is in the possession of Mr Gerald Morice. So far as can

be judged from the quotation, the elderly Lupino's memories are largely corroborated from contemporary evidence, but he goes on to say that Micheli later presented this show at Savile Row, which is not borne out by the facts (though Martinelli was associated with it). The interest of this manuscript need not be stressed, but it awaits critical examination; there are certain obvious inaccuracies, such as naming Astley as the proprietor of Ranelagh.

Some of the advertisements for this theatre are quoted in *Notes and Queries*, 1864.

83. This theatre advertised sparingly; the most useful sources available in the British Museum are *The World* from December 26, 1789; *The Gazeteer* from February 4, 1791; *The Morning Herald* from November 25, 1791; *The Morning Chronicle* from December 21, 1791; and *The Times* for January 22 and March 19, 1791. These runs are not complete, and a number of advertisements cut from newspapers without indication of date or provenance (a mortal sin), that throw valuable light on the Fantoccini, are now in the collection of Mr Gerald Morice.

The repertory at this theatre is analysed in detail in George Speaight, "Le Théâtre des Variétés Amusantes en Londres," in *Revue d'Histoire du Théâtre*, (Paris, iv, 1953). The originals of the repertory presented at this theatre are little known in England, but are valuably described in Martin Cooper, *Opéra Comique* (1949).

84. Carnevale was fortunate in his investments. The next year he won a prize of £20,000 in the lottery, though he had unfortunately sold two-thirds of the ticket (Horace Walpole, *Letters* to the Misses Berry, March 5, 1791). His wife was a singer at the Opera House in the Haymarket, and when this theatre had been burnt down in 1789 Carnevale was suspected—probably quite unjustly—of having set fire to it himself to pay off a grudge against Gallini, the manager; see H. B. Wheatley, *Round About Piccadilly* (1870).

85. For the history of this theatre see L. H. Lecomte, *Histoire des Variétés Amusantes* (Paris, 1908). The first theatre of that name flourished from 1778 to 1789.

86. *The Thespian Dictionary* (1805).

87. Here, for the record, are the names of the composers whose works were drawn upon: Anfossi, J.C. Bach, Bertoni, Clementi, Coursieaux, D'Alyrac, Giardini, Giordani, Giorgini, Gogni, Gretry, Haydn, Monseignie, Paisiello, Piccini, Pleyel, Pozzi, Sacchini, Sarti, and Stamitz. Most of these names are now known only to musical historians, but in their day they were the contemporaries and rivals of Haydn.

The names of some of the singers and musicians at the Italian Fantoccini were recorded:

With the third Fantoccini troupe at Panton Street were M. Gabriel, Mme Dubois, and Mr and Mrs Castegna.

With the fourth Fantoccini troupe at Piccadilly were Signoras Patti, Zilbetti,

Bertellemme, and Cramperini, and Signori Livittini, Muligi, and Moccholi.

Artists at Savile Row included Raimondi and Mr Mountain as leader of the band, and Mr Cardinal and the Beluggis singing.

Perhaps musical historians will be able to identify some of these performers.

88. Haydn's London Notebook was translated and reprinted in H. E. Krehbiel, *Music and Manners from Pergolesi to Beethoven* (1898).

89. This fine house, at the north end of the Row, had originally been built as a garden pavilion for the Earl of Burlington; it was for many years the home of the Alpine Club, and is well illustrated in Hanslip Fletcher, *Changing London* (1933).

In the early thirties of this century I can recollect occasionally dining at an inexpensive restaurant in Savile Place, immediately behind the Alpine Club; this lofty and spacious room (in my recollection, even at that date adorned with murals of some kind) had been built as an extension to his premises by Squibb and was the original Great Room that was converted into the Savile Row Theatre (see Wheatley's *Piccadilly*).

90. Quoted in Mollie Sands, *Invitation to Ranelagh* (1946). The performances here were advertised in *The Gazeteer*, April 29 to August 12, 1796, and May 1 to July 1, 1797.

91. In December 1796 at Covent Garden, and in December 1797 and February and December 1798 at the Royalty, under Astley's management.

92. Illustrated by Duchartre, von Boehn (Figs. 328–331), and Nicoll (Figs. 191, 192).

93. Advertised in *The Public Advertiser*, December 5, 1775, to April 24, 1776. All the particulars in this section are drawn from advertisements in *The Public Advertiser*, except where otherwise noted. For a note on Ambroise in Paris see Magnin, p. 182.

94. See Georg Jacob, *Geschichtedes Schattentheaters im Morgen- und Abendland* (Hanover, 1925).

Earlier in the eighteenth century the father of Henry Angelo, the noted fencing master, had seen a shadow show at the Venice carnival, where it was known as *le tableau mouvant*. He constructed a replica for himself, which was greatly admired by Gainsborough, Wilson, and other artists, and in about 1758 he gave a private performance of a little French play before the English royal princes (*Reminiscences* of Henry Angelo, 1830).

95. This effect was produced by a *giuoco di luce*; see McPharlin, Chapter IV. There is a good description of how to make one of these charming toys in *The Boy's Own Book of Indoor Games and Recreations*, edited by Morley Adams (1912).

96. Oxberry's *Theatrical Banquet, or the Actor's Budget* (1809), vol. ii, p. 129.

97. *The Favourite Airs . . . in the Ombres Chinoises* (1780), partly reproduced in McPharlin, p. 56; and *A Favourite Song in the Broken Bridge Scene at the Ombres Chinoises in Panton Street*, reproduced in *Puppetry* (1939).

98. There is a good collection in the Cooper Union Museum for the Arts of

Decoration in the United States, some of which are illustrated in McPharlin, Chapter V. *The Boy's Own Book of Indoor Games* (see note 95) contains clear diagrams of the construction of this type of figure.

99. Under the influence of the Patagonian Theatre there sprang up quite a crop of puppet theatres presenting ballad operas and musical burlesques. I have noted the Lilliputian Theatre (late the Angel and Crown), in Whitechapel in 1778; the Miniature Theatre in Rice's (late Hickford's) Rooms in Brewer Street in 1790; and the Scenic Theatre, opposite Villiers Street, in the Strand in 1797.

Chapter VII

1. The detailed documentation from newspaper advertisements that we have been able to bring to the story of short seasons at fashionable London theatres is not practical—or possible—when dealing with the performances of travelling showmen at fairs and inns all over the country during a period of a hundred years. I have, therefore, felt compelled to limit the references provided in this section to a general statement of my basic authorities. I regret the necessity for this, but I am sure that a proliferation of notes in every other line of the text would have proved an intolerable irritant to any other than highly specialized readers.

My basic authorities for this chapter are the following collections of newspaper cuttings, throw-aways, and playbills dealing with the London fairs preserved in the Guildhall Library: The Osborne Collection (Gr. 5.1.16), the Kemble Collection (A.6.6), the Bartholomew Fair Collection (Gr. 2.1.7), the J. H. Burn Collection (MS. 1514), a Fairs Collection (A.5.2), and the Smithfield Court Book (MS. 95), to which should be added the Fillinham Collection of Fairs and a volume of Bartholomew Fair cuttings (C. 70.h.6) in the British Museum.

As secondary authorities I have used the following, which are largely based on, but occasionally supplement, the above:

William Hone, *Every-Day Book* (1826).
Thomas Frost, *The Old Showmen* (1874).
Thomas Frost, *Lives of the Conjurors* (1876).
Henry Morley, *Memoirs of Bartholomew Fair* (1859).

My provincial examples are largely drawn from Sybil Rosenfeld, *Strolling Players and Drama in the Provinces, 1660–1765* (1939).

Detailed references are provided for any statements not based upon the above authorities.

2. A. Primcock (James Ralph), *The Touchstone* (1728), reprinted as *The Taste of the Town, or a Guide to All Public Diversions* (1731).

3. From papers of the Vice-Chancellor's Court at Oxford in the Bodleian Library. The full inventory is as follows:

10 Boxes with Figures and Pieces of Figures Show Boards Sceens Machines Sconces Show Cloaths and other Lumber . . .

Box No. 1 . . . 13 Figures
2 12 Figures
3 15 Figures
4 8 Figures undress and Lumber
5 Pieces of Old Figures
6 Scenes and machines
7 Scenes and machines
8 Scenes and machines
9 Scenes and machines
10 Show Cloaths and Lumber
12 Pannells of Painted Boards.

4. This bill, in the Harvard Theatre Collection, is described in detail in "The Earliest-known English Playbill," by William Van Lennep, *Harvard Library Bulletin*, vol. i, No. 3, 1947. Dr Van Lennep suggests that the absence of the usual *Vivat Rex* inscription on this bill indicates that it belongs to the period of the Commonwealth. The appearance of Punchinello, however, at any time before the Restoration is most improbable, and, in fact, it can be shown that puppet playbills did not invariably carry the royal superscription (compare note 4, Chapter VI). Dr Van Lennep's claim for Harvard as the possessor of the earliest-known English playbill must, therefore, be rejected in favour of the Devoto bill (see note 8, Chapter V).

A remarkable cache of puppet playbills, between about 1690 and 1710, that have recently been identified in American libraries will be reproduced and discussed in a forthcoming book by Dr James G. McManaway, of the Folger Shakespeare Library. Performances by John Harris, Matthew Heatley, and Crawley are all represented.

Nicoll, *Early Eighteenth-century Drama* (1929), records that Harris was at Punch's Theatre on Tower Hill in 1721, and perhaps also in 1719 (see *Ahasuerus*).

5. Thomas Gibbons, *An Account of a Most Terrible Fire . . . at Burwell* (1769), taken down from the recollections of Mr Thomas Howe, who was present.

6. *Authentic Memoirs of the Celebrated Miss Nancy DxWSxN* (*c.* 1761).

7. *Memoirs of Harry Rowe*, constructed from materials found in an old box after his death, by Mr John Croft (York, *c.* 1800). This partly provided the basis for W. Camidge, "The Life and Character of Harry Rowe," printed in Burdekins' *Old Moore's Almanac* (York, 1894). Rowe's pseudo-publications are:

Macbeth: a Tragedy written by William Shakespeare, with Notes by Harry Rowe (York, 1797; second edition 1799). Each of these editions carries a different portrait of Rowe as frontispiece.

No Cure No Pay, or the Pharmacopolist, by Harry Rowe . . . with Notes by a

Friend (York, 1797). Another edition of this is titled *The Sham Doctor . . .* with notes by John Croft (n.d.).

For John Croft's and Alexander Hunter's responsibility for these productions see *Biographia Dramatica* under Rowe, and Robert Davies, *A Memoir of the York Press* (1868), p. 309.

8. In his will, made on his deathbed and preserved at Somerset House, he left all his possessions to his wife, Alice.

9. An important bill of Jobson's is reprinted in *Soho and Its Associations*, by Clinch and Rimbault (1895).

10. S. W. Ryley, *The Itinerant* (1808–27), vol. vi, p. 184.

11. Useful information on Jobson and Flockton is to be found in *A Peep at Bartholomew Fair* (*c.* 1830). According to E. W. Brayley, *Accounts of the Theatres of London* (1826), Flockton performed at one time at the Lyceum in the Strand; this must have been after 1765.

12. It is often stated that the puppet showmen were prosecuted for presenting plays with speaking dialogue. The origin of this story is a short paragraph in *The Monthly Mirror* for September 1797:

> Several prosecutions are to be commenced against Flockton, Jobson, and other of the managers of Bartholomew Fair, for having encroached on the *regular theatres*, particularly in the article of dialogue, which is expressly against the Licensing Act. The *resemblance*, indeed, is sufficiently striking to incur the penalties.

It should be noted that this does not expressly refer to puppets at all, and of the two showmen named, Flockton was dead and Jobson did not show at Bartholomew Fair in 1797! I do not know of any other reference to this prosecution, and I suspect the paragraph may be facetious.

13. Henry Fielding, *The History of Tom Jones* (1749), Book 12, Chapters 5, 6, 7. Horace Walpole, *Letters* to Horace Mann, March 11, 1750. See also *The Torrington Diaries* for June 16, 1781.

14. Theatric monarchs, in their tragic gait,
Affect to mark the solemn pace of state.
One foot put forward in position strong,
The other, like its vassal, dragg'd along.
So grave each motion, so exact and slow,
Like wooden monarchs at a puppet-show.

ROBERT LLOYD, *The Actor* (1760)

15. Quadrio, see note 35, Chapter II.

Abbé Prévost, *Le Pour et le Contre* (1734), vol. iii, p. 256. I have not been able to trace the newspaper advertisement to which he refers; it may have been issued by Fawkes, who was playing at James Street that year.

The French-Latin *Dictionnaire de Trévoux*, edition of 1771; this performer may have been John Riner, who, according to Magnin, was presenting rope-dancing and puppets in Paris in 1726.

16. Plümicke, *Entwurf einer Theatergeschichte von Berlin*, p. 109, quoted by

Flögel, i, 6, and Magnin, vi, 2. For the popularity of English marionettes in eighteenth-century Germany see Hans Netzle, *Das süddeutsche Wander-Marionetten Theater* (Munich, 1938), p. 10.

17. See note 2.

18. Edward Popham, "Pupæ Gesticulantes," in *Selecta Poemata Anglorum Latina* (1774). The free prose translation is my own.

19. Joseph Strutt, *The Sports and Pastimes of the People of England* (1801).

20. This impression of a Bartholomew Fair audience is drawn from *A Walk to Smithfield* (1701); there is a manuscript transcript of this rare tract in Guildhall MS. 1514. The description of the show is taken from a frequently quoted handbill issued by Mat. Heatley and preserved in the British Museum (Harl. MSS. 5931 (272)); a convenient reprint is in Hone.

21. *Punch's Puppet Show*, a "turn up" published by Robert Sayer, "1792." There are strong grounds for believing that the date on this booklet is a misprint for 1772; it is No. 14 in a series of "Harlequinade Turn Ups," dated April the 20th; No. 13 in the series was published on March 23, 1772, and No. 15 on June 10, 1772. It is reproduced in full in *Theatre Notebook*, VII, 1953.

22. James Grassineau, *Musical Dictionary* (1740).

23. Jonathan Swift, *Mad Mullinix and Timothy* (1728).

24. To "sell a bargain" was a form of jest which consisted in naming the "parts behind" in irrelevant answer to any question.

25. See note 18. Popham, who became a clergyman, omitted these lines from the second edition of 1779.

26. Henry Fielding, "The Pleasures of the Town," a mock-puppet show in *The Author's Farce* (1730).

27. Joseph Baretti, *Tolondron: Speeches to John Bowle about his Edition of Don Quixote* (1786). This unexpected source provides a most interesting comparison of English, Italian, and Spanish puppets, with special reference to their common use of the squeaker.

28. (Edward Ward), *The Prisoners' Opera* (1730).

29. *Politicks in Miniature* (1741); a satire on the corruption of politics in the form of a puppet play.

30. Compare the passage from Southey, quoted in Chapter VIII, Section 4.

31. For a detailed discussion of this question see George Speaight, "Pull Devil, Pull Baker," *Notes and Queries*, vol. 198, No. 7, 1953.

32. The earliest allusion that I have noted is a caricature of the Newcastle Administration entitled "Punch's Opera with the Humours of Little Ben the Sailor," published in 1756, and reproduced in McPharlin.

33. Sir John Hawkins, *History of Music* (1776), ii, 135, and iv, 388.

34. *The General Advertiser*, September 22, 1752.

35. Baretti, *Tolondron*. See note 27.

36. George Alexander Stevens, *The Adventures of a Speculist* (1788), vol. ii, p. 32. This turn was probably first given in the fifties.

Chapter VIII

1. *Hudibras Redivivus, or a Burlesque Poem on the Times* (1705), vol. ii, Part 4.

2. Jonathan Swift, *A Preface to the B——p of S——m's Introduction to the Third Volume of the History of the Reformation* (1713).

3. Compare the showcloth in Hogarth's "The Election," Plate 2, and in John Nixon's "Edmonton Fair," a watercolour in the Victoria and Albert Museum, reproduced in *The Connoisseur*, vol. xxvi, 1926, showing Flockton's booth in 1788. See also the illustration "from an old print" in Hermann Rehm, *Das Buch der Marionetten* (1905), p, 169.

4. Quoted in Frost, p. 200.

5. *Sports and Pastimes*, p. 167.

6. Southey (see note 17).

7. There are two descriptions of the origin of this book. A note by Cruikshank was printed in the catalogue of an Exhibition of his works held at Exeter Hall in 1863, and reprinted in the "sixth edition" of *Punch and Judy*, published by George Bell and Sons in 1881. Payne Collier's story was told in *An Old Man's Diary, 1832–3* (1871–72), vol. iv, p. 77. Though they differ in details, the two stories largely corroborate each other. Some particulars of Septimus Prowett, to whom the ultimate credit is due, are given in Thomas Balston, *John Martin* (1947), p. 96.

8. The bibliography of *Punch and Judy* has been excellently treated by Paul McPharlin in an article in *The Colophon*, New Series, vol. i, No. 3. Students referring to this should note that later research has revealed the existence of another "third edition, printed for W. H. Reid, 15 Charing Cross" in 1832, which is actually the sheets of the second edition with a cancelled title-page. Mr Arthur W. Ashby has a bibliography of Payne Collier in preparation.

9. Payne Collier's life has still to be written, but a useful summary is contained in H. B. Wheatley, *Notes on the Life of John Payne Collier* (1884). Mr Sydney Race has exposed a number of Collier forgeries in the pages of *Notes and Queries* during recent years.

10. As far as I know, these are the only actual forgeries. Collier, in *An Old Man's Diary*, admitted that he wrote the ballad "Punch's Pranks" himself. The "allegorical" version is said to be quoted from an article in *The Morning Chronicle* of September 22, 1813, but no such article appears in the paper of that date. It may, of course, have appeared somewhere else, but on internal evidence the whole story sounds spurious. The "Sonnet to Punch" (which was introduced into the second edition) has not been accepted as genuine by any editor of Byron's poems. Apart from these flagrant inventions, there are a number of misquotations and bowdlerizations throughout the text, and every reference requires checking. See George Speaight, "Payne Collier and Punch and Judy," in *Notes and Queries*, I, 1, 1954.

11. For notes on the authorship of this book see *Notes and Queries*, 1876, pp. 333 and 354. R. B. Brough was a journalist and dramatist; the burlesques that he wrote with his brother achieved some success in their day, and he was also a fierce radical with a deep, vindictive hatred of wealth, rank, and respectability. He was the friend of G. A. Sala and Edmund Yates, a sensitive, poetical, sickly bohemian, who died at the age of thirty-two. According to Hain Friswell, the illustrations were by Charles ("Shadow") Bennett, but Cuthbert Bede believed that both text and illustrations were by Brough. They are signed with the identical pictorial owl used by Brough in his illustrations to *Diogenes* at this time, and although it is difficult to dispute Friswell's statement, based on personal knowledge, I think that Brough is clearly entitled to take any credit there may be for the pictures.

The text was frequently pirated in children's books during the sixties and seventies, and both text and illustrations were reissued by Nelson in 1919, but this—in many ways the best script of the show ever written—still remains comparatively unknown.

12. The most important subsidiary authorities for the Punch and Judy play that I have used are the following:

(*c.* 1808.) A print of "Punch's Show," published by I. Green, with a revolving disc of characters. (Described in George Speaight, *Juvenile Drama* (1947), p. 212.)

(*c.* 1810.) Mrs C. Maxwell, *Easter, or a . . . Description of All the Public Amusements of London.* Illustrated. (A most interesting poem describing a Punch street show with many of the typical characters of the eighteenth-century marionette plays—"Jane Shore and the baker, the king and the queen," and so on. The accuracy of Mrs Maxwell's observation is, however, open to doubt, for she imagined that the puppets were moved "by wires below," and with some reluctance I have felt that her undated evidence is not quite strong enough to be quoted without corroboration. She may have been guilty of some confusion in her mind between the marionette plays of the fairs and the show in the street. So far as it goes, however, her poetical description entirely supports my theory of the descent of Punch and Judy from the eighteenth-century popular marionette shows.)

1821. An article in *The Literary Speculum*, reprinted in Oxberry's *Dramatic Biography* (1826), vol. v, and quoted by Payne Collier and—more fully—by Stead.

1823. William Hone, *Ancient Mysteries Described.*

1824. "Stanzas to Punchinello," in *The New Monthly Magazine*, vol. x, signed "H." These pleasant verses, by Horace Smith, were reprinted in *The Mirror*, 1824, in his *Poetical Works* (1846), and as a separate illustrated broadsheet, reproduced in *The Puppet Master*, 1947.

1825. "Bernard Blackmantle" (C. M. Westmacott), *The English Spv*, vol. ii. Illustrated by Robert Cruikshank.

1826. "Punch and Judy: a Philosophical Poem" in 51 stanzas by "Bougersdickius," in *The European Magazine*, New Series, vol. ii.

1826. A letter on "Punch in the Puppet Show" signed W.S. in Hone's *The Every-Day Book*, vol. ii.

1827. An article in *The Pocket Magazine*. It seems possible that this was from the pen of Payne Collier.

(*c.* 1828.) (G. Smeeton), *Doings in London*. Illustrated by Robert Cruikshank. (Yet another imitation of *Tom and Jerry*.)

1830. Prince Pückler-Muskaw, *Briefe eines Verstorben*; translated as *The Tour of a German Prince* (1832). (Although the letter describing Punch is dated November 25, 1826, it seems to have been rewritten before publication after checking it with Payne Collier, and its value as an independent testimony is therefore reduced.)

1840. Charles Dickens, *The Old Curiosity Shop*. Illustrated by "Phiz." (Introducing the famous characters of Codlin and Short in Chapters 16, 17, and 18.)

1841. *Punch, or the London Charivari*, No. 1. (After the first inspiration of its choice of name, the magazine and the puppet have proceeded on their separate ways. The first number, however, pays some handsome compliments to its namesake.)

1853. Thomas Miller, *Picturesque Sketches of London Past and Present*. Partly reprinted, with a commentary by Gerald Morice, in *The Puppet Master*, vol. iv, No. 3, 1950. (A valuable description of the show as remembered from his boyhood in *c.* 1820.)

1856. Routledge's *Every Boy's Book*. (Apparently the earliest instructions for children on how to mount a show at home; these were frequently reprinted, often with a text based on Brough, in successive editions of *Every Boy's Book*, *Every Little Boy's Book*, and *The Boy's Treasury* throughout the sixties and seventies.)

1863. *Punch and Judy*: a penny chapbook published by Clarke. (The introduction is lifted from Brough, but the text differs considerably.)

1866. Frank Bellew, *The Art of Amusing*. (How to do Punch at home. See note 36, Chapter II.)

1879. Professor Hoffmann (Angelo John Lewis), *Drawing Room Amusements*. (How to do Punch at home, with the Brough-Routledge text.)

1895. An article describing Professor Jesson's show in *The Strand Magazine*. (The photographs are valuable, but the text is only an abbreviated version of Payne Collier's.)

(*c.* 1900.) A leaflet issued by Thomas Dean, "Performer of Punchinello," with an outline of the play as presented by himself. In the Guildhall Library.

1901. *Punch and Judy*, as performed in all nurseries in Europe, Asia, Africa, and America. Published by Nisbet.

(1932.) *Punch and Judy*, told by Jessie Pope and based on the performance of W. H. Jesson, with many photographs. (A sad but revealing pictorial record of Punch's show in its decline, before the modern revival had touched it.)

I have not thought it necessary to list the many modern texts adapted from Payne Collier, or the even more numerous chapbooks and juvenile picture-books of Punch and Judy, which add nothing to our knowledge of the show.

Unless otherwise noted, statements made in this chapter are based upon examination of the above authorities, plus the more important ones mentioned in the text. A clue to date or author has been provided wherever this seemed necessary. With this section we pass, however, to a period within living memory, and I must increasingly abandon the security of the documented reference for statements that can rely only upon my own observation.

13. Walter Scott, *The Bride of Lammermoor* (1818), refers in its opening paragraphs to "Punch and his wife Joan." A correspondent in *Notes and Queries* in 1877 recalled that it used to be Punch and Joan in the North of England fifty years earlier. The playbill for *Harlequin's Vision*, the Drury Lane pantomime of 1817–18, included Punch and Joan in its cast, but in a review of this show by Keats in *The Champion* of January 4, 1818, he refers to them as Punch and Judy. This is the earliest reference to Judy that I have seen, followed by a *History of the Coronation* satire of 1821.

14. Magnin, fifth book, Chapter II, Part 3.

15. In *Punch's Petition to Mr S——n* (1758) (see note 68, Chapter VI) he begs assistance "for his poor wife (who is now near being a real Ghost) and his helpless babes (who will, without timely succour be as bad as the Babes in the Wood)."

16. This theory was advanced in F. M. Cornford, *The Origin of Attic Comedy* (1914). Mr Cornford sought to show that the old Greek Comedy, the Atellan Farce, the English Mummers' Play, and Punch and Judy were all derived from an ancient Fertility Ritual; and that the Punch and Judy drama was not a series of disconnected incidents, but the "debris of an old fixed plot" featuring a Combat, a Death, and a Resurrection (the healing of Punch by the Doctor). If Mr Cornford had known that the Doctor did not make his appearance in the show till the nineteenth century I cannot believe he would have persisted in his argument. I am afraid that his theory must be dismissed as fanciful.

17. Robert Southey, *The Doctor* (1834), Chapter 23.

18. Works of Shakespeare: final note to *Richard III* and note to *Henry V*, Act IV, Scene 10. See also notes to *Twelfth Night*, Act IV, Scene 2, and *Hamlet*, Act III, Scene 10.

19. See note 18, Chapter VII.

20. References to the Devil's victory over Punch during the ninteenth

century are found in Hone, *Ancient Mysteries* (1823); Cruikshank, *Points of Humour* (1824); *The Every-Day Book* (1826); Miller, *Picturesque Sketches of London* (1853); and Maurice Baring, "Punch and Judy," in *The London Mercury* (1922), reprinted in *Punch and Judy and Other Essays* (1924). For a full consideration of this question see George Speaight, "The Devil in the Puppet Show," *Puppetry*, 1940.

21. *The Life of Mansie Wauch* (1828), Chapter III.

22. Madame de la Nash introduced a dance between Somebody and Nobody in 1748, and Jobson had a Mr Nobody in 1780. There is a very valuable chapter on these stock figures of popular legend in Charles Mitchell's edition of *Hogarth's Peregrination* (1952).

23. Stead, p. 89.

24. The Punch and Judy show has inspired innumerable artists, and it would be quite impossible—even if it served any useful purpose—to provide a complete list of these illustrations here. The following *select* hand list of the more important early illustrations of Punch and Judy may, however, be of some interest; illustrated books referred to in the text or in note 12 are not repeated here:

1785. By Thomas Rowlandson. "George III and Queen Charlotte driving through the Broadway, Deptford." Original watercolour in the possession of Mr Minto Wilson; reproduced in Adrian Bury, *Rowlandson's Drawings* (1949). (See above, p. 179.)

1785. By Samuel Collings. Original drawing in the Guildhall Library. Engraving published by Carington Bowles and Bowles and Carver; reproduced in Stead. (See above.)

1795. Probably by Isaac Cruikshank. Engraving published by Laurie and Whittle. (See above.)

1798. By Thomas Rowlandson. "Views of London, No. 6: the Hackney Turnpike." Engraving published by Ackermann; reproduced in Grego, *Rowlandson*, i, 349.

1799. By Thomas Rowlandson. "Borders for Rooms and Halls," strips of small scenes for cutting out and pasting up. "Pray remember the Puppet Shew Man" appears in one of twenty-four sheets in the series. Engraving published by Ackermann. An unidentified print in my possession appears to be trimmed from another sheet in this series; it represents the familiar view of a crowd gathering round a booth in the street. A variant of this scene, issued as a magic-lantern slide, is reproduced in *The Puppet Master*, vol. iii, No. 7, 1951.

1801. By Ann Dibdin. To illustrate *Observations on a Tour through almost the Whole of England*, by Mr [Charles] Dibdin. (This seems to be the earliest representation of a glove-puppet show performing in a country setting.)

(*c.* 1804.) By Thomas Rowlandson. Original watercolour of a street performance in the possession of Mr Gilbert Davis; reproduced in Bernard Falk, *Thomas Rowlandson* (1949).

1805. By Robert Sayer, in *The Foundling Chapel Brawl*, second part, published by the author.

1811. By Robert Cruikshank. Original watercolour offered for sale by Elkin Mathews in 1948, and reproduced in his catalogue of the same year. Engraving published by Laurie and Whittle as a broadsheet to illustrate the text of *The Humours of Bartleme Fair* as sung by Mr Matthews. (This is a late and unusual illustration of Punch as a glove puppet at Bartholomew Fair.)

1813. By William Mulready. Oil-painting exhibited at the Royal Academy. The original sketch for this is at the Victoria and Albert Museum.

1821. By I. A. Atkinson. Original watercolour in the British Museum Print Room; reproduced (without identification) on the dust-wrapper of Stead. Engraving published by Rowney and Forster. (This pleasant picture is chiefly remarkable for the fact that the puppets are apparently working themselves, without anyone inside the booth! A typically pretty studio composition, of no documentary value whatever.)

1824. By George Cruikshank, in *Points of Humour*, Part 2; reproduced in Ruari McLean, *George Cruikshank* (1948).

(*c.* 1825.) Illustration of a street show in *A Schoolboy's Visit to London*, published by E. Wallis. This picture was also incorporated in a game *Scenes in London* from the same firm. It appears to be the earliest representation of a live dog Toby.

1827. By George Cruikshank. The original drawings for *Punch and Judy* are now in the Princeton University Library; they include one sketch, of Punch pulling the horse by the tail, that was never used in the book. There are four sheets of rough sketches made by Cruikshank, almost certainly at Piccini's performance, in the Victoria and Albert Museum; these include a picture of a masked Harlequin puppet, and portrait sketches of what are probably John Payne Collier and Piccini himself. Sets of india-paper proofs are at both Princeton and the Victoria and Albert, and the latter contains a coloured set of the plates signed by the artist. A few sets of the engravings for *Punch and Judy* were bound up, and sold without any printed text.

1828. By Benjamin Robert Haydon. "Punch, or May Day." Original oil-painting in the Tate Gallery; many reproductions, including a postcard published by the Gallery.

(*c.* 1830.) By Sir George Scharf. Original pencil drawings in the British Museum Print Room.

1836–37. By George Cruikshank, in *The Comic Almanack*, July and November; reproduced in *The Puppet Master*, vol. iv, No. 3, 1950.

1838. By F. Branston, in Peter Parley's *Tales about Christmas*. An early illustration of a live dog Toby, smoking a pipe.

1840. By Thomas Webster. Original oil-painting exhibited at the Royal Academy. Large engraving published by the Art Union of London.

1850. By John Leech, in *The Illustrated London News*, December 21; reproduced in Stead. (An early illustration of Punch at a drawing-room party. Many other pictures of Punch by Leech were published in *Punch*, some of which are reproduced in McKechnie.)

1851. By William Frith. "Ramsgate Sands." Original oil-painting in the possession of Her Majesty the Queen. A replica in the Russell-Cotes Art Gallery, Bournemouth. Many reproductions. (An early illustration of Punch at the seaside.)

(*c.* 1860.) By Arthur Boyd Houghton. Original oil-painting in the Tate Gallery; postcard reproduction published by the Gallery.

1871. By Gustave Doré. Pen-and-ink sketch, reproduced in Pleiades Art Books, *Doré* (1947).

From the seventies onward innumerable sketches of Punch and Judy appeared in the illustrated magazines. With the rise of photography in the eighties their numbers are increased by the valuable records of many early photographs of the show (see, for example, Peter Quennell, *Victorian Panorama* (1937), Plate 60, and Paul Martin, *Victorian Snapshots* (1939), p. 54).

25. The earliest use of the term 'professor' in this sense seems to have been by Foote in 1773; there is a jesting allusion by Robert Brough in his "Papernose Woodensconce" volume of 1854. The title was adopted also by acrobats, and probably by other initiated exponents of hidden mysteries. It was used in a similar sense in Italy.

26. Walter Wilkinson, *Vagabonds and Puppets* (1930).

27. J. Holden Macmichael, *The Story of Charing Cross* (1906).

28. Davenant had referred to "Op'ra-Puppets" in 1663 (see note 17, Chapter V), and Aaron Hill to "some opera fit for Punch's stage" in 1710 (see note 3, Chapter VI); Powell's mock-operas may have helped to popularize the term. Ballad operas frequently appeared on the puppet playbills during the eighteenth century, and Fielding's *The Author's Farce* well illustrates the puppet-show technique of breaking up the dialogue with little songs to popular airs; this style partially survived in Collier's text. The showcloth in Hogarth's "Southwark Fair" of 1733 is lettered "Punches Opera," and a caricature of 1756 uses the same title (see note 32, Chapter VII). Many other eighteenth-century examples could be quoted. On September 10, 1818, Sir Walter Scott wrote to Lady Abercorn that "I would much sooner write an opera for Punch's puppet show."

According to Granville's preface to *Genuine Works in Verse and Prose*

(1732), the title of opera "is now promiscuously given to every farce sprinkled here and there with a song and a dance."

29. A remarkable outsize Punch, which is some three feet high when fully extended, has been preserved in the collection of Mr Edward Kersley. This fantastic figure must have been operated on a rod, and it can never have been very agile, but with its rolling eyes and vast beaked nose it still presents an extraordinary appearance.

30. 2 and 3 Victoria 47, S.57. During the debates in the House of Lords Lord Ellenborough and the Earl of Haddington pleaded for "the never-to-be-forgotten and most celebrated show of Punch." In reply, the Government spokesman assured the House that although the street performances of Punch might be technically liable to police interference under the Act, he was sure that magistrates would take care that its powers were not improperly exercised. The pleasant story, repeated by Mayhew's showman and other writers, that Punch was formally excluded from the Act is unfortunately a legend.

31. "Round the Resorts," compiled by Gerald Morice in *The World's Fair*, November 1 and 29, 1952; October 24 and 31 and November 21, 1953; and October 30 and November 13, 1954.

32. P. J. Stead, *Mr Punch* (1950), p. 87. Other modern studies of Punch are by McKechnie, and Dion Clayton Calthrop, *Punch and Judy: a Corner in the History of Entertainment* (1926). Modern fantasies on the Punch theme include "Evelyn Douglas" (John E. Barlas), *Punchinello and his Wife Judith: a Dramatic Poem* (Chelmsford, 1886); Conrad Aiken, *Punch: the Immortal Liar* (New York, 1921); Russell Thorndike and Reginald Arkell, *The Tragedy of Mr Punch* (1922); and Frank Baker, *Playing with Punch* (1944).

33. Isaac D'Israeli, "The Pantomimical Characters," in *Curiosities of Literature*. This first appeared in the edition of 1817.

34. *Politicks in Miniature*. See note 29, Chapter VII.

35. Bragaglia has recorded much incidental information about the Pulcinellas, both puppet and human, of the eighteenth and nineteenth centuries, and lists many scenarii; but he gives no hint of a playing script for street puppets. See also Pietro Toldo, "Nella Baracca dei Burattini," in *Giornale Storico della Letteratura Italiana*, vol. vi (1908).

36. Ferrigni. This was written in about 1884 (see note 31, Chapter II).

37. Carlo Racca (Akkar), *Burattini e Marionette* (Turin, *c.* 1921).

38. F. Mercey, "Le Théâtre en Italie," in *Revue des Deux Mondes* (1840). Quoted by Sand. Bragaglia dismisses Mercey as a romancer.

39. Here is a selection of the more accessible illustrations (in addition to the several interesting prints reproduced by Bragaglia):

(*c.* 1700.) By Gabriele Bella. A View of the Piazza San Marco, Venice (reproduced in Nicoll, Fig. 149).

(*c.* 1720.) In the Album de Grevenbroch in the Museo Civico, Venice (reproduced in Nicoll, Fig. 179).

1761. By Paoli Posi (in the Victoria and Albert Museum).
(*c.* 1770.) By Gaetano Gandolfi (in the Victoria and Albert Museum).
(*c.* 1780.) By Francisco Maggiotto (reproduced in Stead, p. 33, and in von Boehn, p. 343).
(*c.* 1780.) By Lasinio (reproduced in von Boehn, p. 316).
1785. By Zompini (reproduced in von Boehn, p. 344).
1809 *and* 1815. By Pinelli (reproduced in McPharlin, p. 117).
(*c.* 1830.) Artist unknown (reproduced in Joseph, p. 59).
(*c.* 1840.) By Lenghi (in the Victoria and Albert Museum).

40. *Polichinelle*, drame en trois actes, publié par Olivier et Tanneguy de Penhöet et illustré par Georges Cruishanck (Paris, 1836). (The translators and editors of this work are said to have been Olivier Mainguet, the nephew of Du Mersan, and Anatole Chabouillet, the future curator of the Cabinet des Médailles.)

Polichinelle, farce en trois actes, publiée par Jules Rémond et illustrée de vignettes par Matthieu Gringoire [George Cruikshank] (Paris, 1838). (I have not seen this.)

Punch and Judy, célèbre drama quignolesque anglais pour la prime fois adapté en France à l'usage des thériaqueurs et montreurs de puppes par Papyrus and Martine, suivi des Paralipomènes de Punch par Emile Straus, Icônes de Henry Chapront (Paris, 1903).

41. J. B. Gouriet, *Personnages célèbres dans les rues de Paris* (1811), vol. ii: "Personnages d'Imagination."

42. Eugénie Foa, *Mémoires d'un Polichinelle* (1840). A further scrap of dialogue is preserved in another children's romance, Octave Feuillet, *La Vie de Polichinelle* (1846).

43. De Neuville, p. 42.

44. Ernest Maindron, *Marionnettes et guignols* (Paris, 1901).

45. Here is a selection of some of the more accessible illustrations:

(*c.* 1810.) "Le Polichinel du pont des arts" (reproduced in Paul Ginisty, *Le Théâtre de la rue* (1925).
(*c.* 1820.) (Reproduced in von Boehn, Fig. 307.)
(*c.* 1825.) (Reproduced in von Boehn, Fig. 308.)
(*c.* 1830.) (Reproduced in Chesnais, p. 113.)
(*c.* 1850.) Old Marionette and glove-puppet figures (reproduced in Chesnais, pp. 160–161).
(*c.* 1850.) By Jules David, "La Comédie du Chat," inside and outside the booth (reproduced in Maindron).
(*c.* 1850.) By A. G. Descamps. Watercolour in the Victoria and Albert Museum.

46. Magnin, sixth book, Chapter V, Part 2.

47. Reported by W. W. Gill in *Notes and Queries*, 1939.

48. See note 18.

49. The earliest appearances of these diverse theories that I have noted are as follows: (1) Mrs Thrale, *Diary*, June 27, 1786; (2) Tom Brown, *Commonplace Book* (1707); (3) *Notes and Queries*, 1869; (4) *Notes and Queries*, 1852 (this ingenious piece of philological whimsy is said to have been the inspiration of Martin Tupper); (5) Quadrio, *Storia d'ogni Poesia* (1744); (6) Baretti, *Tolondron* (1786); (7) *Notes and Queries*, 1941. The article on Punch in the *Encyclopædia Britannica* serves at least one useful purpose in giving most of these conjectures an airing.

Chapter IX

1. For this section see the sources listed in note 1, Chapter VII.

2. From a privately printed description of Bartholomew Fair, signed J.J.A.F. (probably J. Fillinham).

3. "To slang" was a cant expression meaning "to exhibit anything in a fair or market" during the eighteenth century (George Parker, *Life's Painter of Variegated Characters* (1789), p. 144). During the nineteenth century it became used to describe a travelling show of any kind, and more particularly "the slangs" signified the controls or strings of a marionette. The term is still in use among showmen of the old school.

4. On Grey see Mayhew, *London Labour and the London Poor* (1861), vol. iii, "The Fantoccini Man," reprinted in *Mayhew's London* (1949); J. P. Robson, *The Life and Adventures of Billy Purvis* (Newcastle, 1849), Chapter XVIII; *A Month's Vacation*, printed for William Cole (*c.* 1825), quoted in Andrew Tuer, *Pages and Pictures from Forgotten Children's Books* (1898); and McPharlin.

5. G. A. Sala, "Things Departed," in *Household Words* for January 17, 1852, reprinted in *Gaslight and Daylight* (1859); A. R. Bennett, *London and Londoners in the Eighteen-fifties and Sixties* (1924). Some attractive sketches of street Fantoccini are among the drawings of George Scharf (B.M. Print Room, folio 21); a number of these shows are illustrated in *Puppetry*, 1944–45, p. 62.

6. Hone, vol. i, for August 14. See also Chambers for March 30.

7. Playbill in the British Museum. See also bills for Marler and Dicks in the Fillinham Public Gardens Collection at the Guildhall Library.

8. Mayhew, "The Chinese Shades," reprinted in *Mayhew's Characters* (1951). See also Chambers for March 30; *The Galanty Show* (1864), containing the dialogue of three plays; and Dean's *New Moveable Book of the Popular Performance of the Galanti Show* (*c.* 1861), with figures and text based on a decadent street performance.

9. See William Hone, *Ancient Mysteries Described* (1823), Chapter 8; C. Maxwell, *Easter* (see note 12, Chapter VIII); and MacFarlane (see note 27).

10. A few attractive examples are reproduced by von Boehn, Figs. 299–301; there are many others, Italian, French, and English.

11. This season was advertised in several London papers; a useful run is in *The Times*, September 17, 1828, to May 11, 1829; it was reviewed here on September 20 and November 22, and in *The Morning Advertiser* for September 20.

12. A useful run of advertisements, with an illustration and a review, is in *The Illustrated London News* from January 10 to July 5, 1852. See also *The Ladies' Companion and Monthly Magazine*, March 1852; Henry Morley, *Journal of a London Playgoer* (1866), for January 17 and February 7, 1852; Mayhew's "The Fantoccini Man"; *The Practical Mechanic's Journal* (1852); *The Theatrical Observer*, July 20, 1852; and *The Dramatic Register* for 1853 (quoted in *Puppetry*, 1936, p. 78). Reviews appeared in *The Times* for January 13, February 11, March 2, April 20, April 27, May 4, December 7, 1852.

Brigaldi (or Bragaldi) had presented a rather similar programme in New York in 1837–38; see McPharlin.

13. Illustrated in *The Illustrated London News*, August 14, 1858; a water-colour view of the theatre is reproduced in E. Beresford Chancellor, *Life in Regency and Early Victorian Times* (1926), p. 59. The "reconstruction" in *Puppetry*, 1934, p. 53, is of a different building, that was probably never a puppet theatre. There are good Cremorne Collections, with playbills of the Marionette Theatre, in the British Museum and the Chelsea Public Library; see Warwick Wroth, *Cremorne and the Later London Gardens* (1907). The figures from this theatre were eventually bought by one of the Middletons in 1872.

14. For Barnett see G. A. Sala, *Life and Adventures* (1895), and E. L. Blanchard, *Life and Reminiscences* (1891). Two of O'Neill's plays for the Royal Marionettes were adapted for human actors and published in "Cumberland's British Theatre," vol. xlviii—*Aladdin* (No. 39) and *Ali Baba* (No. 399).

15. *The Referee*, January 29, 1888. "Dagonet" was George R. Sims, and this description was reprinted in *Dagonet Abroad* (1895).

16. For Colla see advertisements in *The Times*, May 19–June 16, 1888, and review on May 21; *The Referee*, May 20 and June 17, 1888; and cuttings in the Enthoven Collection.

17. For Prandi see advertisements in *The Times*, June 8–October 31, 1888, and reviews May 11 and June 8. (See also note 38.)

18. The information in the last three sections of this chapter is largely drawn from personal interviews and from the pages of *The World's Fair*; in particular the Puppet Column that Gerald Morice has contributed since 1938 to this paper provides a source of material that is of inestimable value to the puppet historian, and to which all future students of this period are referred. It must, however, be recognized that many of the stories recorded are unsupported by any proper documentation, and their exact accuracy, and in particular their dates, must be viewed in that light. In addition the columns of *The Era*, over a period of some

fifty years, disclose a mass of fascinating detail that I have been unable to do more than sample.

19. Printed in *Twelve Comic Songs of Other Days* (W. Paxton, n.d.), and as No. 3304–5 of *The Musical Bouquet* (1874). There is an excellent account of this song in the Rev. Thomas Horne, *Humorous and Tragic Stories of Showman Life* (c. 1905).

20. There is a biography of John Collier (1708–66) in the *D.N.B.*, and by H. Fishwick in his *Works* (Rochdale, 1894). A bibliography of his early editions is given in J. P. Briscoe, *The Literature of Tim Bobbin* (1872); the first edition was in 1746, and it had been reprinted nearly seventy times by the end of the nineteenth century.

21. A version of *Maria Martin*, introducing Tim Bobbin, that was originally used by barnstormers and may have been used by marionettes is printed in *Barnstormer Plays*, edited by Montagu Slater (1928). This has been revived recently by John Wright's Marionettes.

22. One of Clunn Lewis's plays, *The Village Lawyer*, is published in "Puppet Plays and Pamphlets," edited by Gerald Morice (*c.* 1938).

23. Ryley (note 10, Chapter VII), vol. vi, Chapter XXIV, describes a visit to this show in *c.* 1810. See also Mayhew's "The Fantoccini Man" and T. Hannam-Clark, *Drama in Gloucestershire* (1928).

24. "An Unknown Victorian Puppet Theatre in the North of England," in *Puppetry*, 1946–47.

25. A. E. Peterson, "The End of a Quest," in *The Puppet Master*, vol. ii, No. 3, 1948.

26. "In Praise of Puppets," quoted from an unidentified magazine in *The World's Fair*, August 31, 1940.

27. There had, however, been puppet theatres in the City. Writing in about 1830, Charles MacFarlane, in *Popular Customs . . . of the South of Italy* (1846) (originally published in *The Penny Magazine*, 1834–45), recalled how by the end of the eighteenth century puppets in England had declined in favour and the show "was considered fit for none but children and poor people." He remembered, however, that

> in the early part of the present century there was a theatre of the kind in the vicinity of Fleet Street, and another in some street or lane in the heart of the city. I well remember seeing *Romeo and Juliet* played at one of these houses, to the evident delight of an audience which certainly did not consist entirely of children.

No other record of these theatres seems to have survived; it is possible that MacFarlane was thinking of the Little Theatre in Catherine Street, off the Strand, where Gyngell had performed in 1816, and which remained the home of occasional exhibitions of automata and other such sights until the forties (see Andelle), when it was converted into Jessop's notorious night saloon.

28. Throw-away in the Enthoven Collection. This season was advertised in *The Times*, July 23, 1883, to March 19, 1884, and reviewed August 2, 1883.

29. For the full and fascinating story of this visit see McPharlin, Chapter X.

30. An excellent illustrated account of a typical performance of this period is given in *The Children's Variety Entertainment*, by Thomas Holden, verses by Eric Wells (1880).

31. In the eighties Charles de Saint-Genois took the name of "John Hewelt," his brother Alfred that of "Dickson," and the Pajots became "Walton."

32. Edmond de Goncourt, *Journal*, for April 5, 1789; Lemercier de Neuville, *Histoire anecdotique des Marionnettes modernes* (1892), Chapter IV.

There is a certain mystery about Holden's early appearances. When he led the break-away from Bullock's troupe in the United States in 1874 he put into the bill the sketch *Robin Rough Head, or Plowman turned Lord*, "originally performed by him in London for 200 nights." When was this performed? It must have been before March 1873, when Holden joined Bullock's company for the American tour. It seems as if Holden must have had a London season of his own before Bullock opened in 1872. The issue is in doubt, and the discovery of one fugitive playbill could revolutionize the theory I have advanced here of the sequence of the marionette renaissance. J. Holden is recorded as a marionette performer in *The Era* as early as 1864, and Holden's Comic Manikins were established in 1872; these were being presented by Thomas's brother, John, at the South London Palace in 1875; *The Entracte* of May 22 hailed them as the feature of the bill, "a wonderful show which will without doubt be witnessed by everybody on the Surrey side." Thomas probably went into partnership with John on his return from America in 1877; there were several members of the family, and it is not easy to distinguish them. Thomas gained most of the glory, but, according to Mr Wilding, "the cleverest manipulator of all the Holdens was Jim, but he was no talker." See McPharlin for details of his family connexions.

33. Richard Barnard wrote his memoirs in 1913, and the MS. is still in the possession of his family. Some abbreviated extracts appeared in *The Performer* for August 21, 1919, but it is greatly to be hoped that these fascinating reminiscences will one day be printed in their entirety.

Barnard's name sprang into public notice in 1891, when the Westminster Aquarium entered a claim for libel against a Mr Parkinson, a member of the L.C.C., who had objected to the "indecent actions" of Barnard's harlequinade figures there. The innocent puppets were produced in evidence, and the judge could not resist offering them seats on the bench, to the accompaniment of "much laughter in court." The marionettes were completely vindicated, and the theatre-hating councillor had to pay £250 damages, doubled on appeal. See *The Times,* June 26–27, 1891, and H. Findlater Bussy, *Sixty Years of Journalism* (1906).

Some of Barnard's figures were described in "Some Peculiar Entertainments," in *The Strand Magazine*, vol. xi (1896).

34. For the construction of Victorian marionettes see H. W. Whanslaw,

Everybody's Marionette Book (1935), and *Specialized Puppetry* (1948), and Nicholas Nelson and J. J. Hayes, *Trick Marionettes* (U.S.A., 1935).

35. From a pamphlet printed in France in 1887, and quoted in Chesnais, p. 208.

36. The pipe-smoking Mother Shipton from the Clunn Lewis troupe, in the possession of M. Leopold Dor, is said to have belonged originally to Middleton and to be 200 years old, but even if such claims could be proved the figure would certainly have been restrung in the nineteenth century. The Tim Bobbin from the Clowes-Tiller troupe bears a mark on the crown of its head that may, possibly, indicate that it was originally wire-controlled.

37. This theory was advanced by M. Leopold Dor in the catalogue of an Exhibition of Puppets, mostly from his own fine collection, held at the Musée Galliera in Paris in the summer of 1939. It is supported by Chesnais.

38. Continental marionette-makers do not appear to have adopted the all-strung figure until the end of the nineteenth century. To this day the folk-puppet theatres of Sicily, France, and Belgium still use marionettes controlled by an iron rod to the centre of their heads; Prandi's marionettes at the Crystal Palace, as described and illustrated in *Black and White* for May 27, 1893, were manipulated in this way by "an extremely substantial rod of iron about six feet long," terminating in "a wood cross bar, from which strong, but very supple threads run to the hands and feet." Arthur Symons advised visitors to the Costanzi Marionette Theatre in Rome, in 1897, to sit not too far from the stage, where "we shall have the satisfaction of always seeing the wires at their work." (See note 1, Chapter X.)

39. A fine collection of marionettes from the Barnard, Chester and Lee and other troupes is in the possession of Mr Waldo Lanchester, and is displayed at the Puppet Centre, Stratford-on-Avon; some thirty figures from the Clunn Lewis troupe belong to M. Leopold Dor; a collection of D'Arc's figures—after being offered without success to every museum in the British Isles—was sold by auction within the past ten years, and is now believed to be in America; a selection of figures from the Clowes and Rozella troupes belongs to Mr H. W. Whanslaw; the Tiller-Clowes troupe is held by Mr Gerald Morice and myself.

English Victorian marionettes are preserved at the Kingston-upon-Hull Museum and at the Stranger's Museum, Norwich; there is also a set of Punch and Judy figures in the London Museum, and some contemporary glove puppets by Mary Bligh-Bond in the Victoria and Albert Museum.

Chapter X

1. First printed in *The Saturday Review*, July 17, 1897. Reprinted in *Plays, Acting, and Music* (1903).

2. Reprinted in *On the Art of the Theatre* (1911). Further articles on the

puppet by Gordon Craig will be found in *The Mask*, vol. vii, 1915; in *The Marionnette* (1918), the monthly magazine edited by him in Florence, which lasted only a year; and in *Puppets and Poets* (1921), No. 20 of "The Chapbook."

3. Illustrated in *The Illustrated London News*, March 6, 1909. See J. A. Fuller-Maitland, *A Door-keeper of Music* (1929), Chapter XI.

4. Described by G. K. Chesterton in "A Drama of Dolls," reprinted in *Alarms and Discursions* (1910).

5. Joseph gives a valuable sketch of these early puppet experiments. Although the detail of this general world history of puppetry is unreliable, it provides a useful survey of its subject.

6. See Olive Blackham, *Puppets into Actors* (1948), Walter Wilkinson, *The Peep Show* (1927), and many others.

7. Its present address: 23 Southampton Place, London, W.C.1. *The Puppet Book*, edited for the E.P.A. by L. V. Wall (1950), is the best guide to the theory and practice of puppetry in education.

8. Its present address: 206 Radstock Way, Merstham, Surrey.

9. Jan Bussell, *The Puppets and I* (1950) and *Puppet's Progress* (1953), provides an interesting autobiography and an eloquent defence of his profession. See also *Wooden Stars* (1947), a photographic record of the Lanchester Marionettes by Douglas Fisher; and C. W. Beaumont, *Puppets and the Puppet Stage* (1938), a fine collection of photographs of contemporary puppets from all over the world.

10. The future historian of the twentieth-century puppet theatre will find his raw material conveniently collected in the journals of the British Puppet and Model Theatre Guild and of the Educational Puppetry Association, and in the Puppet Columns of *The Worlds' Fair* and *The Stage*. There will be no lack of material, but much need for sifting the wheat from the chaff. This task may be easier in a century's time, when another hand may pick up the pen that I now lay down.

APPENDICES

A. PUPPET SHOWMEN IN ENGLAND, 1600–1914

This attempts to list the names of every puppet-show proprietor who played in England before 1914. Inevitably there must be hundreds of names that have never been recorded and dozens that have eluded my search, and of the list here presented, alongside the important performers, there are ranged many modest entertainers with no claim to fame beyond a chance reference in a parish register or court record. It seemed, however, best, if I was to include a list at all, to make it as complete as possible.

Each entry provides no more than a skeleton of its subject's career, with the years or approximate decades between which he worked and the places at which he appeared. In general, I have not attempted to differentiate between different members of the same family, nor have I included general biographical or theatrical information on their careers; the appearances recorded are confined to puppet performances.

The sources of my information will almost always be discovered in the notes to the text, under the appropriate chapters, but in the cases of a few seventeenth- and eighteenth-century performers I have added a reference if this is not mentioned elsewhere in this volume.

The abbreviations B.F. and S.F. stand for Bartholomew Fair and Southwark Fair.

1600–60

Barker, Anthony	1640	Coventry.
Browne, Robert	1638	Coventry.
	1639	Norwich.
Cloys, Bartholomew	1623	Licensed.
	1624	Coventry.
Cooke, William	1633	Hired a licence.
Costine, William	1632–33	Coventry.
ffussell, Henry	1632–33	With William Costine.
Hall, George	1638–39	With Robert Browne.
Hunter, Thomas	1632–33	With William Costine.
Jones, John and Ann	1630	Upton-on-Severn with a forged licence.
Jones, Richard	1630	With John Jones.
	1638	With Robert Browne.

Luppino, Georgius Guilemus	161–	There is a family tradition in the Lupino family that an Italian puppet player of this name came to England in the reign of James I (Stanley Lupino, *From the Stocks to the Stars* (1934)).
Maskell, Thomas	1635	Norwich.
	1636	Manchester.
Morgan, Fluellen	1633	With William Cooke.
Mossock, Ann	1638	Coventry.
Payne, Richard	1630	With John Jones
Pod, Captain	1600	B.F.
	1614	Dead.
Sands, William and John	1623	Licensed.
	1630	Bridport.
Taylor, Robert	1638	With Ann Mossock.
Tomson, Christopher	1639	Coventry.
"Young Goose"	?	Strutt claims that a motion-man of this name is referred to in *Gammer Gurton's Needle*. This is not true. The allusion may, however, occur in some other play of the period.

1661–1800

Ambroise (Ambrogio)	1775–77	Panton Street (Ombres Chinoises).
	1778	Dublin.
Antonio	1778	Panton Street (Ombres Chinoises).
Armishell, Richard	1674	Stourbridge Fair.
Arnold, Samuel	1776	Bought puppets from C. Dibdin's *Comic Mirror*.
	1776	Marylebone Gardens.
Appleby	1792	B.F.
Astley, Philip	1777	Panton Street; took over from Ambroise.
	1778–79	Piccadilly (Ombres Chinoises).
	1779–90	Astley's Amphitheatre (Ombres Chinoises).
	1809	Olympic (Ombres Chinoises).
Austin, Robert	1683	Norwich.
Baker, Mrs	177–	(T. Dibdin, *Reminiscences* (1827), i, 96.)
Ball, Oliver	1675–78	Norwich.
Ballarini	1778	With Antonio.
Bannister	1790–97	B.F.

Bellayne, Benjamin	1676	Norwich.
Birch, Thomas	1762	Brixham.
Blackmore	1790	B.F.
Blower	1791–93	B.F.
Bologna	1662	Covent Garden.
		Whitehall.
Bornal	1796	B.F.
Bradford, Robert	1667	Norwich.
Braville	1776–77	St Alban's Street (Ombres Chinoises).
Carnevale	1790	Savile Row.
Carter	1800	B.F.
Catchpole	1799	B.F.
Charke, Charlotte	1738	James Street.
	1739–40	James Street.
	1745	With Russel.
Child, John	1735	Ipswich.
Chipperfield	166–	There is a family tradition in the Chipperfield family that an ancestor was a puppet showman in the reign of Charles II (R. M. Saunders, *The English Circus* (1952)).
Clark	1761	York (T. Gent, *Contingencies of Life*).
	1800	B.F.
de Coeurs, Jacob	1685	Norwich.
Collyer, Henry	1736–42	Kent.
Cook, John	1767	Stourbridge Fair.
	1773	London.
	1773–78	Stourbridge Fair.
	1801	B.F.
Crawley	170–	B.F., S.F.
	170–	B.F. (Tony Aston, *Supplement to Cibber* (1747)).
Dallman, Peter	1670–85	Norwich.
Davidge	1792	B.F.
Devoto, Anthony	1667–74	Charing Cross.
	1672–77	B.F.
Dibdin, Charles	1775–76	Exeter Change.
	1780	Little, Haymarket.
Diswell	1794	B.F.
Dixon, Rowland	175–	Ingleton, Yorkshire (Southey, *Doctor* (1834), Chapter 23).
Ellis, John	1774–76	Abbey Street, Dublin.
	1776–81	Patagonian Theatre, Exeter Change.

Ellis and Co.	1800–1	B.F.
Exon	1792–1810	B.F.
Fawkes, Isaac	1725	S.F.
	1726–27	James Street.
	1731	Died.
Fawkes, junior	172–	Bath and Gloucester.
	1732	Opera Room, Haymarket.
	1734	James Street.
	1740	B.F.
	1742	James Street.
Fletcher, Edward	176–	Hereford.
	1772	Died at Cleobury Mortimer.
Flint, widow	1794	Succeeded Flockton.
	1795–1803	B.F.
	1802	Sadler's Wells.
Flockton	1762	Panton Street.
	1776–93	B.F.
	178–	Lyceum, Strand.
	1787	Leytonstone. Peckham.
	1788	Edmonton. Stourbridge Fair.
Foote, Samuel	1758	Drury Lane.
	1773	Little, Haymarket.
Frost	1738–40	Norwich.
Gabriel	1778	With Antonio.
Gaynes	177–	Cassino Rooms.
Godwin	1733–34	Norwich.
	1739	Canterbury.
	1747	B.F.
Green	1701	Strolling without a licence.
Griffin	174–	Brought up Nancy Dawson.
Harris, John	169–	B.F.
	1721	Tower Hill.
	1723	Oxford.
Haynes, James	1683–87	Norwich.
Heatley, Matthew	170–	B.F.
Hill	1754	S.F.
Holinds	1799	B.F.
Howard, Moses	1735–41	Stourbridge Fair.
Howis	1796–97	B.F.
Humphreys	1796–99	B.F.
Iliff, Edward	1791–92	Savile Row.
Jobson	1759	Canterbury.
	1778–94	B.F.

	177–	Covent Garden.
Jonas	1790–99	B.F.
Karby, John	1733	Norwich.
Lacon	173–	Tunbridge Wells; succeeded by Jobson.
Logee	1792	B.F.
Manuelli	1781	Worcester, Bath, Bristol.
Martin, Mrs	1728	Nag's Head, James Street.
Martinelli	1780–81	Piccadilly with Micheli.
	1791–92	Savile Row.
	1796–97	Ranelagh.
	1796	Covent Garden.
	1797-98	Royalty.
Masena	1790	B.F.
Meniucci	1776–77	With Braville.
Micheli	1780–81	Piccadilly.
Monte, John	1685	With Jacob de Coeurs.
Morello, Charles	1790–98	B.F.
de la Nash, Madame	1748	Panton Street.
Noland	1798	B.F.
Parker, Robert	1673	Stourbridge Fair.
Parsloe	1752	S.F.
Perico, Carlo	1770–72	Panton Street.
Plat	1733–34	With Godwin.
Portenary	1792	B.F.
Powell, Martin	1709–	Bath.
	1710	St Martin's Lane.
	1711–13	Covent Garden.
	1714	Spring Garden.
	1717	B.F.
Powell, junior	1725	S.F., with Fawkes.
	1726	James Street, with Fawkes.
	1726	S.F., with Yeates.
Powell	1792	B.F.
Quinborrough, Robert	1678	Norwich.
Raynor	1740	With Frost.
Rebecqui	1800	Worcester.
Reynolds	1747	With Godwin.
Robinson, Thomas	1791	Savile Row.
Robust	1800	B.F.
Rowe, Harry	176––97	Yorkshire.
Russel	1745	Hickford's Room, Brewer Street.
Samuel	1793–94	B.F.
Salmon, Mrs	170–	St Martin's, Aldersgate.

	171–	Horn Tavern, Fleet Street.
Saraband, Mrs	170–	May Fair.
Seward	1744	Moorfields and May Fair.
Sharpe	177–	With Gaynes.
Shepheard, Robert	1727	Burnt to death at Burwell.
Shepherd, William	1734–40	Stourbridge Fair.
	1736	Ipswich.
	1738	Norwich.
Smith, Thomas	1731	Licensed.
Sonne, Elizabeth	1677	Norwich.
Southby	1794	B.F.
Sturmer	1794–95	B.F.
Terwin	1734	S.F.
	1740	With Fawkes.
Thompson, John	1720–35	Stourbridge Fair.
	1721–23	Norwich.
	1761	Canterbury.
Tollett	1721–23	With Thompson.
Trimer, Benjamin	1680	With Peter Dallman.
Wells	1792	B.F.
White, Thomas	1769–76	Stourbridge Fair.
	1790	B.F.
Williams	1773	Chester.
Wilson	1791–96	B.F.
Woodham	1738	With Frost.
Yates, George	1779–80	B.F.
Yeates, senior and	1725–52	B.F.
junior	1725–34	S.F.
	1728	Spittalfields.
	1728–38	Bow Fair.
	1731	Tottenham Court Fair.
	1735	Royal Exchange.
	1739–40	With Charlotte Charke.
	1752	James Street.

1801–1914

Alexander (Douglas)	189––1942	Birmingham, and Punch.
Andelle	1839	Pantheon, Catherine Street.
Archibald	189–	Drawing-room show.
Ashington	188––190–	Yorkshire and Lancashire.
Bailey, Henry	188–	With portable theatre and ghost show.
Barnard, Richard	1867–72	With Middleton's.

	1872–73	With Springthorpe's, Cassidy's, and Simms.
	1874–77	With Bullock's.
	1877–78	With Holden's in Europe.
	1878	In partnership with Wilding at the Westminster Aquarium.
	1879–80	Toured Europe for Montague.
	1881–89	Touring Continent.
	1890–98	Westminster Aquarium, Crystal Palace, and variety circuits.
	1899–1925	Show carried on by his children, with tours to Australia, America, and S. Africa.
Barnett, Morris	1852	Royal Marionette Theatre.
Baylis, Sam	186–	Yorkshire and Scarborough.
Benson, Valentine	190–	At exhibitions, piers, etc.
Bennett	190–	Later manager of Worcester Theatre.
Bentley	189–	Nottingham.
Bolton, Arthur "Judge"	190–	Yorkshire, and Punch.
Bonheur, Franz	190–	New Century Marionettes.
Booth, Tom	190–	
Bourne	1880–1914	And Punch.
Bowman	190–	Four brothers.
Brigaldi	1852–53	Royal Marionette Theatre.
	1852	Manchester and Liverpool.
	1852–53	St James's Theatre.
	1853	Adelaide Gallery.
	1857–6–	Cremorne Gardens.
Brown	189––191–	Hull.
Bryant, George	187–	Bristol.
	1875–89	London music-halls.
Bullock, W. J.	1868–71	Dublin.
	1872	Liverpool.
	1872–73	St James's and Egyptian Halls.
	1874	U.S.A.
	187–	Touring provinces.
	1887	Agricultural Hall.
Buxton, Henry	186–	Touring provinces.
Calver, Edward and Walter	1835–6–	Leeds, Sheffield and North Country fairs.
Campbell, Fred and Fanny	186–	Their daughter married W. Tiller.
Candler	1825	Street Fantoccini.

Cardoni	185–	East End of London.
Case	185–	Wilding senior worked for them.
Cassidy	187–	Harry Wilding and Barnard worked for them.
Chappel	189–	See J. and G. Radford.
Chester and Lee	1868–1931	Mostly in London music-halls.
	1884	Channel Islands. Agricultural Hall.
Clapton	185–	
Clowes	185––73	With Simms.
	1873–1916	Toured South of England.
Colla	1888	Hengler's Cirque.
Cooper	188–	The Imperial Marionettes.
	1881	Cheltenham.
	1882	Russia.
	1888	Alexandra Palace.
D'Arc	1862	Waxwork modeller with Springthorpe's at Hull.
	1867	Added marionette performances to his waxwork show at the Rotunda, Dublin.
	1888	Irish Exhibition, Olympia.
	1894	Toured China and Japan.
	1895	Resumed Dublin performances.
	1907	On the halls.
	1884–	Waxwork show at Cardiff.
Delvaine (Fanning)	1877–1948	English music-halls.
De Marion	190––3–	Music-halls.
Dicks	1824–28	Toured abroad.
	1828	St Helena Gardens.
	1828	Vauxhall.
Du Garde	189–	See J. and G. Radford.
Edwards	1867	A. 1. Marionettes.
Fountains	190–	
Frisby	182–	His daughter married Middleton.
Fuller	1878	Westminster Aquarium.
Gerard	188–	Toured Continent.
Glennie	190–	Liverpool.
Glindon	1856	Adelaide Hall, and Princes Theatre, Glasgow.
Grey	182–	Street Fantoccini.
	1823	Vauxhall, and Sadler's Wells.
	182–	Preston.
	1832	Arrived in New York.
Gray, George	191–	

Gregory	1801	B.F.
Gulliver	190–	
Gyngell	1794–1804	With Flint.
	1816	Little, Catherine Street.
	1816	B.F., Edmonton, and Croydon.
	1817	Dover.
Hartley	188–	With Marshall.
Haydon (or Haydee)	187–	Related to Delvaine.
Hodson	187––1915	At one time with Ashington.
Holden, Thomas	186–	Comic Manikins, and Champion Marionettes
	1873	With Bullock to U.S.A.
	1874	In U.S.A. with ex-Bullock troupe.
	1877–	Touring Continent.
	1890–	English music-halls.
Holmes	1801	B.F.
Howlett, Carl	190–	Worked on Continent with Holden.
Howard	190–	
Jackson	1826	New Bagnigge Wells.
Jennion	1887	Paragon, Mile End Road.
	1888	Alhambra, Brighton.
	1889	Westminster Aquarium.
Jewell, Jesse	1889	Toured Holland.
	1894	Earl's Court.
	1904	To U.S.A.
Johnson, Jack	189–	Later with portable theatre.
Jukes	189–	Manchester.
Kearn	189–	See J. and G. Radford.
Lalette, Lily	1911	Sunderland.
Lawrence	1874	With Bullock in U.S.A.
	1877	Set up in London.
	188––97	Toured English fairs.
	1912	Sold up.
Lee, Clarence	1882	Agricultural Hall; see Chester and Lee.
Lee, Nelson	1823	Newcastle Races.
Leech	1804	B.F.
Letta	190–	Scotland.
Lewis, Clunn	189–	Toured Kent and Sussex.
Lewis, J. H.	185––96	Toured North of England fairs.
	1907–1–	Music-halls.
Leyland, Tom	189–	Toured Lancashire.
Linton	190–	
Maffey	1825–	Dublin and Ireland.
	1828	Tour of provinces.

	1828–29	Argyll Rooms.
	1829	Surrey Theatre.
Mander	188–	Toured fairs.
Marchetti	1884	St James's Hall.
Marler, William	1829	Chalk Farm Tavern.
Marlow, John Hunter	1893	Died.
Marshall	1887	"Ally Sloper" show at Tottenham Club.
Martinek, G.	?	Twenty-four marionettes with wire controls, probably Italian, found at Latchington, Essex. Now in possession of Waldo Lanchester.
Maynard	190–	
Middleton	1830	"Established upwards of 100 years."
	1831	B.F.
	1834	B.F.
	1838	Hyde Park Fair.
	184–	Carried on by widow Frisby.
	186 – 7–	Touring provinces.
	1881	All branches of family united in U.S.A.
Milton, Arthur	189–	Music-halls.
Montague	1879	Holden's ex-manager. In partnership with Gerard bought Springthorpe's show, and employed Barnard for Continental tour.
	1880	Show stranded in Paris.
Morris, Bert	191–	
Mumford	184–	Glasgow Fair.
Newman	190–	
Nimbo	1900	Hull; figures in Hull Museum.
O'Brien	190–	
Paine	188–	With waxworks.
Paris, Thomas	1810	B.F.
	183–	Street Galanty Show.
Perry	1802	B.F.
Pettigrove, Britton	1881–82	With Cooper's Imperial Marionettes.
	1885–86	Albert Palace, Battersea.
Pollintio	190–	
Prandi	1888	Earl's Court.
	1893	Crystal Palace.
Purvis, Billy	1822	With Grey.
	1823–45	Toured North of England.
Radford, J. and G.	187–	Grand Star Marionettes.
Rebmuh (J. W. Humber) and Ward	1895–1905	Marionette and conjuring show.

Rothe, T.	1907–	Drawing-room show.
Rozella, M. (Elsbury)	188–	Drawing-room show.
Seward	1796–1812	B.F.
	181––5–	Cheltenham.
Short	190–	
Simms	185–	Clowes and Barnard joined this show.
Sinclair	1892–	Agricultural Hall, and Punch.
Skinner, Thomas	191–	Toured South Wales.
Springthorpe	186–	Waxwork show in Dublin, and Concert Hall at Hull.
	187–	Widow and children touring in Ireland and England with marionettes.
	1879	Show bought by Montague and Gerard for European tour.
Stanley, Lindrea and Fred	189–	Toured provinces, and Punch.
Sunniway	187–	
Testo	188––191 -	Toured South Wales.
Tiller	186––9–	Ambrose, senior.
	1894	Walter in partnership with Clowes.
	1895–1914	Walter touring fairs.
	1903–15	Ambrose, junior, touring.
Wallace	190–	Burgess Hill.
"Old Waxy"	1843–60	Sunderland, waxworks and marionettes.
	1860–1904	Show continued under same name.
Whatman	188–	Royal Victoria Hall.
Whiteley's	1885	Provided marionette pantomimes for private parties.
Wilding	186–	Wilding senior.
	188–	Harry Wilding worked for many big companies.
	189––1941	Harry Wilding toured Midlands.
Willard	190–	
Wycherley	1881–82	With Cooper's Imperial Marionettes.
	1882–	Took over sole management.

Punch and Judy Men, 1801–1914

Bailey	187–	Buxton, and music-halls.
	1899	Crystal Palace.
Bourne	189–	Head-carver and puppet-maker.
Bullivant, A. R.	191–	Forest Gate.
Candler	1903	Halifax.

Codman	187–	Llandudno, and music-halls.
	189–	Liverpool.
Davis	190–	London.
Dawson, "Pep"	1829	Partner of Old Wild.
Dean, Thomas	190–	Marylebone.
Fern	190–	Edinburgh.
Gardner and Brewer	1868	"From Windsor Castle and Crystal Palace" in New York.
Green	188–	Blackpool and Rhyl.
Herring, Paul	183–	London.
Jesson	189–	London.
Kitlee	191–	London.
Macklin, Jim	183–	London.
Manley and Brewer	1869	New York.
	1906	Tower Street.
Manvers	1866	To New York.
Matthews	1828	"From the Surrey Theatre and Vauxhall" in New York.
Mowbray	188–	Notting Hill.
North, Claude	190–	Clacton.
Ody, Joe	180–	Wiltshire; a Merry Andrew at fairs, perhaps with puppets.
Piccini	179–-182–	London.
Pike	182–-3–	London.
Portland, James	191–	Finsbury Park.
Smith	185–	Poplar.
	191–	Margate.
Staddon	188–	South-west coast.

B. PLAYS PERFORMED BY PUPPETS IN ENGLAND

This attempts to list every play acted by puppets in England between 1500 and 1914 of which any record has been left. Ballets, *divertissements*, and scenic spectacles are not included.

The first column gives the name of the play, sometimes reduced to a common denominator from several different entries. The second column gives the year, or the approximate decade, of its performance by puppets. The third column the name of the showman responsible, or where that is not known the place of performance. When more than one performance by the same puppeteer has been recorded only the earliest is normally listed. In the case of folk-plays, where much of our information is from literary references, a clue to the source of these has been provided, if it is not recorded elsewhere. I have not thought it necessary to list the authority for information that is based on actual playbills, advertisements, or official records. References to the textual notes should elucidate the source of any doubtful entry.

Finally, whenever I have been able to trace what appears to be a performance of the same play in the human theatre I have listed in column four its author and—where appropriate—the composer of the music (when different from the librettist), and in column five the date of its first performance with human actors. The abbreviation B.O. stands for ballad opera.

Folk Plays: Biblical

The Life of King Ahasuerus, or the History of Esther	1654	(E. Gayton, *Notes on Don Quixote*, p. 270.).
	1719	Harris.
Babylon	1607	(*Lingua*, iii, 6).
Bel and the Dragon	1643	(*Actors' Remonstrance*).
The Chaos of the World	1623	Sands.
	1647	B.F. (S. Butler, *Hudibras*, I, 1, 563).
The Creation of the World	1623	Sands.
	1638	Taylor.
	1639	Tomson.
	1644	(Milton, *Areopagitica*).
	1651	(Randolph, *Hey for Honesty*, I, 2).
	1675	Ball.
	1676	Belloyne.
	1682	B.F. (*Wit and Drollery*).
	1699	B.F. (Tom Brown, *Letters*, to G. Moult).
	1701	B.F. (*Walk to Smithfield*).
	170–	Crawley.
	170–	Heatley.
	1705	B.F. (*The Wandering Spy*).
	1709	Powell.
	1712	Powell (as *The State of Innocence*).
	1717	Powell.
	1733	(Hogarth, *Southwark Fair*).
	175–	Dixon.
	175–	(G. A. Stevens, *Speculist*, II, 32).
	1752	Yeates.
	1756	Stretch (*Humble Petition of T. Punch*).
	179–	Rowe (Rowe, *Macbeth*).

The Destruction of Jerusalem	1605	(Marston, *Dutch Courtezan*, III, 1).
	1614	(Jonson, *Bartholomew Fair*, V, 1).
Dives and Lazarus	1654	(Gayton, *Notes on Don Quixote*).
	1682	B.F. (*Wit and Drollery*).
	1705	Heatley.
Jephthah's Rash Vow	1701	B.F. (*Walk to Smithfield*).
	1744	Seward.
	1749	(Fielding, *Tom Jones*, XII, 7).
Jonas	1600	Fleet Bridge (Jonson, *Every Man Out of His Humour*, II, 1).
	1605	(Marston, *Dutch Courtezan*).
Judith and Holofernes	1663	Lincoln's Inn Fields (Pepys, August 6).
	1664	B.F. (John Locke, *Letters*).
Nebuchadnezzar	1711	Powell (as *The Virtuous Wife*).
	175–	Dixon.
Nineveh	1600	Fleet Bridge (Jonson, *Every Man . . .*).
	1605	(Marston, *Dutch Courtezan*).
	1607	(*Lingua*).
	1609	(*Every Woman in Her Humour*, V, 1).
	1610	(Beaumont and Fletcher, *Wit at Several Weapons*, I, 1).
	1611	(H. Peacham, *Coryat's Crudities*).
	1614	(Jonson, *Bartholomew Fair*).
	1658	(A. Cowley, *Cutter of Coleman Street*, V, 11).
Noah's Ark	1703	Crawley.
	175–	Dixon.
	1818	Leverge Gallanty Show (Hone, *Ancient Mysteries*, 231).
The Prodigal Son	1604	(Shakespeare, *Winter's Tale*, IV, 2).
	169–	Harris.
	1818	Leverge Gallanty Show (Hone).
The Resurrection	150–	(Lambarde, *Places in England and Wales*, under Witney).
Sodom and Gomorrah	1614	(Jonson, *Bartholomew Fair*).
Solomon and the Queen of Sheba	1671	Norwich.
	1728	(Swift, *Mad Mullinix*).
	1731	(Swift, *Strephon and Chloe*).
	175–	Griffin.
	1756	Stretch (*Humble Petition of Punch*).
	1760	(Goldsmith, *Second Letter on Coronation*).

	1773	(G. A. Stevens, *History of Master Edward*).
	1773	(Goldsmith, *She Stoops to Conquer*, III).
Chaste Susannah, or the Court of Babylon	1654	(Gayton, *Don Quixote*).
	1655	B.F. (D'Urfey, *Wit and Mirth*).
	1711	Powell.
	175–	Dixon.
The Witch of Endor	1728	(Swift, *Mad Mullinix*).

Folk-plays: Historical and Legendary

Arden of Faversham	1736	Collyer.
	1742	German puppets.
	184–	Middleton and Frisby.
	188–	Clunn Lewis.
Friar Bacon and Friar Bungay	169–	Harris.
	1711	Powell.
	1740	Charke and Yeates.
Bateman, or the Unhappy Marriage	169–	B.F., S.F.
	1713	Powell (as *The Unfortunate Lovers*).
	1728	(Ralph, *Taste of the Town*).
	1748	de la Nash.
	175–	Dixon.
King Bladud, Founder of the Bath	1711	Powell.
The Constant Lovers, or the Blind Beggar of Bethnal Green	1712	Powell.
	1725	Powell, junior.
The Fall of Caleb the Great Enchantress, or the Birth of St George	1713	Powell.
The Children in the Wood	1714	Powell (*Second Tale of a Tub*).
	175–	(Stevens, *Speculist*).
	1758	Stretch (*Punch's Petition*).
	1777	East Grinstead (Letter from James Northcote in Whitley, *Artists in England 1700–1799*).
	1825	Grey (henceforth as *The Babes in the Wood*).
	1862	Sunderland.
	1872	Bullock.
	187–	D'Arc.
	188–	Wilding.

	188–	Tiller.
	188–	Middleton.
	189–	Bolton.
	189–	Testo.
	189–	Ashington.
	1896	Rebmuh and Ward.
Crispin and Crispianus	1742	German puppets.
Dido and Æneas	1735	Sheppard.
	1763	(*British Magazine*, October).
Dorastus and Fawnia, or the Royal Shepherd and Shepherdess	1728	Martin.
The Duke of Guise	1600	(*Blind Beggar of Bethnal Green*, IV).
(or *Duke of Lorraine*)	1603	(Dekker, *Wonderful Year*).
	1728	(Swift, *Mad Mullinix*).
	1731	(Swift, *Strephon and Chloe*).
The Great Earthquake in Jamaica	1692	S.F. (Evelyn, September 15).
Queen Elizabeth	164–	(Davenant, *Long Vacation*).
	169–	Harris.
	1726	Powell, junior, and Yeates.
	1761	Clark.
The Unhappy Favourite, or	1738	Charke.
the Earl of Essex	1743	Canterbury.
Faustus	1710	Powell (*Tatler*, 115).
	1712	Powell (as *Faustus's Trip to the Jubilee*).
	1728	(Swift, *Mad Mullinix*).
	1728	(Ralph, *Taste of the Town*).
	1734	Fawkes.
	179–	Rowe (Rowe, *Macbeth*).
St George and the Dragon	1725	Yeates.
	1727	Shepheard.
	1728	(Swift, *Mad Mullinix*).
	175–	(Stevens, *Speculist*).
The Glorious Princess, or Virtue Triumphant	1747	Godwin and Reynolds.
The Gunpowder Plot	1614	(Jonson, *Bartholomew Fair*).
	1762	(G. A. Stevens, *Bartholomew Fair*).
Henry VIII and Anne Boleyn	1711	Powell (*Spectator*, 14; see *Whittington*).
	1738	Charke.
	179–	Rowe (Rowe, *Macbeth*).
Hero and Leander	1614	(Jonson, *Bartholomew Fair*).
	1711	Powell (as *Heroic Love*).

Jane Shore	1683	Austin.
	169–	B.F.
	1751	James Street.
	175–	Griffin.
	175–	Dixon.
	1761	Clark.
	181–	(Maxwell, *Easter*).
	1812	West End Fair.
	188–	Wilding.
Julius Cæsar	1600	(*Blind Beggar of Bethnal Green*).
	1603	(Dekker, *Wonderful Year*).
	1605	(Marston, *Dutch Courtezan*).
	1609	(*Every Woman in Her Humour*, V, 1).
	1756	Stretch (*Humble Petition of Punch*).
	1779	Jobson.
The Lancashire Witches	169–	Harris.
London	1600	(Jonson, *Every Man Out of His Humour*, Prologue).
	1607	(*Lingua*).
Mother Lowse	1714	Powell (*Second Tale of a Tub*).
Lysander	1712	B.F. (*Spectator*, 377).
The Magician's Fate	1712	Powell.
The Last Year's Campaign (Victory of Malplaquet)	1710	Powell.
Maudlin, the Merchant's Daughter of Bristol	1667	Bradford.
The British Enchanter, or the Birth of Merlin	1711	Powell.
Merry Tom	1678	Quinborrough.
The Siege of Namur	1695	(Tom D'Urfey, *Don Quixote*, III).
The City of Norwich	1597	Stratford-on-Avon.
	1600	(*Blind Beggar of Bethnal Green*).
	1611	(H. Peacham, *Coryat's Crudities*).
	1614	(Jonson, *Bartholomew Fair*).
Patient Grissel	1655	B.F. (D'Urfey, *Wit and Mirth*).
	1667	B.F. (Pepys, August 30).
	1774	(Tom Warton, *History of English Poetry*).
King Philip and Queen Mary	1728	(Swift, *Mad Mullinix*).
	1739	Charke and Yeates.
Robin Hood	1714	Powell (*Second Tale of a Tub*).
Rome	1600	(Jonson, *Every Man Out of Hi Humour*, Prologue).

Fair Rosamond	1655	B.F. (D'Urfey, *Wit and Mirth*).
	1677	Sonne.
	169–	Harris.
	1748	de la Nash.
	175–	Dixon.
	1763	(Stevens, *History of Master Edward*).
The Seven Champions of Christendom	1712	Powell (announced, but not performed).
The Seven Wise Men of Greece	1756	Stretch (*Humble Petition*).
	179–	Rowe (Rowe, *Macbeth*).
Mother Shipton, and the Downfall of Cardinal Wolsey	1712	Powell (announced).
	1728	(Ralph, *Taste of the Town*).
The Siege of Troy	1712	Powell (as *The False Triumph*).
	1731	(Swift, *Strephon and Chloe*).
	1734	Terwin.
	1858	See Pantomimes (nineteenth-century).
Tamberlaine	1600	(*Blind Beggar of Bethnal Green*).
The Universal Monarch defeated, or the Queen of Hungary Triumphant	173–	Fawkes.
Valentine and Orson	1712	Powell (announced).
Whittington, thrice Lord Lord Mayor of London, and his Cat	1668	S.F. (Pepys, September 21).
	1670	Norwich.
	169–	Heatley.
	1711	Powell.
	1737	Collyer.
	1739	Godwin.
	1748	de la Nash.
	1762	B.F. (Stevens, *Bartholomew Fair*).
	1810	Seward.
	188–	See Pantomimes (nineteenth-century).
The World's Abuses	1638	Browne.

Comedies, Farces, and Dramas (Eighteenth-century)

Amphitryon, or the Two Sosias	1738	Charke (announced)	Dryden	1691
The Conjuror	1787	Flockton		
The Enchanted Island	1788	Flockton		
The Ghost	1780	Flockton	? Mrs Centlivre	1767
Henry the Fourth	1738	Charke	From Shakespeare	
Henry the Eighth	1738	Charke	From Shakespeare	
The Inconstant Lover	1735	Child	? G. Farquhar	1701

The Miller of Mansfield	1738	Charke	R. Dodsley	1737
The Mistake, or the Constant Lover Rewarded	1740	Charke and Yeates	Vanbrugh	1705
The Old Debauchees, or the Jesuit Caught	1738	Charke	H. Fielding	1732
Retaliation	1779	Patagonian	L. Macnally	1782
Richard the Third	1738	Charke	From Shakespeare	
The Rival Queens, or the Death of Alexander the Great	1784	Flockton	Nat Lee	1677
The Royal Offspring, or the Maid's Tragedy	171–	Salmon		
The Sailor's Return	1782	Flockton		
The Tinker in a Bustle	1786	Flockton		
The Town Miss	1752	Parsloe	? D. Garrick	1747
	1779	Yates		
The Unnatural Brother, or the Orphan Betrayed	1712	Powell		
Virtue Rewarded	1742	German puppets (See *La Buona Figliuola*)	From Richardson	1741

Burlesques and Satires

The Apotheosis of Punch	1779	Patagonian	L. Macnally	
The Arcadian Brothers	1852	Brigaldi	"Hugo Vamp"	
Bombastes Furioso	1852	Brigaldi	W. B. Rhodes	1810
The British Admiral (*Keppel*)	1779	Patagonian		
Chrononhotonthologos	1776	Patagonian	H. Carey	1734
The Covent Garden Tragedy	1734	Fawkes	H. Fielding	1732
	1738	Charke		
	1748	de la Nash		
The Death of Common Sense	1781	Patagonian		
Doctor Adelphi	1780	Patagonian		
Piety in Pattens	1773	Foote	S. Foote	1777
	1776	Arnold		
The Pleasures of the Town	1734	Yeates	H. Fielding	1730
Poll Practice, or the Secrets of Suffrage	1852	Brigaldi	"Hugo Vamp"	
Poor Robin's Dream, or the Vices of the Age Displayed	1711	Powell		
Punch à la Romaine, or a Classical Education	1852	Brigaldi		
The Sixth Act of Romeo and Juliet	1852	Brigaldi		
Roscius in Spirits, or the Rival Tenants	1852	Brigaldi		
Tom Thumb	1734	Fawkes	H. Fielding	1730

	1777	Patagonian	Kane O'Hara		1780
The Town Rake, or Punch turned Quaker	1711	Powell			
	1728	Yeates			
The United Services	1852	Brigaldi			

Ballad Operas, Comic Operas, and Operatic Burlesques

The Beauteous Sacrifice	1712	Powell			
The Beggar's Opera	1780	Patagonian	John Gay	B.O.	1728
The Beggar's Wedding	1734	Fawkes	C. Coffey	B.O.	1729
	1738	Charke			
Britons strike Home	1740	Fawkes	E. Philips	B.O.	1739
The Camp at Coxheath	1779	Patagonian			
The Cooper	1778	Patagonian	T. Arne		1772
The Country Wedding, or the Fulham Waterman Defeated	1740	Charke and Yeates			1739
Damon and Phillida, or the Rover Reclaimed	1738	Charke	C. Cibber	B.O.	1729
The Deserter	1777	Patagonian	C. Dibdin	Monsigny	1773
The Dragon of Wantley	1738	Yeates	H. Carey	J. Lampe	1737
	1777	Patagonian			
The False Triumph, or the Destruction of Troy	1712	Powell			
	1726	Powell, jun.			
The Flitch of Bacon	1781	Patagonian	H. Bate	W. Shield	1778
The Generous Freemason, or the Constant Lady	1740	Charke and Yeates	W. R. Chetwood	B.O.	1730
The Harlot's Progress	1733	Yeates			
	1736	Collyer	Theo. Cibber		1733
Heroic Love, or the Death of Hero and Leander	1711	Powell			
	1726	Powell, jun.			
Hob in the Well	1739	Godwin	J. Hippisley	B.O.	1729
The Honest Yorkshire Man	1740	Charke and Yeates	H. Carey	B.O.	1735
The Irish Widow	1781	Patagonian	D. Garrick	M. Arne	1767
The Jovial Crew	1778	Patagonian	R. Brome	B.O.	1731
Linco's Travels	1780	Patagonian	D. Garrick	M. Arne	1767
Love in a Village	1778	Lilliputian	I. Bickerstaffe	B.O.	1762
The Lover his own Rival	1737	Yeates	A. Langford	B.O.	1736
	1740	Charke and Yeates			
Midas	1776	Patagonian	Kane O'Hara	B.O.	1762
	1778	Lilliputian			

The Milkmaid	1775	Dibdin	C. Dibdin		
The Mock Doctor	1738	Charke	H. Fielding	B.O.	1732
	1779	Patagonian			
The Nuptials of Venus	1780	Patagonian			
Orpheus and Erudice	1712	Powell			
The Padlock	1776	Patagonian	I. Bickerstaffe	C. Dibdin	1768
	1787	Flockton			
The Politicians	1780	Patagonian			
The Purse, or the Benevolent Tar	1797	Scenic Theatre	J. C. Cross	W. Reeve	1794
The Quaker	1778	Patagonian	C. Dibdin		1777
The Rake's Progress	1740	Charke and Yeates	From Hogarth	B.O.	
The Recruiting Sergeant	1776	Dibdin	I. Bickerstaffe	C. Dibdin	1770
	1777	Patagonian			
The Scold Outwitted	1780	B.F.			
The Shipwreck	1779	Patagonian	From Shakespeare and Dryden	Smith	
Thomas and Sally	1776	Patagonian	I. Bickerstaffe	T. Arne	1760
	1781	Manuelli			
The Triumph of Fidelity	1790	Miniature			
True Blue	1780	Patagonian	H. Carey		1739
The Two Misers	1779	Patagonian	Kane O'Hara	C. Dibdin	1775
Venus and Adonis	1713	Powell			
The Waterman	1778	Patagonian	C. Dibdin	B.O.	1774
	1780	Micheli			
	1781	Chinese Academy			
	186–	Middleton			
	187–	Bullock			
The Widow in Tears	1791	Savile Row	Dibdin	Shield	

Pantomimes (Eighteenth-century)

The Birth of Harlequin	1754	Bence			1735
The Emperor of the Moon	1777	Patagonian			
The Enchanter	1776	Patagonian			
The Fairy Queen	1752	Yeates			1730
Harlequin Conjuror, or Pantaloon Dissected	1754	Hill			
Harlequin Mercury	1781	Patagonian			
Harlequin's Revels	1778	Lilliputian			
Hecate, or Harlequin from the Moon	1777	Patagonian	James Love		1763
The Lunar Ambassador	1778	Patagonian			
The Magicians	1781	Patagonian			

The Miller's Daughter	1777	Patagonian		
The Necromancer	1759	Jobson	? J. Rich	1728
The Peasants	1778	Patagonian		
The Rambles of Harlequin	1780	Patagonian		
The Witches, or Harlequin Sailor	1776	Patagonian	? James Love	1762

Dramas (Nineteenth-century)

Alonzo the Brave	186–	Middleton	H. M. Milner	1826
The Beggar's Petition	188–	Wilding	G. D. Pitt	1841
Ben Bolt	1862	Sunderland	J. B. Johnstone	1854
Bitter Cold	188–	Tiller		1865
Black Beard the Pirate	1862	Sunderland	J. C. Cross	1798
Black-eyed Susan	187–	Bullock	D. Jerrold	1829
	187–	Middleton		
	188–	Wilding		
	189–	Brown		
The Bottle Imp	1852	Brigaldi	R. B. Peake	1828
	1860	Sunderland		
The Brigand Chief	187–	Bullock	J. Planché	1829
	187–	Middleton		
Briton and Boer	190–	Wilding	F. Cooke	1900
The Brother's Revenge	188–	Wilding		1854
The Castle Spectre	1863	Sunderland	M. G. Lewis	1797
	189–	Brown		
The Charcoal Burner	187–	Bullock	G. Almar	1832
	187–	Middleton		
	188–	Wilding		
	188–	Clowes		
Charles Peace	190–	Wilding		
Clari, the Maid of Milan	1862	Sunderland	J. Planché	1823
The Colleen Bawn	1862	Sunderland	D. Boucicault	1860
	188–	Wilding		
	188–	Middleton		
The Corsican Brothers	1862	Sunderland	D. Boucicault	1852
Cramond Brig	1862	Sunderland	From Scott	1826
The Crippen Horror, or Tracked by Wireless	1910	Wilding	Bert Wilding	
The Dead Witness	188–	Wilding	From Dickens	1863
The Death Ship	188–	Wilding		
Dick Turpin	188–	Wilding		1835
	188–	Tiller		
	189–	Brown		
The Dream at Sea	188–	Wilding		
Drink, or Father, Dear Father, Come Home	188–	Wilding	C. Reade	1879
Driven from Home	188–	Tiller	G. Macdermott	1871

The Duel in the Snow	188–	Wilding	E. Fitzball	1860
East Lynne	188–	Tiller	From Mrs Henry Wood	1866
	188–	Wilding		
	189–	Ashington		
The Eddystone Elf	188–	Wilding	G. D. Pitt	1834
The Face at the Window	189–	Wilding	F. B. Warren	1897
The Factory Girl	188–	Wilding		1852
	188–	Tiller-Clowes		
Faith, Hope, and Charity	188–	Wilding	E. L. Blanchard	1845
The Fall of Algiers	1863	Sunderland		1825
Fallen among Thieves	188–	Wilding	From A'Beckett	1882
The Floating Beacon	187–	Bullock	E. Fitzball	1824
	187–	Middleton		
The Flying Dutchman	1863	Sunderland	E. Fitzball	1827
	189–	Brown		
The Forest of Bondy	189–	Brown	W. Barrymore	1814
Forget-me-not	188–	Tiller	W. Tiller	
George Barnwell	1863	Sunderland	G. Lillo	1731
Grace Darling	185–	Clapton	E. Stirling	1838
The Grandfather's Clock	188–	Wilding	E. Bertrand	1879
The Grip of Iron	188–	Wilding	A. Shirley	1892
Guy Fawkes	189–	Brown	G. Macfarren	1822
Guy Mannering	1852	Brigaldi	Walter Scott	1816
The Haunted Castle	189–	Bolton		
The Haunted Churchyard	189–	Brown		
The Haunted House	189–	Brown		
The Haunted Inn	190–	Skinner	R. Peake	1828
The Haunted Tower	189–	Brown		
The Hunter of the Alps	187–	Bullock	W. Dimond	1804
	187–	Middleton		
	188–	Chester and Lee		
The Hut of the Red Mountain	1863	Sunderland	H. Milner	1827
The Ice Witch, or the Frozen Hand	1860	Sunderland	J. Buckstone	1831
The Inchcape Bell, or the Dumb Boy of the Rock	1863	Sunderland	E. Fitzball	1828
The Innkeeper of Abbeville	1863	Sunderland	E. Fitzball	1822
The Italian's Revenge	188–	Wilding		
Jack Ketch	189–	Brown		
Jack Sheppard	188–	Wilding	J. Buckstone	1839
	188–	Middleton		
Lady Audley's Secret	188–	Wilding	From Miss Braddon	1863
	188–	Tiller		
Leah, the Jewish Maiden	188–	Wilding	A. Daly	1863
London by Night	188–	Wilding	C. Selby	1868
Lost in London	188–	Wilding	W. Phillips	1867
The Maid and the Magpie	1859	Sunderland	I. Pocock	1815

Maria Martin, or the Murder at the Red Barn	1860	Sunderland		1828
	186–	Middleton		
	188–	Wilding		
	188–	Tiller-Clowes		
	188–	Tiller		
	188–	Chester and Lee		
	189–	Brown		
	189–	Clunn Lewis		
	189–	Hodson		
	189–	Ashington		
Mazeppa	1863	Sunderland	From Byron	1823
Michael Earle, the Maniac Lover	188–	Wilding	T. E. Wilks	1839
The Miller and His Men	185–	Calver	I. Pocock	1813
	187–	Bullock		
	188–	Middleton		
	188–	Wilding		
The Miser and the Three Thieves	186–	Middleton		
The Mistletoe Bough	188–	Tiller	C. Somerset	1834
	188–	Middleton		
	188–	Wilding		
A Momentous Question	188–	Wilding	E. Fitzball	1844
The Murder at the Roadside Inn	188–	Wilding	E. Fitzball	1833
My Poll and My Partner Joe	1859	Sunderland	J. Haines	1835
	187–	Bullock		
	188–	Middleton		
Notre Dame, or the Gipsy Girl of Paris	188–	Wilding	From Hugo	1871
Obi, or Three-fingered Jack	1860	Sunderland		1860
	189–	Brown		
The Old House at Home	188–	Wilding		1860
Othello	188–	Middleton	From Shakespeare	
Paul Clifford	189–	Brown	E. Fitzball	1835
Peep O'Day Boys	188–	Wilding	E. Falconer	1861
Poor Jo (from *Bleak House*)	187–	D'Arc	From Dickens	1875
	188–	Wilding		
	188–	Tiller		
Queen's Evidence	188–	Wilding	G. Conquest	1876
The Red Rover	189–	Brown	E. Fitzball	1829
Rob Roy	1862	Sunderland	From Scott	1818
The Robber's Wife	1863	Sunderland	I. Pocock	1829
Robin Rough Head, or Ploughman turned Lord	187–	Holden	T. Holden	
	188–	Middleton		
Romeo and Juliet	181–	"In the city"	From Shakespeare	

Sea and Land, or the Smuggler's Daughter	1861	Sunderland	M. Lemon	1852
The Sea of Ice	188–	Middleton	Dennery	1853
	188–	Wilding		
The Seven Clerks	188–	Middleton	T. Wilks	1834
The Silver King	188–	Wilding	H. A. Jones	1882
Simon Lee, or the Murder of the Five Fields Copse	188–	Tiller	G. D. Pitt	1839
Sixteen-string Jack	1860	Sunderland	T. Wilks	1842
Spring-heeled Jack	189–	Brown	W. Travers	1868
Sweeney Todd, the Demon Barber of Fleet Street	188–	Wilding	G. D. Pitt	1847
	188–	Middleton		
	188–	Tiller		
	188–	Testo		
	189–	Bolton		
	189–	Brown		
A Tale of Mystery	188–	Wilding	T. Holcroft	1802
Temptation	188–	Wilding	W. Townsend	1842
The Ticket of Leave Man	188–	Wilding	Tom Taylor	1863
Timour the Tartar	1863	Sunderland	M. G. Lewis	1811
	189–	Brown		
Two Little Shoeblacks	189–	Wilding		
Two Little Vagabonds	189–	Wilding	G. Sims	1896
Uncle Tom's Cabin	1853	Ethiopian Marionettes	From Mrs Beecher Stowe	1852
	1862	Sunderland		
	186–	Middleton		
	188–	Tiller		
Under the British Flag	189–	Tiller	J. Curtin	1896
Valentine and Orson	1863	Sunderland	T. J. Dibdin	1804
The Vampire's Bride	188–	Middleton	J. Planché	1820
Vendetta, or the Corsican's Revenge	189–	Wilding	W. Calvert	1888
The White Horse of the Peppers	1862	Sunderland	S. Lover	1838
The Wife of Seven Husbands, or a Legend of Pedlar's Acre	188–	Wilding	G. Almar	1831
	188–	Middleton		
The Wild Woman of the Wreck	188–	Tiller		
The Wizard of the Moor	1860	Sunderland	H. Gott	
The Woodcutter's Daughter	189–	Skinner		

Comedies and Farces (Nineteenth-century)

The Area Belle	189–	Bentley	W. Brough	1864
As You Like It	188–	Middleton		

The Bath Road	1863	Sunderland		1830
Deaf, Dumb, and Blind	1861	Sunderland		
The Election, or the Choice of a Husband	1831	Middleton		
Excelsior, or the Noble Spaniard and the Slave	1874	Middleton		
The Illustrious Stranger	1862	Sunderland	J. Kenney	1827
Jobson and Nell	1863	Sunderland		
The Lottery Ticket	1862	Sunderland	S. Beazley	1826
The Married Batchelor	1863	Sunderland	P. O'Callaghan	1821
Mr Ferguson, or the Determined Lodger	1838	Middleton		
The Oldham Recruits	1861	Sunderland		
The Rival Lawyers, or the Old One Outwitted	1830	Middleton		
St Patrick's Day, or the Scheming Lieutenant	1862	Sunderland	R. B. Sheridan	1775
The Secret Panel	1862	Sunderland		
The Swiss Cottage, or Why Don't She Marry?	1852	Brigaldi	A. H. Bayley	1851
The Two Gregories, or Where Did the Money Come From?	1852	Brigaldi	T. J. Dibdin	1821
	1862	Sunderland		
The Two William Thompsons	1863	Sunderland		
The Village Lawyer, or Baa!	184–	Middleton and Frisby	W. Macready	1787
	1861	Sunderland		
	189–	Clunn Lewis		
Whose Wife is She?	1852	Brigaldi	"Hugo Vamp"	

Pantomimes and Extravaganzas (Nineteenth-century)

Aladdin, or the Wonderful Lamp	1852	Brigaldi	"Hugo Vamp"	
	189–	Testo		
Ali Baba and the Forty Thieves	1852	Brigaldi	"Hugo Vamp"	
	189–	Testo		
Beauty and the Beast	185–	Calver		
	1862	Sunderland		
	187–	Holden		
	188–	Middleton		
	188–	Wilding		
	188–	Pettigrove		
	188–	Imperial		
	1889	Jewell-Holden		
	189–	Rebmuh and Ward		

Blue Beard and His Wives	187–	Holden		
	188–	Wilding		
	1888	D'Arc		
	189–	Testo		
	189–	Ashington		
Cinderella	188–	Middleton		
	188–	Wilding		
Don Giovanni, or the Spectre on Horseback	1852	Brigaldi	T. J. Dibdin	1817
Fusbos the Great	188–	Pettigrove		
The Golden Pippin, or the Judgment of Paris and the Siege of Troy	1858	Brigaldi	"Hugo Vamp"	
Harlequin and Little Tom Tucker	1863	Sunderland		
Harlequin Father Christmas	1885	Whiteleys		
Harlequin O'Donoghue, or the White Horse of Killarney	1860	Sunderland		
Jack and the Beanstalk	188–	Middleton		
	189–	Testo		
Mother Goose, or Harlequin and the Golden Egg	1860	Middleton	T. J. Dibdin	1806
The One-eyed Monster	1864	Baylis		
The Prince and the Peri, or the Talisman of Oramanes	1857	Brigaldi	"Hugo Vamp"	
The Queendom of Ladyland	1864	Brigaldi	"Hugo Vamp"	
Red Riding Hood	1872	Bullock		
	188–	Middleton		
	188–	Wilding		
	189–	Ashington		
	189–	Whatman		
Robinson Crusoe	188–	Wilding		
	1895	D'Arc		
Sinbad the Sailor	1885	Pettigrove		
	189–	Ashington		
Whittington and His Cat	188–	Middleton		
	188–	Wilding		
	189–	De Marion		
The Yellow Dwarf	1885	Whiteleys		

Foreign Plays and Operas

These were announced under French, Italian, or English titles. I have normally taken the English form wherever possible. The term *scenario* indicates that a skeleton plot with a similar title has been recorded for the Commedia dell' Arte.

Aïda	1893	Prandi	Ghislanzoni	Verdi	1871
Amor	1888	Prandi			
L'Amore Discorde	1790	Savile Row		Coursiaux	

Art overcome by Virtue	1776	Haymarket			
L'Attaque du Convoi	1828	Maffey			
La Bataille de Cronstadt	1829	Maffey			
Le bon Valet	1791	Savile Row	de Pompigny		1784
La Buona Figliuola	1781	Micheli	Goldoni	Piccinni	1760
	1791	Savile Row			
Le Bureau des Gazettes	1791	Savile Row			
Le Bureau des Mariages	1792	Savile Row			
The Danaides, or the 99 Victims	1829	Maffrey	de Chavagnac and Desaugiers	Parody on Salieri	1819
The Death of Don Juan	1828	Maffey	*Scenario*		1657
Les deux Chasseurs et la Laitière	1790	Savile Row	Anseaume (from La Fontaine)	Duni	1763
Les deux Jumeaux	1776	Haymarket	*Scenario*		166–
	1790	Savile Row	Florian		
Le Devin du Village	1791	Savile Row	Rousseau		1752
La Doppia Metamorfose	1790	Savile Row			
The Enchantress Circe, or Art conquered by Art	1770	Perico	*Scenario*		16—
	1776	Haymarket			
	1779	Panton Street			
L'Erreur du Moment	1790	Savile Row	de Monvel	Dézède	1773
The Fable of the Bear	1777	Haymarket			
	1779	Panton Street			
Les fausses Consultations	1790	Savile Row			
Five Harlequins by Magic Art	1770	Perico	*Scenario*		16—
Il Furbo caricato	1791	Savile Row	*Scenario*		16—
Le Gardien	1792	Savile Row			
Georges Dandin	1791	Savile Row	Molière		1668
Happiness in Love	1776	Haymarket			
Arlequin avalé par la Balance	1828	Maffey			
Harlequin of All Work, or 1, 2, 3, 4, 5, 6	1828	Maffey			
Harlequin Bandit Chief, or the Innocent Condemned	1776	Haymarket	*Scenario*		1727
Harlequin Chimney Sweep, or Les Fourberies d'Arlequin	1770	Perico	*Scenario*		1720
	1776	Haymarket			
	1780	Micheli			
	1790	Savile Row			
	1828	Maffey			
Harlequin and Columbine in Hell, or the Judgment of Pluto	1776	Haymarket			

	1779	Panton Street		
	1780	Micheli		
Harlequin Companion of the Devil	1776	Haymarket		
Harlequin's Deception	1780	Micheli		
Harlequin Duke of Athens	1781	Micheli	*Scenario*	1679
Harlequin French Tailor and Spanish Knight	1776	Haymarket	*Scenario*	1680
	1779	Panton Street		
Harlequin Great Sorcerer, or his Birth from an Egg	1770	Perico	*Scenario*	173–
	1776	Haymarket		
	1779	Panton Street		
	1780	Micheli		
	1781	Manuelli		
	1791	Savile Row		
Arlequin Juge et Partie	1828	Maffey	*Scenario*	1667
Harlequin King of the Enchanted Island	1770	Perico	*Scenario*	1722
Harlequin's Love Triumph by Magic Art	1780	Micheli	*Scenario*	16—
Harlequin Master and Servant	1770	Perico	*Scenario*	1717
Harlequin and Pantaloon, the Magical Combat	1770	Perico		
	1776	Haymarket		
	1779	Panton Street		
Arlequin President, or le Coffre Infernal	1828	Maffey		
Harlequin Prince by Magic	1770	Perico	*Scenario*	1668
	1776	Haymarket		
	1792	Savile Row		
	1828	Maffey		
Harlequin Spy and Fool at Court	1770	Perico	*Scenario*	1716
Harlequin Statue	1829	Maffey	*Scenario*	1716
Harlequin swallowed by a Whale	1829	Maffey		
Arlequin Valet	1791	Savile Row	*Scenario*	1680
Harlequin Vanquisher of Turks	1770	Perico		
Harlequin Villain and Hangman	1770	Perico	*Scenario*	1667
Harlequin's Voyage and Disasters	1829	Maffey	*Scenario*	1721
Harlequin the Wizard Conqueror	1779	Panton Street		
L'Heureux Retour	1790	Savile Row		

The Invitation of the Statue of Loyola	1779	Panton Street	*Scenario*		1657
The Magician, or the Intrepid Harlequin	1828	Maffey	*Scenario*		17—
Li Medici per Amore	1780	Micheli			
Le Médecin malgré lui, or Harlequin compelled to be a Doctor	1780	Micheli	Molière		1666
M. de Pourcogneac	1791	Savile Row	Molière		1669
Nanette à la Cour	1780	Micheli	Favart	Pasticcio	1755
Nero	1770	Perico	*Scenario*		1681
Les petites Affiches	1790	Savile Row	Plancher-Valcour	Pasticcio	1780
Le Philosophe imaginaire	1790	Savile Row	Bertati	Paisiello	1779
Pytagoras, or Harlequin the Deliverer	1828	Maffey			
Le Retour du Pierrot	1790	Savile Row			
Richard Cœur de Lion	1828	Maffey	Sedaine	Grétry	1784
The Rival Magicians, Circe and Atlas	1779	Panton Street			
	1780	Micheli			
Roberto il Diavolo	1888	Colla	Scribe	Meyerbeer	1831
	1888	Prandi			
Rodope	1888	Prandi			
Le Roi et le Fermier	1792	Savile Row	Sedaine	Monsigny	1762
Samson	1770	Perico	*Scenario*		173–
La Serva Padrona	1776	Marylebone Gardens			
	1780	Micheli	Federico	Pergolesi	1733
La Sonnambula	1852	Brigaldi	Romani	Bellini	1831
The Spiteful Lovers	1780	Micheli	*Scenario*		162–
The Triumph of Love	1777	Haymarket	*Scenario*		1636
	1780	Micheli			
Les trois Recettes	1790	Savile Row	? de Monvel	Pasticcio	
The Universal Deluge	1888	Colla			
	1888	Prandi			
Vesuvius	1888	Prandi			
A Visit to Paris	1828	Maffey			
Le Voyage supposé	1792	Savile Row			
Zemire et Azore, or Beauty and the Beast	1829	Maffey	Marmontel	Grétry	1771
Zoroaster, or Harlequin's Judgment	1780	Micheli	Mazzinghy	Bach	

Divertissements of the Ombres Chinoises

The most important seasons are indicated as follows:

(*a*) 1775–76, Ambroise, Panton Street,
(*b*) 1776–77, Braville and Meniucci, St. Alban's Street.
(*c*) 1777, Ambroise, Panton Street.
(*d*) 1778, Gabriel, Antonio, and Ballarni, Panton Street.
(*e*) 1778–79, Astley, Piccadilly.
(*f*) 1779–90, Astley, Amphitheatre.

An African Lion Hunt	*c e f*
Beasts of the World	*a*
The Beggar and his Wife	*e*
The Broken Bridge	*b c d e f*
The Butchers	*a*
A Cat and Dog Fight	*a*
The Cobbler, and the Cat's Escape with the Dinner	*c d e f*
Duck Hunting	*a b c d f*
The Dutch Woman	*f*
The Farmyard	*e*
Gibraltar	*f*
The Hen	*c*
The Highwayman's Escape	*a*
The Housebreakers	*c*
The Joiners	*a*
The Knifegrinder	*e f*
The Lame Spanish Beggar	*a*
The Magical Valet	*c*
The Magician Knave	*a*
Le Malade Imaginaire	*c*
Metamorphoses of a Magician	*a b c d e*
Mount Vesuvius	*f*
The Public Gardens in Paris	*a b c d e*
A Spanish Bull Fight	*c*
The Spanish Don in Paris	*a*
The Spanish Sharpers	*a*
The Storm at Sea	*a b c d e f*
Sunrise	*a*
The Venice Dock Yard	*b c d e f*
The Weaver or Militiaman	*e f*
The Whale versus the Capodollio	*b f*
Winter Scene	*b c*
The Woodcutters	*c e*

INDEX

Note. This index covers the text of the book (pp. 11–270); information in the Appendices regarding puppet showmen and plays is not duplicated here.